LETTERS AND PAPERS

RELATING CHIEFLY TO THE

Provincial History of Pennsylvania,

WITH SOME

NOTICES OF THE WRITERS.

by Thomas Balch.

PRIVATELY PRINTED.

PHILADELPHIA:

CRISSY & MARKLEY, PRINTERS, GOLDSMITHS HALL, LIBRARY ST.

1855.

PREFACE.

Some time ago, the Historical Society of Pennsylvania passed a resolution, requesting me to edit certain letters written by Chief Justice Shippen. The duty was begun, but in the course of its execution, other materials were tendered to me, consisting in part of the 'Shippen MSS.' in the archives of that Society, in part of masses of letters, accounts, and other papers in the possession of descendants of some of the families prominent in the Province. The interest which had been created by the occupation itself, and the desire to add something to the stores of the future historian of this State, induced me to sift with care these miscellaneous MSS. and to print such as were of some, even though not remarkable, value.

The greater portion of them are purely private in their character. I therefore thought it well to print only a very-small number of copies, so as to prevent any, except those connected by 'kindred 'ties,' from obtaining the volume.

I have endeavored to make the genealogical notices, and also the notes appended to the letters, full and accurate. In my efforts, I have been greatly assisted by Mr. J. F. Fisher, Mr. Edward Shippen, Mr. Joseph Swift, Dr. G. W. Norris, Mr. Samuel Powel, and other gentlemen. To them are due the best thanks, not only of myself as Editor, but of all who prize an honorable ancestry, such as the following pages disclose.

Some of the letters relate to public affairs, and aid in supplying gaps in Pennsylvania history. At a future day I will print extracts from these.

Philadelphia, March, 1855.

GENEALOGICAL NOTICES

OF

THOSE FAMILIES

WHOSE MEMBERS HAVE, MORE OR LESS, CONTRIBUTED

TO THE

FOLLOWING CORRESPONDENCE.

WILLIAM SHIPPEN,* of Yorkshire, England, (gentleman,) had issue—

Two sons, which died young:

A daughter, m. to Mr. Leybourne, of Yorkshire; she died there:

He had also, WILLIAM SHIPPEN, afterwards Rector of St. Mary's Church, Stockport:

EDWARD SHIPPEN, b. 1639, who emigrated to America, and was the founder of the family here.†

* MS. Pedigrees which formerly belonged to the late Judge Yeates, Judge Shippen, E. S. Burd, &c. Bible Entries of Joseph Shippen, (son of Edward, the emigrant,) now in possession of Col. John Hare Powel. Hazard's Reg. IV. 241, (reprinting from the Portfolio:) 'A gentleman of fortune and family, in the county York.'

† It will be seen by the following pages that Mr. Griswold has been misled (*Republican Court*, p. 15) as to the pedigree of Edward Shippen.

The particulars of the first William Shippen's parentage, birth, marriage, death, or place of residence are unknown. In the Memoirs of James Logan,* his son Edward is made to say, that 'Alethey' was, at the time of his birth, the residence of his father. This, however, is presumed to be a misprint, or an error of the copyist; there being no such place, as far as ascertained. It is conjectured, from the name, that the family was originally of Flemish or Dutch extraction; a conjecture to which some countenance is given by the circumstance that the part of Yorkshire in which Mr. Shippen is supposed to have lived,—that lying between Pontefract and Wakefield,—had many Flemish families settled in it; so much so, that Bigland, says,† 'The Don.' 'This last part is called the Dutch River, 'being a canal cut by Cornelius Vermuiden and his Dutch 'and Flemish settlers.'

That the vicinity of Pontefract or Wakefield was his place of residence, appears reasonably certain from the fact, that his son, 'William, was elected to the scholarship in Uni-

* Edward Shippen was father-in-law to Thomas Story, and went early into Pennsylvania from Boston, whither he had gone from England in 1675. There he was persecuted for his religion, as a Friend, and received from the zealots in power, a public whipping. He was very successful as a merchant in Philadelphia, and amassed a large fortune, etc. He retained a strong interest towards his fellow professors in old England. In a letter to William Ellis, dated 27th of Seventh Month, 1699, he alludes to his having forwarded for poor Friends, a present of gold. "I have sent by our dear Friend, Aaron Atkinson, 12¾ ozs. of gold. It cost here £76 10s. currency. I suppose it will sell in London for something above £50 sterling, the which I have desired Aaron to sell; and I leave the disposing of it to thee and him, among poor Friends, where there is most need, and where it may be most helpful." He adds, "and if there be a meeting at Alethey, where I was born, I desire to know; and whether they be in want."—*Memoirs of James Logan, by Wilson Armistead.* London, 1851, p. 39, (n.)

† '*History of Yorkshire,*' p. 900, London, no date.—*Thorne.*

'versity College, Oxford, to which natives of Yorkshire are, 'alone, eligible; and a preference is given in the first in-'stance, by the college statutes, to all persons who are either 'natives of those localities, or who have been educated at the 'Grammar School, in one of those two towns.'*

1653, May 26, his son, the Rev. WILLIAM SHIPPEN, was matriculated at University College, Oxford.

1656, January 29: took his degree of A. B.†

1657, July 22, elected to Scholarship.

1659, June 16, elected Fellow of Union College.

1659, received degree of A. M.

1663, elected Proctor.

1668, resigned.

'He was afterwards Proctor of the University, 1664,‡ 'and at length Rector of Stockport in Cheshire; and author 'of "the Christian's Triumph over Death," a sermon 'preached at the funeral of Richard Leigh, Esq. He is 'D. D. not of this University, if I mistake not, but by the 'diploma of Dr. Wm. Sancroft, Archbishop of Canter-'bury.' §

The family here have no information as to the date of his birth or marriage. He died in 1693, and was buried under the chancel of the Church. From what Lord Mahon says, || he was probably not a man of wealth, but left rather an indifferent estate.

* Rev. Dr. Gresswell to Bishop Doane. MS. in possession of Mr. J. Francis Fisher.

† 2 Wood's Fasti Oxon. 125.

‡ Ibid, 111, 157.

§ Extracts from Printed Register of Oxford. Dr. Gresswell. MS. 2 Wood *cit. ante*, 125.

|| History of England, (3d ed.) III. p. 30

In the Bible-entries of his nephew, Joseph Shippen, son of Edward, it is stated, 'My relations in England are my 'uncle, William Shippen's children:

'1. ROBERT SHIPPEN, Doctor of Divinity.

'2. WILLIAM SHIPPEN, Doctor of Law, and a parliament-man.

'3. EDWARD SHIPPEN, a Physician.

'4. JOHN SHIPPEN, a Spanish merchant.'

1. ROBERT SHIPPEN, of Brazennose College, Oxford, received 1693, July 22, the degree of A. M.

1699, July 4, made D. D., and was subsequently principal of Brazennose, and Vice Chancellor of Oxford University. There is said to be a fine bust and monument of him, yet remaining in that College. There appears to have been a certain degree of intimacy between Robert and his cousin Joseph; but his letters, as well as those of Joseph, are lost. His bookplate is preserved in the American branch of the family, and bears underneath the coat of arms, the following inscription:

"Robertus Shippen. S. T. P."
"Coll. Æn: Nas: Principalis."

2. WILLIAM SHIPPEN, the "downright Shippen" of Pope,* the famous leader of the Jacobites, m. Frances Stote, d. of Sir Richard Stote.† Of him and his wife Lord Mahon thus speaks:

'Shippen, whom the public voice still proclaimed as 'the great leader of the Jacobites, was thought by them

* I love to pour out all myself, as plain
As downright Shippen, or as old Montaigne.
POPE.

* Burke's Landed Gentry. *s. v.* Bewicke. Mr. Burke calls him 'William Shippen, the patriot.'

'so weak as to be left out of all their consultations.* Shippen, at this time,† was sixty-eight, and his energy, perhaps, much impaired.‡ But as it seems to me, even his earlier reputation grew much more from his courage, his incompatibility, his goodhumored frankness of purpose, than from any superior eloquence or talent. Horace Walpole, the younger, describes his speeches as spirited in sentiment, but generally uttered in a low tone of voice, with too great rapidity, and with his glove held before his mouth: § certainly not the portrait of a great orator. It is said, that he had some skill in poetry, yet it does not seem that he was known or prized by any of the eminent men out of the House of Commons. His father was Rector of Stockport, and his paternal inheritance had been small: he acquired, however, an ample fortune by marriage. His wife was extremely penurious, and, as a relation gently expressed it, "with a peculiarity of temper,|| and unwilling to mix in society. She was much noticed by Queen Caroline, but steadily declined all connection with the Court. Shippen, himself, like Pulteney, was not free from the taint of avarice; when not attending Parliament, he lived chiefly in a hired house on Richmond Hill, and it is remarkable, that neither of these distinguished politicians, though each wealthy, possessed that chief pride and delight of an English gentleman, a country seat." '¶

* History of England, III. p. 30. (3d ed.) and auth's cit.

† 1740.

‡ Stuart papers. Lord Sempill's Letter, June 13th, 1740.

§ Coxe's Memoirs of Walpole. I. 672.

|| Judge Willes, her grand nephew. Coxe's Walpole, I. 673. Shippen survived her several years, in full possession of her fortune.

¶ Coxe's Walpole, I. 673. As to Pulteney, see Pope to Swift, May 17, 1739—Swift's Works, XIX. 291.

Whether or not, Lord Mahon, who claims to present a fair and impartial narrative to his readers, has done full justice to Shippen, may be a question. That Shippen possessed, in a high degree, all the virtues ascribed to him by the historian, is, of course, unquestionable. The courage and integrity which animated him in such dangerous and agitated times, were truly noble; such as neither danger could daunt, nor temptation undermine, nor discouragement diminish.* With what a fine spirit does he protest against a

* 'For my part I am not ashamed nor afraid to affirm, that thirty 'years have made no change in any of my political opinions; I am 'now grown old in this house, but that experience which is the con-'sequence of age has only confirmed the principles with which I 'enter'd it many years ago; time has verified the predictions which 'I formerly utter'd, and I have seen my conjectures ripen'd into 'knowledge. I should be therefore without excuse, if either terror 'could affright, or the hope of advantage allure me from the decla-'ration of my opinions; opinions, which I was not deterred from 'asserting, when the prospect of a longer life than I can now ex-'pect might have added to the temptations of ambition, or aggra-'vated the terrors of poverty and disgrace; opinions, for which I 'would willingly have suffered the severest censures, even when I 'had espoused them only in compliance with reason, without the 'infallible certainty of experience. Of truth it has been always 'observed, Sir, that every day adds to its establishment, and that 'falshoods, however specious, however supported by power, or esta-'blished by confederacies, are unable to stand before the stroke of 'time: Against the inconveniences and vexations of long life, may 'be set the pleasure of discovering truth, perhaps the only pleasure 'that age affords. Nor is it a slight satisfaction to a man not 'utterly infatuated or depraved, to find opportunities of rectifying 'his notions, and regulating his conduct by new lights. But much 'greater is the happiness of that man, to whom every day brings a 'new proof of the reasonableness of his former determinations, and 'who finds, by the most unerring test, that his life has been spent 'in promotion of doctrines beneficial to mankind. This, Sir, is the 'happiness which I now enjoy, and for which those who never shall 'attain it, must look for an equivalent in lucrative employments, 'honorary titles, pompous equipages, and splendid palaces. These, 'Sir, are the advantages which are to be gained by a seasonable 'variation of principles, and by a ready compliance with the pre-'vailing fashion of opinions; advantages, which I indeed cannot 'envy, when they are purchased at so high a price.'—*Debates in Parliament*, (1741–2,) pp. 102, 103.

standing army, though his earnest efforts against 'a burden 'heavy and dangerous to the people' had so often failed. 'Sir; I now stand up to make my anniversary oration 'against a standing army. I have made one and twenty

Shippen's character and conduct are so well illustrated in the report of the proceedings, when he was sent to the Tower, that I can not forbear giving it. *Parlt. Debates*, 1717, Dec. 4, p. 20, &c.

'In this speech, Mr. Shippen overshot himself so far in his ex- 'pressions, as to give too much advantage against him, to such as 'perhaps were not over-backward to lay hold of it: His words that 'gave the offence were to the following purpose, *That the second 'paragraph of the Kings' speech seemed rather to be calculated for the 'meredian of* Germany, *than* Great Britain; and that *'twas a great 'misfortune, That the King was a Stranger to our language and con- 'stitution.* These expressions gave offence to several members, and 'in particular to Mr. *Lechmere*, who having taken them down in 'writing, urged, 'That those words were a scandalous invective 'against the King's person and government, of which the house 'ought to shew the highest resentment, and therefore moved, That 'the member who spoke those offensive words should be sent to the '*Tower*.' Mr. *Lechmere* was seconded by Mr. *Cowper*, brother to 'the Lord Chancellor, and back'd by Sir *Joseph Jekyll*, and some 'others: Upon which Mr. *Robert Walpole* said, 'That if the words 'in question were spoken by the member on whom they were 'charged, the *Tower* was too light a punishment for his rashness; 'but as what he had said in the heat of this debate might have 'been misunderstood, he was for allowing him the liberty of ex- 'plaining himself.' Mr. *Snell*, Mr. *Hutchinson*, and some other 'gentlemen, spoke also in behalf of Mr. *Shippen*, intending, chiefly, 'to give him an opportunity of retracting or excusing what he 'had said; which Mr. *Shippen* not thinking proper to do, several 'speeches were made upon the question, Whether the words taken 'down in writing were the same as had been spoken? A gentleman 'having suggested, That there was no precedent of a censure passed 'on a member of the house, for words spoken in a Committee, Sir '*Charles Hotham* produced instances of the contrary; and, on the 'other hand, Mr. *Shippen* having maintained what he had ad- 'vanced, it was, at last, resolved by a majority of 196 voices 'against about 100, That the words taken down in writing were 'spoken by Mr. *Shippen*. It was then about nine o'clock in the 'evening, and it being moved and carried, That the Chairman leave 'the chair; Mr. *Speaker* resumed his place, and Mr. *Farrer* 'reported from the said Committee, 'That exceptions having been 'taken to some words spoken in the Committee, by *William Ship- 'pen*, Esq., a member of the house, the Committee, had directed 'him to report the words to the house.' Which being done accord- 'ingly, and candles ordered to be brought in, Mr. *Shippen* was 'already, of which fifteen have never been seconded, and 'this will probably be the sixteenth.'* Not the less, though, was he bound to do his duty.

But courage, integrity and good temper, though sufficient to render him a prominent actor amongst the Jacobites, were not enough to constitute him their leader in a body like the House of Commons; that too, during a long service of many years, with such men as Walpole, Pultney, Stanhope, Barnard, as associates and antagonists. He must have had, as the debates fully show, both the sagacity and the eloquence of an accomplished statesman.

Perhaps Lord Mahon's judgment was warped by the fact, that Shippen was at the head of the commission appointed to examine and sift General Stanhope's accounts, as Envoy and as Commander-in-Chief.† However candid or correct his recital may be as to other matters, it looses those characteristics whenever the individual or the subject touches the house of Stanhope or the American Revolution.‡ His partiality for his family is a weakness excusable in the eyes of many; and harmless, except where it presents his story

'heard in his place, and then withdrew. After this it was moved, 'that the question might be put, 'That the words spoken 'by *William Shippen*, Esq., (a member of this house) are highly dishonor- 'able to, and unjustly reflecting on his Majesty's person and govern- 'ment." Which occasioned a debate that lasted 'till past 11 o'clock; 'when the question being put, was carried in the affirmative by 175 'voices against 81; and thereupon ordered, 'That *William Ship- 'pen*, Esq. be, for the said offence, committed prisoner to his Ma- 'jesty's Tower of *London*, and that Mr. *Speaker* do issue his war- 'rant accordingly.'—*Debates in Parliament*, 1717–21, (Dec. 4, 1717,) p. 20.

* Parlt. Debates, 1739. p. 138. See also his speech in favor of Triennial Parliaments.—*Debates in Parliament*, 1716, p. 454.

† 1 Mahon's Eng. 109.

‡ Some of the errors as to this country, to be found in his work, have been exposed by that learned and accurate American Antiquary, Mr. Peter Force, in an able and severe critique.

to the injury of others. Such is the case as to the character which he has drawn of this 'Parliament man;' * and though not disposed, to use his own words, and say 'that it implies not merely literary failure, but moral guilt;'† we may at least protest against the manner in which he appears to 'lower the fame of a political adversary.'‡

3. EDWARD SHIPPEN, of Brazennose College, received 1693, July 22, the degree of A. M. He was a Physician, and is supposed to have married, Frances, d. of Peter Leigh, of Lyme, widow of Sir Gilbert Clarke.§

4. JOHN SHIPPEN, was, as already stated, according to his cousin Joseph's bible-entries, a Spanish merchant; and was baptized 1678, July 5, by his father, in Mary's Church, at Stockport; and was British Consul at Lisbon.

It would also seem that he had a daughter named ANNE; for Edward Willes, son of the Lord Chief Justice Willes, m. Anne niece of William Shippen, M. P. She d. 1799, leaving issue.‖

* 'Honest Will Shippen,' as he was called, or 'Downright Shippen,' as Pope terms him, was a zealous Jacobite member of parliament, possessed of considerable talents, and a vehement opposer of Sir Robert Walpole's government. He, however, did justice to that able minister, for he was accustomed to say, 'Robin and I are honest men; but as for those fellows in long perriwigs' (meaning the Tories of the day,) 'they only want to get into office themselves.' He was the author of a satirical poem, entitled, 'Faction Displayed,' which possesses considerable merit.—D. [Shippen was born in 1672, and died in 1743. Sir Robert Walpole repeatedly declared, that he would not say who was corrupted, but he would say who was not corruptible—that man was Shippen. His speeches generally contained some pointed period, which he uttered with great animation. He usually spoke in a low tone of voice, with too great rapidity, and held his glove before his mouth. —*Horace Walpole's letters, ed. by Lord Dover*, I. 101, (note.) London, 1840.

† 1 Mahon. Introd. 2.

‡ 1 Mahon. Introd. 2.

§ Burke's Land. Gent. *s. v.* Tatton.

‖ Burke's Land. Gent. *s. v.* Willes.

EDWARD SHIPPEN, son of the first mentioned William, and the founder of the family in America,

1639, was born in Yorkshire, England,

1668, emigrated to Boston : persecuted into removing

1693–4, to Philadelphia, where,

1712, October 2d, he died, Æ. 73.

Of his history in England, nothing is known except that he was bred to mercantile pursuits, in which he engaged after his arrival in Boston: very successfully too, as it appears, that he was, on removing to Philadelphia, computed to be worth at least £10,000 stg.—a sum by no means inconsiderable in those days, particularly in a new country. His sagacity and ability largely increased his fortune during his residence in Philadelphia.

1669. He was a member of the Ancient and Honorable Artillery Company, and in

1671, married Elizabeth Lybrand; which marriage, it is conjectured, led to his embracing Quakerism: and, so zealous was the convert, that we find

1677, Aug't 16. Governor Coddington of Rhode Island, in a letter from Boston, under this date, mentions that on the 9th of that month, Shippen, together with others, was arrested for attending Friends meeting, and 'publickly 'whipped, and again on the next day of Public worship, 'when he suffered in the same way.' That Shippen had the courage not only to suffer as a martyr, but also to defy his oppressors, is shown by the following extract from Thomas Story's Journal.*

* Thomas Story's Journal. London 1718, pp. 195–6. See also pp. 223–26. See also Southey's Com. Place Book.

1699. 'And the next day, accompanied by some friends, 'we went to Boston: near which, on a green, we observed a 'pair of gallows; and being told, that was the place where 'several of our friends suffered death for the truth, and had 'been thrown into a hole, we rode a little out of our way to 'see it: which was a kind of pit, near the gallows, and full 'of water, but two posts at each end, which had been set 'there by Edward Shippen of Philadelphia, a reputable 'Friend, formerly of Boston: who would have erected some 'more lasting monument there, with leave of the magistrates, 'but they were not willing: since it would too frequently 'and long bring to remembrance that great error of their 'ancestors, which could not now be repaired: so that he had 'only leave to put down those posts, to keep the place in 'remembrance, till something further might be done, at a 'time when it might be less obnoxious.'

Great as were the persecutions which he, together with his unfortunate fellow 'sectaries,' endured at the hands of the Pilgrim Fathers and their descendants, yet he continued in Boston; for

1687, Sept. 12, during Andross' usurpation, he presented a petition to Sir Edmund, upon consideration of which the following order was made:

'That whereas Edward Shippen of Boston, Merchant, 'hath by his petition set forth that for many years past he, 'and those under whom he claims, have been possessed of 'a certain house and ground wherein he now liveth: one 'other house and ground in the occupation of Thomas 'Savage: one other house and ground in the occupation of 'George Dawson: several warehouses and grounds belonging 'thereto; and about four acres of ground in pasture; all 'within the town of Boston; and moreover petitions to have 'them confirmed to him: Whereupon the Governor, Sir 'Edmund Andross, ordered them to be surveyed, so that a 'patent for them might be granted unto him.'*

Besides the above mentioned houses, warehouses, lots and pasture, there belonged to Mr. Shippen several wharves, somewhere near Fanueil Hall, known in the last century as 'Shippen's Wharves;' but now far inland, and covered by well built streets, in consequence of the extensive fillings up, which have so much expanded the limits of Boston.

1689–90, March 14. It appears from the record of the Council and General Court, 'that Mr. Edward Shippen, 'now intending a journey to Pennsylvania, be desired to pur'chase fifty barrels of gunpowder, if there to be had; and 'more, if it can be bought at a reasonable rate.' A very singular commission: one more suitable to the ancient artilleryman than the twice-flogged Quaker.

1692, June 16. Mr. Shippen is mentioned as the bearer of letters from Easton, Secretary of Rhode Island,† to Addington, Secretary of Massachusetts.‡

1693–4. The persecutions of the Quakers in Boston reached such a pitch, that Mr. Shippen was driven into taking refuge in Pennsylvania.§

It may have been that he was banished, such having been a usual mode of punishing the Quakers; or as these 'jail'ings, whippings, and banishments' were frequent, and occurred 'in season and out of season,' not only in conse-

* Petitions of this kind were abundant about this time, as Governor Andross denied that the holders of Real Estate had any legal claim to it. *J. B. Felt.*

† Mr. Shippen had married his second wife in Rhode Island, about a year before this, as will be presently seen.

‡ Mr. J. B. Felt says he can find no further records.

§ Dr. W. E. Horner says, 'he was invited by Penn.' *Address, &c. in* Hazard's Reg. X. 66.

quence of provocations by the Quakers themselves, but on the mere 'appearance of a meteor in the heavens,' Mr. Shippen may have grown 'weary of well doing' as a martyr, and so betaken himself to a government less disposed 'to promote the Reformation of manners.'*

It would seem to have taken him about a year to effect the disposal of his estate in Boston, and transfer it to Philadelphia. In this latter city, Mr. Shippen's wealth and character speedily obtained for him such position and influence, that

1695, July 9th, he was elected speaker of the Assembly: and William Penn named him in the Charter,

1701, Octr. 25, as the first Mayor of the City of Philadelphia. Penn, as is well known, gave the most anxious consideration to his selection of officers to govern the new city. He thoroughly appreciated the importance of a correct choice. It was, to borrow a military phrase, the base-line of his operations. The success of his whole enterprise turned upon it: the consciousness of which, apart from any other motives, political or philanthropic, was sufficient to stimulate him to the utmost caution and deliberation in his choice of incumbents. In Shippen, he found a man of courage, energy, integrity, intelligence and sagacity; whose unspotted moral character was ample earnest to the citizens, that the executive power would be exercised with the strictest justice and fidelity; whose active business habits and bravery equally assured them of the chief magistrate's resolution

* Oldmixon. Vol. I. p. 112. 'Another persecution. I must not 'forget, that upon the appearance of a meteor here, the magistrates 'wrote a circular letter to the Elders and Ministers of every town, to 'promote the reformation of manners—a good work certainly with 'or without a comet, which if it prognosticates any thing, I should 'rather incline to think it ought not to be applyed to a new perse-'cution of Baptists and Quakers, whom they did not indeed hang, 'but ruined many honest men, says the Reverend historian, by 'fines, imprisoments and banishment,' &c.

and promptness: whilst his high social position gave dignity to the office.

1702–4. He was President of the Governor's Council. In this last year, he contracted his third marriage, which led to his separation from the Society of Friends. After which he appears to have retired altogether from public life; except that he continued to advise upon public affairs, as we find from Penn's letter, dated 24th 5th mo. 1712, where Mr. Shippen is addressed, in connection with I. Norris, T. Story, &c.*

1712, Octr. 2: He died in Philadelphia, aged 73.

No one could wish to detract in the slightest degree from Penn's merits; but we are taught to render 'honor to 'whom honor is due.' In doing so, we must needs say that a great, if not the greatest portion of the glory of building up the Commonwealth which was 'founded by deeds of 'peace' is due to Shippen, Norris, and Logan, and men like them: the men, who here, in the new country itself, fostered commerce, developed the resources of the province, set the best of examples, by disdaining no proper toil in their respective vocations, yet neglected not the refinements and graces of letters and polite society.†

* 1 Watson's Annals, 83. He also served in the City Councils. Watson makes an error, I. 523. He says that in 1709, Mr. Shippen petitioned Common Council to remit a fine of £7 10 for an assault and battery on Thos. Clark, Esq., one half remitted on his paying other half. It was Edward Shippen, *Junr.*—*Minutes of Council*, p. 63.

† The following extracts serve to show the style in which Mr. Shippen lived:

'There are very fine and delightful gardens and orchards in most 'parts of this country; but Edward Shippen, who lives near the 'capital city, has an orchard and gardens adjoining to his Great 'House, that equalizes, if not exceeds, any I have ever seen; having 'a very famous and pleasant summer-house erected in the middle 'of his extraordinary fine and large gardens abounding with tulips, 'pinks, carnations, roses (of several sorts), lilies, not to mention

1671. EDWARD SHIPPEN'S first wife was Elizabeth Lybrand of Boston. They had issue,

1. FRANCES, b. at Boston, Feb. 2, 1672. d. April 9, 1673.
2. EDWARD, b. " Octr. 2, 1674. d. Nov. 2, 1674.
3. WILLIAM, b. " Octr. 4, 1675. d. 1676.
4. ELIZA, b. Augt., 1676 d. an infant.
5. EDWARD, b. at Boston, Dec. 10, 1677–8.
d. at Philadelphia Dec'r. 26, 1712:

He married Anna Francina Vanderheyden, near Bohemia River, Maryland, daughter of Matthias and Anna Margaret Vanderheyden.* They had issue, one daughter, Margaret, m. to John Jekyll, Esq. a younger Brother of Sir Joseph Jekyll, (Master of the Rolls and Secretary of State to Queen Anne,) then Collector of the port of Boston. After Mr. Jekyll's death, she lived, as a widow till about the year 1750, in Philadelphia,† where she died. She was handsome, wealthy

'those that grow in the fields.'—*Gabriel Thomas' Account of Pennsylvania*—London, 1698. p. 43.

'This venerable edifice long bore the name of "the Governor's 'House." It was built in the early rise of the city—received then 'the name of "Shippey's Great House," while Shippen himself was 'proverbially distinguished for three great things—"the biggest '"person, the biggest house, and the biggest coach."

'It was for many years after its construction beautifully situated, 'and surrounded with rural beauty, being originally on a small emi- 'nence, with a row of tall yellow pines in its rear, a full orchard of 'best fruit trees close by, overlooking the rising city beyond the 'Dock creek, and having on its front view a beautiful green lawn, 'gently sloping to the then pleasant Dock creek and Drawbridge, 'and the whole prospect unobstructed to the Delaware and the 'Jersey shore. It was indeed a princely place for that day, and 'caused the honest heart of Gabriel Thomas to overflow at its recol- 'tion, as he spoke of it in the year 1698.'—*Watson*, (2 ed.) I. 368.

* Her sister Ariana was m. to James Frisby, of Sassafras River, Md. Mrs. Shippen was godmother to their child, Francina Augustina Frisby.—*MS. pedigree compiled by Judge Brice of Baltimore, now in possession of Dr. Caspar Morris, of Philadelphia.*

† In Second street, just below the Shippen or Government House, in a house still standing; after her death the residence of Thomas Fisher, grandfather to J. Francis Fisher, Esq.

and very fashionable.* Of her descendants there is found only the following.

1758, July 19. Fanny Jekyll was m. to William, son of Edward Hicks, Esq.†

A Mr. Jekyll also appears as one of the subscribers to the 'Falls Fishery,' 1763.‡

* 'I have also preserved a card of admission, of the year 1749, 'addressed to Mrs. Jeykell, a lady of pre-eminent fashion and 'beauty, the then leading lady of the ton. She was the grand-'daughter of the first Edward Shippen, a mayor, merchant, and 'Quaker. She was married to the brother of Sir Joseph Jeykell, 'the secretary of Queen Anne; and when in her glory in Philadel-'phia, she dwelt in and owned the house next southward of "Ed-'"ward Shippen's great house" in south Second street, where is 'now Nicholas Waln's row.'—*Watson*, (2 ed.) I. 285.

† Chief Justice Shippen to his Father. July 20, 1758.

‡ The MS. list of subscribers, the rules to govern them, and 'a 'bill of fare' of one of their entertainments, are worthy of preservation. They are as follows:

'A List of Gentlemen proposed to be subscribers to the Mount Regale Fishing Company for 1763.

His Honour The Governor,
1. Mr. Gilbert Berkley,
2. Mr. Benj. Chew,
3. Mr. Will. Coxe,
4. Mr. John Coxe,
5. Mr. Redmond Conyngham,
6. Mr. David Franks,
7. Mr. Tench Francis,
8. Mr. John Gibson,
9. Mr. T. Gilbert,
10. Mr. B. Levy,
11. Mr. Arch. McCall,
12. Mr. John Lawrence,
13. Mr. John Relfe,
14. Mr. Edward Shippen,
15. Mr. Richard Stevens,
16. Mr. George Smith,
17. Mr. Jos. Swift,
18. Mr. Tilghman,
19. Mr. T. Lloyd,
20. Dr. Shippen, Jr.,
21. Mr. Allen,
22. Mr. Bache,
23. Mr. Clymer,
24. Mr. Chapman,
25. Mr. Clifton,
26. Mr. Dickinson,
27. Mr. Turbutt Francis,
28. Mr. Hopkinson,
29. Mr. Jeykill,
30. Mr. Kidd,
31. Mr. Chalmers,
32. Mr. Meredith,
33. Mr. R. Morris,
34. Mr. Nixon,
35. Mr. Nesbit,
36. Mr. Robt. Ritchie,
37. Mr. Smythe, lawyer,
38. Mr. Joseph W. Shippen,
39. Mr. Jos. Shippen, Junr.,
40. Mr. Willing,
41. Mr. Peter Wikoff,
42. Mr. Alex. Wilcox.

'*Falls Fishery, at Peter Robinson's.*

'To be commenced on Thursday, the 6th of June, and to continue

6. JOSEPH, b. at Boston, Feb. 28, 1678–9. of whom, more presently.

7. MARY, b. May 6, 1681. d. 1688.

8. ANNE, b. at Boston, June 17, 1684. m. at Phila. 10th

'every other Thursday, till the last Thursday in September, inclu-'sive. Tickets to be sent to any Ladies or Gentlemen, Strangers 'that are in town, by the managers, not exceeding gentlemen at 'one time.

'The Wine and Spirit to be provided in bottles with sealed corks, 'and to be sent to Peter Robinson, who is to be allowed a profit, on 'each bottle of Wine, 1s. 6d., on each bottle of Spirit, 0s. 6d., and 'on the whole quantity of Sugar bought of 4d. per lb., and 6d. per 'head for each person present, for the tea table, the Company to 'find the Tea.

'Mr. Robinson to furnish Lemons, and to be allowed 50 per cent. 'profit.

'Dinners to be prepared for 30 persons by Mr. Robinson, who is 'to be allowed 1s. 6d. per head, whether that number be present or 'not. If more than that number be present, he is to be paid at '1s. 6d. per head.

	£	*s.*	*d.*
'A small round of Beef, stuffed, - - - -	0	8	4
'A loin of Veal, 12½ lb. a 8d., - -	0	8	0
'8 Chickens, roasted, - - - - -	0	8	0
'2 Tongues, a 2s. 6d., - - - -	0	5	0
'Beef Steaks, 10 lb. a 8d., } These two to be sent out	0	6	8
'Live Fish, if to be had, } undressed.			
'Beans, Peas and Sallad, - - -	0	5	0
'Cherry Pie, - - - - -	0	2	6
'4 Quarts Rasberries or Strawberries, - -	0	5	6
'1 Cream Cheese, - - - - -	0	1	3
'1 doz. large Spoons, - - - - -	0	6	0
'½ Gallon Spirit, - - - - - -	0	3	9
'Biscuits, - - - - - - -	0	1	6
'1 Loaf Sugar, which you must send to Mr. Meredith's for,	0	6	3
'Lemons,			
'Bread, - - - - - -	0	2	8
	3	2	5
'For my trouble, - - - - -	0	15	0
	£3	17	5

'MR. BURNS:—Please procure the above articles against Tuesday 'next, and I will take care to see you paid for them, and am

Your humble servant,

'Philada., July 2d, 1763. NATHL. CHAPMAN.

July, 1706. Thos. Story, d. *s. p.* She was buried in Friends' New Burying Ground, in Phila.

Mr. Story was first Recorder of the City of Phila., Master of the Rolls, and Keeper of the Great Seal. He came out from England in 1699. By his marriage, he received a large property; part of which was the large house in Second street, afterwards sold to James Logan, afterwards pulled down to afford the site, in part, of the present Bank of Pennsylvania. After her death he returned to England, and subsequently reconveyed this estate by his will to his wife's family.* In 1706, he was chosen Mayor, but on refusing was fined £20 by the Council.† His career is so well known

'Dr. Sir:—Please to pay Mr. Burns £3 17s. 5d. for the within 'Bill for Mt. Regale Fishing Cympany, and charge it to that ac- 'count. I am, sir,

Your most humble servant,

'To Joseph Shippen, Esq. NATHL. CHAPMAN.

Philadelphia, 8th July, 1763.

'Received, August 16, 1763, of Joseph Shippen, Jr., £3 17s. 5d. 'in full of the within account. JAMES BYRNE.'

This was a different 'Fishing Club' from that still in existence.

* Edward Shippen to Chas. Willing.

'*Lancaster, 8th April,* 1754.

'Dear Sir:—Your favor of the 27th ulto. did not come to hand 'till last Saturday night. Kepler keeps letters sometimes a month 'in his drawers. I have several letters by me from uncle Thomas 'Story, in which I can find nothing relating to the London Company 'except the following paragraph, dated at Carlisle, in Cumberland, 'in April, 1742: "I have about one hundred and two shares of the '"lands and interest in the London Company, which my friend, '"John Estaugh, very well knows cost me very dear, and much '"trouble. I am thy loving uncle, Thomas Story."

'I think you have a copy of the will or else I would trouble the 'bearer with it. I have no other papers or writings relating to 'that affair. We enjoy our health very well, and are going next 'week to pay our children a visit at Shippensburgh. We conclude 'with our best regards to yourself, sister and cousins, as if parti- 'cularly named.

Your affectionate brother-in-law,

EDWARD SHIPPEN.'

† *Minutes of Councils*, p. 42.

through his Journal, that it is unnecessary to say more of him. He was not regarded as a sufficiently fashionable match, by some of the family.*

1690. EDWARD SHIPPEN, m. 2dly. at Newport, R. I. Rebecca Richardson, widow of Francis Richardson of New York, merchant, by whom, he had issue,

Elizabeth, b. 1691. d. 1692, about which time also Mrs. Shippen died.

1704. EDWARD SHIPPEN. m. 3dly. Elizabeth James, widow of Thomas James, of Bristol, England, (her maiden name was Wilcox,) by whom he had

John, died an infant.

William. d. 1731, aged about 25 years. He d. *s. p.* and left the large estate, bequeathed to him by his Father, to a half brother or sister ex parte materna, through whom it was transmitted to the Powel family, and formed the principal portion of their landed estate.†

* Extract from a letter of Isaac Norris, now (1855,) in possession of Dr. G. W. Norris:

'11th 5 mo. 1706.

'T. Story and Ann Shippen were married yesterday. Ned was 'at the wedding, but Joe appears so disgusted, that nobody can 'reconcile his actions to reason. He went to New Castle to be out 'of the way.'—*See also Life of Logan*, p. 19, (cit. ant.)

† Mr. Fisher's MSS., Judge H. Shippen's MSS., &c.

Joseph Shippen, before mentioned,* was b. in Boston, February 28, 1678–9; m. at Boston, July 28, 1702, Abigail Grosse, dau. of Thomas and Elizabeth Grosse. She d. June 28, 1716, at Philadelphia.

In 1704 he removed to Philadelphia; thence, after his first wife's death, to Germantown, where he resided in the house now known (1855) as 'the Buttonwood Tavern,' until his death, which occurred in 1741. After the death of his first wife, he m. 2dly. Mrs. Rose Plumley, by whom he had no issue. She was the mother of Sarah Plumley, who was m. to his son Edward.

Of his first wife, Abigail Grosse, but very little is known. Her connexions in Boston appear to have been most respectable. Tradition says, with what foundation cannot now be accurately ascertained, that she was a near kinswoman of Gov. Bowdoin's wife. During a long series of years her children kept up a friendly intercourse with their relatives.

Augt. 9, 1725. Edward Shippen, (the above mentioned son of Abigail and Joseph,) then on a visit to Boston, writes to Miss Plumley, to whom he was engaged and afterwards married:—'All last week I was visiting my friends. 'I believe there never was a more loving and kind people 'in the world. My grandmother lives handsomely, but has 'nothing to spare except good will and kindness, until she 'dies. All my aunt's and uncle's daughters are extraordi-'narily well married. They get me to dinner at one place 'to-day, then make me promise to dine at another to-mor-'row, and to sup at another; and so they carry me about.

* *Ante*, p. xxi.

'I have a maiden aunt who lives with my grandmother, the 'very image of my own mother. Both of them bid me 'remember their kind love to you.'

Nov. 26, 1753. Edward Shippen, (eldest son of Abigail and Joseph,) writes to his 'Dear Cousin,' Thomas Fayerweather, at Boston, a most confidential letter as to family affairs, in reply to one of the same character.

Octr. 5, 1774. Chief Justice Shippen, writing to his father at Lancaster, says—'Cousin Tom Greenough from 'Boston dined with me last week. He made me promise 'to transmit to you his hearty love.'

Octr. 16, 1775. Mr. Fayerweather, then at Cambridge, (near Boston,) writes to the same Edward Shippen, thanking him for a letter of introduction presented by 'Cousin Burd.'

A Mr. Erving appears to have been a near kinsman. The same Mr. Erving would also seem to have been a brother-in-law of Governor Bowdoin.*

Of Mr. Shippen himself there remain but few memorials.† The only letter from him which has been preserved, so far as is known, is the following. It shows him to have been an industrious, energetic man. It was written, as will be seen, when he was more than sixty years of age.

* 'She was certainly related to Gov. Bowdoin by his mother; 'also to the Ervings, (Mr. Erving, our minister to Spain some years 'ago, and Col. Erving of the U. S. Army were of this family.')—*Mr. Fisher's MSS.* 'Gov. Bowdoin m. Elizabeth Erving.'—*Hon. R. C. Winthrop.*

† The following notice of 'the Buttonwood,' appeared in the editorial columns of the *Germantown Telegraph, March 13th*, 1855:—

'An Old Soldier.—A few days ago, one of the old trees which 'had for some years given up the ghost, standing in front of the 'Buttonwood Hotel, opposite this office, was removed, and we pre-'sume 'cast into the burning.' The other, which had been its 'companion for about eighty years, still stands, alive and well, in 'all the majesty of its prime, it having recovered from the disease 'which so seriously attacked this kind of tree all over the country, 'some five or six years ago.'

'*July* 15*th*, 1740.

'SON EDWARD:—I have finished my hay and have 'reaped my wheat. I am getting it in to-day, and am cut-'ting my rye, and must pay my men. When you was here 'last, I told you I must come to town for rent. You said 'you would help me to get it. Joe has been here since, 'and I told him the same. So I desire you will speak to 'him and bring me up £20 this afternoon, for I cannot 'leave my people.

'I am your loving father,

'JOSEPH SHIPPEN.'

Mr. Shippen may be justly included amongst 'the men 'of science' of his day. He was a member of 'The Junto,'* and bestowed much attention upon such pursuits; amongst others, practical anatomy.†

Mr. Shippen had by his first wife the following children:

1. EDWARD, b. in Boston, July 9th, 1703; of whom more presently.
2. ELIZABETH, b. in Philadelphia, April 17, 1705; d. June 8th, 1714.

* 'The Junto was instituted by Dr. Franklin in 1727, for mutual 'information and the public good. Nearly, if not all, were born in 'the same year, 1706. The association consisted of Benjamin 'Franklin, Joseph Shippen, Hugh Roberts, William Coleman, Philip 'Syng, Enoch Flower, Joseph Wharton, William Griffiths, Luke 'Morris, Joseph Turner, Joseph Trotter, Samuel Jervis, Samuel 'Rhodes, Joseph Brintnall; also Nicholas Scull, William Parson, 'and Thomas Godfrey.—*Hazard's Register*, XV. 184. See also Sparks' Franklin, I. 83.

† 'It is most probable that here he (the elder Shippen) acquired 'those ideas of the importance of the study (Practical Anatomy), 'which induced him to press upon his son the propriety of making 'himself master of the science, in order to the establishment of 'those lectures he afterwards so ably delivered.'—*Contributions to the Medical History of Pennsylvania by Dr. Caspar Morris*, 4 *Haz. Reg.* 332.

His portrait is in the possession of Miss Burd, at her house in Chestnut street.

3 JOSEPH, b. in Philadelphia, Nov. 28th, 1706; d. June 1793. He m. Mary Kearney. His only son, Joseph,* d. July, 1766. His daughter Kitty was m. to a Mr. Wallen of Jamaica, and d. shortly afterwards. In 1742 (Oct. 5th,) he was elected to the City Council, in which he served for some years.† He went, in the family, by the name of 'Gentleman Joe,' by reason of the gay, luxurious life which he led; and which, as appears from his brother's letters,‡ wasted his patrimony. He subsequently removed to Germantown, where he died.

4. WILLIAM, b. August 31, 1708; d. Decr. 29, 1710.

5. ANNE, b. August 5, 1710; m. to Charles Willing. Of her more hereafter.

6. WILLIAM, b. October 1, 1712. Of him more hereafter.

7. ELIZABETH, b. Sept. 28, 1714; d. Decr. 3, 1714.

* Most probably the 'Joseph W. Shippen' who subscribed to the Fish Club, (*ante*, p. xx.)

† *Minutes*, 417.

‡ EDWARD SHIPPEN TO CH. J. SHIPPEN, AT PHILADELPHIA.

'*Lancaster*, 15*th December*, 1753.

'DEAR SON:—That evening I left you I lodged in Germantown 'with my poor disconsolate brother. I let his wife know she must 'instantly change her most unkind behaviour to him or he would 'become broken-hearted, and then she would lose soon a most 'affectionate husband, and their children a most tender father.

'The Doctor is to sell the house wherein T. L. lives, and Mr. Mo- 'land is to be paid, and one or two more, and then my brother's 'creditors are all to be called together and some method proposed 'for payment, and when his creditors meet, it will be proper for 'yourself and Mr. Plumsted, and also the Doctor, to be present, 'that the creditors may be prevailed upon to give time for the dis- 'posal of things; for this is not a proper season to sell.' Also *Edward Shippen to Thomas Willing*, Lancaster, 11th January, 1754.

EDWARD, the eldest child of Joseph and Abigail Shippen, was b. in Boston, July 9, 1703; m. at Philadelphia, Sept. 20, 1725, to Sarah Plumley, dau. of Charles and Rose Plumley. She was born in Philadelphia, Nov. 8, 1706; d. April 28, 1735. They had issue,

1. ELIZABETH, b. Aug. 17, 1726; d. Aug. 29, 1726.
2. JOSEPH, } twins—b. Sept. 1727.
3. WILLIAM, } twins—d. same month.
4. EDWARD, b. Feb. 16, 1728–9: afterwards Chief Justice of the State of Pennsylvania.
5. SARAH, b. Feb. 22, 1730: afterwards the wife of Col. James Burd.
6. JOSEPH, b. Octr. 30, 1732: afterwards Colonel under, and Secretary to, the Province of Pennsylvania.
7. ROSE, b. Sept. 10, 1734; d. an infant.

Mr. Shippen m. 2dly, August, 1747, Mary Gray, dau. of William and Mary Gray. She was b. in London, January 13th, 1705–6, and d. at Lancaster, May 3d, 1778. The two or three of her letters yet remaining, and the affectionate terms in which she is always mentioned by her husband and step-sons, warrant us in believing her to have been a most estimable woman.* By her, Mr. Shippen had no children.

Mr. Shippen was brought up as a merchant by James Logan, and was in business (1732)† first, as Logan & Shippen, and afterwards, in 1749, with Thomas Lawrence in the

* 'Peggy and the baby are well. Molly is its name, for mam-'my's sake.'—*Ch. J. Shippen to his Father, Augt.* 25, 1757. Col. Shippen also called a daughter 'Mary,' after her.

† I have before me a curious bill against 'the Proprietors,' 'for 'sundrys sent to Stenton for the Delawares,' Sept. 7th, 1732.

fur trade, as Shippen & Lawrence.* He was elected, October 3, 1732, to, and served for many years, in the City Council, and in 1744 was Mayor of the City. In May, 1752, he removed to Lancaster,† where he was appointed Prothonotary, and continued such till 1778. He had large transactions as paymaster for supplies for the British and Provincial forces, when commanded by Gen. Forbes, Gen. Stanwix, and Col. Bouquet; and managed them with so much integrity as to receive public thanks.‡ He was a county judge

* The following extract from Mr. Swift's MSS. serves to show the profits realized on merchandise in those days. It is taken from a letter dated 20th September, 1747, written by Mr. John Swift to a correspondent in England:

'The China I sold altogether at 167½ pr. ct.; Damasks, 26 yds. 'sold at 75*s.*; ditto 40 yds. 133*s.* 4*d.*; broad Don Camblett 132*s.*; 'Boyled ditto £8 5*s.*; Silk Camblettees 82*s.* 6*d.*; Women's thimbles '12*s.*; Lovers' knots, No. 20, at 80*s.*, yd. wd.; Stanetts 88*s.*; Serpentines, No. 22, at 88*s.*; plain Camblettees, 41 yds. at 85*s.*; 'Tammys at 58*s.* The men's gloves won't sell. Sealing Wax 5*s.*; 'black Ribbon 16*s.*; Duke William Ribbon, and the platted Ribbons 'sold at 200 pr. ct.; Caps of all sorts at 175 pr. ct.; Men's stockings, No. 1, at 47*s.*; shaded duroys at 44*s.*; stars and garters, No. '31, at 88*s.*; plain Camblettees, No. 32, at 60*s.*; Ivory Combs at '200 pr. ct.; Horn ditto at 2*s.* 9*d.*; Ink powder at 9*s.* and 10*s.* pr. 'doz.; 3-4 Checks at 2*s.* 3*d.*, 2*s.* 2*d.*, 2*s.* 1*d.* aud 2*s.* pr. ell; 6-4 'ditto 4*s.* 2*d.* pr. ell: yd. wide ditto at 2*s.* 7*d.* pr. ell; new fashioned Diapers, 15 yds. at 41*s.*; Flowered quilting, 20 yds. at 54*s.*; 'Spotted Rugs at 200 pr. ct.; Felt Hats at 200 pr. ct.; Pins at 'above 200 pr. ct.; India Pictures at 10*s.*; Chamber Glasses at 70*s.*; '2 of the large Sconces I sold for £23; the works of charity at 29*s.* 'each. The Dowlas sold at 175 pr. ct.; Long Lawns at 175 pr. ct.; 'Printed Calicoes, 12½ yds. sold at 55*s.*, 54*s.* and 53*s.*; do. 2 colors, '18 yards, 80*s.*; purple ground, 18 yds. 85*s*; Linen handkf. 2*s.*; 'Chintz Ponabaggarrees at 28*s.* and 30*s.*; the ½ ps. Chintz Dorgurrees at 24*s.* and 25*s.*; Niccanees at 32*s.*; Cotton Romals at '23*s.*; Silk Romals at 80*s.* and 82*s.* 6*d.*; Bandannahs at 53*s.* and '54*s.*, all sold; Nuns thread sells but low at don the number; 'Rolled tapes, No. 19, at 10*s.*; do. 29, at 18*s.*; Dutch pretties 14*s.*; 'Writing paper 20*s.* and 28*s.*, only three rms. unsold. Shallons, No. '23, at 80*s.*; do. No. 22 at 75*s.*, 4 ps. unsold.'

† Hence generally designated as 'Edward Shippen, of Lancaster,' to distinguish him from the others of the same name.

‡ Chief Justice Shippen to his Father, in a letter dated *May* 10*th*, 1760, expresses great gratification at 'having settled your accounts,

under both the Provincial and State governments. In early life he laid out Shippensburg, with so much judgment as to its situation and advantages for settlers, that it speedily grew to be a flourishing village. In 1746–8 he was one of the founders of 'The College of New Jersey,' at first located at Newark, subsequently (1753) at Princeton, now so well known and honored as NASSAU HALL, and was one of its first Board of Trustees; a position which he resigned in 1767, after twenty years' service.* Nor was this his only service to the cause of education; the value of which his own accomplishments enabled him fully to appreciate.†

'and received the thanks of the General:' and in another, dated *May 28th*, 1760, he says, 'General Stanwix told me, he never saw 'fairer accounts, and that his Majesty himself and the whole army 'were greatly indebted to you.'

* *Catalogus Collegii Neo-Cæsariensis*, MDCCCLIV.

† He was also one of the subscribers to the Philadelphia Academy, which became afterwards the University of Pennsylvania.—*Charles Thomson to Col. Shippen*, January 31, 1755.

He was, amongst other things, a fine French scholar,—a rare species of knowledge in those days,—and got, through his son Edward, many of the letters found in French vessels, taken by the privateers.

EDWARD SHIPPEN, JR., TO HIS FATHER.

'*Philadelphia, June 23d*, 1758.

'HON'D SIR:—You wrote me to send you the French letters that 'came in the prize. I would cheerfully have procured them for you 'if there had been any, but the French Captain, when he struck, 'threw overboard every letter. There is a French flag of truce 'taken in our bay, by the Spry privateer, as she was running sugars, 'but you know she can contain no letters.

'We have no news, but are in daily expectation of hearing from 'Louisburg. Our kind love to mammy, sister, &c.

'I am, dear sir, your affectionate and dutiful son,

'EDWARD SHIPPEN, JR.'

Some of these letters are quite curious. Amongst them is one, translated by Mr. Wm. Duane, which gives some insight into the manners of the day, and the intercourse then existing between the people of France and her colonies.

'*Near Louisburg, May* 26, 1744.

'SIR AND DEAR FRIEND:—I have just received the letter of the '11th of last February, in duplicate, which you do me the honor

His public duties as a citizen, Mr. Shippen, as is shown by the foregoing condensed statement, discharged in a manner eminently praiseworthy and honorable. In his private intercourse, he showed himself virtuous and upright. Mr.

'to write me. The critical time in which we now are here, to learn 'by the first vessels that will arrive from Europe the declaration of 'war between France and England, which appears inevitable, and 'the fear that the Dutch will join this latter crown against us, ac'cording to the last news which we have just received of the engage'ment of our Brest squadron, joined to that of Spain, against Ad'miral Mathews, to which is added that the Toulon squadron is 'about to carry over the Pretender into England with some troops 'to support his party in that nation and place him on the throne, 'no longer permit me to spend this year in France, as I had previ'ously signified to you, and I cannot even think of making this 'voyage until we have a certainty of peace at least with the mari'time powers, so that this motive prevents my deciding positively 'upon the proposal that you make me, besides the fact that you do 'not tell me if the 50,000 French money that are asked for are pay'able in cash at the celebration of the marriage, or if it is meant, 'as I suppose, that this sum shall be discharged in many payments 'made annually. This is what you would oblige me by explaining 'in your first (letter) in reply.

'I can assure you, my dear friend, in advance, that this alliance 'is infinitely flattering to my daughter and myself, and that we are 'very sensible of the honor which Mons. and Madame De Launcey 'do her in asking her in marriage for their nephew. If it were not 'for this uncertainty of war I would not hesitate to go to France 'next spring, if the parties should agree after having seen each 'other, and I do not think that there would be the least obstacle on 'my daughter's part, if the gentleman is known to you. See, my 'dear friend, if he intends waiting until we shall have a certainty 'of peace; without that, I cannot expose myself to proceeding to 'France, and in one word that is the essential point of all. The 'business may perhaps be arranged in the interval of time that will 'elapse until I receive your reply thereupon. This is what I can 'do for my daughter. I will give her for a dower the fifty thousand 'livres French money that are demanded of me, payable 10,000 in 'cash at the celebration of the marriage, and the 40,000 remaining 'four years afterwards in one payment, and I will pay besides an 'annual income of two thousand livres in France, (and every year 'in advance,) by way of interest for the long time that I take for 'the payment of the 40,000 livres. And you will observe that if I 'gave the 50,000 of the dowry in cash, I would still have to make 'use of it in real estate that will not produce the income that I offer 'above, and which seems to me much more advantageous to the 'gentleman.

Lawrence blames him for being 'too religious.' His piety never degenerated into ascetecism.*

As a husband and a father he was affectionate and indulgent; manifesting at all times a tender solicitude for the temporal advancement and moral health of his children. He was most anxious to preserve their love for each other in its fulness and integrity after his death. To prevent, therefore, its being impaired by anything concerning the distribution of his property after his death—that most prolific source of alienation and controversy in families—he submitted his proposed will to his two sons; who, to their

'Finally, if my proposal suits the parties interested, you have 'only to acquaint me with it promptly, and draw up the form of 'the contract which they wish to have made, which you will have 'the kindness to send me in duplicate, that I may make my arrange-'ments thereupon, and send you a positive answer.

'It now remains for me to give you all the thanks that I owe you 'for the continued proofs that you give me and my daughter of 'your friendship. I assure you that our gratitude on this account 'is most lively, and no one has a more inviolable attachment.

'Sir and dear friend,

'Your very humble and very obedient servant,

'DISSAT.

'Accept also Madame Thomas Des Veaux' thousands of assurances 'of respect from my daughters and all my family. Present them 'also, I pray you, on behalf of my daughters and myself, to Mon-'sieur and Madame De Launcey.

'The vessels wherein this present (letter) and its duplicate will 'go, having postponed their departure until to-day the 10th of June, 'we have just learnt by two ships from Nantes and two from Bor-'deaux, which arrived at the Cape two days ago, that the king of 'France has declared war against England, and that he also wishes 'that the Dutch should declare themselves for or against. Behold 'all that I feared besides has happened; so, my dear friend, there 'is no longer any way of thinking of the project of marriage in 'question, now that they are unwilling to await the return of peace, 'which perhaps will be nearer at hand than they suppose. God 'grant it! DISSAT.'

* The first mention which I find of Mr. Shippen's participating actively in church affairs is, that, September 17th, 1730, he took his seat as an elder in the Synod of Philadelphia.—*Records Presbyterian Church*, 98.

honor be it said! fearing that he had not given their sister quite enough, suggested an addition to her portion. A codicil, prepared by his son Edward, increasing her share in his estate, was accordingly signed.*

Mr. Shippen's advanced age prevented his taking any very active part, except as a committee-man, during the Revolution. His judgment was fixed as to the rights of the Colonies, and his sentiments were warmly expressed in behalf of his country, not only during that eventful contest, but throughout that long period of oppression and resistance which preceded the final struggle.† He did not live to hear of the surrender of Cornwallis, but his faith in the success of the righteous cause seems to have never once wavered.‡

EDWARD, the eldest son of Edward Shippen and Sarah Plumley, was b. Feb. 16, 1729, at Philadelphia.

'EDWARD SHIPPEN,§ the subject of this memoir, followed 'the honorable course of his father, and fully sustained the 'reputation derived from him. Having completed his ele-'mentary education with distinguished diligence and success,

* Judge Yeates to his father-in-law, (Col. Burd,) Sept'r 25th, 1781.

† See his letters *passim*.

‡ His portrait, also, is in the possession of Miss Burd.

§ There are various biographical sketches of him; one of which, taken from the National Portrait Gallery, is reprinted here, as being better than any which I could present. It follows that written by Dr. Charles Caldwell, *Portfolio*, 1810. *Hazard's Reg.* IV. 241, as to Judge Shippen's lienage, and accordingly makes the same error in confounding Edward Shippen, of Lancaster, with Edward, who emigrated to America. I give Dr. Caldwell as the writer of this sketch, in the *Portfolio*, (reprinted in *Hazard*,) on his own authority: *Autobiography of Dr. Caldwell*, 430, (Philadelphia, 1855.) His portrait, by Stuart, is in the possession of Miss Burd, at her residence in Chestnut street.

'he commenced the study of the law under the direction of 'Tench Francis, Esquire, then the attorney-general of Penn-'sylvania. In 1748, Mr. Shippen, having prosecuted his 'legal studies for about two years, went to London to com-'plete them in the Temple. In our day, this is no longer 'necessary; nor indeed are our American youth required to 'go abroad for instruction, in any of the learned professions 'more than in the mechanic arts. After spending two years 'in London, not in frivolous dissipated pursuits, but in the 'acquirement of the knowledge of his profession and the 'general cultivation of his mind, Mr. Shippen was admitted 'a barrister of the Middle Temple; and he returned to 'Philadelphia, to commence his career of life, and enter 'upon the duties of a lawyer and a citizen. He was so 'occupied, when the war of our revolution interrupted the 'civil pursuits of our citizens, and suspended, more or less, 'their private business.*

'On the happy conclusion of this momentous struggle, 'the departments of government, as well as the occupations 'of the people, returned to their regular action and course. 'To furnish the judiciary with men of suitable qualifications, 'as to character and knowledge, was obviously an object of 'primary importance. Professional learning and moral 'integrity in the administration of the laws, were indispen-'sable to secure the public confidence for the courts of

* CH. J. SHIPPEN TO EDWARD SHIPPEN, AT LANCASTER.

'*December* 31*st*, 1776.

'HON'D SIR:—I did not receive your favor of the 16th inst. till 'yesterday. It has been laying in Dr. Shippen's house ever since 'it came—the Doctor himself having rode to Bethlehem at the time 'of the alarm.

'I still keep my family near town, at my place near the Falls of 'Schuylkill, where I purpose to spend the winter, keeping only a 'maid servant in the house in town, to prevent its being filled with 'soldiers.'

'justice; and in searching for them, Mr. Shippen could not 'be overlooked. He was accordingly appointed president 'of the court of common pleas of the county of Philadel- 'phia, a place of high trust; and was also the presiding 'judge of the court of quarter sessions for the city and 'county. These appointments were made under the consti- 'tution of the state, adopted in 1776. A more perfect 'organization of the judiciary was made by the constitution 'of 1790.

'In 1791, Mr. Shippen was appointed one of the judges 'of the supreme court, whose jurisdiction extended over the 'whole state, and whose duties and powers called for the 'highest grade of professional learning and talents, as well 'as of personal character and public confidence. On the 'election of Chief Justice M'Kean to the executive chair of 'the commonwealth in 1799, Judge Shippen succeeded him 'on the bench, and was appointed Chief Justice by Gover- 'nor M'Kean, who was perfectly well acquainted with the 'qualifications the office demanded, and with the fitness of 'the person he selected for it. Chief Justice Shippen con- 'tinued to perform the duties of his exalted station with 'undiminished ability, and unimpaired confidence and 'respect, until the close of the year 1805, when the infirmi- 'ties of age, he being then nearly seventy-seven years old, 'admonished him to retire to repose. A few months after 'his resignation of office, on the sixteenth day of April, '1806, he found his final resting place, placidly leaving the 'world, in which, from his earliest youth, he had been con- 'spicuous for his virtues and usefulness. The volumes of 'our judicial reports are enriched with many of his opinions, 'of great importance; and these are now received with the 'same respect which they commanded when they were sus-

'tained by his personal and official influence and authority. 'Much of our law which is now well settled, was, at the 'period of his judicial administration, in a state of uncer-'tainty, long usages sometimes interfering with positive 'legislative enactments. Principles were to be established 'suitable to our system of jurisprudence, and constructions 'to be given to doubtful laws. His sound mind, his excel-'lent legal education and great experience, his cool temper 'and discriminating sagacity, were all admirably calculated 'for the performance of such functions; and he did perform 'them in a manner to satisfy his contemporaries, and to be 'approved and unshaken to this day. Judicial qualifications 'and services are not of a character to catch the multitude, 'or to be the subjects of popular applause; but there is no 'officer concerned in the administration of the affairs of a 'people, whose duties are more anxious and arduous to him-'self, or more important to the community, than those of 'the judge. The preparatory education and long study; 'the painful and attentive experience, which are indispen-'sable for the attainment of the qualifications befitting the 'bench; the habits of close and careful investigation; the 'faculty of discovering the true ground of controversy, of 'distinguishing between real and apparent resemblances, 'between sound reasoning and ingenious sophism; the 'firmness never to yield principles to expediency, nor to 'sacrifice or disturb the great system of jurisprudence for 'particular cases; and withal, to hold a perfect command 'over every feeling that might irritate the temper or mis-'lead the judgment, present to our contemplation a combi-'nation of rare and valuable qualities, deserving our highest 'consideration and respect. The laws must be sustained 'with independence and intelligence, or it is in vain that 'they are wise and salutary; justice must be rendered faith-

'fully to the parties who appeal for it to the judicial tribu- 'nals, or it is a mockery to promise them protection and 'redress. The active, efficient, vital operations of the gov- 'ernment are performed by the courts. No man is so high 'or so humble as to be beyond their reach; they bring the 'laws into every man's house, to punish or to protect them.* 'Such are the responsibilities of a judge. It was on the 'judgment seat of the law, that the high qualities of Chief 'Justice Shippen were brought into their best exercise and 'use. He seemed by nature as well as education to have 'been especially prepared for this station. Patient, learned, 'discriminating and just, no passion or private interest, no 'selfish or unworthy feeling of favor or resentment ever held 'the slightest influence over his conduct or decisions.

'Few situations expose the temper to more irritating 'trials than that of a judge. He must occasionally encoun- 'ter ignorance, impertinence, stupidity, obstinacy, and chi- 'canery, and he must take care that they do not move him 'from his line of duty. The bland and equal temper of 'Chief Justice Shippen never forsook him amidst such 'trials, but, on the contrary, threw a charm over his manner 'of repelling or submitting to them. The young and the 'timid advocate was encouraged by his kindness, and flat- 'tered by his attention. He knew and practiced the lesson 'of Lord Bacon, that "patience is one of the first duties of 'a judge;" and he felt that he was bound to hear every 'party and every advocate, before he decided his cause. A 'suitor might go from his court disappointed by the judg- 'ment, but he could not be dissatisfied with the judge.

* Possibly the writer of the above sketch may have had in his mind, whilst penning some of the foregoing sentences, Hooker's magnificent Apostrophe to Law; (*Eccles. Polity*, Book I. p. 194, Am. ed. 1844.)

'Of the private character and deportment of Chief Jus-'tice Shippen, it may be truly said that he has left few imi-'tators of his manners. His politeness was of the kind 'that has its foundations in a well regulated temper and the 'best feelings of a benevolent heart, polished by a familiar 'intercourse, from his birth, with refined society. He com-'bined, in a remarkable degree, benignity with dignity, con-'ciliating the affections while he commanded a perfect 'respect; and, as a valuable citizen, and an accomplished 'lawyer and judge, remarkable for the great extent and 'minute accuracy of his knowledge, he must ever be con-'spicuous, among those worthies who have won, by their 'virtues and their talents, an imperishable name.'

Judge Shippen was, as has been alleged, a loyalist, and Mr. Sabine, whose research and impartiality entitle his opinions to the most respectful consideration, has so regarded him. It seems to me, that setting aside the fact of his having been subsequently appointed Chief Justice, and the bearing which that has as showing the esteem in which he was held by his contemporaries, his letters show him to have been, if a loyalist, one of the most moderate kind. He was evidently a man of quiet and peaceable temper; shrinking not only 'from war and war's alarms,' but even from the less dangerous and exciting strife of party politics.* The boyish folly of his son,† who allowed himself to be misled by his elder companions, no doubt contributed largely, if not altogether, to the belief in the loyalism of his father; but, even in this matter, the comments made by Judge

* Mr. Wharton (State Trials, p. 46) has given us a most vivid picture of the manner in which, in the times of political strife just after the Revolution, the Pennsylvania judges, as well as those of other States, wielded their high offices to serve their respective parties. To no such censure was the judicial career of Mr. Shippen obnoxious.

† See post, letters, p. 255.

Shippen in his letter to his father at Lancaster, show the real feelings and spirit of the man; and the manner in which Gen. Washington disposed of it may be considered as proving, that the sentiments which that great patriot entertained concerning Judge Shippen, were not those with which he regarded active or well known loyalists.*

Many persons in the Colonies regarded the taxation and other oppressions of their country, as proceeding wholly from the Ministry, and not from the Crown. They termed the war 'a wicked ministerial war,' and whilst disposed to venture everything for their liberty and rights, they were not prepared to recognize the necessity of a separation. It was to this class, including many 'men of undoubted 'patriotism,' I believe Judge Shippen to have belonged.†

Mr. Shippen married a daughter of Mr. Tench Francis,

* Sparks' Washington, III. 343.

† Mr. Sabine, in his manly and impartial essay prefixed to his *Loyalists*, has so fully considered this subject that a reference to it is sufficient for the purposes of these notices. One short extract from it (p. 67) will serve to show that even ardent *Whig leaders* were not without doubts as to the wisdom of a separation.

'All, both Whigs and Tories, were born and had grown up under 'a monarchy; and the abstract question of renouncing it or of con'tinuing it was one on which men of undoubted patriotism differed 'widely. Very many of the Whigs came into the final measure of 'separating from the mother country with great reluctance, and 'doubt and hesitation prevailed even in Congress. Besides, the 'Whig leaders uniformly denied, that Independence was embraced 'in their plans, and constantly affirmed, that their sole object was 'to obtain concessions, and to continue the connection with England 'as hitherto; and John Adams goes further than this, for, says he, '"*there was not a moment during the revolution, when I would not have* '*given everything I possessed for a restoration to the state of things* '*before the contest began, provided we could have had a sufficient security* '*for its continuance.*" If Mr. Adams be regarded as expressing the 'sentiments of the Whigs, *they* were willing to remain Colonists, 'provided they could have had their rights secured to them; while 'the Tories were contented thus to continue, *without* such security. 'Such, as it appears to me, was the only difference between the two 'parties *prior* to hostilities, and many Whigs, like Mr. Adams, would 'have been willing to rescind the declaration of independence, and 'to forget the past, upon proper guarantees for the future.'

with whom he studied.* Of her family I have obtained the following information.

The first of the family of Francis, of whom the American descendants have any account, was

* The following letter is characteristic of the 'manners of the 'time,' as to marriages:

WILLIAM ALLEN TO EDWARD SHIPPEN, AT LANCASTER.

'DEAR SIR:—Your son delivered me your favor, by which I ob-'serve that he has requested your consent to his marriage, and that 'you would be so good as to give him your assistance in setting him 'forward in the world; and, by what you write, I perceive he has 'signified to you that Mr. Francis would expect that something 'should be done for him which would bear a proportion to what he 'gives his daughter. I have perused the estimate of what you 'intend for both your sons, and have well weighed the reasons you 'give for your conduct on the occasion, and I have made so free as 'to confer with my mother about the affair, and to communicate the 'contents of your letter. As both she and I have had a sincere 'regard for you and your family, and have heartily wished their 'welfare, and as you have been pleased to regard us in that light 'by communicating your thoughts on the occasion, I shall, with the 'freedom and candor of a friend, give you my sentiments; which, 'however, are submitted to your better judgment. And, as you 'know your own circumstances better than I possibly can, you can 'more rightly determine what is expedient for you to do.

'I would first mention that you seem to think there is danger of 'your removal from your offices, and that you hold them by a pre-'carious tenure. To this give me leave to answer that Sam Blens-'ton was the only prothonotary ever removed in the Province, as 'far as I can learn; and it was done because he set himself against 'and insulted government to a high degree. I very well know that 'Mr. Hamilton was of opinion that he could not be legally removed, 'and told Governor Thomas that Sam would contest it; but he, 'being a proud, rich fellow, was either ill advised or did not think 'it worth while to have any contention about it. The office of pro-'thonotary is, in its nature, during good behavior, and until a 'person is legally convicted of ill behavior, he cannot, in my opin-'ion, be legally ousted from the office. Ill behavior may be made 'out in sundry ways, such as notorious crime, neglect of the records, '&c. In some conversation with Mr. Francis on this subject, on a 'former occasion, I found he was of opinion that the office was for 'life. All of them in England are on that footing. Bordly, of 'Maryland, was removed, and he brought his action against the 'person appointed in his place, and recovered damages against him. 'But, in case the Proprietor should contemplate such a step, can 'you believe that your interest with the present Governor and his 'friends, your alliance with Mr. Francis and his family, to say no

Philip Francis,* Mayor of Plymouth in 1644, during the civil war. He was a Royalist, and it is said, that the subsequent preferment of his son and grandson in the Church of Ireland was owing to his services in the cause of the King. His son,

The Very Rev. John Francis, D.D., was Dean of Leighlin, about the close of that century, a position which he held

'more, would not be sufficient to prevent anything of the sort being 'put into execution? Believe me, I think you are as safe from any 'danger of removal as I am from being dispossessed of the house in 'which I live. Your prudence is such that you will ever recommend 'yourself to the Proprietor and his friends.

'I have dwelt thus long upon this matter in order to set it in a 'right light. As, therefore, you have an honorable subsistence for 'yourself; and as, when you made application for the office, you 'very handsomely said, that your object in asking it was that you 'might have it in your power to do something for your children; 'these considerations make me presume so far as to give you my 'opinion that what you propose to make over to your son upon his 'marriage, is not sufficient. It is not equal to the fortune which 'Mr. Francis gives his daughter; and as you have the name about 'town of having a good estate, and own sundry houses, the world 'will think it strange, if, on the marriage of your eldest son, you do 'not give him a house to live in; and, if this match should be bro-'ken off, where, do you think, is he like to succeed, when it is told 'that his father disregarded him so much that he would give him 'little or nothing. I think it will be putting a slight on your son, 'who is generally well thought of, and who, if no accident happens 'to depress, will make a figure in the Province.

'I observe, likewise, the estimate you make of what you intend 'to give your son Joseph. If a house to each of them were added '—that where Evans lives, and that where Mr. Burd did live—it 'would be of service to them, and would not be missed by you.

'My mother joins me in opinion as to this matter. But I beg 'leave to assure you, that nothing would have induced me to be 'thus free, were I not persuaded that you would be so kind as to 'believe it to proceed from my hearty friendship and good will. 'Your son knows not the contents of this. I think it not advisable 'for me to say anything of the affair to Mr. Francis for many very 'good reasons, too tedious to mention.

'I beg leave to assure you that I am, sir,

'Your affectionate friend, kinsman and humble servant,

'WILL. ALLEN.'

* The coat of arms is—'Per bend or and sa. a lion ramp. counterchanged. *Crest.* An eagle displ. erm. beaked and membered or.

until 1704 at least; when he appears to have sat in the Convention at Dublin.* He seems to have been a scholar and a great collector of books, and the itinerant Bibliopole, John Dunton, who was very grateful for his patronage, describes him as a very eloquent preacher. His son,

The Very Rev. JOHN FRANCIS, was Dean of Lismore, 1722, and held besides, the Rectory of St. Mary's Church, Dublin; from which, it is said, he was ejected for his Jacobitism. From this, it is inferred, that he inherited the attachment to the Stuarts, to which the advancement of his family in the Church of Ireland has been attributed.

He married MISS TENCH, a lady of good family, and by her had, amongst others,

TENCH, of whom more hereafter, as head of the American branch of the family.

RICHARD, an eminent lawyer, author of a work, 'Maxims 'in Equity,' well thought of and esteemed by his professional brethren. It has been frequently reprinted.†

PHILIP, who entered the Church. He abandoned the Tory principles of the family, became the chaplain to Lord Holland, and obtained through his influence a Rectorate

* Ware's History of the Church in Ireland.

† Maxims of Equity, &c. By Richard Francis, of the Middle Temple, Esq. First American Edition. By William Waller Hening, Counsellor at Law, Editor of the Statutes at Large of Virginia, &c.
RICHMOND:
1823.

Preface to the First American Edition.

Francis's Maxims have long held a distinguished rank among books of authority. They were first published in London, in 1728, in a thin folio volume; and although the *title pages* of 1739 and 1746, purport to be the *second* and *third editions*, yet, all the books are of the same impression. [See Clarke's Bibliotheca Legum, or Law Catalogue, p. 275.] In 1791, an octavo edition was published in Dublin.

in Suffolk. He received the degree of D.D. 1762, from the University of Dublin, and died in 1773.*

He is most bitterly satirized by Churchill, in 'The Author,'† and, it is said, not very highly esteemed by his American relatives, whom he visited. But he was a man of fine talents and learning, as exhibited in his translations of Horace, Demosthenes, and other publications, amongst which were several Plays, which have received a fair share of commendation.

His son, b. 1740, at Dublin, was the celebrated SIR PHILIP FRANCIS,‡ K. G. C. B., now generally supposed to have been the author of JUNIUS.

TENCH FRANCIS, above mentioned, emigrated to Maryland shortly after the year 1700. He had received a learned and legal education in his own country, and established himself in Kent County, where, 1724, he m. ELIZABETH TURBUTT, a lady of great beauty and good family. But he was soon attracted to Philadelphia as a better field for his talents. In 1744 he was made Attorney General, and held the position till 1752; and from 1750 to 1754, he was Recorder of the City.

* Rose (*Biog. Dict.*) says, that Gibbon was for a short time one of his pupils, and that his Rectory at Barrow in Suffolk, and also the chaplainship of Chelsea College, were the rewards of his services as a political writer.

† The Editor of Churchill's Works, London, 1804, seems, in a prefaratory note to 'The Author,' to cast a doubt upon the supposed reference to this Dr. Francis; and attributes Churchill's enmity, if Dr. Francis be the person spoken of, to political feelings.

‡ For a sketch of Sir Philip, see *Rose's Biog. Dict.* s. v.

He was highly considered as a man, a lawyer, and a scholar. He was also something of an author. One of his pieces on 'Paper Currency,' is printed in Pownall's work on the Colonies, and has received the praise of political economists of the present century, as showing him to have been far in advance of his times.*

He died Aug. 14, 1758.

His children were,

1. JOHN, b. 1725; d. unm.
2. ANNE, b. 1727; d. 1771. She was m. to JAMES TILGHMAN, Secretary of the Land Office in Pennsylvania.† They had a large family, among whom were,
   - TENCH, a Colonel in the Revolutionary army, aid to Gen. Washington, &c.
   - ANNE, m. to Wm. Hemsley, Esq.
   - ELIZABETH, m. to James Lloyd, Esq.

* The portraits of himself and wife, also of James Tilghman and wife, the latter holding Chief Justice Tilghman, then a child, are in possession of Miss Burd.

† From an exceedingly curious MS. 'account of births and 'deaths, &c.' of various Maryland families, I extract the following:

Richard Tilghman, (whose pedigree is given in the MS. to Richard Tilghman, living 1399 in the reign of Henry IV,) b. 1626; m. Miss Foxley. He came to Maryland in 1675, was bred a surgeon, and was one of the signers to 'have justice done' on Charles I, and left England for fear of the consequences. His tenth child,

Richard, m. 1672 Anna Maria Lloyd, and had, with others,

James Tilghman, m. Ann Francis.

Anna Maria, second dau. and fourth child of Matthew Tilghman and Anne his wife, was born on the 17th day of July, 1755. She m. Col. Tench Tilghman, one of Gen. Washington's aids-de-camp, whose likeness, with that of the General and the Marquis de Lafayette, was taken by order of the Legislature of Maryland, and suspended in the room occupied by the House of Delegates, where it now remains. They had children,

Margaret, who m. Tench Tilghman, of Talbot county, Maryland, and d. leaving one son, Tench.

Elizabeth, who m. Nicholas Goldsborough, of Talbot county, Maryland.

WILLIAM, afterwards Chief Justice of Pennsylvania,* m. Margaret Allen.

PHILIP, who entered the English Navy, and married a daughter of Admiral Milbank.

3. MARY, b. 1729; d. 1801; m. WILLIAM COXE, of New Jersey, by whom she had a large family. Among them were,

TENCH, of some note as an author and politician, m. Miss McCall.

JOHN, a Judge of the District Court.

WILLIAM, an eminent pomologist.

DANIEL W., m. Margaret Burd.

SARAH, m. to Andrew Allen, Esq.

REBECCA, m. to Dr. Wm. McIlvaine, an eminent physician.

4. TENCH, b. 1730; d. 1800; m. 1762, ANNE, eldest dau. of Charles and Anne Willing. They had issue,

1. JOHN FRANCIS, b. 1763; m. Abby, dau. of Hon. John Brown, of Rhode Island, and was the father of the Hon. JOHN BROWN FRANCIS, Senator of the United States, Governor of Rhode Island, &c.
2. THOMAS WILLING FRANCIS, b. 1767, an eminent merchant in Philadelphia. He m. Dorothy, dau. of Hon. Thomas Willing, by whom he had a large family, of whom now survive only,

ELIZABETH, m. to her cousin, the Hon. John B. Francis, above mentioned.

* See Mr. Binney's eloquent eulogium, *Appendix to* 16 *Sergeant & Rawle's Reports.*

Anne, m. to Hon. James A. Bayard, U. S. Senator from Delaware.

3. Sophia Francis, m. to George Harrison, Esq., of Philadelphia. She d. 1851.

4. Charles Francis, b. 1771; d. unm. 1845.

5. Elizabeth Powel Francis, b. 1777; m. 1806 to Joshua Fisher. She still survives. She is the mother of Mr. J. Francis Fisher, who m. Elizabeth, dau. of the Hon. Henry Middleton, Governor of South Carolina, and Minister to the Court of St. Petersburg.

Mrs. Middleton was the dau. of Col. Julines Hering, of Jamaica, whose wife was Mary Helen, dau. of John Inglis, and Mary McCall, of Philadelphia.

5. Elizabeth, b. 1733; d. 1800; m. John Lawrence, by whom she had one child,

Elizabeth, m. to James Allen, son of Chief Justice Allen.* They had,

James, who d. s. p.

Anne Penn, m. to James Greenleaf.

Margaret, m. to Chief Justice Tilghman.

Mary, (still living) m. to Harry Walter Livingston, of Livingston's Manor, New York.

6. Margaret Francis, b. 1735; d. 1794; m. to Edward Shippen, Chief Justice, as above mentioned. They had issue,

1. Elizabeth, m. to Edward Burd, Major in the American Army during the Revolution, son of Col. James Burd and Sarah Shippen.

* *Sabine's Loyalists.* s. v. Allen.

They had issue,

EDWARD SHIPPEN BURD, m. Miss Sims.

MARGARET, m. to D. W. Coxe.

SARAH, still living.

2. SARAH, m. to Thomas Lea, and had,

ROBERT.

MARGARET, m. to Dominick Lynch, of New York. They had six children.

JANE, m. to Julius Izard Pringle, of S. C., and has issue.

DOMINICK, m. Antonia Arquimba, of Port Mahon.

MARGARET SHIPPEN, m. to Stewart C. Maitland, of Scotland.*

GEORGE HARRISON.

3. EDWARD, m. Elizabeth Footman. They had,

EDWARD,

MARGARET,

ELIZABETH,

RICHARD,

MARY,

FANNY.

4. MARY, m. Dr. Wm. McIlvaine. They had,

WILLIAM,

EDWARD BLOOMFIELD,

MARIA,

MARGARET.

5. JAMES.

6. MARGARET, m. April 8, 1779, to Gen. Arnold.†
They had issue,

* Burke's Landed Gentry.

† Arnold of Little Messenden Abbey. Burke's Landed Gentry.

EDWARD SHIPPEN, Lieut. 6th Bengal Cavalry, and Paymaster of Muttra; d. at Dinapoor in India, Dec. 13, 1813.

JAMES ROBERTSON,* Major General, K. H. and K. Crescent, m. Virginia, dau. of Bartlett Goodrich, Esq., of Saling Grove, Essex.

* Lieut. Gen. Robertson Arnold died in London on December 27th, 1854. He was a second son of Benedict Arnold by Margaret his wife, daughter of Chief Justice Shippen, of Pennsylvania. He entered the corps of Royal Engineers in 1798, and served more than half a century. He married Virginia, daughter of Bartlett Goodrich, Esq., of the Isle of Wight, and for his military services was created a Knight of Hanover, was appointed Aid-de-camp to William IV, and was presented with a costly sword.

The above-named officer was the second of five children which Arnold's second wife, Miss Shippen of Philadelphia, bore him, viz: Edward, James Robertson, George, Wm. F., and Sophia. His first wife bore three sons, viz: Benedict, Richard and Henry. Benedict, the eldest, an officer of artillery in the British army, died young in the West Indies. Henry entered the King's service after his father's defection, and was a lieutenant of cavalry in the American Legion. He lived afterwards at Troy, New York, with his aunt Hannah, and was engaged in mercantile pursuits. At a subsequent period he removed to Canada, where he is now a man of property. He received half pay and a grant of lands from the British government. Richard in 1782 was also a lieutenant of cavalry in the American Legion, commanded by his father. In almost every particular his history is identical with that of his brother Henry.

James Robertson entered the British army in 1798, and rose to the rank of Colonel of Engineers. He was stationed at Bermuda from 1816 to 1818, and from the last-named year until 1823, was at Halifax, and the commanding officer of engineers in Nova Scotia and New Brunswick. While thus in command he was at St. Johns, and on going into the house built by his father, in King street, which is still standing, he wept like a child. He was a small man; his eyes were of remarkable sharpness, and in features bore a striking resemblance to his father. A gentleman, who has been in service with him, and was intimately acquainted with him, speaks of him in terms of high commendation, and relates that he has often heard him express a strong desire to visit the United States. Since the accession of Queen Victoria, he has been one of her majesty's aids-de-camp. In 1841, he was transferred from the engineer corps and appointed Major General, and a Knight of the Royal Hanoverian Guelphic Order. See *Sabine's Loyalists*. s. v. Arnold.

George, Lieut. Col. 2d Bengal Cavalry; d. in India, Nov. 1, 1828.

William Fitch, of Little Messenden Abbey, county Bucks, a magistrate for Bucks, late Capt. 19th Lancers, b. June 25, 1794; m. May 19, 1819, Elizabeth Cecilia, only dau. of Alexander Ruddach, Esq., Capt. R. N., of Dorkney and of the island of Tobago, and has issue,

Edward Glaburn,
Margaretta Stewart,
William Trail,
Elizabeth Sophia,
Georgiana Phipps,
Louisa Russell.

Sophia Matilda, m. to Col. Pownall Phipps, E. I. C. service; related to the Mulgrave family, and has one son and two daughters.

Arms.—Gu. three pheons, arg. on a chief of the second, a bar nebulée, az.

Crest.—A demitiger, sa. bezantée, maned and tufted or, holding a broad arrow, stick, gu. feathers and pheon, arg.

Motto.—Nil desperandum.

7. Rachael Francis, b. 1737;. m. 1st, Mr. Relfe;* 2dly, Matthew Pearce, by whom she had several children.

* 'Feb. 19, 1760.
'My sister, Rachel Francis, is to be married in a fortnight to Mr. 'John Relfe.'

3

8. TURBUTT FRANCIS, b. 1740; d. 1797. He was a Colonel in the British Continental army, and distinguished in the French and Indian wars. He m. Rebecca, the only dau. of Samuel Mifflin, and by her had,

   TENCH.

   SAMUEL, who took the name of his grandfather Mifflin, and m. Elizabeth Davis.

   REBECCA, who m. Mathias Harrison. Their dau. is Rebecca, widow of the late James McMurtrie, Esq.

9. PHILIP, b. 1748; m. his first cousin, on the maternal side, a Miss Goldsborough, of Maryland. He left descendants by a daughter, m. to a Mr. Thomas, of Maryland, whose son,

   PHILIP FRANCIS THOMAS, was a few years since Governor of Maryland.

"The marriage of one of the daughters of Chief Justice Shippen to the notorious General Arnold, has given occasion to many injurious reflections, which, as they regard the lady as well as her family, may be pronounced not only unkind, but ungenerous. She was, indeed, unfortunate enough in such an alliance, and her memory should have been spared the additional hardship of baseless insinuations. For these, I would refer to the life of Arnold, in an anonymous publication entitled 'Washington and his Generals,' and to the posthumous memoirs of Aaron Burr, by Matthew L. Davis.

"It was reserved to a late period to account in any way for the treason of Benedict Arnold by a suggestion of the influence of the family with which he was associated by marriage, or of the beautiful young woman of whom every domestic tradition gives a character the reverse of 'gay and frivolous,' 'artful and extravagant.'

"I am allowed here to quote the words of an excellent lady, still living, whose reminiscences have been kindly furnished to me, a lady to whose personal and intellectual attractions the most malignant of Mrs. Arnold's detractors bears evidence. She says: 'I may add my recollections of 'my mother's general opinion of Mrs. Arnold, often ex'pressed to others as well as to myself. Being intimately 'acquainted with Mr. Shippen's family, she well understood 'their several characteristics, and would dwell with pleasure 'on the affectionate and exemplary conduct of Mrs. Arnold, 'both before and after her marriage. She used to say that 'Miss Peggy Shippen was particularly devoted to her father, 'making his comfort her leading thought, often preferring 'to remain with him when evening parties and amusements 'would attract her sisters from home. She was the darling 'of the family circle, and never fond of gadding. There 'was nothing of frivolity either in her dress, demeanor, or 'conduct, and though deservedly admired, she had too much 'good sense to be vain.' * * * 'I have often heard 'her speak with deep feeling of the sad fate of this most 'excellent woman; of her great purity of mind and princi'ples,' &c. * * * 'This estimate of Mrs. Arnold's 'character was also confirmed by my brother, who was inti'mately acquainted with the family of Mr. Shippen. He 'always spoke of her with emphatic and distinguished *respect* 'for her highly estimable qualities of mind and heart, and 'he deplored for her the lamentable conflict she must have 'endured on discovering her husband's treason, between 'love for her country and her father's family, and grief for 'her husband's base conduct. Thus have I been accus- 'tomed, all my life, to hear Mrs. Arnold spoken of as a 'suffering and innocent victim.'*

* Additional testimony is to be found in the letter in which Arnold addressed her. He says:

'DEAR MADAM:—Twenty times have I taken up my pen to 'write to you, and as often has my trembling hand refused to obey 'the dictates of my heart—a heart which, though calm and serene 'amidst the clashing of arms and all the din and horrors of war, 'trembles with diffidence and the fear of giving offence when it 'attempts to address you on a subject so important to its happiness. 'Dear Madam, your charms have lighted up a flame in my bosom 'which can never be extinguished; your heavenly image is too 'deeply impressed ever to be effaced. My passion is not founded 'on personal charms only: that sweetness of disposition and good- 'ness of heart, that sentiment and sensibility which so strongly 'mark the character of the lovely Miss P. Shippen, renders her 'amiable beyond expression, and will ever retain the heart she has 'once captivated.

'On you alone my happiness depends, and will you doom me to 'languish in despair? Shall I expect no return to the most sincere, 'ardent, and disinterested passion? Do you feel no pity in your 'gentle bosom for the man who would die to make you happy? 'May I presume to hope it is not impossible I may make a favorable 'impression on your heart? Friendship and esteem you acknow- 'ledge. Dear Peggy, suffer that heavenly bosom, (which cannot 'know itself the cause of pain without a sympathetic pang,) to ex- 'pand with a sensation more soft, more tender than friendship. A 'union of hearts is undoubtedly necessary to happiness; but give 'me leave to observe that true and permanent happiness is seldom 'the effect of an alliance formed on a romantic passion, where fancy 'governs more than judgment. Friendship and esteem, founded on 'the merit of the object, is the most certain basis to build a lasting 'happiness upon; and when there is a tender and ardent passion 'on one side, and friendship and esteem on the other, the heart '(unlike yours) must be callous to every tender sentiment, if the 'taper of love is not lighted up at the flame.

'I am sensible your prudence and the affection you bear your 'amiable and tender parents, forbids your giving encouragement to 'the addresses of any one without their approbation. Pardon me, 'dear madam, for disclosing a passion I could no longer confine in 'my tortured bosom. I have presumed to write your papa, and 'have requested his sanction to my addresses. Suffer me to hope 'for your approbation. Consider before you doom me to misery, 'which I have not deserved but by loving you too extravagantly. 'Consult your own happiness, and if incompatible, forget there is

"In a memoir intended to circulate only within the limits of our relationship, it may be permitted to the descendants of a family which has at all times been respected for its virtues, to defend their loyalty to the government under which they were born.

"Attached, as they were, by the strongest ties, to the land of their fathers, they were not less jealous of their hereditary rights as freemen; and were not found backward in maintaining them by every effort short of that kind of resistance which the laws they revered called treason. And if they doubted the security which liberty and property might obtain under democratic forms of government, or of the possibility of successful resistance by arms to the mighty power of England, they might well be pardoned for hesitation to embark in a struggle which, should it end in defeat, might be followed by severe oppression, if in success, by the convulsions of an unsteady, disjointed, weak confederacy.

"It should be recollected, too, that here in Pennsylvania, the most prosperous of all the colonies, the government of the Proprietaries had been particularly mild and generous, to which much consideration was deservedly due. And whatever cause of complaint we might urge, as *Englishmen*, against the parliament as violating old *Magna Charta rights*, that *our charter of Pennsylvania*, under which we accepted our lands and provincial privileges,

'so unhappy a wretch; for may I perish if I would give you one 'moment's inquietude to purchase the greatest possible felicity to 'myself. Whatever my fate may be, my most ardent wish is for 'your happiness, and my latest breath will be to implore the blessing of heaven on the idol and only wish of my soul.

'Adieu, dear madam, and believe me unalterably,

'Your sincere admirer and devoted humble servant,

'B. ARNOLD.

'*Sept.* 25, 1778.

'MISS PEGGY SHIPPEN.'

reserved to King and Parliament the right of taxation by duties on commerce. It might be doubted, therefore, with some reason, how far warlike resistance was in any respect justified. A large part of our most respectable inhabitants were opposed to such measures on principle; and if the influence of wealth increased their timidity, it was not without excuse, when its possessors measured their own pecuniary risks with that of a large proportion of the most flaming patriots.

"Success has added the justification which belongs to it, to the cause of the republicans, and toryism is a name of reproach. But the writer, who has no disposition to detract in any way from the honors justly due to those who carried through our revolutionary struggle, would only ask for those who, in those trying times, still loved England, and all its time-honored institutious, and feared to lose by severance from their mother country, the regulated liberty and stable rights they most held dear, that they should not be branded *all* as traitors.

"The writer has never seen any evidence that the family of Shippen sympathized with those who would have oppressed their country. Some of them joined the American armies; and those who did not, and especially Mr. Edward Shippen, submitted to the powers de facto, and gave in his declaration of neutrality, or whatever was the assurance of submission required.

"While Philadelphia was held by the British army, civilities were reciprocated with them by the families of wealth and birth who remained in the city, and the young ladies did not reject the homage of the accomplished officers. Among them was the handsome and brilliant Major André, who, endowed with all the gifts and tastes which win the regard of the sex, devoted them all to please the beautiful Margaret Shippen, and although I believe there was no thought of love between them, a mutual regard and friendship was established and maintained till the sad catastrophe which involved the fate of both. He was her Knight at the celebrated fete of the Meschianza,* and, it is said, kept up with her a correspondence of courtesy, under cover of which he conveyed his communications to her husband. Of this, however, *only one letter*, offering to procure for her in New York some articles of dress, is presented as evidence. But even if this supposition be well founded, it is not, I believe, by any one, pretended that she was cognizant or in fault.

"Soon after the evacuation of Philadelphia by the British, the military command of the city was bestowed on General Arnold.

"At that time no suspicions of his patriotism had been whispered. Scarcely any soldier had done so much to sustain the martial renown of his country; and yet, notwithstanding the adventurous expedition led by him through the northern wilderness of Maine to the siege of Quebec, which, it is thought, would have been captured if his advice had been followed; his brilliant feats on the lakes and in Connecticut; his gallant charges at Saratoga, which decided the victory; all this had no influence in silencing personal enemies, who might, perhaps, have been more patriotic if not more just, if they had overlooked some acts, the very worst of which, as proved before a court martial, were not greatly injurious to his country, and such, perhaps, as always have been and will be committed by some who manage the commissariat of an army.

"It is noted that on his trial by court martial in January,

* Gent's Mag. vol. 48, (1778), pp. 330, 353.

1780, he made a most invidious comparison between his own services and those of his chief accuser, whose wavering fidelity he contrasts with his own sterner patriotism, when, at that very time, he had been for eight months in correspondence with the enemy. This correspondence was not, I presume, at that time even guessed at. It may not unreasonably be supposed to have been begun under a sense of deep resentment at the charges made against him while his wounds were still bleeding from so many a hard-fought field. For three years he had been the object of attacks. From influences which we cannot now trace, his promotion was stopped; juniors put over him, who had done no such deeds as his; honorable commands withheld, which he thought his due; his pride as an officer galled to the utmost, till he was driven to the project of abandoning the service of his country, from which he neither expected gratitude nor justice. *I* do not say that he was in the right; that he did not merit the distrust and neglect that he was treated with; *but only this*, that he might have persuaded himself fully that he was an injured and persecuted man. In matters of rank, no one feels so keenly as a soldier. His pride is more than woman's vanity, and many a one has abandoned a cause with far less reason than Arnold. *His* was a bad nature, and he went further: *he betrayed it.* I have the opinion of a most candid and honest historian (Mr. Sparks) to confirm my own, that had Arnold obtained the honors he fought for, or been pardoned his official irregularities; had his great public services been permitted to cover his private misconduct, he had never been the betrayer of the country for which he had already done so much.

"The coldness and resentment arising from what (whether justly or not) he very naturally thought persecution, inclined him to seek his society elsewhere than in that circle of which his enemies formed a conspicuous part; and he found, it is likely, in the high breeding and refinement of our 'little 'aristocracy,' a charm which was new to him. It was not long before he became captive to the fascinations of the beautiful Margaret Shippen, and to the great distress of her family, she returned his love.* Tradition tells us that the connection was violently opposed, not so much from political feeling as from distrust of the man, objection to his origin, and dislike of his private character, as far as it was known. Arnold was not, in fact, a gentleman. His birth and early education were low; and his peddling and smuggling trade with the islands, and his traffic in cattle and horses, could neither have improved his manners nor his morals. He was reckless, daring and unprincipled; qualities fit enough to make a great soldier, but not to secure the confidence of an honorable parent, who looks for something better in the partner of a darling child.

"It is, however, most probable that anecdotes, repeated, after his disgrace, (perhaps invented then or embellished,) to illustrate his mercenary, mean, and treacherous disposition, were not at that time known in Philadelphia, where he arrived, crippled with honorable wounds, and glorious with laurels won by exploits such as no officer in the army then could boast of. More likely is it that then were circulated traits of generosity and kindness, such as his conduct in educating, at his own expense, the orphans of Gen. Warren, which fact alone goes to show that his lavish expenses were not wholly selfish.

* The recollections of Miss Margaret Shippen, a first cousin of Mrs. Arnold, entirely confirm this. She had heard from Mrs. Burd and Mrs. Lea, that their father never liked Arnold from the first, and was not friendly to the match; but that it was encouraged by a lady, a Mrs. P., who thought highly of him, and had great influence over the mind of the young lady.

"However defective in private honor or real patriotism, no one of our American Generals had so many opportunities of displaying feats of brilliant courage, that there can be no doubt that the imagination of Miss Shippen was excited and her heart captivated by the oft-repeated stories of his gallant deeds. For these alone she loved and married him; not for the splendor of his military rank and the show of his establishment, which must have contrasted greatly with what she had lately seen during the British occupation; not for the means of gratifying personal vanity, for Arnold was poor and she enjoyed all that wealth could give; still less to win him from the cause to which every honorable thought should bind him. Never could she have believed that treason would one day wither those glorious laurels. Never could her influence have been used to weaken his attachment to the cause to which he had devoted himself. Against the wishes of her family, she chose a hero for her husband; and had her influence been of any avail, it would have preserved him in the ways of honor. He dared not make her the confidante of his projected treason, or we may be sure he would have 'found a counsellor on his pillow to urge him to 'the imitation of republican virtue, and stimulate him to 'follow the rugged path of a revolutionary patriot.'

"What can be meant by the writer who ventures to say 'there is no reason to think she ever utter'd a word, or made 'a sign to deter him,' while he 'utterly rejects the theory 'that she was the instigator of the crime,' and admits 'that 'she never tempted or counselled him to ruin?' Every testimony *but one*, which we have hereafter to consider, pronounces her innocent—nay, utterly ignorant and unsuspicious of his designs. What word, then, or sign, could she have used? what 'guardianship exert to protect him from 'the tempter?'

"We have the evidence of Cols. Hamilton and Varick as to the condition of this unhappy lady on the discovery at West Point. Frantic with grief, she touched the heart of every one around her. Crushed to the earth in her affections and her honor; the pride of her heart, the credit of her name, the honorable inheritance of her child, all at once destroyed; the husband whom she had loved to regard as a patriot hero, the very Paladin of the war, now only to be despised and hated. In this cloud of agonizing thought, she threw herself on the compassion of that great man who always did what was right, and he gave her not only his pity and protection, but what was better, the assurance of his respect and confidence. WASHINGTON told her he was perfectly sure of her innocence, and offered her an escort, whether she chose to follow her husband, or return to her father's house. Be it remembered, she decided on the latter course; and, had it rested with her, she would, it is probable, never have rejoined the husband who had so utterly forfeited her esteem.

"Since the above was first written, I have been furnished with the reminiscences of the lady whose words I have before quoted in confirmation of my statements. Those who know her intimately, as I have done from my childhood, will give them the highest value for truthful accuracy, right feeling, and just appreciation. It is Mrs. James Gibson, who writes as follows:

'I propose now to relate an anecdote on this subject, 'which is fresh to my own knowledge and recollection.

'Major Franks, of the Revolutionary army, was a well 'known acquaintance of my parents. He was respected and 'welcomed wherever he went, for his social good humor and 'manly candor. In one of his visits to Philadelphia, where 'his near relations resided, he was often at my father's; and 'one day, when dining with other gentlemen at our house, 'and my father and the others had returned to the parlor, 'my mother detained Major Franks to converse with him 'respecting Mrs. Arnold, whom she had recently heard very 'unjustly spoken of. He entered upon the subject with 'alacrity. Mamma said to him, "Tell me, Major Franks, '"what is your opinion and belief concerning her know-'"ledge of her husband's plans." He quickly replied, '"Madam, she knew nothing of them—nothing! She was '"as ignorant of them as a babe." His manner was solemn 'and earnest, and I began to think it might be proper for 'me to withdraw, but he said, "Don't let Betsy go—I have '"nothing to say that she may not hear." Of course, I 'gladly resumed my seat at the table, and he went on:— '"Madam, I am glad you have mentioned this subject. I '"have much to say. I am much distressed by it. Within '"a few days I have heard, for the first time, things said of '"her that are contrary to truth—false!—utterly false! '"You know I was one of Gen. Arnold's aids. He paid '"me the compliment to assign me the particular duty of '"protecting Mrs. Arnold; of attending to her safety, her '"general welfare, and her health. I was, in the General's '"family, laughingly called '*the nurse!*' Her health was '"then delicate; and while Gen. Arnold was in command '"at West Point, he frequently sent her to different, some-'"times distant parts of the country, on that side of the '"river. He always sent a guard with her, besides her '"female attendant, and gave me very particular charge '"over her welfare. He spoke of her suffering in the

'" bustle of the camp, and wished her to be relieved from '" it during the summer. I obeyed, nothing doubting, but '" considering him a pattern for a husband, although other '" and far different motives for sending her away on these '" excursions afterwards came to light. But, madam, she '" knew nothing of his projects. In truth, she was subject '" to occasional paroxysms of physical indisposition, at- '" tended by nervous debility, during which she would give '" utterance to anything and everything on her mind. This '" was a fact well known amongst us of the General's '" family; so much so as to cause us to be scrupulous of '" what we told her or said within her hearing. General '" Arnold was guarded and impenetrable towards all around '" him, and I should believe her to have been ignorant of '" his plans, even without my knowledge of this peculiar '" feature in her constitution; but *with it*, such a strong '" corroborative proof, I am most solemnly and firmly con- '" vinced that General Arnold never confided his detestable '" scheme to her. *He could not have ventured to do it.* '" He was, moreover, too well aware of her *warm patriotic* '" *feelings. You know*, madam, *how completely she was* '" *American at that important period.* Madam, I can aver '" solemnly, she was totally ignorant of his schemes." '*

"Here we have evidence above suspicion, not only of her innocence, but of her patriotism.

"The following facts are vouched for as known in the family at the time, often privately repeated, but never mentioned beyond its most intimate circle till the publication of the base calumny contained in the memoirs of Aaron Burr.

"Mrs. Arnold having determined to go to her father in

* The true historical view has been taken by Mr. Hubbell, in his tragedy of "Arnold," a poem creditable to his judgment as to events, and to his literary taste.

Philadelphia, set out in her carriage to travel there by easy stages. On her way she stopped to spend the night at Mrs. Prevost's, (an old acqnaintance,) afterwards the wife of Col. Burr, and at that time on terms of tender friendship, if not indeed engaged to him.

"This fact is told by Burr's biographer, and no doubt, after his narration; but he does not say that Burr himself met her at Mrs. Prevost's, and when she left the house in the morning, offered his escort, which he pretended might be useful to her in the then excited state of the public mind on the subject of the treason. Still less does he tell, what his friend would not have ventured to repeat, that on the way he made love to this afflicted lady, thinking to take advantage of her just feelings of indignation towards her husband, to help him in his infamous design. Yet this is the fact, if our tradition be true. And indignantly repelled, he treasured up his revenge, and left a story behind him worthy of his false and malignant heart, to blast this amiable lady's fame, when there might be no one to disprove or deny it. After telling us she set out from West Point *to join her husband in New York,* he says, that on arriving at Mrs. Prevost's, (who was a loyalist,) she there threw off the mask, admitted she had been playing a part which wearied her, and 'avowed that by her persuasions and unceasing perseverance, she had *herself* brought the General into an arrangement to surrender West Point,' &c., &c. That this statement is false, utterly false, even the most unfriendly writers admit. Known facts contradict it. Is it not almost incredible that any man could invent such a calumny with such a motive? Yet it is so. One who was second in the nation, and had almost reached its highest honor, was capable of this baseness: and his name might well, for this and other acts, be handed down to perpetual infamy, deserved as well as by the traitor Arnold.

"On Mrs. Arnold's arrival in Philadelphia she decided on a separation from her husband. She could not endure the thought of a return to one whom she could no longer honor; but this course was not permitted to her. After a short residence with her family, whose affectionate attentions were beginning to soothe her troubled heart, she received a new shock in the peremptory order of the Executive Council to leave the State. The following is a copy from the minutes.

'In Council,
'*Philadelphia, Friday, October 27th,* 1780.

'The Council taking into consideration the case of Mrs. 'Margaret Arnold, (the wife of Benedict Arnold, an at- 'tainted traitor with the enemy at New York,) whose resi- 'dence in this city has become dangerous to the public 'safety; and this board being desirous, as much as possible, 'to prevent any correspondence and intercourse being carried 'on with persons of disaffected character in this State and 'the enemy at New York, and especially with the said Bene- 'dict Arnold; therefore, *Resolved,* That the said Margaret 'Arnold depart this State within fourteen days from the 'date hereof, and that she do not return again during the 'continuance of the present war.'

"Her father, her friends, all sought a reversal of this decree of exile. Her wish for a separation was represented; her word pledged to hold no correspondence with her husband; every assurance and security offered on the part of her father, that no communication should be held with him but what should pass open through the hands of the government; but entreaties were in vain. Private enmity or hidden influence was at work, and this urgent request was denied. Perhaps the baffled seducer, by secret representations, may have thus contrived to drive away the witness of his villainy; or it may be that the occasion was seized by some enemy in power to gratify an old grudge against the members of a family suspected of 'Incivism,' and hated for their aristocratical pretensions. Or, the impulse may have come from without; from some revolutionary society, or the Committee of Public Safety, too much resembling a similar institution in the times of French democracy, potent for evil, but not always for good, now exciting popular fury, and again driven by the fiend it had raised.*

"If we had all the history of the times, it might perhaps be found, that like the excitements about the emigrés and their friends, raised from time to time to effect some local object, or legislative vote in Paris, our politicians could get up an outcry against the tories and the Quakers, when such

* Since the above was in type the following letter has been sent to me, which more than confirms the statements above made.

MAJOR EDWARD BURD TO HIS FATHER, COL. JAMES BURD.

'*Lancaster, Nov.* 10*th*, 1780.

'You have doubtless heard of the unfortunate affair of Mrs. 'Arnold. We tried every means to prevail on the Council to permit 'her to stay among us, and not to [compel her] to go to that infer- 'nal villain, her husband, in New York. The Council seemed for a 'considerable time to favor our request, but at length have ordered 'her away. Yesterday was the day she was to have set off, and 'Mr. Shippen, intending to accompany her the greatest part of the 'way, could not be up at this Court.

'This circumstance has involved the whole family in the deepest 'distress. Mr. Shippen had promised the Council, *and Mrs. Arnold* '*had signed a writing to the same purpose*, engaging not to write to 'Gen. Arnold any letters whatever, and to receive no letters without 'showing them to the Council, if she was permitted to stay.

'However, this did not answer the purpose we hoped for. If she 'could have staid, Mr. Shippen would not have wished her ever to 'be united to him again. It makes me melancholy every time I 'think of the matter. I cannot bear the idea of her re-union. The 'sacrifice was an immense one at her being married to him at all. 'It is much more so to be obliged, *against her will*, to go to the arms 'of a man who appears to be so very black.'

a warming up was thought salutary; that even a mob could be brought down from Byrne's tavern, headed by that stalwart landlord, to convince a jury not quite ready enough to find a verdict on the evidence before them. But whatever stories of the kind may be preserved by memory, or in private diaries, it is perhaps well to suppress them for the reasons given by Charles Thomson for destroying his papers.

"At all events, this amiable lady, though true to honor and her country, was forced to leave her father's house, and urged perhaps by the advice of friends, and the entreaties of a husband once dearly loved,* she returned to him and shared his fate in evil, as she had before in good report.

"In after life, wherever she was known she was admired and respected.† Her letters to her family, still preserved, tend to prove her to have been an excellent woman in every relation, and she had the satisfaction of forming the characters of several virtuous and honorable children.

"She deeply felt her separation from her native land and family, and lived in seclusion, from which she had no temptation to go into society, where there were no charms nor honors for her.‡ She must, indeed, have wished her name

* Miss Margaret Shippen recollects her cousins Burd and Lea speaking several times to her of their sister's state of distress and vacillation at this period, hardly resolving to accompany her husband to England, though wishing to be persuaded there was some palliation of his guilt, and that his conduct had not been so thoroughly base and treacherous as it was generally thought.

† Arnold, generally slighted, and sometimes insulted, though indulged by his royal master, from policy, with notice and honors, could hardly have sustained his social position, but for the charms and virtues of his wife, which, we are told, procured her sympathy and friendship everywhere but among her countrymen.

‡ Five years after her departnre, she returned to see her father and family; but she was treated with so much coldness and neglect, even by those who had most encouraged her marriage, that her feelings were deeply pained. 'She never could come again.' She

forgotten by all but those who loved her; though, alas! it will be preserved in history to excite a momentary pity for her undeserved misfortunes; unless, indeed, the cruel calumny which I have noticed and disproved should be perpetuated. Even if it were true that she thought, as she might have done, that her husband was a persecuted man, and shared a revenge which she supposed just, such sympathy might surely have been pardoned. The revival now of such tales is, it must be admitted, uncalled for and unkind, and it is to be hoped they will never be repeated.* At any

died in the winter of 1796, at an early age for one of a long-lived race. Her sisters would have brought her younger children to this country; but they refused, and wisely. Two of her sons reached high military rank; her daughter Sophia was a religious and exemplary woman. Her letters speak of General Arnold's uniform kindness, but plainly show that "her heart was broken."

* The following extract of a letter addressed to Miss Schuyler by Alexander Hamilton, on the 25th September, 1780, shows, in part, what ruin, in addition to the loss of his own fame, the treason of Arnold scattered around him:

'Arnold hearing of the plot being detected immediately fled to 'the enemy. I went in pursuit of him, but was much too late, and 'could hardly regret the disappointment when, on my return, I saw 'an amiable woman, frantic with distress for the loss of a husband 'she tenderly loved—a traitor to his country and to his fame—a 'disgrace to his connections. It was the most affecting scene I ever 'was witness to. She, for a considerable time, entirely lost herself. 'The General (Washington) went up to see her, and she upbraided 'him with being in a plot to murder her child. One moment she 'raved, another she melted into tears. Sometimes she pressed her 'infant to her bosom, and lamented its fate, occasioned by the im-'prudence of its father, in a manner that would have pierced insen-'sibility itself. All the sweetness of beauty, all the loveliness of 'innocence, all the tenderness of a wife, and all the fondness of a 'mother, showed themselves in her appearance and conduct. We 'have every reason to believe that she was entirely unacquainted 'with the plan; that the first knowledge of it was when Arnold went 'to tell her he must banish himself from his country and from her 'forever. She instantly fell into a convulsion, and he left her in 'that situation. This morning she is more composed. I paid her 'a visit, and endeavored to soothe her by every method in my 'power, though you may imagine she is not easily to be consoled. 'Added to her other distresses, she is very apprehensive the resent-'ment of her country will fall upon her (who is only unfortunate) rate, a controversy on such a subject is deprecated, and a public refutation is not to be thought of.

"The above is written for the satisfaction of the numerous members of a family, who will all feel an interest in relieving the character of a beautiful* and amiable woman of their race from the charge of participation in or approval of an odious treason. They will be disposed to believe the story as handed down from her nearest relations, and contemporary friends. Further proofs will not be called for, and would not, perhaps, be forthcoming. There is, it is supposed, no documentary evidence, for all the papers of Mrs. Arnold were seized by the republican authorities, and if they still exist, are not accessible to those who would wish to vindicate her."

JOSEPH SHIPPEN, the second son of Edward Shippen, of Lancaster, was b. Oct. 30, 1732, was graduated at Nassau Hall 1753, entered the Provincial army, in which he rose to the rank of Colonel, and served in General Forbes' expedition, which resulted in the capture of Fort Du Quesne. After the troops were disbanded he went to Europe, partly on a mercantile adventure, but as it appears from the letters, (p. 185, &c.) chiefly for the advantages to be derived from foreign travel. He returned to Philadelphia somewhere in December, 1761, and was shortly afterwards (Gordon says January 2, 1762,) appointed Secretary to the Pro-

'for the guilt of her husband. I have tried to persuade her that 'her fears are unfounded; but she will not be convinced. She re-'ceived us in bed, with every circumstance that interests our sym-'pathy; and her sufferings were so eloquent that I wished myself 'her brother, to have a right to become her defender.'—*See Life and Writings*, I, p. 268, 275, 276.

* Her portrait, by Sir Thomas Lawrence, now in the possession of the Misses McIlvaine, shows her to have been a remarkably beautiful woman.

vince, in which office he succeeded the Rev. Richard Peters. About 1773 he removed to the country, near Kennett Square, in Chester county, a step which he was induced to take by reason of the expenses incident to a large family, and his own state of health, being, at that time, and for some years, quite infirm.* The latter I take to have been the true reason for his not serving in the Revolutionary army. Thence he removed to a place which he purchased in Chester county, and which, in honor of his mother, he called Plumley. He was appointed Judge of Lancaster Court in 1789, and d. Feb. 10th, 1810, having served his country, and filled with honor many reputable stations; esteemed by all who knew him as an eminently just and upright man. No words are too strong to describe the tender and affectionate character of his relations with his family. I have before me a letter, written by his wife during her last illness, addressed to her husband, with directions 'to be opened after my death.' Amongst other things, she makes a request that he would give a sum of money, not large, to a female friend of hers in needy circumstances, in such a manner as to prevent any suspicion of the source from which it came;† but the language in which

* EDWARD SHIPPEN TO JAMES BURD, AT TINIAN.

'*Lancaster, March 9th,* 1777.

'DEAR MR. BURD:—I received a letter yesterday for Col. Ship-'pen, who was just returned from Philadelphia, having got better 'by Doctor Shippen's assistance. One thing in particular helped 'him, which was taking 9 ounces of blood from him. * * * *

'I am, dear Mr. Burd, your affectionate, loving father,

'EDWARD SHIPPEN.'

In another letter, shortly prior in date to this, one of his children says—'But I will not ask you to write, as I know your right arm 'trembles so much.'

† I ought perhaps to add, that not only was this request faithfully complied with, but that the pains taken by Col. Shippen and one of his sons, to have the bounty reach its object in the way desired by the donor, are the best of testimonials to the affectionate regard which was had for the wishes of the wife and mother.

the letter is couched, could have proceeded only from a heart, in which early love had been strengthened and ripened into conjugal devotion by long years of well-deserved confidence.

It was the same as to his children. A letter from his daughter Mary, concerning her proposed household arrangements after marriage, then about to take place, proves that no detail, which concerned the welfare of his child, was without interest to his parental bosom.

On Col. Shippen's public career it is unnecessary further to dwell. To his service as a soldier, he added the accomplishments of a scholar and of a man of taste;* and was not

* '*London, Sept.* 1*st*, 1763.

'DEAR SIR:—Your very kind favor of the 11th October last, 'reached me in the month of January following, just on my arrival 'at Rome, after having been a whole year longer away from thence 'than I ever at first thought of. After having wrote you my letter 'of the 10th May from Florence, by which I see you were informed 'of the deplorable situation I was in for the first five months of that 'year, I went very slowly picking up; but, as you may easily sup-'pose, my strength and spirits were so much reduced by the long, 'close confinement to my bed, the strict diet I was obliged to keep, 'and especially the cruel incisions the surgeon had made on my 'ancle, I still found myself unable to apply closely to my work for 'a long time, notwithstanding all the inclination and longing 'I had to do so. Every time I set down to the slightest studies, 'though but for a quarter of an hour, there came a giddiness and 'feverishness upon me that forced me to leave off. My first appli-'cation was to serve my worthy and honored patrons in the copies 'they desired, as far as lay in my power; and as, just at that time, 'Lord Fordwich had ordered up from Leghorn to Florence the pic-'ture that Mr. Mings had painted for him, of a Holy Family, and 'was so obliging as to give me leave to copy it. I thought myself 'happy in having such an opportunity of studying upon my favorite 'master, since he was gone from Rome, and the season of the year 'was not proper for me to go thither to seek for other studies. I 'concluded also that nothing could be more agreeable to you and 'my other friends than the copy of so capital a piece. The agree-'ableness of the climate of Florence, the extraordinary kindnesses 'of Sir Horace Mann, which I shall always have a most grateful 'remembrance of, especially for that shown me in my illness, and 'the honorable notice taken of me by all the English nobility and destitute of some talent in versification. The following lines, said to have been of his composition, are here printed,

'gentry that were there, as well as by many of the Florentine noblemen, were great engagements to me to stay, so that, with all these advantages, I got through the copy (notwithstanding the great weakness that still hung upon me) in about two months, after having been obliged to make my excuses for not serving the Duke of Grafton, and several others, whom, even by Sir Horace's advice, I was obliged to refuse, because of my weak constitution, which absolutely forbad my undertaking much fatigue. Indeed, nothing but such a study after Mings could have made me go through with so large a copy, and in so short a time, and I thought it a happy instance of my cure, that after so much labor I was not again laid up with a fresh fit of my usual violent pains. As you and the gentlemen were pleased to give me such liberty to suit my own taste and turn, I saw nothing else at Florence so suitable for me to copy as the Venus by Titian, and a celebrated picture of Hannibal Caracci, in the Prince Corsini's palace, of Venus lamenting over the dead body of Adonis. In a reasonable time I got this picture done, and sat about the Titian, when, just as it was dead colored in, the fire broke out in the gallery, and put everything there in confusion, and stopped the work of copying there, upon that picture, for some time. If it had been in the winter season, I should, immediately upon this, have proceeded to Rome, and pursued my studies there, not to lose time; but as there were still two months before it was reckoned safe for me to go that way, and as I had a very favorable opportunity of passing that interval in a journey to Bologna, Parma and Venice, I resolved to embrace it, considering those places, for different merits, as much the object of a student's attention as even Rome itself, in a certain degree. I also considered, that while I was thus not losing my time, I should be improving my health, which all my friends were of opinion required such exercise and change of air, after so long and cruel confinement, and such close application as I had given the whole summer. Perhaps you will have heard already from the worthy gentlemen at Leghorn, that Mr. Matthews, having left their service some months before, and coming to Florence, accompanied me in this tour, after having consulted those gentlemen, who were pleased not to disapprove of it, but on the contrary favored us both with the kindest and most honorable letters of recommendations for all the places where we were to go in. The particular kindness of Mr. Murray, at Venice, made my stay there much longer than I ever imagined, for which I am in great measure obliged to you, good sir, and Mr. Allen, by your speaking so advantageously of me when you were there. The little enjoyment I have had of my health, you are sensible, must naturally have taken off much of my pleasure for a longer stay, and especially the dread of being laid up at every return of the summer, if I persisted to stay at Rome, not as an effort of poetical genius, but because they perpetuate the names of the belles of his day:

'where only my studies required me to stay, since I attribute my 'having (thank God) been so well of late, more to the exercise I 'have had in travelling about, than to any amendment in my con-'stitution. On my return from Venice to Florence, I had but just 'time to finish my copy of Titian's Venus. I hastened to Rome to 'make as much as possible of the short time that remained for me 'there, and thought myself happy in getting done a copy of Guido's 'finest Herodias in Cardinal Corsini's palace, and another picture 'which I composed as a study of my own. Just after I had got 'over these two pieces, Mr. Patoune, a gentleman, a particular 'friend of Mr. Crispin's, was pleased to offer me his company to 'England. I therefore could not but embrace it, particularly with 'Mr. Crispin's advice, and be thankful to Providence that had 'thrown such a lucky offer in my way, and thus, thank God, I am 'at last safe arrived at the mother country, which we Americans are 'all so desirous to see, and which I could not but desire as much, 'or more, than Italy itself. After leaving Rome I went to Leghorn 'for a few days, as well to pay my last personal respects to the 'worthy gentlemen there, (whose favors and friendship I shall 'always gratefully remember, as well as the good Mr. Crispin's,) as 'to see about the dispatch of the pictures I had got ready for Ame-'rica, and luckily there then offered a New England schooner, that 'loaded all the copies already mentioned, as the gentlemen will have 'informed you, except the Herodias, which unhappily did not reach 'Leghorn in time, and now lay there for another opportunity. I 'hope they will all arrive safe, and give satisfaction to my worthy 'patrons, as have been my endeavors, and as I am in duty bound to 'do. If I have not been able to serve them with more copies, I 'hope, from your and their generous sentiments, it will be consi-'dered how much my studies in Italy have been interrupted by my 'infirmities, from the very first. I was too uneasy and too uncer-'tain of my health to pretend going through a regular course, '(which, by the way, if I could have kept on at Rome, would have 'engaged me to apply more to drawing than painting of copies,) so 'that I have been glad to pick in any way as much improvement as 'my health and time would permit, and flatter myself I shall be 'allowed to have acquired as much as any other in my circumstances 'could have done, though not near so much as I could wish. I am 'very sensible of my own wants in regard to painting, and it will be 'the labor of my whole lifetime to supply them. Your useful hints 'upon this subject I take in the kindest part; and for the friendly 'intentions you have, I value them as much as if they came from 'Mings himself. You will give me leave always to consider you, 'dear sir, and Mr. Jn. Allen, among my best and most honored 'friends, as well as his worthy father, and the Governor; and it

Lines written in an Assembly Room.

'In lovely White's* most pleasing form,
What various graces meet!
How blest with every striking charm!
How languishingly sweet!

'will always be my study to deserve the continuance and benefit of 'your friendship and good will. As to the price of the copies, and 'the manner how I am to satisfy those gentlemen for the generous 'assistance I have had in money from them, I desire before all 'things to consider what is suitable and agreeable to them. They 'are too generous not to make all the allowance that my circum- 'stances may deserve; and as to myself, I had much rather that 'some friend would take upon him to settle the first particular, than 'pretend to rate my own labors, when in their service to whom I am 'in honor and gratitude so much obliged; but as I have the happi- 'ness of meeting here Mr. Allen himself, the principal of my 'patrons, to whom, of course, I shall endeavor to give satisfaction 'in this and every other point, it is the less necessary for me now 'to tire you with a longer detail. I trust wholly in your good 'nature for an excuse for my not answering your kind letter before I 'left Italy, and hope you will ascribe my unpunctuality rather to 'my being so hurried and unsettled in the last months of my stay 'there, than to any forgetfulness of duty and obligation, which I am 'constantly sensible of, though I should unfortunately fail of giving 'you such proofs of them as you may strictly expect. It was the 'greatest pleasure to me to hear of my good friend, Mr. John Allen's, 'safe return home, and I beg you'd make my hearty compliments 'to him and all friends, with my particular respects to Governor 'Hamilton, who makes me proud of the honor he has done my first 'two copies, as you are pleased to mention. My sincere compli- 'ments wait no less on all your worthy family, assuring you that I 'am, with all gratitude and esteem,

'Dear sir, your most obliged, humble servant,

'BENJ'N WEST.

'My dear sir, I have one favor to beg of you, that is, on the arri- 'val of the case in which the three copies are, they may be care- 'fully taken out, and the case fastened up again, as it is full of 'things I am desirous not to have seen, as they are little particulars 'belonging to painters. I hope you will pardon me for this liberty.

'To JOSEPH SHIPPEN, Jr., Esq., in Philadelphia.'

* Sister of Bishop White.

'With just such elegance and ease,
Fair, charming Swift* appears;
Thus Willing,† whilst she awes, can please;
Thus Polly Franks endears.

'A female softness, manly sense,
And conduct free from art,
With every pleasing excellence,
In Inglis‡ charm the heart.

'But see! another fair advance,
With love commanding all;
See! happy in the sprightly dance,
Sweet, smiling, fair M'Call.‡

'Each blessing which indulgent Heaven
On mortals can bestow,
To thee, enchanting maid, is given,
Its masterpiece below.

'In Sally Coxe's§ form and face,
True index of her mind,
The most exact of human race
Not one defect can find.

'Thy beauty every breast alarms,
And many a swain can prove
That he who views your conquering charms,
Must soon submit to love.

* Ellinor White Swift, eldest daughter of Mr. Joseph Swift.

† Most probably Miss Abby Willing.

‡ Miss Katharine Inglis and Miss Margaret M'Call, dau. of Samuel M'Call and Ann Searle, (post, lxxxviii) They lived together about fifty years, the greater portion of the time in Pine street, (No. 91,) opposite St Peter's church.

§ Mrs. Andrew Allen.

'With either Chew* such beauties dwell,
Such charms by each are shared,
No critic's judging eye can tell
Which merits most regard.

''Tis far beyond the painter's skill
To set their charms to view;
As far beyond the poet's quill
To give the praise that's due.'

Some mention of two of Col. Shippen's brother officers will, perhaps, tend to a better understanding of the following letters. Lt. Col. Lloyd was of a family which participated largely in the management of the early affairs of the Province. He was lost at sea, on his way from Boston to Charleston, somewhere about 1770.

Dr. John Morgan was the son of a respectable Welsh gentleman, who settled here at an early day. He studied medicine with Dr. Redman, and was Apothecary to the Pennsylvania Hospital, an office which he held for about a year, and relinquished for the purpose of going on Forbes' expedition, in which he held a Lieutenant's commission, but acted chiefly as Surgeon, and, as appears by Col. Burd's report to the Governor, did 'his duty very well.' On his return, he became the coadjutor of Dr. Shippen in founding a Medical School in Philadelphia; a project which had been, in fact, a long-cherished idea of his own, and which had chiefly induced him to visit Europe, to pursue his medical studies.† His thesis, delivered on obtaining his degree,

* Eldest daughters of Benj. Chew, Esq. One became Mrs. Phillips, the other Mrs. Carroll.

† Dr. Morgan's letters, &c., now in Dr. G. W. Norris' possession.

was printed at Edinburgh in 1763; and is esteemed by high professional authority, an excellent and able production. After this he traveled in Europe for two years or more, and was admitted to the Royal Society in 1765.* He returned to Philadelphia, and his subsequent career is well known.†

JOSEPH SHIPPEN, above mentioned, m. Sept. 29, 1768, JANE, dau. of John and Jane Galloway, of Anne Arundel county, Maryland.‡ He d. at Lancaster, Feb. 10, 1810.

* Mr. Sam. Powel's diary has the following entry:—'1765, Dec., 'paid for yr. admission fee to the Royal Society, £21.'

† Col. Shippen also took an interest in scientific pursuits. 1768, Jan. 19, he joined the Am. Philos. Soc.

‡ Dr. Caspar Morris, of this city, has kindly favored me with the following note concerning Mrs. Shippen's family:

'The Mr. Galloway mentioned in Mr. Shippen's letter (*post*, p. '309,) was Mr. Joseph Galloway, brother of Miss Jenny Galloway, 'afterward Mrs. Shippen. His son John died of consumption. 'Mrs. Linn died at Cumberland, Maryland, within a year or two, 'leaving several sons and daughters, a good estate and honorable 'reputation.

'Mr. Samuel Galloway was the head of the family, and lived at 'Tulip Hill. He had one son and two daughters. The son was Mr. 'John Galloway, who inherited the Tulip Hill estate, and left it to 'his only child, a daughter, who married Virgil Maxcy, Solicitor of 'U. S. Treasury, and subsequently Minister to Brussels. He was 'killed by the explosion of Com. Stockton's great gun on board the 'Princeton. He left two daughters; one married to Francis Mar- 'koe, of Washington City, and the other to Colonel G. W. Hughes, 'of the Topographical Engineer corps. The latter is the possessor 'of the Tulip Hill estate, having on it one of the finest old mansions 'in the State of Maryland. One of the daughters of Mr. Samuel 'Galloway married Mr. Ringgold, and her son married Miss Cad- 'walader, of this city, and was the father of Commander Ringgold, 'of the U. S. Navy, and Major Ringgold, who fell in the Mexican 'war. The other daughter was the Mrs. Cheston mentioned so hon- 'orably by Mr. S. She was the grandmother of Mrs. Morris, and 'was a woman of extraordinary worth and loveliness. The farm is 'now in my possession, and still maintains the same character given 'it by Mr. Shippen. The oysters of the old lady were famous 'indeed. Her son was a man of whom it might be said, if of any, 'that he possessed the "Virtus intacta, nescia sordida, intaminatis 'fulget honoribus," which Horace considers the highest glory of 'man. The name of Galloway is now extinct, except as it is borne

She was b. Sept. 1745, and d. at Plumley, Chester county, Penna., Feb. 17, 1801. They had issue,*

1. Robert, b. July 10, 1769; d. Dec. 31, 1840; m. Priscilla Thompson, and had, (with Beale Bordley, Jenny, Joseph and Anna, *d. unm.*,)

Mary, m. to James Maxwell, have issue,

Robert,

Park.

Sarah, m. to Robert Patterson.

Hannah, m. to William Ewing.

John, m. his cousin, Margaret Swift, and have issue,

Elizabeth,

Samuel Swift,

Edwin J.

Charles, m. Martha Eddowes, have issue,

Priscilla, m. Rev. C. A. Staples.

Robert,

Ellen,

Mary, m. C. Cullum.

Margaret, m. Rev. N. A. Staples.

Richard, m. Magdalena Black, have issue,

Harriet, m. E. P. Hastings.

William,

'by Mr. Galloway Cheston, and my son Galloway C. Morris, and 'Dr. Joseph G. Shippen, of Pottsville. Mr. Benjamin Galloway 'was another son of Mr. Samuel Galloway. He was educated at 'Eton College, and read law at Lincoln's Inn. He returned home 'and married a Miss Chew, and settled at Hagerstown, and died 'childless.' I may also add, that the Galloways settled in Maryland prior to the year 1640; and that Joseph Galloway, the well-known Loyalist, was a cousin of Mrs. Shippen.

* Her portrait, by Benjamin West, is in the possession of Mr. John Shippen, of Pottsville. His portrait is in the possession of his son, Dr. J. G. Shippen, of Pottsville.

MARY ANN,
ROBERT,
MARGARET.
ELIZABETH,
THOMPSON,
MARGARET, m. to J. Black, have issue,
BORDLEY,
WM. H. H.,
JANE.

2. JOHN, b. Oct. 31, 1771; m. Abigail Reynolds. They d. leaving one son,
EDWARD BURD YEATES SHIPPEN, d. at Hagerstown, Maryland, aged 19.
3. MARY, m. to Samuel Swift. Of her, more hereafter.
4. MARGARET.
5. JOSEPH GALLOWAY, M. D., b. Dec. 25, 1783; m. Anna Maria Buckley, dau. of Daniel Buckley, of Lancaster county, Penna. They have,
HARRIET AMELIA,
JOSEPH, M. D.
EDWARD, of Philadelphia, m. Augusta Chauncey, dau. of Major Levi* and Priscilla Decatur Twiggs,† and have issue,
ELIZABETH BORDLEY TWIGGS,
SARAH BURD,
FRANCES STOCKTON, d. 1853.
ANNA MARIA, m. to William Newell, of Schuylkill county, Penna., have issue,
WILLIAM HARMAR.

* Major Levi Twiggs, U. S. Marine Corps, killed at the storming of Chapultepec, Mexico, 1847.

† A niece of Com. Stephen Decatur.

6. HENRY, b. Dec. 28, 1788; d. March 2, 1839; m. Elizabeth Wallace Evans. Judge Henry Shippen, President of the Sixth Judicial District, was educated for the bar, and was in very successful practice at Lancaster, when the war of 1812 interrupted his forensic career by rousing him to his country's defence.* During the

* The following letter, though of more recent date than any elsewhere printed in this volume, will not, I am sure, be without interest:

JUDGE HENRY SHIPPEN TO HIS SISTER, MRS. SWIFT.

'*Lancaster*, *October* 23*d*, 1812.

'DEAR SISTER:—It was my intention to have gratified myself with 'a visit to my dear brother and sister this week, but having been 'pressed to act as one of the judges at the late election, I agreed to 'do so, not knowing at that time that it would oblige me to attend 'also at the Presidential Election, on the 30th inst. Court sits here 'so soon after, that I must postpone my pleasure till some time in 'December.

'Your letters have evinced so much anxiety about my being 'ordered to march against our enemies, that I could not avoid being 'sensibly affected by them, although I have too long neglected an-'swering them, owing to a multiplicity of matters, that have of late 'occupied me. I have no expectation of receiving orders till next 'spring, and even then it is quite uncertain. If it should turn out 'otherwise, I shall go readily, and try to see all my friends before 'leaving this on an expedition.

'I have heard from brother of your trips to Pottsgrove, German-'town, Ormiston, &c., of which you have said nothing; neither does 'brother mention anything about his prospects and success in busi-'ness. I always knew there was nothing selfish in either of your 'dispositions; but I should always be very glad to hear more about 'yourselves.

'I cannot help frequently casting a retrospective eye on former 'times, recollecting with pleasure the days of my youth or child-'hood, which I spent in the country, surrounded by my friends, in 'peace and innocence, tranquillity and happiness. How little did 'I then know of the world, its vices and vicissitudes! When read-'ing the history of Rome and the villanies of her tyrants, I ima-'gined it was the tale of other times, now gone and past forever, the 'likeness of which was no more known. When reading the sudden 'reverses of fortune in a novel or play, I conceived it to be merely 'the illusions of fancy, far beyond anything in real life. How mis-'taken the ideas and notions of my childhood! I now often, alas! 'too often, see the reverses of fortune, instances of misery, oppres-'sion of the unfortunate and unprotected, the cruelty and malice of attack on Baltimore he proved his valor and patriotism, but lost for some years the vigor of an uncommonly strong constitution by sufferings produced by inflammatory rheumatism. He at last recovered, resumed his profession, married, and removed to Meadville, where he resided for many years, beloved and respected in no common degree. His judicial appointment embraced five counties, and its onerous duties seem to have been discharged in a most creditable manner.* He is said, by those who knew him, to have been a man of most benevolent disposition, high moral principle, and engaging manners. They had,

FRANCES, m. to Edgar Huidekoper.

EDWARD,

'the wealthy, equaling if not exceeding anything I have met with in 'the effusions of the most fanciful writer. A man who, some years 'ago, stood high in character, wealth and importance, as a merchant 'in Philadelphia, bearing a commission of the Peace, now lies, the 'victim of oppression, and the picture of misery and wretchedness, 'in a solitary room in Lancaster prison, for a debt he is unable to 'pay. This is but one among many instances that come within my 'observation in the course of my profession. How thankful should 'we be to a kind Providence for his goodness in keeping us above 'the frowns of fortune. And how thankful should I be to my dear 'good father for urging me to a profession which affords me fre-'quent opportunities of alleviating the distresses of the unfortunate, 'at the same time that I am following my professional duties and 'making my livelihood. But a truce, for a message this minute 'comes to invite me to come and drink tea with Mrs. Grubb, at Mrs. 'Zantzinger's. That charming woman has been spending a few 'days with Miss Juliana. You have frequently joked and pressed 'me about entering into a matrimonial engagement. Could I find 'another just like her, I should not be long in making a choice, so 'far as related to myself.

'Weddings have of late become very fashionable at Carlisle and 'Harrisburg, but Lancaster remains statu quo—none talked of.

'Adieu, my dear sister, as I must cease so as to accept my invi-'tation. Yours, affectionately,

'H. SHIPPEN.'

* Several of his decisions are to be found in *Haz. Reg.*

HENRY,
EVANS W., m. Katherine Y. McElwee.
RUSH R., (Rev.) now of Chicago.
SARAH, m. to Rev. Thos. J. Mumford.
WILLIAM,
FRANKLIN,
JOSEPH.

Of the families of Swift and M'Call, which have been already and will be again mentioned, I have gathered the following information, which may be appropriately inserted here:

SAMUEL M'CALL,* of Glasgow, merchant, m. a dau. of Robert Dundas, of Arnistoun. She was a sister of Lord Arnistoun, and an aunt of Viscount Melville. They had issue, (with others,)

ROBERT, who emigrated to America, and settled in Virginia. He had,

SAMUEL, who m. his cousin Ann, as hereafter mentioned.

Another son, (WILLIAM, as is said,) whose dau. Catharine Flood M'Call, was living in Richmond, Virginia, in 1821, when Mr. Swift called upon her. She was, as is believed, the last of the Virginia branch.

* These notices are prepared from various MS. letters, deeds, powers of attorney. &c., in the possession of Mr. Swift, Mr. Harry M'Call and Mr. Riché; and from information derived through a gentleman in England. *M'Call Arms.*—Gu. a fesse chequy ar. and of the field, surmounting two arrows in saltire ar. points upward, all between three buckles of the same, and within a bordure indented or. *Crest.*—A boot, thereon a spur, all ppr. *Motto.*—Dulce periculum.

GEORGE, who settled in Philadelphia.

JAMES, from whom descended James M'Call, Esq., of Braehead and Glyntown, now or lately Lt. Col. 8th Hussars.

GEORGE M'CALL settled in Philadelphia some time during the year 1701, (as is conjectured); but, however this may be, in

1710, he bought a large tract of land, some ten thousand acres, situated on the Schuylkill river and Manahatany creek, which he called Douglas Manor. He was a merchant in high standing, and acquired large wealth.

1716, August 9th, he m. ANN YEATES, dau. of Jasper Yeates, a gentleman of the highest consideration and character in the Province; who was one of the Council, and part of the time held that office whilst a member of the Assembly. He did much to compose the differences between the two bodies, frequently acting on Committees of Conference. One of his descendants, Judge Jasper Yeates, as will be hereafter seen, married the daughter of Col. James Burd.

Mr. M'Call d. 1740.

She d. 1744. They are both buried in Christ Churchyard. Their portraits are in the possession of the Misses M'Call, in Chestnut street.

They had, (with MARGARET, WILLIAM and JENNY, who d. *young or unm,)*

1. CATHARINE, m. to John Inglis,* for many years Col-

* Mr. Inglis' portrait, painted by Peale about the year 1770, for the City Dancing Assembly, of which Mr. Inglis was a manager from its institution till within a few years of his death, is now in the possession of Mr. Fisher. Mr. Inglis' arms were: Az. a lion rampant ar. on a chief ar. three stars az. *Crest.*—A demi-lion ar. in his dexter paw a mullet or. *Motto.*—Recte faciendo securus.

lector of the Port, and also member of Common Council, to which he was elected Nov. 11, 1745. They had,

JOHN INGLIS, m. Barbara ———. He was afterwards Rear Admiral in the British Navy. He lived at Red Hall, near Edinburgh.

SAMUEL INGLIS, who m. Ann ———, and d. 1783, leaving Rebecca, who d. shortly after her father, as did also his widow.

GEORGE INGLIS, of Abingdon, Montgomery county; *d. unm.* 1833.

KATHARINE, *d. unm.* 1821.

MARY, m. to Col. Julines Hering, of Jamaica.* They had, besides Mrs. Middleton, mentioned heretofore (p. xlvi),

ANNA MARIA, m. to the late Earl of Scarborough, and d. leaving the present Earl and two daughters.†

ELEANOR, m. to Sir John Milbanke, Bart.

CATHARINE, m. to Mr. Gordon.‡

OLIVER, m. but *d. s. p.*

ANN, m. to Gilbert Barkly, merchant, who d. 1771. They had one child, Katharine Barkly, who lived (July 12th, 1804) with her uncle, Admiral Inglis.

2. JASPER M'CALL, a merchant, who m. Magdalen Kollock, of Delaware. He d. 1747. His widow subsequently m. JOHN SWIFT, for many years Collector of the Port.

* His arms were, 'Vert, on a bend ar. a cinquefoil between two 'lions pass. of the field.' For a notice of Col. Hering's descent, see *Burke's Commoners.* s. v. Beckford of Fonthill. Mr. Fisher has the portraits of Col. Hering and his wife.

† See *Burke's Peerage.*

‡ Her two dau. married into the family of Miles.—*Burke's Landed Gentry.*

John Swift was the eldest of the two sons of John Swift and Mary White, his wife, who emigrated to Pennsylvania, and purchased lands in Philadelphia county, which he represented for many years in the Assembly.* He came from London† to this city, and was of a family which sprung originally from Yorkshire. Mrs. Swift was the sister of the John White to whom John Swift's letters are addressed; a man of considerable wealth, of high character and excellent social position. He took a most affectionate interest in the welfare of his two nephews, John and Joseph, and had them sent out to him in England, where they were educated, the younger, Joseph, having been a graduate of one of the two great Universities; though it is not now known of which.‡ Though their uncle offered them a home in England, yet they preferred to take care of themselves, and 'seek their fortunes' in the new world.§ Some years, however, before Mr. White died, he made over to them his fortune, upon condition that they should pay to him a given annuity; a condition which was not only fulfilled, but when, on one occasion, he wanted something more than usual, his request was answered by a bill of exchange for double the amount he asked for.

* Proud. II. 150, &c.

† Mr. Swift's coat of arms was, 'Or. a chev. barry nebulée ar. 'and az. between three roebucks courant ppr.' Mr. White's arms are generally used by the Swift family.

‡ Some of Joseph Swift's Latin and Greek books are still kept in the family; but the inscriptions in them do not mention the University at which he was educated.

§ John Swift to Grosvenor Bedford, Oct. 11, 1748, speaks of 'the 'indolent and luxurious life which I led at Croydon,' (Mr. White's residence,) 'as not suitable to my circumstances, whatever it might 'be to my inclinations.'

April 12, 1748. 'My ambition and inclination lead me to settle 'in England, but I think it is better for me to stay here, where 'there is a certainty of advantage in business.'

Of Mr. White I have not been able to obtain many particulars. A great deal of his plate and china still remain in the family.* There is also a curious medal now in the possession of Mr. Joseph Swift.† His portrait, by Sir Joshua Reynolds, hangs at Swarthmore, and represents a portly, fashionably-dressed gentleman, who, to judge from his physiognomy, was by no means deficient either in character or in love of good cheer.

Mr. White's letters were unfortunately destroyed some years since. Tradition represents him to have been descended from a family which had held high civic honors in the city of London, and also distinguished position in the English church.

* The arms, as painted on the china and engraved on the silver, are: Gules, a bordure sable charged with eight estoiles or; on a canton ermines, a lion rampant sable. *Crest.*—On the china, an ostrich, but on the silver a stork.

† A friend, with some numismatic propensities, inquired in *Notes and Queries*, (ix. 399, x. 15, 94,) concerning this medal. It is of *silver*, about two inches in diameter. On the face is a bust of Queen Anne, crowned with laurel; legend, D. G. MAG. BRI. FR. ET HIB. Reverse, full length figure of Britannia, holding a lance and an olive branch; ships sailing and laborers ploughing in the background; legend, COMPOSITIS VENERANTUR ARMIS, MDCCXIII. Tradition represents it to have been given to Joseph Swift, on some occasion, whilst he was at the University,

Mr. W. D. Haggard (x. 94) thinks this tradition 'incorrect,' because the medal 'was struck on the Peace of Utrecht. There were 'two medals struck, one much smaller than the other. The larger 'one in *gold* was presented to each member of the House of Lords; 'the smaller one in *gold* to each member of the House of Commons. 'I have seen a medal of the same description, but of a size between 'the two; *ex. rare.*'

Mr. Haggard has overlooked the fact that the medals of which he speaks are of *gold*, whilst this is of *silver*. Another correspondent, (E. H.) of Notes and Queries, (x. 15,) suggests that 'an examination 'of the records of Oxford or Cambridge might show, that a medal 'was presented to the writer of the best copy of verses upon the 'Peace of Utrecht.' This may perhaps have been the case; that the medal was thus given to a member of the family of Mr. White or Mr. Swift, perhaps to Mr. White himself, who is said to have received his degree at Oxford.

John Swift returned to Philadelphia some time in November or December, 1746,* and entered into business as a merchant. He served for many years in the City Council,

* John Swift's letter-book, from which I have already extracted matter calculated to exhibit life and society in Philadelphia, as it was more than a century since, has in it also a letter, part of which is curious as showing what our ancestors, on the other side of the water, desired to obtain as the rarities of our country. It is addressed to Mr. John White, at Croydon, in Surry, dated April 27th, 1749. After speaking of a couple of silver sauceboats, which he had had made as a present to his uncle, partly, however, for the sake of showing the skill of the silversmith, he says:

'I have also sent you four flying squirrels by Capt. Arthur, who 'has promised to take care of them. They are in a wire cage, 'which I had made last summer for the purpose, and I have pro- 'vided for them a good store of nuts. You are to pay Capt. Arthur 'for their passage with a good bowl of punch at the Coffee House, 'if they get to you safely, which I hope they will. It gives me a 'great deal of uneasiness, that I have not been able to procure some 'rattlesnakes to send you. I have sent eight to Mr Bedford, which 'were all that I could anyways muster up. The season is now 'coming on for them, and I have four doctors and two iron-works 'engaged, by solemn promises, to get all they can for me, besides 'several frequenters of the market, and they shall none of them 'have any peace till I am supplied with a sufficient quantity. Mr. 'Bedford seemed to have set his heart so very much on having 'some, and I have said so much to him about them, that I was 'ashamed to put him off any longer. I hope you will be so good as 'to excuse me until I get some more.'

In the letter, by the same vessel, advising Mr. Bedford of the shipment of the rattlesnakes, he mentions that 'there is a small 'bundle of French vipers among them.' Terrapins were sent so frequently, that I doubt not but that they were as much esteemed by the Philadelphia epicures of that day as they are by the philosophers of the present.

The names of Grosvenor Charles Bedford, and his brother, Horace Walpole Bedford, are of course familiar to the readers of Southey's Life and Letters. I suppose, from the dates, place of residence, names, &c., that these gentlemen were the sons of the friend of Mr. Swift and Mr. White.

John Swift married without obtaining his uncle's consent beforehand. From several letters on the subject I extract the following, which give a quiet but amusing account of the affair. Mr. White's dissatisfaction did not prevent his bestowing one half of his fortune on Mr. Swift, as already related.

CH. J. SHIPPEN TO COL. SHIPPEN.

'*London, September 14th*, 1749.

'You tell me of John Swift's wedding. The reason of his conto which he was elected Dec. 4, 1757. He was generally known as 'the old Collector.'* He d. 1802. By his wife, Magdalen, he had issue,

JOHN WHITE, JACOB, and MARY, *d. unm.*

ALICE, m. 1st, to Robert Cambridge Livingston, by whom she had,

ROBERT SWIFT, THOMAS FERGUSON, JOHN SWIFT, JAMES DUANE, and MARIA, m. to John C. Stevens, Esq.

'cealing it, was that his uncle, Mr. John White, might give his con- 'sent to the marriage before he heard that it was actually consum- 'mated; in which, however, poor Swift was disappointed, for the 'old gentleman had not the letter to ask his consent before he 'received that which gave an account of his being married. I met 'Mr. White in the Coffee House and wished him joy, but he gave 'me a short answer: that it was no joy to him, and thought that, 'as Swift had no other dependence but on him, the least he could 'have done would have been to ask his consent before he took such 'a step. However, I hope he will not carry his resentment so far 'as to prejudice the poor fellow, who, I believe, is very deserving.'

JOHN SWIFT TO OSGOOD GEE, ESQ., AT BECKENHAM, KENT.

'I should have acquainted you of my being married, while it was 'new, but could never catch myself in a humor to do it, and answer 'your letter at the same time. I make no doubt but you, and all 'the rest of my friends, were surprised to hear it. I am sensible 'that it must appear, to people that know me, to be a very strange 'way of proceeding, not to consult my uncle about it, but I was got 'so far in love (without intending it) that I could not bear the 'thought of being refused, because nothing in this world could have 'made me happy, if that had been the case. I must now look upon 'Philadelphia as my home, but have not given over the thought of 'seeing England once again, and having the pleasure of being your 'guest at Beckenham. Pray make my compliments to Mrs. Gee, 'and all your good family. I have sent two small kegs of pickles, 'the produce of this country, of which I beg your acceptance, and 'hope they will prove good. They are in a box, which I have sent 'to my uncle's, under the care of Mr. Elliot, a young gentleman 'that came over with me from London, and we have lived together 'in the same house these two years. If it should fall in your way 'to be acquainted with him, you will find him to be a very sensible, 'modest, deserving young fellow, and an agreeable companion. He 'is a son of my Lord Minto's, of Scotland.'

* His portrait is now in possession of Miss Magdalen P. Swift.

She m. 2dly, (in New York,) James Craufurd, Esq., Colonel of the Guards, Equerry to the Queen, and Governor of Bermuda, by whom she had no issue. He was a friend of George Selwyn.*

JOSEPH, who commanded a troop of horse (Loyalist) during the Revolution.† He went to Nova Scotia, where he married, but subsequently returned to Philadelphia with his wife, and here d. 1826. He had nine children. He was 'the handsome as ever but 'stuttering as usual Captain Joe Swift,' mentioned in Miss Franks' letter to her sister, a part of which is printed in the Republican Court.

CHARLES, at one time Register of Wills, m. 1st, Mary Riché, by whom he had, (with Mary d. young,)

THOS. RICHE,

MAGDALEN PEEL,

SARAH, m. to her cousin, James Duane Livingston.

CHARLES, who changed his name to Charles Swift Riché.

JOHN, for several years Mayor of the City.

Mr. Swift m. 2dly, Mrs. Inman, by whom he had,

ROBERT, LEWIS,‡ and HENRY.

* See mention of him and his brother in Mr. Jesse's entertaining volumes 'George Selwyn and his Contemporaries,' iv. 103, iii. 380. Mr. Griswold (Republican Court, p. 32) says that Gov. Craufurd, after his marriage, resided in New York till his death.

† Mr. Sabine, in his *Loyalists*, has a brief notice of him.

‡ Mr. Lewis Swift is now in possession of the old family property, called 'Croydon Lodge.'

3. Anne M'Call, b. April 7, 1720; m. her cousin, Samuel M'Call. He was employed by the government, as I find from his letter, (*Dover, May* 28, 1765,) in some matters of consequence, and is called, in one of the letters, 'Major M'Call.' They had, with Anne, Catharine, Margaret, Eleanor and Isabel, who *d. unm.*,

Mary, who m. a British officer, named Dow, and had two children,

Samuel, d. young, and Anne, returned to Philadelphia, where she lived with her aunts, and *d. unm.* 1841.

4. Samuel, b. Oct. 5, 1721; d. 1762. He was a merchant, and appears to have served in no other public capacity than that of member of Council, to which he was elected Oct. 6, 1747. He m. Ann, dau. of Capt. John Searle, and had issue,*

George, Margaret, Eleanor and Mary, *d. unm.*

Catharine, m. Tench Coxe, *d. s. p.*

John Searle M'Call, of the island of St. Christopher, merchant, *d. unm.* 1786.

Ann, m. to Thomas Willing, as hereinafter mentioned.

5. George, b. April 16, 1724; d. 1758. His wife was the Mrs. Lydia M'Call in Watson's list of belles. She d. 1762. They had,

Mary, Catharine, and Lydia, all of whom *d. unm.*

* MS. in Chief Justice Tilghman's handwriting.

6. Mary, b. March 31, 1725; m. to William Plumstead, (son of Clement Plumstead, well known in the early annals of the Province,) repeatedly elected Mayor of the City, 1750, &c. They had,

William, Clement, Anne, and Catharine, who *d. unm.* and

George, who m. Miss Ross, and had,

William, Mary, Clement, and Margaret.

7. Archibald, b. June 28, 1727; d. 1799. He lived at the corner of Union and Second streets. He was the first East India merchant of his day. He m. 1762, Judith Kemble, of Mount Kemble, in New Jersey,* and by her (who d. 1828, aged 86) had issue, several children, which *d. young;* and Samuel, Harriet, Richard and Robert, *d. unm.* Also,

Mary, b. July 28, 1764; d. March 23, 1848; m. to Lambert Cadwalader, Colonel in the American army during the Revolution. They had,

John, d. young.

Thomas, m. Maria Gouverneur, of New York.

Archibald, b. Oct. 11, 1767; d. 1843; m. Elizabeth Cadwalader, half sister of the late Gen. Thomas Cadwalader, and had, with others,

George M'Call, Col. U. S. A., m. Miss M'Murtrie.

* For an account of the Kembles, one of whom m. Gen. Gage, B.A., of Boston memory, see *Burke's Land. Gentry*, s. v. Van Corllandt.

GEORGE, b. May 2, 1769; d. April 17, 1799; m. Miss Clymer, dau. of George Clymer, one of the signers of the Declaration.

ANNE, b. May 12, 1772; d. 1845; m. to William Read, Esq.

WILLIAM, m. Elizabeth Sitgreaves, of Easton.

PETER, b. March 23, 1776; d. 1809; m. Sarah Gibson, and had,

JOHN GIBSON, d. leaving issue, and

PETER, lately Mayor of the City, m. Miss Mercer, of Virginia.

HENRY, b. Sept. 27, 1788, still surviving; m. Lise Jones, of Louisiana, and has,

RICHARD, m. Olivia Wilson.

HARRY, m. Charlotte Wilcocks.

JONES, m. Angele Longer.

8. MARGARET, b. April 6, 1731; d. 1804; m. 1759, to JOSEPH SWIFT, younger and only brother of John Swift, above mentioned. He was b. June 24, 1731, and d. December 26, 1806. They are buried in the same tomb in Christ Church-yard. Their portraits are at 'Swarthmore,' formerly his residence, now that of his gr. son, Mr. Joseph Swift.

Joseph Swift was a merchant, and in business for many years with his brother. He was elected to the City Council, along with George Clymer, on the 6th of October, 1767, in which he served until his death in 1806.* His character

* He seems to have taken some interest in politics. '*May 1st,* '1776.—This has been one of the sharpest contests, yet peaceable, 'that has been for a number of years, except some small disturbance 'among the Dutch, occasioned by some unwarrantable expressions 'of Joseph Swift, viz., that except they were naturalized, they had 'no more right to a vote than a Negro or Indian.'—*Christopher Marshall's Diary*, 77. At night Mr. Swift's residence was threatened by a mob; but, as he was not there, no damage was done.

is so well described by one of his contemporaries, as to require no further words from me.

'With a constitution delicate in the extreme, he executed 'his many duties with an energy and steadiness only to be 'expected from a stronger frame. In his private dealings 'he was exemplarily just. In the City Magistracy, which 'he filled for some time, he was a firm though gentle curb 'to evil-doers, a support and protector of those who did well. 'In various offices of our commercial, charitable and reli-'gious institutions, particularly those of the Protestant 'Episcopal Church, of which he was an invaluable member, 'he honored himself and served his constituents by a faith-'ful and judicious execution of the trusts.'

I may add, that his acquirements as a scholar often brought his pen into requisition, when public papers were to be prepared; an instance of which may be found in the address by the Philadelphia merchants to the Speaker of the New Jersey Assembly. They had,

Ellinor White, John, William, George, Martha and Margaret, *d. unm.* Ellinor was famous in her day as a belle, but died young.

Mary, now living at the advanced age of 92 years. She was the intimate friend of her cousin, Eleanor Elliot, who afterwards m. Admiral Digby, and went to England, and with her she maintained for many years, until Mrs. Digby's death, a constant and affectionate correspondence. Mrs. Digby's letters were filled with details of society and life in England; but, after her death, Miss Swift destroyed them. Mrs. Digby, amongst other things, sent out two pictures representing different views of her husband's residence, one of which is at Swarthmore, the other is in the possession of Mr. Swift's eldest daughter. They were painted (as appears by the inscriptions on them) by Robert Sherburne, 1790.

JOSEPH, who m. and left two daughters, Mrs. Crawford and Mrs. Morrison.

ELIZABETH, still living.

SAMUEL, b. 11th Jan. 1771, who m. Feb. 11, 1795, Mary Shippen, dau. of Col. Joseph Shippen. She was b. May 17, 1773, and d. June 2, 1809. He d. at Germantown, Nov. 28, 1847. They are buried in one tomb in the graveyard of the ancient Episcopal Church at Oxford. She, as appears both from her letters and the testimony of those who knew her, was faithful, judicious and affectionate in all her several relations in life. He was graduated at the University of Pennsylvania, and studied law with Judge Yeates; but preferring the independence of a country life, lived at his country place, in Philadelphia county. Educated a Federalist, he nevertheless espoused the Democratic policy, which he occasionally advocated in articles greatly esteemed at the time for their vigor, candor, research and polish. He possessed much natural poetical talent, which he cultivated and exercised, up to his decease, for the amusement and gratification of his family, though he never cared to seek a wider circle. Many of these pieces are preserved by his children. They had issue,

MARGARET, m. to John Shippen, and has issue, (*ante*, p. lxxvi.)

WILLIAM, *d. unm.*

MARY, m. to M. Brooke Buckley. They have issue, one son,

EDWARD SHIPPEN.

JOSEPH, m. Nov. 24, 1831, Eliza Moore Willing, dau. of George Willing, hereafter mentioned. She d. Sept. 9, 1840. They had, (with GEORGE, who d. young,)

EMILY, m. Thomas Balch. Oct. 5, 1852.

MARY.

SAMUEL, m. Mary Royer, and has issue.

ELIZABETH,

SARAH,

EDWIN,

JANE, m. to John Swift, (not a kinsman.)

9. ELEANOR, b. July 8, 1732, m. to Andrew Elliot,* then

* Mr. Elliot, already spoken of, (*ante*, p. lxxxvi,) is frequently mentioned in John Swift's letter-book, from which I extract a paragraph, written whilst Mr. Elliot was on a visit to London. The letter is addressed to Grosvenor Bedford, Oct. 25, 1749. 'If you 'frequent the Pennsylvania Coffee House, you will probably meet 'with a tall, thin Scots gentleman, with a pimply face. He answers 'to the name of Elliot, and is an intimate friend of mine, one for 'whom I have a particular regard, on account of several valuable 'qualities I have discovered in him, we having lived together in the 'same house for nearly two years.' Mr. Elliot was elected to the City Councils, Oct. 7, 1755, along with Chief Justice Shippen and Thomas Willing, and served in that body for several years. There is a sketch of him in Mr. Sabine's *Loyalists*, to which I will only add, that the Pennsylvania property, derived through his marriage, was confiscated and sold.

a resident in Philadelphia, afterwards Lt. Gov. of New York. She had but one child, (a few days after whose birth she died),*

ELEANOR, m. 1st, January 14th, 1774, to James Jauncey, Jr., of New York; and 2dly, about 1784, to Admiral Digby, who served on our coast during the Revolution. She *d. s. p.*†

After his first wife's death, Mr. Elliot m. 2dly, Elizabeth Plumstead, (sister of William Plumstead, who m. Mary M'Call,) and had two daughters,

* The portrait of Mrs. Elliot and her dau. Eleanor, taken whilst a child, by West, are at Swarthmore. Mrs. Buckley has a miniature of Mrs. Digby, taken after she went to England to reside.

† In the defence of Admiral Graves (*Pol. Mag.* 1784, vi. 20, &c.) is a curious account of the battle which he *intended* to fight with the Count de Grasse, and thereby relieve Lord Cornwallis; an extract from which, as it relates to Admiral Digby, I make.

'The 24th, in the evening, Rear Admiral Digby came from Europe 'with the Prince George of 98, Canada of 74, and Lion of 64 guns; 'and upon the 11th of October arrived the Torbay of 74, and Prince 'William of 64 guns, from Jamaica, in pursuance of Sir George 'Rodney's orders.

'Mr. Digby bore himself a commission for commanding in North 'America, and brought to Mr. Graves Admiralty orders, dated the '9th of June, for his proceeding with the London to Jamaica and 'for putting himself under the senior officer on that station, if senior 'to himself. However, the London could not be spared at this 'crisis, when another engagement was in contemplation; and the 'officers both of fleet and army appearing desirous of the same 'Admiral's continuing to direct the naval operations, and no one 'more so than Mr. Digby himself, (the next in rank upon the sta- 'tion,) Mr. Graves went on with the maritime command, although 'superseded, with the same ardor and alacrity as before.

'The utmost, and very uncommon exertions had indeed hitherto 'been made throughout all the marine departments to get every one 'of the ships ready again for sea, but some cross accidents inter- 'vened to retard them; in particular, the Alcide, by falling aboard 'the Shrewsbury, had carried away her bowsprit and foreyard, just 'as she was repaired in her damages from the late fight. All, how- 'ever, except the Shrewsbury, Montagu, and Europe, went down 'with the help of evening tide to Sandy Hook the 17th, when the

ELIZABETH, m. to Earl Cathcart. She was the grandmother of the late General Cathcart, who was killed in the Crimea.

AGNES, m. to Sir David Carnegie.

'Admiral gave out his line of battle;* the next morning they em-'barked their troops; and on the morning of the 19th, the three 'last-named ships joining the rest, and taking in their lot of soldiers, 'the whole armament getting safe over the bar, hurried away for 'the Chesapeake. It consisted of 25 ships properly of the line, 'there being three of 98 guns, fourteen of 74, one of 70, and seven 'of 64, besides two of 50, with 7149 land forces on board, to which 'the general would have added another regiment or two, but there 'was not room for them.

'On the 24th, when near Cape Charles, (the hithermost headland 'of the Chesapeake,) the scouting vessels brought intelligence of 'Lord Cornwallis having surrendered some days before. His lord-'ship had opened a treaty the 17th, settled the terms the 18th, and 'signed them the 19th. * * * *

'This made him (Admiral Graves) determine to lose no time in turning over the North American command to Mr. Digby, in pur-'suance of the Admiralty's order; and as his own ship was not

---

* 'LINE OF BATTLE.—The Princessa to lead with the starboard, and the Bedford with the 'larboard tacks on board.

FRIGATES.	RATE.	SHIPS.	COMMANDERS.	GUNS.	MEN.	
'Sybil	3d	Princessa	Rear Adm. Samuel Drake Capt. Knatchbull	70	577	Robt. Digby, Esq., Rear Admiral of the Red.
'Britannia	—	Alcide	—— Charles Thompson	74	600	
	—	Lion	—— Fooks	64	500	
	—	Canada	—— Hon. Wm. Cornwallis	74	600	
'Perseverance 'to repeat 'signals	2d	Pr. George	Rear Admiral Digby Capt. J. Williams	98	768	
	3d	Resolution	—— Lord Robert Manners	74	600	
'L'Enfer *fire sh.*	—	Intrepid	—— Pye Molloy	64	500	
'Felicity	—	Montagu	—— Bowen	74	600	
	4th	Warwick	—— Hon. G. K. Elphinston	50	350	Thomas Graves, Esq., Rear Admiral of the Red and Commander in Chief.
	3d	Pr. William	—— G. Wilkinson	64	500	
'Rattlesnake	—	Centaur	—— Inglefield	74	650	
'Carysfort	—	Europe	—— Child	64	500	
'Volcano *fire sh.*	—	Robuste	—— Cosby	74	600	
'Orpheus to re-'peat signals	2d	London	Rear Admiral Graves Capt. Kempthorne —— Morice	98	800	
'Amphion	3d	Royal Oak	—— Burnett	74	600	
'Conflagration 'fire-ship	—	America	—— Samuel Thompson	64	500	
	—	Shrewsbury	—— Knight	74	600	
	—	Torbay	—— Gidion	74	600	
'Blonde	4th	Adamant	—— David Graves	50	350	
'Lively	3d	Ajax	—— Charrington	74	550	Sir Samuel Hood, Bart. Rear Admiral of the Blue.'
'Salamander 'fire-ship	—	Prudent	—— Barkley	64	500	
	—	Monarch	—— Reynolds	74	600	
'Pegasus to re-'peat signals	2d	Barfleur	Rear Adm. Sir Sam. Hood Capt. Alex. Hood	98	768	
'Ostrich	3d	Invincible	—— Saxton	74	600	
	—	Belliqueux	—— Brine	64	500	
'La Nymphe	—	Alfred	—— Bayne	74	600	
'Santa Margaritta	—	Bedford	Commodore Affleck Capt. Thomas Graves	74	617	

SARAH SHIPPEN, dau. of Edward Shippen, of Lancaster, (*ante*, p. xxviii) was m. to Col. James Burd. He was the third son of Edward Burd, a gentleman who lived on his estate of Ormiston, near Edinburgh, Scotland, by his wife, Jane Halliburton, a dau. of the Lord Provost of Edinburgh. Both Col. and Mrs. Burd d. at his estate of Tinian, near Harrisburg. They had issue, (with ALLEN, *d. young*, and ELIZABETH, *d. unm.*)

SARAH, m. to Judge Jasper Yeates.
EDWARD, m. to Elizabeth Shippen.*
MARY SHIPPEN, m. to Peter Grubb, Esq.
JANE BURD, m. to George Patterson, Esq.
MARGARET BURD, m. to Jacob Hubley, Esq.
JAMES BURD, m. Elizabeth Baker.
JOSEPH BURD, m. 1st, Kitty Cochrane; 2d, Harriet Bailey.

All the children of Col. and Mrs. Burd (except Joseph) rejoiced in respectably-sized families; but as the ramifications appear to be extensive, and as the materials before me are such as I can but little trust, I will not attempt to trace them. Some of their grand-children either are, or were, or intermarried with persons of character and position: the

'required for the security of the West Indian squadron on their 'passage, although he had offered to accompany them for that pur- 'pose, he sailed on the 10th at eight in the morning, singly, for his 'own destination.'

* As this page is passing through the press, the following announcement appears in the newspapers, of the death of the last surviving child of Major Burd:

'This, 11th day of June, SARAH BURD, daughter of the late 'Edward Burd, Esq., in the 70th year of her age.'

late Edward Shippen Burd, Judge Charles Smith, of the Supreme Court of this State, Burd Patterson, Esq., Redmond Conyngham, and others.

Col. Burd was for many years in the military service of the Province;* but, as the following letters speak so fully of his career, it is unnecessary to enter into a more particular account of his life and character, except as to his service in the Revolutionary army. It seems, that he was very active at the beginning of the Revolution in his efforts to raise troops, and was greatly disappointed and somewhat mortified at not having received a commission as Brigadier General.† However, he accepted a Colonelcy, to which he

* The following extract from a letter from Edward Shippen, Esq. to Col. James Burd, dated 'Lancaster, October 6, 1759,' is curious as showing that nearly a century ago 'the western trade' was of consequence, and the subject of feeling:

'Your kind favor of the 18th inst., several days ago, and I am much 'pleased to hear of your and Col. Shippen's good health, and that 'you are going on so fast with the roads through that rugged coun- 'try to the mouth of Red Stone creek, which empties into the Mo- 'nongahela. This will give the Virginians and the worthless Mary- 'landers a fine opening to Pittsburgh, and I am glad enough of it 'on every account except one, that the former will have an easy 'way to transport their goods to, and bring back the peltry from the 'Ohio, and as they will then find the sweets of the Indian trade, '(tho' for my part I should call them the sours,) we may reasonably 'expect they [will] not suffer us to go out of our limits down that 'river.'

† JOSEPH SHERER TO COL. JAMES BURD, AT TINIAN.

'*Philadelphia, August 27th,* 1776.

'DEAR COLONEL—I received yours of the 19th, and it gives me 'great pleasure to hear of your welfare, as well as also the spirit 'with which you have conducted matters, indeed. I hardly could 'expect that you could have fitted out two companies as well as you 'have done, and as for arms, here they are not to be had; notwith- 'standing there is a great deal comes here, there is a demand for 'them to the continental troops, so that our troops belonging to the 'State, can have few or none. * * * * I must conclude, and 'with all esteem, I subscribe myself,

Your most obedient, humble servant,

JOSEPH SHERER.

was elected Sept. 18th, 1775.* Dissensions in his battalion, and reluctance on the part of his soldiers to serve anywhere else than in their own immediate neighborhood, induced him to resign. The letters appended in the note give the substance of the story. It was a source of deep regret, as besides being 'fond'† of a military life, he had anticipated some reputation by exercising, in behalf of his country, the professional experience and knowledge which he possessed.‡

EDWARD SHIPPEN TO COL. BURD, AT TINIAN.

'*Lancaster, August 28th*, 1775.

'DEAR MR. BURD:— * * * I suppose the slight you have 'received from those from whom you deserved due respect, is the 'reason of your resignation. However, say as little about it as 'possible, for fear of making the breaches wider, as our family have 'resigned themselves to doing. I know it is expected from those 'who do not muster, that they shall pay. Let us put our trust 'in God, repent of our sins, mend our lives, and pray to him for a 'deliverance out of the hand of our murdering enemies, for the 'battle is not to the strong. * * * * Doctor Smith says that 'General Tryon has told Lord Dartmouth, in a late letter, that the 'measures of Parliament won't do; they must be stopt.'

* ELECTION OF FIELD OFFICERS.

'Colonel James Burd.
'The election held at Wm. Dickey's.
'*September* 18th, 1775.

† *Post*, p. 175.

‡ COL. BURD'S LETTER OF RESIGNATION, TO GEN. MIFFLIN.

'*Tinian, December 27th*, 1776.

'SIR:—I had the honor to be favored with your orders last night, 'dated 23d instant, previous to which I had resigned the command 'of the battalion; but this morning, by Capt. Crouch, have for-'warded your orders to Major Cornelius Cox, who at present com-'mands the battalion, (Lieut. Col. Murray being taken prisoner at 'Fort Washington.) I think it my duty to give you my reason for 'resignation, and the more especially at this time of public . 'If I had had an opportunity of a personal conference, I think I 'could have convinced you that I not only had reason for this step, 'but a necessity for so doing. I would inform you that the space 'occupied by my battalion is very long, between forty and fifty 'miles in length, and broad withal, that it requires time to commu-'nicate any order, and inconvenient to get the whole battalion to-'gether, especially at this season of the year. However, in conse-

To return to the child of Joseph and Abigail Shippen, next in order.

ANNE SHIPPEN, dau. of Joseph and Abigail Shippen, b. August 5, 1710; m. January 21st, 1731, to CHARLES WILLING. He was b. in Bristol, England, May 18,

'quence of the orders you refer to, I gave out orders for the 'whole battalion to meet in their districts on Monday, the 9th inst., 'the middle of which I attended myself; and further directions for 'all the officers of the battalion to meet me at Garber's Mill, on 'Tuesday, the 10th inst., to make report of their proceedings. Ac- 'cordingly, on Tuesday they all met me, and this part was all of the 'volunteers which were to be found, upon which I gave orders in 'writing, and sent them to every company in the battalion, that the 'whole battalion should rendezvous at Middletown on Monday, the '16th inst., in order to march by divisions to join General Wash- 'ington; and those that were not provided with arms, &c., I pro- 'mised to have them provided at Philadelphia; that neither money 'nor anything should be wanting. I attended, ready to march with 'the battalion from Monday, the 11th, to Sunday night, the 22d, 'and not one man turned out but ten, seven of whom were officers, 'myself included, (except a small company of volunteers commanded 'by Captain Bloler, of thirty-three, officers in) whom I 'marched off. Least I should stand in the way, I thought proper 'to resign, offering at the same time my personal attendance, and to 'render any service acceptable, upon notice being given me of such 'being wanting. You will no doubt expect I should give some rea- 'sons for such conduct in the battalion at this time. I cannot sug- 'gest any, unless the following may be the reasons: that three com- 'panies have already marched to camp, one of which, viz: Captain 'James Murray, still remains there; that Captain John Murray has 'one, which renders the battalion so weak, that they have not more 'or very few men more left than are sufficient to attend to their cat- 'tle, &c.; or a late prejudice against myself. I have commanded 'the battalion ever since our troubles began, with pleasure to my- 'self, and to the battalion seemingly, for anything I knew to the 'contrary, and have been able to comply with all orders heretofore 'given me, which was not the case in the last instance to which 'you allude; and from what I have already said, I make no doubt 'I will stand unimpeached in your judgment, and that of my supe- 'rior officers, judging that you all know that I have done every 'thing in my power. After making an apology for troubling you 'with such a long scrawl, I beg leave to subscribe myself,

'Sir, your most obedient, humble servant,

'JAMES BURD.

'To the Hon. Brig. Gen. THOMAS MIFFLIN.

1710, and d. in Philadelphia, Nov. 30, 1754, in which place she also d. June 23, 1790.*

CHARLES WILLING was the son of Thomas Willing, of Bristol, merchant, b. Jan. 16, 1679, by Anne Harrison, his wife, whom he m. July 16, 1704. She d. Sept. 11, 1747. She was, paternally, the grand-dau. of Gen. Harrison, the Regicide,† and maternally the dau. of Dorothy Mayne, her-

'I put it to vote on the 18th, if I should not march with them, 'and it was carried against me that I should not. On Saturday 'morning I was on my journey to go to Lancaster to see you. The 'officers advised I should not proceed, but remain to endeavor to 'get the battalion to march. This they thought more advisable for 'the good of the service.'

* The portraits of himself and wife are in the possession of Dr. Charles Willing. There is also a portrait of Mrs. Willing at Berkley, on the James River, Virginia.

† As the 'Regicide' is occasionally mentioned, and as an error (hereafter corrected in these pages,) concerning the ancestry of the late President Harrison, frequently occurs in the public prints or in works of standing, (e. g. the *Republican Court*,) I here print a notice of him, in which I have followed these authorities:

Howell's State Trials. London, 1816, vol. V. pp. 998, 1008, 1230, &c.

The High Court of Justice, by James Caulfield. London, 1820, pp. 63, &c.

Major Gen. Thomas Harrison was born at Newcastle-under-Line, in the county of Stafford. Whatever was his father's situation in life, he did not neglect his son, who, after receiving a grammatical education, was articled to an attorney, named Hocelker, in good estimation in Clifford's Inn, who had an employment under the King, and (Lord Clarendon says) discharged his duty faithfully. After serving his clerkship,* Harrison joined the company of students in the law, that became, under the command of Sir Philip Stapylton, guard to the Earl of Essex, the parliament general. He rose gradually until he reached a Majority, and in 1646, at the surrender of the old Palace at Woodstock, was one of the Commissioners to receive it. He gained the good opinion of Col. Sydney (Lord Lisle's son), at whose request the Commons, January, 1646–7, voted that he should accompany Lord Lisle, Sir John Temple, and Col. Sydney to Ireland, where his conduct was so meritorious, that he was included in the resolution of thanks, and was raised to a Colo-

* The Court said to him on his trial, 'You are versed in proceedings of law.'

self the dau. of Simon Mayne, another of the Regicides. She was certainly a woman of talent and of uncommon education for the times in which she lived. Some verses of

nelcy. He became so conspicuous that he was appointed one of the Commissioners of the Army to treat with Parliament as to a good understanding between them; and had so much interest that, when in November following, his regiment threatened to mutiny, he obtained their pardon; for which they showed their gratitude by gallant service at Preston, in Lancashire, where the Duke of Hamilton was defeated.

When it was decided to try the King, Col. Harrison was fixed upon to bring him from Hurst Castle to Windsor. Lord Clarendon says, that he received his royal charge with all outward respect and uncovered; and, during the entire journey, his conduct was dignified, though watchful. He frustrated the King's attempt to escape at Bagshot. When Charles, who dreaded assassination, expressed to him some apprehensions of secret violence, he answered 'that, 'whatever the Parliament resolved to do, would be very public, and 'in a way of justice to which the world will be witness.' The part he took in the trial was characteristic, and he set his hand and seal to the warrant of execution.

In 1650 he became a Major General, and was sent to Ireland, where he again distinguished himself; but came over with Cromwell to assist at the consultation with Fairfax as to his scruples about commanding the army against the Scots, which terminated in Fairfax's resignation.

In October, 1651, Harrison made a brilliant figure in drawing out the train-bands and other bodies of men, to the number of 8,000, in Hyde Park, preparatory to his going north with Cromwell to meet the Scots. At the battle of Worcester, his conduct gave the greatest satisfaction to the General and the whole army.

In the dissolution of the Long Parliament, Harrison was completely duped by Cromwell; but soon discovering the abuse of his friendship by him with whom he had so often fought and prayed together, he instantly broke with him. Cromwell regarded him as a dangerous rival for power. Harrison held him as one who had betrayed the public trust, which made his heart swell high for vengeance. In December, 1655, in consequence of his refusal to subscribe to the new government, the Protector took his commission from him and sent him prisoner to Carrisbrook Castle, from which he was discharged in 1656; but his opposition to the government involved him in new difficulties, and he was shortly after sent as a prisoner to Pendennis Castle. Upon his release, he joined Lord Grey of Groby in the scheme of destroying the Protector, siezing Monk, and erecting the kingdom of Christ.

At the Restoration, Major General Harrison was siezed by Col. Bowyer, at the head of a party of the Staffordshire militia. He hers, of a religious character, are yet extant; and the handwriting is remarkably fine. The late Mr. Thomas Willing gave to his son-in-law, Major Jackson, a book which had be-

might have avoided this, as he knew what was designed against him; but 'he considered it,' he said, 'an act of desertion to the 'cause to leave his house,' and so remained quietly awaiting the event. He was conveyed to the Tower, and thence to Newgate for trial, having been absolutely excepted from pardon by a clause in the Bill of Indemnity, and was, October 10, 1660, indicted as Thomas Harrison, late of Westminster, in the county of Middlesex, gentleman. He defended himself exactly as might have been expected of a man of his fearless, resolute spirit, who had never feared death. He told the Court, that the king's death was not a thing done in a corner, but that the sound thereof had been heard in most nations; that he would not, of himself, offer the least injury to the poorest man or woman that went upon earth; but what he did was out of conscience to the Lord. He maintained the authority of the commissions under which he acted, and instead of usurping an authority, it was, he said, done in the fear of the Lord. The Court here interrupted him, and Lord Finch told him, 'he must not 'be suffered to run into these damnable excursions to make God the 'author of the damnable treasons committed.'

Nothing intimidated, he argued then, that he had done no wrong, because the act was authorized by Parliament, to which that Court was inferior, and therefore he was not to be questioned for it; citing a case alike to it in Richard the Second's time. Upon being told that 'his countrymen would cry out and shame him,' he answered—'May be so, my Lords. Some will, but others, I am sure, will not.'

Every plea he offered being overruled, the jury was charged and brought in a verdict of guilty. He was executed at Charing Cross, October 13, 1660. On the scaffold his legs and hands trembled; but he assured those who noticed it, that it was an infirmity to which he had been subject for twelve years, owing to the vast quantity of blood lost by wounds received in the battles which he had fought. Throughout his conduct he exhibited the greatest courage and composure. He parted with his wife and friends with great joy and cheerfulness, as he did use to do when going on a journey or about some service of the Lord. He helped the Serjeant to adjust the rope. In his speech from the gallows, he bade them take notice, that he was brought thither to suffer death for being instrumental in that cause 'which God hath witnessed to my appeals and won-'derful victories: and if I had ten thousand lives, I could freely 'and cheerfully lay them down all, to witness to this matter.'

'Then he was turned off,' says the State Trials, 'and was cut 'down alive; for after his body was opened, he mounted himself, 'and gave the executioner a box on the ear.' Ludlow says—'He 'was so barbarously executed, that he was cut down alive, and saw 'his bowels thrown into the fire.'

longed to her, and has her autograph in it. It is yet in Mrs. Jackson's possession.* Gen. Harrison's portrait, painted on panel by Walker, is now in the possession of Dr. Charles Willing, who also has one of the mourning rings given at the funeral of Anne Harrison;† another, and that given at her mother, Dorothy Mayne's funeral, are in the possession of J. Francis Fisher, Esq. This Thomas Willing was (with others) the son of Joseph Willing, also of Bristol, by his second wife, Ann Lowle, an heiress,‡ whom he m. May 24th, 1676.

Charles Willing came out to this city somewhere about the year 1729, and settled here as a merchant. He was elected Mayor of the city 1748, and again 1754, and died, it is said, of ship-fever, contracted whilst in the discharge of his official duties.§ He was much respected and esteemed,

* The title page is torn out; index, as far as preserved, begins with,

33. Speeches, and his Majesty's last speech at his martyrdom, with many things relating to his death.

II. Messages, 40; only 21 before printed—declaration from Carisbrooke and Isle of Wight.

III. Letters, 36; Answer to Commons' Declaration.

2. *Concerning Matters Sacred.*

1. Papers which passed between His Majesty and the Ministers at Newport, about Episcopacy, 1648, &c.
2. His prayers.

Several things relating to H. M. death; *e. g.* a speech made in Latin by Dr. Lotius, &c.

Verses; *e. g.* "A deep groan at the funerale," &c.

After which follows a copy of Eikon Basilke, &c.

Re-printed in Regis Memoriam, for John Williams, 1649.

† She died Sept. 11th, 1747.

‡ The coat of arms of the Lowle family was:—Sa. a hand grasping three darts, one in pale, two in saltire, argent. *Crest.*—A demi-eagle erm. rising, wings expanded, having a leaf of laurel in its beak. The seal which belonged to Anne Lowle's father, is now in Dr. Willing's possession.

§ Epitaph—

'If to be all the wise and good commend,
'The tender husband, father and the friend,
'At home beloved and blest, esteemed abroad,
'Studious to serve mankind and please his God;
'If these from death one useful life could save,
'Thou had'st not read that Willing fills the grave.'

both as a merchant and a magistrate. The mercantile house founded by his brother Thomas* and himself was, it is said, esteemed the first of its day in the city; as proof of which is mentioned the facts, that Mr. Morris presided at the Merchants' feast (p. 232, *post*) given to the Proprietaries, and that Thomas Willing (son of Charles) walked at the head of the merchants at the famous 'Federal Procession,' in 1788.

I. Thomas Willing, b. Dec. 19, 1731; d. 19th January, 1821; m. Anne McCall, (*ante*, p. lxxxviii.) The epitaph on Mr. Willing's tombstone, in Christ Churchyard, understood to be from the pen of Mr. Binney, gives so copious yet condensed an outline of Mr. Willing's life, character and services, that other comment is unnecessary here.†

'In memory of Thomas Willing, Esquire, born nine- 'teenth of December, 1731, O. S.; died nineteenth of Jan- 'uary, 1821, aged eighty-nine years and thirty days. This 'excellent man, in all the relations of private life, and in 'various stations of high public trust, deserved and acquired 'the devoted affection of his family and friends, and the 'universal respect of his fellow citizens. From 1754 to '1807, he successively held the offices of Secretary to the 'Congress of Delegates at Albany, Mayor of the City of

* Thomas Willing, son of Thomas of Bristol, came to this city somewhere about the year 1726, and established the mercantile relations of which his younger brother Charles afterwards took charge and enlarged, as stated above. He then returned to Bristol, where he died. A miniature of him is in possession of Mr. Fisher. The family Bible of Joseph Willing is in the possession of the present Mr. Richard Willing, to whom father it was given by Ann, dau. of Richard of Bristol, and grand-dau. of Joseph. This Thomas is the person after whom Willington, now Wilmington, Delaware, was originally called.—*Mrs. Montgomery's Reminiscences*, p. 172.

† *Republican Court*, p. 16.

'Philadelphia, her representative in the General Assembly, 'President of the Provincial Congress, Delegate to the Con'gress of the Confederation, President of the first chartered 'Bank in America, and President of the first Bank of the 'United States. With these public duties, he united the 'business of an active, enterprising and successful merchant, 'in which pursuit, for sixty years, his life was rich in ex'amples of the influences of probity, fidelity, and persever'ance upon the stability of commercial establishments, and 'upon that which was his distinguished reward upon earth, 'public consideration and esteem. His profound adoration 'of the Great Supreme, and his deep sense of dependence 'on His mercy, in life and in death, gave him, at the close 'of his protracted years, the humble hope of a superior one 'in Heaven.'*

Thomas Willing and Anne M'Call had issue, (with CHARLES, GEORGE and HENRY, d. infants,)

1. ANN, b. Aug. 1, 1764; m. to William Bingham, Esq., U. S. Senator from Pennsylvania.† They had,

    WILLIAM, who resides in Paris, m. Charlotte, Baroness de Vaudreuil, in her own right.

    ANNE LOUISA, m. to Lord Ashburton, so well known in America as the negotiator of the Webster-Ashburton Treaty.

    MARIA MATILDA, m. to Henry Baring.

* The discussion in Notes and Queries as to 'the fashion of 'Brittainy,' (XI. 255,) causes me to note here, that, in nearly every letter addressed by Mr. E. Shippen, of Lancaster, to his *nephew* at Philadelphia, Mr. Shippen begins, 'Dear *Cousin* Tommy Willing.'

† For a full and glowing account of Mrs. Bingham, one which renders anything else here unnecessary, see Dr. Griswold's *Republican Court.*

FRANCIS BARING,* an eminent London merchant, b. April 18, 1740; created Baronet May 29, 1793; m. 1766, Harriet, dau. of William Herring, Esq., of Croydon, cousin and co-heir of Thomas Herring, Archbishop of Canterbury, by her (who d. Dec. 3, 1804) had issue, with others,

The Rt. Hon. ALEXANDER BARING, 2d son of Sir Francis Baring, Bart., b. Oct. 27, 1774, was raised to the peerage as Baron Ashburton, of Ashburton, county Devon, April 10, 1835, having held office during the previous four months as President of the Board of Trade and Master of the Mint. He was also a Privy Councillor, trustee of the British Museum, and D. C. L. of Oxford. He m. Aug. 23, 1798, Anne Louisa, eldest dau. of the Hon. Wm. Bingham, of Philadelphia, a Senator of the United States, and by her (who d. Dec. 5, 1848) had issue, five sons. He d. May 13, 1848.

WILLIAM BINGHAM, present Lord Ashburton, (Privy Councillor,) b. June 1799; m. April, 1823, Harriet Mary, eldest dau. of George John, 6th Earl of Sandwich, and had a son,

ALEXANDER MONTAGU, who d. an infant, Feb. 5, 1830.

FRANCIS, b. May 20, 1800; m. January, 1833, Clara Hortense, dau. of the late Duke of Bassano, and has issue,

* Burke's Peerage.

1. Alexander Hugh.

2. Denzil Hugh, and a daughter, Mary Louisa Anne.

Frederick, in holy orders, Rector of Itchin-Stoke, Hants, b. June 31, 1808; m. April 24, 1831, Frederica Mary Catharine, 3d dau. of John Ashton, Esq , of the Grange, county Chester, and has issue.

Alexander, b. May 2, 1810, Lieutenant R. N.; d. March 12, 1832, on board His Majesty's ship Alfred, in the Mdditerranean.

Arthur, b. Oct. 8, 1818; d. at Madeira, Feb. 16, 1838, unm.

And four daughters,

Anne Eugenia, m. 1823, to Humphrey St. John Mildmay, Esq., and d. March 8, 1839.

Harriet, m. to Henry Frederick Thynne, who succeeded his father as 3d Marquis of Bath.

Louisa,

Lydia Emily.

Henry Frederick Thynne, Capt. R. N., 3d Marquis of Bath, b. May 24, 1797; m. April 19, 1830, Harriet, dau. of Lord Ashburton; succeeded March 27, 1837; d. June 24, 1837, leaving issue,

1. John Alexander Thynne, 4th Marquis, b. March 1, 1831.

2. Henry Frederick, b. Aug. 2, 1832.

And two daughters,

Louisa Isabella Harriet,

Alice, d. 1847.

Henry, (3d son,) b. 1777; m. April 19, 1802, Maria Matilda, 2d dau. of William Bingham, Esq., of Philadelphia, (who married 2dly, the Marquis de Blaisell, and d. 1852,) by whom he had issue, three sons and two daughters,

Henry Bingham, M. P. for Marlborough, b. March 4, 1804; m. June 30, 1827, Lady Augusta Brudenell, (5th dau. of Robert, 6th Lord Cardigan,) and has issue.

James Drummond.

William Frederick, b. August 12, 1822; m. Nov. 12, 1845, Emily, eldest dau. of Sir R. Jenkins, G. C. B., and has issue.

Anna Maria, m. to William Gordon Coesvelt, Esq.

Frances Emily, m. Aug. 19, 1830, to Henry Bridgeman Simpson, Esq.

2. Charles, b. April 7, 1766; m. 1st, Rose Evans, 2d, Ann Hemphill.

3. Thomas Mayne, b. April 15, 1767; m. Jane Nixon, and d. leaving issue,

Elizabeth, m. to John Stirling, of Scotland. They have (with Andrew, Elizabeth, Dorothea, Mary, and Agnes, *d. young*,)

Anna, m. to Henry S. Cooke.

Thomas Mayne,

William,

John, killed at Inkerman.

Emma.

CHARLES, (M. D.,) m. Miss Tillinghast.
ANNE, m. to Mungo Murray, of Lintore, Scotland.
EMMA, (now deceased,) m. to Capt. James Maitland, R. N.

4. ELIZABETH, b. March 27, 1768, still living; m. to the late Major Wm. Jackson, of the Revolutionary army. They had, (with others, *d. young*,)
ANN,
MARY RIGAL, *d. unm.*
CAROLINE, m. to Mr. Philip Physic.
WILLIAM, m. Martha James, dau. of Dr. Thos. C. James, *d. s. p.*

"Major William Jackson of the Revolutionary army, was born in Cumberland, England, March 9th, 1759, and was brought to Charleston, South Carolina, at an early age. On the paternal side, he was of English, and on the maternal, of Scottish descent; of a highly respectable ancestry.

Having the misfortune to be left an orphan in his childhood, from the property bequeathed to him by his father, under the care of his guardian, Colonel Owen Roberts, he received a liberal and classical education, and was enabled to support himself as an officer during the war of the Revolution.

In June, 1775, then in the 17th year of his age, he entered, as a lieutenant, the first Continental regiment of South Carolina Infantry, then commanded by Colonel Christopher Gadsden, in which he continued to serve until Major General Benjamin Lincoln assumed the command of the southern department of the Revolutionary army, when, on the recommendation of his friend, Colonel Charles Cotesworth Pinckney, General Lincoln appointed him his aid-de-camp, which appointment, with that of Captain in the above named regiment, he held until the close of the war.

Lieutenant Jackson was in the expedition to Florida, in 1778, when the regular Continental regiments under the command of General Howe of North Carolina, aided by Colonel Charles Cotesworth Pinckney, and other distinguished officers, marched from Charleston, crossed the river St. Mary, took possession of Fort Towson, and would have proceeded to St. Augustine, but the British garrison there being reinforced, and their supplies of stores and provisions being nearly exhausted, after some skirmishing with the enemy, they were forced to retreat, which they were enabled to do by the coast navigation, and returned to Georgia, after enduring much suffering and privation.

In May, 1779, Lieutenant Jackson was at the skirmish of Tulefinny, and on the 20th of June following, at the battle of Stone Ferry, at which his guardian, the brave Colonel Roberts was mortally wounded. Before expiring, he took an affectionate farewell of his son, Captain Roberts, who was in action with him, and of his ward, Lieutenant Jackson. Addressing the former, he said: 'My son, take my sword. 'Never sully it. Return to your duty, with a father's blessing.'

On the 9th of October, 1779, Lieutenant, now Captain Jackson, being the day on which his commission as such was given by Congress, was again in action, in the attack made on Savannah by the American and French troops, led by General Lincoln and the Count D'Estaing. During the assault, which lasted an hour, the loss suffered by the allies was frightful, they having had nine hundred men killed and wounded. The assailants were repulsed.

Captain Jackson was in the only sortie made during the siege of Charleston, when three hundred Carolinians and Virginians led by Colonel John Laurens and Lieutenant

Colonel Henderson, rushed into the British entrenchments with unloaded muskets, the sword and the bayonet being the only weapons used, and after a sanguinary conflict in which fifteen or twenty of the enemy were killed, and some few made prisoners, succeeded in regaining the American lines, having had the misfortune to have Captain Moultrie, brother of Colonel Moultrie, slain, and to lose two of their men.

Captain Jackson was at the siege of Charleston, when General Lincoln, after a gallant defence of six weeks, was obliged to capitulate, and surrender the city on the 12th of May, 1780, but not until they had experienced the horrors of famine, the works had been pronounced untenable by General Du Portail, and every effort of patriotism and courage had been exerted by the intrepid Lincoln, and the troops under his command. So near had the British approaches been brought, that Colonel Parker, of the Virginia line, was shot, leaning on the parapet, as Major Jackson, who now ranked as such in his capacity of aid-de-camp, was in the act of delivering him an order from General Lincoln.

After the capitulation of Charleston, General Lincoln and Major Jackson, (who were prisoners on parol,) by order of General Washington, attended as commissioners for the exchange of prisoners, and among others negotiated their own and that of Colonel John Laurens, who, soon after, was appointed special Minister to France, and Major Jackson appointed Secretary to the Mission.

On the 9th of February, 1781, Colonel Laurens and Major Jackson embarked at Boston, in the frigate Alliance, Captain Barry.

Colonel Laurens was completely successful in effecting the

object of his mission.* Owing to his ability and energy, he obtained from the French government a large loan, ample supplies of clothing and military stores, and the co-operation of the French fleet under the command of the Count de Grasse, which contributed to the capture of Lord Cornwallis, and the surrender of Yorktown, in October, 1780.

Colonel Laurens, after the object of his mission was attained, returned to America, and was present at the surrender of Yorktown, where he greatly distinguished himself in storming a redoubt.

According to instructions from Colonel Laurens, Major Jackson proceeded to Amsterdam to receive the funds, which Mons. Necker had sent there, and to superintend the purchase and shipment of the clothing and military stores, all of which arrived safely in America.

How Major Jackson executed the trust confided to him by Colonel Laurens, a letter of the late John Adams, afterwards President, which was published in the Boston Patriot, of the 14th of April, 1810, will show.†

* The American Review, Vol. I, p. 425, contains an account of the proceedings of Colonel Laurens in France, from the pen of Major Jackson, Secretary to the Mission.

† AMSTERDAM, *June* 27, 1787—wrote Congress: 'Major Jackson 'has been sometime here, in pursuance of instructions from Colonel 'Laurens, in order to dispatch the purchase of the goods, and the 'shipping of the goods and cash for the United States, which are to 'go by the South Carolina. But when all things appeared to be 'ready, I received a letter from his excellency Dr. Franklin, inform'ing me that he feared his funds would not admit of his accepting 'bills for more than 15 thousand pounds stl. The accounts of the 'Indian and the goods amounted to more than fifty thousand pounds, 'which shewed that there had not been an understanding sufficiently 'precise and explicit between the Dr. and the Colonel. There was, 'however, no remedy but a journey to Passy, which Major Jackson 'undertook, dispatched the whole business, and returned to Amster'dam in seven days. So that I hope there will be no more delays. 'Major Jackson has conducted, through the whole of his residence 'here, as far as I have been able to observe, with great activity and 'accuracy in business, and an exemplary zeal for the public service.'

After the business in which he had been engaged was completed, Major Jackson returned to America, and was appointed Assistant Secretary at War, his revered friend, General Lincoln being the Secretary of that Department, which office he held until the peace of 1783. As the war had now ceased, and he had attained his 24th year, he was desirous of pursuing some business as a future means of support, and with this view tendered his resignation to General Lincoln, which was accepted in a most kind letter.*

Soon after, Major Jackson sailed for Europe, for the purpose of making arrangements for entering into commercial business in this country, on his return. On informing Gene-

* 'GENERAL LINCOLN TO MAJOR JACKSON.

'*Princeton, Oct. 30th,* 1783.

'I was this morning honored, my dear friend, with the receipt of 'your letter of this date, purporting your wish to resign the office of 'Assistant Secretary at War.

'While my own ease and convenience, in a tone loud and explicit, 'caution me against complying with your request, the more silent 'and pursuasive voice of friendship and justice prevails, and tells 'me (that) I must sacrifice the former to your interest and happi-'ness, and that I must, however reluctantly, as your future pros-'pects in life are involved in the measure, accept your resignation.

'Permit me, my dear sir, before I take leave of you, to return you 'my warmest thanks for your meritorious services in the field as my 'aid-de-camp, as well as for those you have rendered as my assistant 'in the War Office. Those services, I have the pleasure to assure 'you, have been seen also, acknowledged and approved by your 'country. Besides, I have enjoyed real satisfaction in your private 'friendship. Your faithfulness and integrity have hourly increased 'my affection and esteem for you.

'Adieu, dear friend. That the best of Heaven's blessings may 'encircle you, that your path in life may be smooth and prosperous, 'your course through it easy and happy, and that you may finally 'smile in unceasing bliss, is the prayer of

'Dear sir,

'Your affectionate friend,

'B. LINCOLN.

'MAJOR JACKSON.'

ral Washington of his intentions, he received letters from him addressed to persons abroad.*

After his return to America, he was but a short time in business, when by the advice of friends, favored by his own inclinations, he determined to study law, which he did with that eminent jurist, the late William Lewis, of Philadelphia, on whose motion he was admitted to practice law in the Court of Common Pleas, and subsequently in the Supreme Court of Pennsylvania. In the year 1787, he was elected Secretary to the Convention which formed the Constitution of the United States.

On making known to General Washington his desire to enter on the pursuit of his profession, Major Jackson received the following letter from the Father of his Country.†

* One of these was not delivered.

'*Princeton, Nov.* 1*st*, 1783.

'Dear Sir:—Major Jackson has just informed me of his intention to embark next week for Europe. Tho' he has already had the honor to be introduced to you, I could not let him depart without expressing my esteem for his character, and my wish that he may experience any civilities it may be in your power to show him.

'With the most respectful attachment, I have the honor to be

'Your Excellency's most ob't and humble serv't,

'G. WASHINGTON.

'His Excellency, Doct. Franklin.'

† '*Philadelphia, Dec* 26*th*, 1791.

'Dear Sir:—At the same time that I acknowledge the receipt of your intention to enter upon a professional pursuit, and during the ensuing term propose yourself for admittance as a practitioner of law in the Supreme Court of the State of Pennsylvania, I beg you to be persuaded that my best wishes will accompany you in that, or in any other walk of life into which your interest or inclination may lead you.

'That your determination is the result of the best view you have of your circumstances and expectations, I take for granted, and therefore shall say nothing which might embarrass the decision; but with pleasure equal to the justice of it, shall declare to you that your deportment, so far as it has come under my observation, has been regulated by principles of integrity and honor, and that the duties of your station have been executed with abilities, and I embrace the occasion your address has afforded me, to thank you

After the organization of the government, General Washington, then President of the United States, invited him to join his family as his aid-de-camp and private secretary, in which situation he remained with him until the year 1793, accompanying him in his tour through the States.

Major Jackson, after leaving the President's family, was induced to defer the practice of the law, and to embark again for Europe, early in the year 1795, on an agency for the sale of lands for Mr. Bingham, which he successfully transacted, remaining abroad for this purpose nearly two years. On his return to Philadelphia, he was married on the 11th of November, 1795, to the beautiful Miss Elizabeth Willing, sister of Mrs. Bingham, to whom he had been engaged for many years.

On the 14th of January, 1796, President Washington appointed Major William Jackson surveyor of the Port of Philadelphia, which office he held under the administration of his illustrious Chief, and during the Presidency of Mr. John Adams, without reproach, until removed by President Jefferson for his political adherence to the principles of Washington.

One allegation made by Mr. Jefferson for removing Major Jackson from office, was that he had influenced the voting of the subordinates in the Custom House. An original paper signed by all those officers, and now in the possession of his widow, is a complete refutation of the charge.

'for all your attentions, and for the services which you have rendered 'me since you have been a member of my family. Let your departure from it be made *perfectly* convenient to yourself, and believe 'me to be with sincere esteem and regard,

'Dear sir,

'Your affectionate, humble serv't,

'GEO. WASHINGTON.

'MAJOR JACKSON.'

The opinion Mr. Jefferson entertained of the capacity and patriotism of Major Jackson, is shown in a letter which he sent to him on hearing of his intention of visiting Europe. It was not presented, which accounts for its being in possession of Mrs. Jackson, and when Mr. Jefferson displaced him, there was no more reason to doubt his capacity, patriotism, or fidelity in discharge of the duties of his office, than when this letter was written.

For several years succeeding his removal from office, Major Jackson was the editor of the Political and Commercial Register, a paper devoted to the maintenance of the principles of the Federalists, and the policy of Washington, and adverse to the acts of Mr. Jefferson, during his Presidency.

Major Jackson's companions in arms and associates of the Pennsylvania Society of the Cincinnati, having confidence in his ability to do justice to the subject, called on him to deliver an oration in commemoration of Independence, as early as the 4th July, 1786. It was spoken in the Reformed Calvinistic Church, north Fourth street, in Philadelphia, to a crowded audience, who expressed their satisfaction at the manner in which the honor conferred on him, was performed.*

* '*Mount Vernon, 28th Sept.*, 1786.

'Dear Sir:---I have received your letter of the 20th ult., together 'with the Pamphlets enclosed. I consider your sending the latter to 'me as a mark of attention which deserves my warmest acknow-'ledgments.

'I cannot join with you in thinking that the partiality of your 'friends, in assigning to you so honorable a task, prejudiced their 'discernment. The subject is noble, the field extensive, and I think 'it must be highly satisfactory, and indeed flattering to a man, that 'his performance upon such an occasion, is approved of by men of 'taste and judgment.

'With sentiments of great esteem and regard, I am

'Dear sir,

'Your obd't, humble serv't,

'Major Jackson. 'G. WASHINGTON.

In the same Church, as Secretary General of the Society of the Cincinnati, Major Jackson, at the request of the Pennsylvania Society of the Cincinnati, delivered his eulogium on the character of the great Washington, before the President of the United States, the members of both houses of Congress, Mr. Liston, the British Minister, other diplomatic characters, and a large assemblage of the military, citizens and ladies, the church being filled to its utmost capacity.

This, like the oration, was much commended, and like it, at the request of the Society of Cincinnati, was published. The public prints spoke of it as an eloquent production, and the author received numerous testimonials from those who were present, and from absent friends to whom he transmitted the pamphlet.* Among which, was a letter from his father-in-law, Mr. Thomas Willing.

In the years 1818 and 1819, his brother officers of the Revolutionary army appointed him their Solicitor to Congress, to obtain for them an equitable settlement of the half pay for life. Although not successful in effecting his object, owing to the very important and exciting bills then under consideration by Congress, he transacted the business entrusted to his care with zeal and ability, and received many gratifying letters from various members of Congress, from different sections of the Union, regretting the fate of his application, and expressive of the manner in which he had conducted his agency. Among them are letters from General Harrison, late President of the United States, and several of his friends, and the warm friends of the Revolutionary officers, the late Hon. John Sergeant of Philadel-

* See also post, letters, p. 308.

phia; all evincing that Major Jackson, late in life, retained the talent and energy which had characterized his early years.

On the arrival of General Lafayette in Philadelphia, Major Jackson, at the request of the Pennsylvania Society of the Cincinnati and of the citizens, delivered two addresses, one at 12, the other at 1 o'clock, in the Hall of Independence, to our country's distinguished friend and guest, which were approved by those who had entrusted the grateful duty to him, and responded to with feeling by General Lafayette.

After Major Jackson's death, which took place in Philadelphia on the 17th of December, 1828, the Pennsylvania Society of the Cincinnati passed a resolution to wear crape on the left arm for thirty days, and a similar tribute was passed to his memory by the State Society of South Carolina.

Major Jackson had the power, in a remarkable degree, of attaching and retaining the friendship of his early friends and associates, during life, and his character was such as to justify their attachment to him. As a husband, father, friend and citizen, he was ever kind, faithful, indulgent, sincere and patriotic."

5. Mary, b. Sept. 15, 1770; m. to Henry Clymer, and had issue.
6. Dorothy, b. July 16, 1772; m. to Thomas Willing Francis, already spoken of.
7. George, b. April 14, 1774; m. 1st, Maria Benezet, who d. s. p.; 2d, Rebecca Blackwell, only child of the Rev. Dr. Robert Blackwell, for many years Rector of St. Peter's Church, in this city. She was a lady of rare virtues, of remarkable judgment, and great beauty. She d. May 12, 1852. He d. leaving,

MARIA, m. to her cousin, the late Willing Francis, son of Thomas Willing Francis.

HARRIET, m. to the late Henry Ralston.

REBECCA, m. to George P. Thomson.

ELIZA MOORE, m. to Joseph Swift, (as already mentioned.)

DOROTHY, m. to J. W. Wallace.

CHARLES, m. Miss Watson.

8. RICHARD, b. Dec. 25, 1775; m. Eliza Moore.

9. ABIGAIL, b. May 16, 1777; m. to Richard Peters, better known to the legal fraternity as Reporter to the U. S. Supreme Court. They had,

NANCY BINGHAM,

SARAH,

FRANK, m. Maria Millar.

ELIZA, m. to John W. Field.

10. WILLIAM SHIPPEN, b. Feb. 6, 1779; m. Maria Peters, and had,

RICHARD P. and

MARIA, m. to Rev. John Spotswood.*

II. ANN, dau. of Charles Willing and Anne Shippen, b. July 16, 1733; m. to Tench Francis, as already stated. 'She was beautiful, amiable and accomplished,' says an old Bible-entry.

III. CHARLES, b. May 30, 1738; was a merchant in Barbadoes for many years, where he m. May 24, 1760, Elizabeth H. Carrington, of that place. He returned

* A descendant of Sir Alexander Spotswood, the famous Governor of Virginia; from whom also descended Mrs. Gen. Washington, Mrs. Patrick Henry, and others.

to Pennsylvania, and d. at Coventry farm in Delaware county, March 21, 1788.* They had,

ELIZABETH G., b. Sept. 30, 1764; m. to John Forster Alleyne, of Barbadoes. They went to England to live, and had,

HAYNES GIBBES, JOHN GAY, JAMES HOLDER, CHARLES, SARAH, ELIZABETH, CHARLOTTE and MARGARET.†

ANN, b. Aug. 25, 1767; m. to Luke Morris, of Philadelphia. Luke Morris was descended from Anthony Morris, b. at St. Dunstan, Stepney, London, Aug. 23, 1654, who emigrated to Pennsylvania 1683. His son Anthony, b. in London, 1682, was the father of Anthony Morris, b. in Philadelphia, 1705; m. (his second wife) Elizabeth Hudson, a descendant of Edward Hudson, a brother of Hendrik Hudson, the navigator and discoverer, and by her had (with others) Luke, above mentioned. They had, (with ANN, *d. unm.*, ELIZABETH CARRINGTON, and MARGARETTA HARE,)

ABBY WILLING, m. to Justus Johnson.

THOMAS WILLING, who m. Caroline Maria, dau. of George Calvert, of Riversdale, Prince George county, Maryland. George Calvert was a son of Benedict Calvert, who was a son of Charles,

* His portrait by West, the first *professional* performance of that artist, is in the possession of Mr. Charles Willing Littell, at Elton, Germantown.

† *Betham's Baronetage.* s. v. Alleyne.

Lord Baltimore, and half-brother of Frederick, the last Lord Baltimore. He d. 12th May, 1852. She d. 25th Nov., 1842, leaving

Rosalie E.,

Anna M., m. to Francis K. Murray, of Maryland.

George C.,

Julia M.

Susan Sophia, m. to John S. Littell. Of his family I have the following information:

The ancestors of Mr. Littell, on the father's side, were among the earliest settlers of East Jersey. They came from Essex county, England, and were among the founders of Essex county, N. J.; so called in remembrance of the fatherland. To the period of the Revolution they were, generally, occupied in agricultural pursuits. The grandfather of Mr. Littell was a Captain of artillery in the Revolutionary army, in which he continued throughout the war, participating in thirteen skirmishes, and taking part, with his command, in the battles of Springfield, N. J., Germantown, Monmouth, Trenton and Princeton. At the battle of Springfield, at '*Littell's Bridge*,' he derived especial eclât for conduct and intrepidity, and the effectiveness with which he managed a single piece of artillery, keeping the enemy, under Knyphausen, in check, and compelling them, finally, to retire.

For his services during the war, Capt. Littell received no remuneration; nor has any ever been received, or applied for, by his descendants, although it might have been reasonably claimed, for, apart from his services, he devoted his whole patrimony to the cause. He reëntered the army, with his Captain's commission, at the close of the Revolutionary war, and marched, under Gen. St. Clair, in his unfortunate expedition against the North-western Indians.*

The mother of Mr. Littell was the youngest daughter of Thomas Gardiner, and Susan Elton, daughter of Anthony Elton, whose grandfather emigrated from England, it is believed, in 1697. He was an earnest member of the Established Church of that country, and, with many of his descendants, lies in the cemetery of old St. Mary's, at Burlington. The ancestors of his mother, Susan Gardiner, were among the earliest settlers of West Jersey; and very frequent mention is made of them in Smith's History of New Jersey. The first Thomas Gardiner arrived at Burlington in the year 1676, from England. He was a substantial Quaker, one of the founders of the City of Burlington, and a 'Proprietor of 'West Jersey,' and held an honorable place in the government. He was, for many years, a member of the Governor's Council. He died in September, 1694. Smith, in Chap. XII., Hist. N. J., records as follows :—'In September, '1694, died Thomas Gardiner. He arrived early at Bur'lington, went through several public stations in West Jer'sey with a good character, had considerable knowledge in 'variety of business, and was an exemplary member of 'society, civil and religious.'

On page 401 of Smith's History, the death of the son of the above, is thus recorded :—

'In 1712 died Thomas Gardiner, of Burlington, several

* The family coat of arms is as follows:—Sa. a pillar ducally crowned, or. between two wings expanded, and joined to the base of the last. *Crest:* a cock, statant, on an arrow, or. combed and wattled gu. See *Edmonston's 'Complete Body of Heraldry,'* and also *Washbourne's 'Book of Family Crests.'*

'times mentioned before. He was well acquainted with 'public business, a good surveyor, and useful member of 'society: several years one of the Council, Treasurer of the 'Western division, and the first Speaker of Assembly after 'the union of the governments of East and West Jersey.'

Proud, in the 'Introduction' to his 'History of Pennsyl-'vania,' says:—'Thomas Gardiner was a man of eminence 'among the Quakers and early settlers in Burlington and 'West Jersey. He served in several public offices, in the 'government, with honor and fidelity; was very skilful in 'a variety of business; a good surveyor, and a very useful 'member of society; several years one of the Council, Trea-'surer of the Western division, and first Speaker of the 'Assembly, after the union of the governments of East and 'West Jersey, in 1703. He died at Burlington, in 1712.' —*Proud's Hist. Penna.* pp. 159–60.

Speaking of the religious state of the early Quaker settlers of West Jersey, Proud further says:—'Before a house was 'built in the place, they constantly, at stated times, held 'their religious meetings under a tent, covered with sail-'cloth, till John Woolston had got his house ready, which 'was the first framed house in Burlington; at whose house, 'and that of Thomas Gardiner, they afterwards continued 'to hold their meetings, both for Divine worship, and the 'discipline or order of their religious society, till a suitable 'meeting-house was built for that purpose.' And he adds, 'Among the *women* of worthy and eminent character in the 'same society, at this time, appear to have been Elizabeth 'Gardiner, Sarah Biddle,' &c. &c. &c.

IV. Dorothy, m. to Capt., afterwards Sir Walter Stirling, R. N.

A pedigree,* beginning with 'Willielmus, filius Thoraldi, 'who had the lands of Calder in the reign of David I, who 'came to the Throne in 1224,' traces the family down to Sir Walter Stirling, of Faskine, in the county of Lanerk, Knt., a captain in the Royal navy. He was advanced to the rank of a lieutenant in the navy in 1745–6; and commanded a sloop of war in 1757; in 1759 he was promoted to be a post captain, and appointed to the Lynn, a forty-gun ship, and employed in that ship as a cruiser till 1761, when he removed into the Lowestoffe, a new ship, mounting twenty-four guns, and in the month of May, 1762, destroyed two of the enemy's prames, off Gravelines, after killing and wounding a considerable number of the persons on board. His first command, after the peace, was in 1763, when he was appointed to the Rainbow, of forty guns, and ordered to North America, where he continued till 1766, in which year he returned to England; he was then out of commission till 1770, when he was appointed to the Dunkirk, of sixty guns, as captain to Commodore Mackenzie, who commanded on the Jamaica station. He, in 1771, removed from the Seaford, to the Portland, of fifty guns, and soon after returned to England, and was paid off in 1772. In 1778, he was appointed a regulating captain on the impress service; and at the end of the year 1780 was made captain of the Gibraltar, of eighty guns, one of the squadron sent to the West Indies, under the orders of Sir Samuel Hood, to reinforce Lord Rodney. The expedition against the Dutch island, St. Eustatia, taking place soon after his arrival on

* Betham's Baronetage, 1808.

that station, he was chosen to be the welcome messenger of the success, and in consequence received the honor of knighthood; in the summer of 1781, he was appointed commander, with the rank of Commodore at the Nore, and hoisted his broad penant first on board the Conquestador, and afterwards removed into the Prince Edward, of sixty guns; he quitted this command before the end of the year 1782, and in the same year was appointed to the Duke, of eighty guns, under Admiral Kempenfelt. Soon after the action with the French, with an inferior force, they captured many transports full of troops bound for India. He married Dorothy, daughter of Charles Willing, Esq., of Philadelphia, and Anne Shippen;* she died in 1782, aged 45, was buried at Drumpellier, near Glasgow; he died in 1786, buried in a vault, at Hammondsworth, in Middlesex, in the sixty-ninth year of his age, having had issue,

1. Sir Walter, created a Baronet, Nov. 30, 1800.
2. Charles, a captain in the navy,† appointed commissioner of the navy at Jamaica, in June, 1803, who married Charlotte, second daughter of Andrew Grote, Esq., of Blackheath, in the county of Kent, and a banker in London, and had

    Charles,

* COL. SHIPPEN TO COL. BURD, AT FORT AUGUSTA.

'*Philadelphia, Aug. 11th*, 1763.

'Dear Brother:— * * * I heartily congratulate you on 'the safe arrival of our worthy friend Wm. Allen, Esq., with his 'two fine daughters, in England, after an agreeable passage of six 'weeks. They landed at Portsmouth, on the 12th June. This 'news we received yesterday by the packet.

'We also learn that Captain Stirling and his lady were to sail the 'middle of June in a frigate for the Virginia station, and that Mr. 'Lardner had taken his passage in her. * * *

† He was a prisoner during the Revolution, *post*, 283.

ANDREW,
W. FREDERICK,
J. FRANCIS,
C. DOROTHEA.

3. ANNE, who married her first cousin, Andrew Stirling, of Drumpellier, in North Britain, and of London, merchant, the eldest son of William, and the eldest grandson of John Stirling, provost of Glasgow, born in 1677, the eldest brother of her grandfather Walter. She d. June 1, 1830, and had (with DOROTHY, MARY, and ELIZA, *d. young*,)

WILLIAM, b. March 18, 1779.
WALTER, b. 1780.
JOHN, b. Oct. 20, 1786, m. Elizabeth Willing, (*ante*, p. cviii.)
CHARLES, b. 1789.
(SIR) JAMES, b. Jan. 1791, Rear Admiral, R. N.
ANNA, b. Sept. 1792.
DOROTHEA, b. Jan. 1794.
ANDREW, b. Jan. 1795.
ROBERT, b. April, 1796.
EDWARD HAMILTON, b. April, 1797.
MARY, b. Aug. 1798.
AGNES.

Sir Walter Stirling, F. R. and A. S., b. June 24, 1758, d. Aug. 25, 1832, a banker in London, Major-commandant of the Somerset-Place Strand Volunteers, from 1798 to 1803; and July 17, 1803, elected Lieutenant-colonel of the Prince of Wales' Loyal Volunteers; a justice of peace for the county of Kent; a governor of Bridewell and Bethlem hospitals; a Director of the Globe Insurance Office; and high sheriff for the county of Kent in 1804; born June 24, 1758; elected representative in parliament for Gatton, in the county of Surrey, in April, 1798; he married, April 28, 1795, Susanna, only child and heiress of George Trenchard Goodenough, of Broughton Poggis, in Oxfordshire; of Dunstalls, near Shoreham, and of the Grove, near Shooters Hill, both in Kent; and of Bothwood, in the Isle of Wight, Esq., F.R.S., and one of his Majesty's commissioners of taxes, (lineally descended from William of Wickham, Bishop of Winchester, which entitles his heirs to their education at Winchester college, as kin of the founder,) by whom he had issue,*

MARY JANE, b. March 28, 1795, m. to Sir James Flower, Bart.

DOROTHY ANNE, b. May 24, 1796, m. to J. B. Lennard, Esq.

MATHILDA GEORGIANA, b. Feb. 27, 1798, m. to Sir T. B. Lennard, Bart.

* Arms—Argent, on a bend engrailed, azure, between two roses, gules, seeded, or. and barbed, vert. three buckles of the fourth, all within a bordure, of the fifth; above the shield is placed a helmet befitting his degree, with a mantling, gules, the doubling, argent. *Crest*—On a wreath of his liveries a dexter armed arm, issuing out of a ducal coronet, grasping a dagger in fess, all proper; the last hilted and pomelled, or. In an escroll above the Crest, this motto, *Gang forward.* And on a compartment below the shield are placed for *Supporters*—Two hinds, purpure, gorged with ducal coronets, proper, and semée of estoils, argent. *Seat*—Shoreham, Kent. *Residence*—Pall Mall, London. These arms were allowed the late Baronet in consequence of his being a descendant of James Stirling, of Keir, and Janet, daughter and heiress of Andrew Stirling, of Calder. It is worthy of remark that there are now living (1803) four Baronets of this name: Sir Walter Stirling, of Ardoch; Sir John Stirling, of Glorat; Sir James Stirling, of Uppal; and the present Baronet.

WALTER GEORGE, b. March 15, 1802.* Sir Walter George, 2d Baronet, m. 18th August, 1835, Lady Caroline Francis, dau. of John, Earl of Strafford, and has,[1]

WALTER, b. 5th March, 1838.
WALTER GEORGE, b. Sept. 6, 1839.
FRANCES MARY,
HARRIET ANN.

V. MARY, b. Sept. 24, 1740, d. March 24, 1814, m. to Col. Wm. Byrd, of Westover, in Virginia. Her portrait is at Berkley, on the James river. She is the lady mentioned in such complimentary terms by the Marquis de Chastellux.†

Col. Byrd was descended from an ancient family seated at Broxton, in the county of Chester. Two pedigrees, inscribed upon parchment, and emblazoned with the coats of arms of the various families with whom there were intermarriages, are now in the possession of his descendants: one is certified from Herald's College, during the time of

* *Burke's Peerage.*

† '*Travels in America during the years* 1780, 1781, 1782. *Translated by an English gentleman who was in the counury during that period. Dublin*, 1787.

The Marquis says that he set out for Westover, and traveled some twenty-six miles along a very agreeable road, with magnificent houses in view at every instant, 'for the banks of the James river 'are the garden spot of Virginia;' that of Mrs. Byrd, however, surpassed them all in magnificence of buildings, beauty of situation and pleasures of society. Mrs. Byrd he describes as a widow, about forty-two years of age, very agreeable in conversation, who had managed her estate exceedingly well, and speaks of her two daughters who had passed the previous winter at Williamsburgh, where they had been greatly complimented by M. de Rochambeau, and all the French officers. He narrates the troubles she encountered from both of the contending parties.

Queen Elizabeth; the other, also certified by the same high genealogical authority, is of later date.*

The founder of the family in America was William Byrd, generally known as 'the first Col. Byrd.' He was a Captain in the British service, Auditor General of the Colony, Colonel under the Provincial goverment, &c; a man of great hospitality and liberality, and especially 'a generous benefactor to the Huguenots.† He m. Mary Horsemanden in Kent, and had three dau. and one son,

WILLIAM, b. March 28, 1674, d. Aug. 26, 1744.

'His vast fortune' (says Campbell,) 'enabled him to live 'in a style of hospitable splendor before unknown in Vir-'ginia, and to indulge a munificent liberality. His extensive 'learning was improved by a keen observation and refined 'by an acquaintance and corespondence with the wits and 'noblemen of his day in England. His writings display a 'thorough knowledge of the natural and civil history of the 'Colony, and contain faithful and humorous sketches of the 'manners of his age. To him is due the honor of having 'contributed more, perhaps, to the preservation of the his-'torical materials of Virginia, than any of her sons.'

Some of Col. Byrd's writings, particularly that known as the Westover MS. and its burlesque, are now in the possession of the American Philosophical Society of this city. His extensive correspondence belongs to his descendant, Mr. Wm. Byrd Harrison, of Upper Brandon. His portrait

* There are several of these pedigrees in Virginia. Amongst others, one, now in possession of Col. Peyton, deduces the descent of the late Sir John Peyton, of Gloucester, from one of the Knights who accompanied William the Conqueror.

† *Charles Campbell's Hist Virginia*, p. 104, a book which reflects the greatest credit on the author for accuracy and research.

by Kneller, is at Berkley.* He m. 1, Lucy Parke, dau. of the Governor of the Leeward Islands, (from which gentleman also descended Mr. Custis, the first husband of Mrs. General Washington,) and by her had

WILHELMINA, m. to Mr. Chamberlayne of Virginia, and

EVELYN, *d. unm.*

2, Miss Taylor, an heiress of Kensington, in England, and had

WILLIAM, of whom presently.

ANN, , m. to Mr. Carter, of Clives.

MARY, m. to Mr. Carter, of Sabine Hall.

* He lies buried in the garden of his seat, Westover, where a marble moument bears the following inscription: 'Here lieth the 'Honorable William Byrd, Esq. Being born to one of the am-'plest fortunes in this country, he was sent early to England for 'his education, where, under the care and direction of Sir Robert 'Southwell and ever favored with his particular instructions, he 'made a happy proficiency in polite and various learning. By the 'means of the same noble friend, he was introduced to the acquain-'tance of many of the first persons of that age for knowledge, wit, 'virtue, birth or high station, and particularly contracted a most 'intimate and bosom friendship with the learned and illustrious 'Charles Boyle, Earl of Orrery. He was called to the bar in the 'Middle Temple; studied for sometime in the Low Countries; visi-'ted the Court of France, and was chosen Fellow of the Royal So-'ciety. Thus eminently fitted for the service and ornament of his 'country, he was made receiver general of his Majesty's revenues 'here; was thrice appointed public agent to the court and ministry 'of England, and being thirty-seven years a member, at last be-'came president of the council of this colony. To all this were 'added a great elegancy of taste and life, the well-bred gentleman 'and polite companion, the splendid economist and prudent father 'of a family, with the constant enemy of all exorbitant power, and 'hearty friend to the liberties of his country. Nat. Mar. 28, 1674. 'Mort. Aug. 26, 1744. An Ætat 70.' His portrait, a fine old cavalier face, is preserved at Berkley.*—*Campbell*, p. 113.

* Beverley. B. 4. p. 62. thus alludes to the garden at Westover: 'Colonel *Byrd* 'in his garden, which is the finest in that country, has a summer-house set round 'with *Indian* honey-suckle, which all the Summer is continually full of sweet 'flowers, in which these birds delight exceedingly. Upon these flowers I have 'seen ten or a dozen of these beautiful creatures together, which sported about 'me so familiarly, that with their little wings they often fanned my face.'

JANE, m. to Mr. Page, of North river. His son William, better known as 'the third Col. Byrd of Westover,' was Colonel in the British Provincials. He commanded (1758) one of the two Virginia regiments; Gen. Washington commanded the other. He was educated and lived a good deal in England. It was at one time contemplated to give him the command subsequently bestowed on Gen. Stanwix.* He m. 1 Elizabeth Carter, of Shirley, and had

ELIZABETH, m. to 1, Mr. Farley, 2, Mr. Dunbar, 3, Col. Skipwith.

WILLIAM, Captain in the British Guards, *d. young.*

JOHN, m. Mrs. Randolph, of Wilton.

THOMAS, m. Mary Armisted, of Hesse.

OTWAY, m. Ann Mumford.

2, Mary Willing, above mentioned, and had,

CHARLES, m. Sally Meade and removed to Kentucky.

RICHARD, m. 1, Lucy Harrison, of Brandon, and 2, Emily Wilson, of Smithfield, Va.

WILLIAM, m. Susan Lewis, of Gloucester, Va.

MARIA, m. to John Page, of Frederick county, Va.

ANN, *d. unm.*

EVELYN, m. to Benjamin Harrison,† of Brandon,

* Post, p. 153.

† "The common ancestor of the Harrisons of Berkley and of Brandon was Benjamin Harrison of Surrey. He was born in that county 1645, and died 1712. It was long believed by the Harrisons of Virginia, that they were lineally descended from the celebrated Col. Thomas Harrison, the friend of Cromwell and one of the Regicides. This opinion, however, appears to be erroneous. The first of the family in Virginia was the Hon. Benjamin Harrison, a member of the Council in Virginia. He lies buried in the yard of an old church near Cabin Point, in the county of Surrey. The following is his epitaph :—'Here lyeth the Body of the Hon. BENJAMIN HARRISON, '*Esqe.*, who did Justice, loved Mercy, and walked humbly with his

and d. leaving

GEORGE, m. Miss Ritchie, and d. leaving

GEORGE, and

ISABELLA.

WM. BYRD, m. Miss Harrison of Berkley, and has

BENJAMIN,

RANDOLPH,

'God; was always loyall to his Prince and a great Benefactor to his 'Country. He was born in this Parish, the 20th day of September, '1645, and departed this Life the 30th day January, 1712-13.' It is certain that this Benjamin Harrison, born in Southwark parish, Surrey, Virginia, in 1645, during the civil war in England, could not be the son of Col. Harrison, the regicide. He may, however, have been a collateral relation. That this Benjamin Harrison, of Surrey, was the first of the family in Virginia, is confirmed by some ancient wills still preserved. He had three sons, of whom Benjamin, the eldest, settled at Berkley. He married Elizabeth, daughter of Louis Burwell of Gloucester, and was an eminent lawyer and sometime Speaker of the House of Burgesses. He died in April, 1710, aged 37, leaving an only son Benjamin, and an only daughter Elizabeth. The son Benjamin married a daughter of Robert (called King) Carter of Corotoman, in the county of Lancaster. Two daughters of this union were killed by the same flash of lightning at Berkley. Another daughter married —— Randolph of Wilton. The sons of this Benjamin Harrison and —— Carter his wife, were Benjamin, signer of the Declaration of Independence; Charles, a general of the Revolution; Nathaniel, Henry, Colin and Carter H. From the last mentioned, are descended the Harrisons of Cumberland. Benjamin Harrison, Jr., of Berkley, the signer, married a Miss Basset. Their children were Benjamin, Carter B., sometime member of Congress, and William Henry, President of the United States, one daughter who married —— Randolph, and another, who married —— Copeland. So far the Berkley branch of the Harrisons."

"The second son of Benjamin Harrison of Surrey, first of the family in Virginia, was Nathaniel. His eldest son was named Nathaniel, and his only son was Benjamin Harrison, of Brandon, one of the council of Virginia, at the same time with Benjamin Harrison, Jr., of Berkley, about the commencement of the Revolution. This Benjamin Harrison of Brandon was father of the present William B. Harrison, Esq., of Brandon, to whom I am indebted for most of the foregoing particulars, relative to his ancient and eminent family. See 8 Hening, pp. 66 and 174."—*Campbell*, p. 155.

CARTER,
SHIRLEY.
ABBY, m. to Judge Wm. Nelson.
JANE, m. to Carter B. Harrison of Macon, brother of the late President Harrison.

VI. ELIZABETH, b. Feb. 10, 1742–3, m. to Samuel Powel, of Philadelphia. They had three children, all of whom d. s. p., and Mrs. Powel left the bulk of her estate to her nephew, John P. Hare, hereafter mentioned, on condition that he should change his name to Powel, which he did.

VII. RICHARD, b. Jan. 2, 1744, m. but d. s. p.

VIII. ABIGAIL, b. July 15, 1747, *d. unm.*

IX. JOSEPH, b. Oct. 13, 1749, d. an infant.

X. JAMES, b. Feb. 9, 1750-51, d. Oct. 13, 1801. He served as a Captain during the Revolutionary War, and had the misfortune to be taken prisoner by the British, by whom he was confined on board of one of their prison-ships, where he endured great privations and sufferings.

XI. MARGARET, b. Jan. 15, 1753, m. Nov. 16, 1775, to Robert Hare. She d.   . He was the son of Richard and Martha Hare of Limehouse,* near London,

* Richard and Martha have had, besides the above named Robert,
RICHARD, father of Richard of Bath, who m. a dau. of Sir —— Hollis.
JAMES, (Rev.) m. a dau. of Sir Thos. Clarges, and had
RICHARD, now General Sir Richard Hare Clarges, having changed his name on succeeding to the estate.
CHARLES, Captain R. N., who m.   , and had
CHARLES, R. N., and
CHARLOTTE, m. to Admiral John Alexander.
JOHN, a lawyer of the Inner Temple.

and was b. at Woolwich, in Kent, 28th Jan'y, 1752, (O. S.) landed at Philadelphia June 4, 1773. A Journal of a Tour made by him through the Northern and Eastern Colonies, shortly before the Revolution, has been printed by the Historical Society. He was a member of the convention that framed the Constitution of Pennsylvania, and afterwards Speaker of the Senate. They had issue, (with RICHARD, *d. young*,)

CHARLES WILLING, b. at Westover, April 23, 1778.

MARTHA, b. Aug. 17, 1779, d. 1852.

ROBERT, b. Jan. 17, 1781, m. Harriet, dau. of John Innes Clark of Rhode Island, and had

JOHN INNES CLARK, now Judge of District Court, m. Esther Binney, dau. of Hon. Horace Binney.

LYDIA, m. to Frederick Prime, of New York.

ROBERT HERTFORD, m. Caroline Flemming.

GEORGE HARRISON, U. S. N.

JOHN POWEL, who afterwards changed his name by Act of Assembly, to John Hare Powel, b. April 22, 1786, m. Oct. 20, 1817 Julia de Veaux, dau. of Col. Andrew de Veaux, of South Carolina, distinguished as a Loyalist officer during the Revolution. His wife was Anna Maria Verplank, of New York. Col. de Veaux's other dau. (Augusta,) m. Philip Verplank, of Verplank's Point, N. Y. Mrs. Powel d. Dec. 8, 1845. They had

SAMUEL, m. Mary, dau. of Hon. Robert

Johnston, of Jamaica.* They have issue.

De Veaux, m. Elizabeth Cooke. She d. 1845. He d. 1848, leaving one child.

Henry Baring, m. Caroline, dau. of Hon. Richard H. Bayard, of Delaware. He d. April 4, 1852, leaving one child.

Robert Hare,

Elizabeth and Hertford, *d. young.*

Julia, m. to W. Parker Foulke.

John and Ida.

Of Dr. William Shippen, already mentioned, (*ante*, p. xxvii) I have no further information than such as is already in print, except a few anecdotes. Of his son, I have nothing to add to what is already public. I would suggest, however, that there must be, I should think, some mistake in the notice of him to be found in Dr. Caldwell's autobiography (p. 115)—a work heretofore cited, (*ante*, p. xxxiii.)

I have been unable to trace the connection, if any, of Mr. William Shippen, a member of the Continental Congress from Pennsylvania, or Captain Shippen, killed at the battle of Monmouth,† with Edward Shippen, the founder of the family here. Nor have I succeeded in ascertaining of what kinsmanship was Mr. James Searle, so well and honorably known in our Revolutionary History, both as a member of Congress and by his diplomatic services, and the Mr. John Searle mentioned at p. lxxxviii.

* He made a pedestrian tour through Russia, of which he published an account, and was descended from the family of the Marquis of Annandale.

† "*Hill Family*," by J. Jay Smith, a most entertaining book.

Through the kindness of Dr. G. W. Norris, I have obtained the verses concerning Dr. Franklin, mentioned at p. 264, *post*. I give them as a note.* I also add some

* He thinks the tradition in the family is, that they were written by Miss Hannah Griffiths, a grand-daughter of the first Isaac Norris; but says that Miss Norris, spoken of by Judge Yeates, was quite clever at verses. The verses themselves appeared in the works of Dr. Smith, Provost of the University, (Philadelphia, 1803,)* with some verbal changes, and were by him ascribed to the Rev. Jonathan Odell, (see *Sabine's Loyalists*); but incorrectly, as appears from the Doctor's own account. At first he attributed them to his 'dear, deceased wife,' in whose 'handwriting' was the copy which he 'found on his writing-desk;' then to 'her and her dear friend, Mrs. Ferguson;' and then, on the information 'of B. R. M., Esq.,' to 'Mr. Odell.' There can be no reasonable doubt as to Dr. Smith's being mistaken, and of Judge Yeates, writing contemporaneously, being correct.

Inscription on a curious stove in the form of an urn, contrived in such a manner as to make the flame descend instead of rising from the fire; invented by Dr. Franklin.

'Like a Newton sublimely he soared
To a summit before unattained;
New regions of science explored,
And the palm of philosophy gained.

'With a spark which he caught from the skies,
He displayed an unparalleled wonder;
And we saw with delight and surprise,
That his rod could secure us from thunder.

'Oh! had he been wise to pursue
The track for his talents designed,
What a tribute of praise had been due
To the teacher and friend of mankind.

'But to covet political fame
Was in him a degrading ambition;
The spark that from Lucifer came,
Enkindled the blaze of sedition.

'Let candor then write on his urn,
"Here lies the renowned inventor,
Whose flame to the skies ought to burn,
But inverted, descends to the centre."'

* For this information I am indebted to the kindness of Mr. M'Allister, our well-known local antiquary.

curious verses upon the celebrated Meschianza, written by an ardent loyalist lady, whose sentiments doubtless fully accorded with those of Mr. Galloway.*

I have thus completed these notices and edited these letters and papers with such care and skill as I was master of. My object has been to gather together and preserve information not likely to be much longer attainable, and by accuracy, if possible, of name, date and fact, to correct

* The following lines upon the Meschianza were written by a lady, a member of the Society of Friends, residing at the time in Philadelphia.

Answer to the Question 'What is it?'

A shameful scene of dissipation,
The death of sense and reputation;
A deep degeneracy of nature,
A frolic 'for the lash of satire;'
A feast of grandeur fit for kings,
Formed of the following empty things:—
Ribbons and gewgaws, tints and tinsel,
To glow beneath the historic pencil;
(For, what tho' treason now stands neuter,
How will it sparkle—page the future.)
Heroes that will not bear inspection,
And glasses to reflect reflection;
Triumphant arches raised on blunders,
And true Don Quixotes made of wonders.
Laurels, instead of weeping willows,
To crown the Bacchanalian fellows;
The song of victory complete,
Loudly re-echoed from defeat;
The fair of vanity profound,
A madman's dance—a lover's round.

In short it's one clear contradiction
To every truth (except a fiction);
Condemned by wisdom's silver rules,
The blush of sense and gaze of fools.

But recollection's pained to know
That ladies joined the frantic show;
When female prudence thus can fail,
It's time the sex should wear the veil.

some errors which already prevail. Whether or not I have accomplished my object; what have been my shortcomings, either through lack of materials or my own defects; what the value of the facts preserved, must be left to the judgment of others.*

It certainly would have been far easier and more agreeable, and the temptation was great, to have woven these notices and letters into a consecutive narrative; to have attempted to portray in my own fashion the habits, manners and actions of these people; how they bore themselves in the trying situations in which many of them were placed; what was their behavior when duties clashed, or when duty conflicted with affection, for it will be seen that of the same family some were Whigs and others Loyalists; what was their social intercourse; what their individual peculiarities; how their joys were tempered and their griefs assuaged; how they lived, and loved, and died. Indeed, portions of such a memoir are already in existence, detached sentences from which appear in the foregoing pages. But as I desired merely, in the present volume, to give nothing but facts, I have rigorously abstained from inserting anything, which did not as *mere matter of fact* illustrate the character of the individual spoken of.

* A few pages of the following letters were not corrected by me before finally passing through the press: hence one or two errors have occurred. The letter dated Sept. 13th, 1753, (p. 23) should have been 1758. The reply of the prisoner (p. 144) should have been—'Que leur dessein etoit d'attaquer toutes nos gardes avancez, 'et de les suivre s'ils pourroient dans les retrenchmens.' 'The 'case of the Court of Chancery' (p. 1, et seq.) is in the appendix to 1 Dallas Rep. 509, from a certified copy. The MS. from which that given here was printed, came from the papers of Col. Shippen, for many years Secretary to the Province. Mr. Peters' letter (p. 97) should have been dated at Philadelphia. Some literal or verbal errata also might be made: but they correct themselves to the reader.

LETTERS AND PAPERS

RELATING CHIEFLY TO THE

Provincial History of Pennsylvania,

WITH SOME

NOTICES OF THE WRITERS.

by Thomas Balch.

PRIVATELY PRINTED.

PHILADELPHIA:

CRISSY & MARKLEY, PRINTERS, GOLDSMITHS HALL, LIBRARY ST.

1855.

PREFACE.

Some time ago, the Historical Society of Pennsylvania passed a resolution, requesting me to edit certain letters written by Chief Justice Shippen, then in my possession. The duty was performed, but, when the MS. was ready, I was informed that the publication had been postponed. I then changed my original purpose into collecting and printing 'papers and letters relating chiefly to the Pro- 'vincial history of Pennsylvania,' and for the better understanding of them, to give 'some notices of the families of the writers.' Whilst thus engaged, various materials were tendered to me, consisting in part of the 'Shippen MSS.' in the archives of that Society, in part of masses of letters, accounts, and other papers in the possession of descendants of some of the families prominent in the Province. The interest which has been created by the occupation itself, and the desire to add something to the stores of the future historian of this State, induced me to sift with care these miscellaneous MSS. and to print such as were of some, even though not remarkable, value.

The greater portion of them are purely private in their character. I therefore thought it well to print only a very small number of copies, so as to prevent any, except those connected by 'kindred 'ties,' from obtaining the volume.

I have endeavored to make the genealogical notices full and accurate. In my efforts, I have been greatly assisted by Mr. J. F. Fisher, Mr. Edward Shippen, Mr. Joseph Swift, Dr. G. W. Norris, Mr. Samuel Powel, and other gentlemen. To them are due the best thanks, not only of myself as Editor, but of all who prize an honorable ancestry, such as the following pages disclose.

Some of the letters relate to public affairs, and aid in supplying gaps in Pennsylvania history. At a future day I will print extracts from these.

Some few copies of the letters and papers have been struck off without the 'notices of the writers,' as the latter were such as only concerned the members of their respective families.

A few of the following pages were not corrected by me before finally passing through the press; hence one or two errors have occurred. The letter dated Sept. 13th, 1753, (p. 23) should have been 1757. The reply of the prisoner (p. 144) should have been—'Que leur dessein etoit d'attaquer toutes nos gardes avancez, 'et de les suivre s' ils pourroient dans les retrenchmens.' 'The 'case of the Court of Chancery' (p. 1, et seq.) is in the appendix to 1 Dallas Rep. 509, from a certified copy. The MS. from which that given here was printed, came from the papers of Col. Shippen, for several years Secretary to the Province. Mr. Peters' letter (p. 97) should have been dated at Philadelphia.

Through the kindness of Dr. Norris, I am enabled to give, from the Norris papers, the verses mentioned at p. 264. He thinks the tradition in the family is, that they were written by Miss Hannah Griffiths, a grand-daughter of the first Isaac Norris; but says that Miss Norris, spoken of by Judge Yeates, was quite clever at verses. The verses themselves appeared in the works of Dr. Smith, Provost of the University, (*Philadelphia*, 1803,*) with some verbal changes, and were by him ascribed to the Rev. Jonathan Odell (see *Sabine's Loyalists*); but incorrectly, as appears from the Doctor's own account. At first he attributed them to his 'dear, deceased wife,' in whose 'handwriting' was the copy which he 'found on his wri- 'ting-desk;' then to 'her and her dear friend, Mrs. Ferguson;' and then, on the information 'of B. R. M., Esq.,' to 'Mr. Odell.' There can be no reasonable doubt as to Dr. Smith's being mistaken, and of Judge Yeates, writing contemporaneously, being correct.

* For this information I am indebted to the kindness of Mr. M'Callister, our well-known local antiquary.

V

Inscription on a curious stove in the form of an urn, contrived in such a manner as to make the flame descend instead of rising from the fire; invented by Dr. FRANKLIN.

'Like a Newton sublimely he soared
To a summit before unattained,
New regions of science explored,
And the palm of philosophy gained.

'With a spark which he caught from the skies,
He displayed an unparalleled wonder,
And we saw with delight and surprise
That his rod could secure us from thunder.

'Oh! had he been wise to pursue
The track for his talents designed,
What a tribute of praise had been due
To the teacher and friend of mankind.

'But to covet political fame
Was in him a degrading ambition;
The spark that from Lucifer came,
Enkindled the blaze of sedition.

'Let candor then write on his urn,
"Here lies the renowned inventor,
Whose flame to the skies ought to burn,
But inverted, descends to the centre."'

Philadelphia, March, 1855.

LETTERS AND PAPERS

CHIEFLY RELATING TO THE

PROVINCIAL HISTORY OF PENNSYLVANIA.

THE CASE OF THE COURT OF CHANCERY IN PENNSYLVANIA, WITH THE OPINIONS OF MR. WILLES AND MR. RYDER.*

Upon this foot the Court of Chancery, in Pennsylvania, having been established, continued to exercise jurisdiction in matters of equity proceedings therein, as near, as they conveniently could, according to the known usage or practice of his Majesty's High Court of Chancery at Westminster. Nor were the proceedings of the said Court complained of in any sort, or its authority called in question, until January, 1735, though two Acts of Assembly for establishing the Courts of Law in Pennsylvania, were passed in that interval of time, and fourteen Assemblies (this being the fifteenth,) have been held.

Upon divers petitions presented January 27th, 1735, to the House of Assembly, complaining that the Court of Chancery in this Province is erected in violation of the

* The first part of this MS. is missing. It does not, so far as my reading goes, appear to have been heretofore printed, though the subject has been frequently discussed.

Charter of Privileges, the House came to the following resolution, viz:

Resolved, That the Court of Chancery, as it is at present established, is contrary to the Charter of Privileges granted to the Freemen of this Province.

And upon conferences since had between the Governor and the Assembly, (which two alone without the Governor's Council compose [legislative power] Pennsylvania,) the Assembly have argued from the [authority] of several English law books, that the king at this day cannot, by his commission, erect a Court of Equity.

Your opinion is desired:

Question.—Whether a Court of Equity is not a vital and fundamental part of the English Constitution, incident to and inseparable from it? And whether the power of determining cases on Bill in Equity is not, by the fundamental laws and Constitution of the Kingdom of England, vested in the King as supreme magistrate, and in the Chancellor acting under his appointment?

Answer.—It is pretty difficult to trace out the original foundation of Courts, most of them having their beginning either from necessity or expedience. But it has been always held, that the power of determining cases in Equity was originally vested in the King of England, and that the Chancellor only acted by virtue of a delegated power from him, being appointed at first as his assistant, when causes in Equity began to be so very numerous that the King could not despatch them himself.*

Question 2.—Whatever courts the King may now erect by his commission [in] England, where all necessary courts

* Any one curious as to this point, will find all the learning in Mr. Spence's learned treatise.

are already in being; yet whether King Charles the Second could by law grant sufficient authority by a commission under the Great Seal unto William Penn and his deputies, to erect Courts of Equity in the Province of Pennsylvania; or is it absolutely necessary that the consent of the Legislature there should first be had, in order to the erecting such courts?

Answer.—Though it is held that his Majesty cannot now by his commission erect a new Court of Equity in England, where all proper courts have been long since established, yet I am of opinion that King Charles the Second, when he was erecting a new form of government in Pennsylvania, might, by his Charter, grant to William Penn and his deputies a power to erect new Courts of Equity in that Province, and that the consent of the Legislature there was not necessary to be first had, until Mr. Penn made it so by his Instrument or Charter, of the 28*th October*, 1701.

Question 3.—Whether the unanimous resolution of the Assembly, requesting Mr. Keith to open and hold a Court of Equity for the said Province, with the assistance of his council, laid before him on the [4th May, 1720,] his assent to that request, and establishment of [a Court] pursuant thereto, by the advice of his Council, the subsequent approbation of the Assembly given to that establishment, and the notification thereof to the public in Pennsylvania, by written proclamation under the Great Seal there, may not be called an act of the whole Legislature there, although not rendered in the ordinary form of law, or at least may not be deemed a sufficient signification of the consent of the Legislature thereto?

Answer.—I am of opinion that the unanimous resolution of the Assembly, 4th May, 1720, what was afterwards done by Governor Keith and his committee thereupon, the subsequent approbation of the Assembly, and the proclamation which issued thereupon, sufficiently established the present Court of Chancery, notwithstanding the clause relating thereto in the said Charter of the 28*th October*, 1701, for I think that there has been a sufficient declaration of the assent of the Legislature, to the erecting of such Court.

Question 4.—Whether the original establishment and holding of the Court of Chancery by such devise as aforesaid, after the time of William Penn's Charter of Privileges to the inhabitants, but before the resolve of the Assembly, in January, 1735, can justly be construed as a violation of the sixth clause of the said Charter (whatever that clause may import, seeing it was provided that the Governor and six parts in seven of * * * the Legislature might alter the Charter—or whether a proceeding, heretofore before the Governor and his Council, (not as a Council of State, but as a Court of Chancery, according to equity and stated rules of practice of that Court,) was not a proceeding *in the ordinary court of justice*, and consequently within the reservation in the said sixth clause?

Answer.—I am of opinion that neither the establishment nor the holding of the said Court of Chancery, after the consent of the Assembly so declared as aforesaid, can be construed to be a violation of the sixth clause of the said Charter. But if the Governor and Council, after that Charter, had proceeded to hear cases in equity without such consent of the Assembly, I should have been of opinion that it had been contrary to the said Charter.

Question 5.—Whether since the Assembly have come to their Resolution of January, 1735, it will now be contrary to the Charter of Privileges, or unlawful to continue to hold

the said Court of Chancery, notwithstanding such last mentioned vote, or ought the Court of Chancery to be established by Act of Assembly, and not otherwise?

Answer.—As I am of opinion (that this Court of Chancery was at first legally and rightfully [established] I do not think that it will be contrary to the Chart [er or un-] lawful to continue to hold the same. But I am of opinion that the same may be lawfully held till the whole Legislature have passed an act to the contrary.

J. Willes.*

August 21st, 1736.

Answer to Question 1.—I am of opinion that a Court of Equity is a necessary part of the English Constitution, that relates to the administration of justice: and that the Chancellor appointed by the King, [or] the Keeper of the Great Seal, are, by virtue of their office, entitled to exercise that jurisdiction.

Answer to Question 2.—I conceive that King Charles Second might, by law, grant power to William Penn and his deputies, to erect a Court of Equity in Pennsylvania, without the consent of the Legislature there.

Answer to Question 3.—I conceive this is not an Act of the Legislature there, nor a sufficient signification of their approbation, supposing their approbation was necessary.

Answer to Question 4.—I conceive the establishing the Court of Chancery in the manner above mentioned, was no violation of the sixth clause of the Charter of 1701, both because there was the assent of the Governor, and six parts in seven of the Assembly met, and because the proceeding

* Attorney General, afterwards Lord Chief Justice of the Common Pleas.

in a Court of Equity may be justly called the ordinary course of justice.

Answer to Question 5.—I apprehend the Resolution of the Assembly does not make that illegal which was not so before, therefore that it is not unlawful to hold the [said] Court of Chancery, notwithstanding that resolution.

D. RYDER.*

October 13th, 1736.

A LIST

Of Subscribers for An Assembly, under the direction of John Inglis, Lynford Lardner, John Wallace and John Swift: each subscription, forty shillings, to be paid to any of the Directors at subscribing.†

Alex^r. Hamilton,	James Hamilton,
Tho. Lawrence, Jr.,	Ro. Mackinen,
John Wallace,	Wm. Allen,
Phineas Bond,	Arch^d McCall,
Ch^s Willing,	Jos. Turner,
Joseph Shippen,	Thos. Hopkinson,
Sam. McCall, Junr,	Richd Peters,
George McCall,	Adam Thomson,
Edw. Jones,	Alex^r Stedman,
Samuel McCall, Senr,	Patrick Baird,
Redm. Conyngham,	John Sober,
Jos. Sims,	David Franks,
Thomas Lawrence, Senr,	John Inglis,

* Solicitor General, afterwards Lord Chancellor.

† Printed from the original MS. in Mr. Lardner's possession It will be seen that Mr. Griswold (*Republican Court*, p. 13), has had an incorrect copy placed in his hands.

David McIlvaine,
John Wilcocks,
Charles Stedman,
John Kidd,
Wm. Bingham,
Buckridge Sims,
John Swift,
John Kearsley, Junr,
Wm. Plumsted,
Andrew Elliot,
James Burd,
Wm. Peters,
James Polyceen,
Wm. Franklen,
Hen. Harrison,
John Heuston,
Daniel Boiles,
Ninian Wischeart,
Abram Taylor,
James Trotter,
Samson Levy,
Lynford Lardner,
Richd Hill, Jr.,
Benj. Frill,
Jn. Francis,
William McIlvaine,
Willm Humphreys,
Thomas White,
John Lawrence,
Thos. Græms,
John Cottenham,
John Moland,
Wm. Cuzzens.

(1st Philadelphia Assembly, 1748.)

JOHN SWIFT TO JOHN WHITE, AT THE PENN'A COFFEE HOUSE, BIRCHEN LANE, LONDON.

Philadelphia, July 13th, 1747.

DEAR UNCLE:—When I began this letter, I intended to have given you a true account of two French privateers that were yesterday at Bombay Hook, from whence there came an express to the President here, (Mr. Palmer), which gave an account that they had landed a hundred men at Black Creek, who had plundered the inhabitants of their negroes, and what else they could get; shot a woman in the thigh, and taken her husband prisoner. But I am disappointed, for there is not a word of truth in it, notwithstanding it was as much believed in this town, two hours ago, as the Bible is. Even the Quakers' faith failed them, so that they could not help giving their assent to the truth of it; and it was added, besides, that there were more privateers upon the coast, but this did not gain so much credit. The women, you may be sure, were in great consternation upon hearing that danger was so near them, but it had no other effect upon the men of my acquaintance, than to raise their indignation against a Quaker government.

I am sure I wrote to you by the first opportunity, after the river became navigable, and told you that we had had a severe winter, which prevented my writing to you sooner, which letter went by the way of Ireland, and a copy of it by Seymour, so that if that account can afford you any pleasure, I flatter myself you will receive it. But I did not paint it in all its horrors, as I would have done had I known that accounts of that sort would have been pleasing to you. I know it was not so to me, who felt it. But we have had a spring that has made amends for it. From the latter end of February to the latter end of May, was as fine weather as ever was known in any part of the world, I believe; I never saw anything comparable to it in England, at this season of the year. We had neither frosts nor cold winds, in March, nor too hot weather in May; the latter end of March peach trees were in blossom, and asparagus plenty. The 17th of April I eat tarts made of gooseberries, that were on the trees the day before, at which time all sorts of trees in the woods were green. There was as fair a prospect of great crops of corn, as ever was known; but we have had so much rain for these three weeks last past, that people will be greatly disappointed of their expectations, for instead of a good crop, they will have a very bad one. The rain has mildewed the corn all over the country, and in some places where they cut it early, it has rotted in the field and not been worth carrying in.

JOHN SWIFT, TO JOHN WHITE, PENN'A COFFEE HOUSE, LONDON.

Philadelphia, August 29th, 1747.

DEAR UNCLE:—I am not certain whether this will cover a bill of exchange for £200 or not, the reason of which is that I am obliged to go out of town, to Penn's manor, to-morrow morning, according to appointment, and I do n't know of any body that wants to draw, except Allen & Turner, and they are both in great affliction, for the loss of their relations; Mr. Allen, for Andrew Hamilton, who died yesterday, (after being four days ill of a yellow fever), and was this morning buried at Bush Hill; and Mr. Turner, for his nephew, (a son of Peter Turner's), who died yesterday of the same disorder, and is to be buried this afternoon from his house. I have therefore put the money into the hands of Mr. Abram Claypoole, and desired him to get a bill of them on Monday, if they have not done drawing: I believe it will cost 85 per cent., so that I find there is no advantage to be got by waiting, for which reason I shall, for the future, buy my bills as soon as I receive the money. This is not a country for a man to live in who is fond of this world, when every year he must run the risk of being seized with this vile fever, and hurried away before he has time to look about him, which I think must be a melancholy consideration to a man in good circumstances, that has a family of children he wishes to see brought up. Poor Mr. Hamilton has left two sons, and his wife is so ill of the fever, that it is thought she can't get over it. Jasper McCall, Captain Atwood's wife, and Dr. Kearsley's wife, have all died this week. Mr. Currie is ill, but there is some hope of his recovery.

Memorandum, September 5th, 1747, Mr. Claypoole got a bill of exchange of Allen & Turner, for £200, and enclosed it in the above.

JOHN SWIFT TO JOHN WHITE, AT THE PENN'A COFFEE HOUSE, LONDON.

Philadelphia, September 20th, 1747.

DEAR UNCLE:—The news I have to send you from this place, is as follows: a Spanish privateer, of ten guns, took last week eight vessels belonging to this place, and three to Virginia; she came to an anchor in the Bay. The yellow fever still rages very violently in town, young Samuel Powel died of it this day.

JOHN SWIFT TO JOHN WHITE, LONDON.

Philadelphia, November 29th, 1747.

DEAR UNCLE:—I have sent Mr. Bedford two kegs of pickles and two to Mr. Williams. The success the Spanish privateers had upon our coasts last summer, has much alarmed the inhabitants of this town, and a pamphlet published here a few days ago, setting forth the miserable calamities that may befall us, if something is not done for our security against next spring, has raised a military spirit amongst the people. Yesterday there was a grand meeting of all ranks and conditions at Whitfield building, where they signed an association for forming themselves into a militia for the defence of the city. And there is to be a lottery set on foot immediately, to raise money towards fitting out a vessel, to protect the trade. And a petition will be presented to our worthy Assembly, (who are now sitting), praying them to take it into their consideration, and do something for the common security. I have sent you the pamphlet and a copy of the association, and three papers relating to the Quakers' principles of not defending themselves, which have been of great service to some of them, and convinced them that they have been in a mistake about that matter. Edmunson is acknowledged to have been a great man amongst them.

As the London gentlemen volunteers have no use for their fire-arms, now the rebellion is over, I suppose some of them will be disposed of at a reasonable rate. In that case I should be glad if you would send me one, as I am bound in reason, duty and honor, to have one of some kind or other, and my fowling-piece has no bayonet to it. I can sell it when I leave the country.

JOHN SWIFT TO GROSVENOR BEDFORD, ESQ., AT THE GENERAL EXCISE OFFICE, LONDON.

Philadelphia, March 22d, 1747.

DEAR FRIEND:—I congratulate you upon the acquisition of a son, (may he be a good one,) and that Providence has not suffered any loss to befall you but what may be retrieved. I have had a loss in a lottery as well as you, though not a very handsome one. If you incline to drink any more, please to let it be to my safe return to you, because that is what I wish for most. As my manner of living here, or to speak more properly, spending time, is new to you, I will give you some account of it. Know, then, that I lodge at the house of

Mr. Robert Ellis, whose wife is a cheerful, discreet, .good sort of woman, and though not young, yet still remembers that she has been so, and therefore we agree very well; and there are three young ladies in the house, one of which happens to be a widow, so that we have a variety of conditions. But I am giving you a history of a whole family instead of my own, though so far was necessary to my design, because it is in this family that a great part of my time is past; all my nights, many of my evenings, and the time it takes me to breakfast and dine. My days I spend in giving my attendance on a place I call my store, but it is to very little purpose of late, that I am almost tired of it. I sometimes of an evening go to a club made up mostly of sober, staid elderly gentlemen, who have had their day, and seen the folly of it, and are now satisfied with as much wine as they can drink by eleven o'clock. A bumper is never proposed, but upon some very extraordinary occasion, which I think has never happened since I have been in the country. Do n't you think they are very discreet people? But I have not philosophy to be governed altogether by the example of others. I always find an inclination in myself for one bumper at least, and indulge myself in it, when I am in company that have a relish for it, which sometimes happens; but this is a very sober town, and I am prodigiously afraid of getting an ill name, and am therefore much upon my guard. I sent you by the widow Captain Whyte, a small keg of mangos and one of peaches, and some terrapins, which I hope you will receive. I am ashamed that I have not yet got the rattlesnakes to send you, but indeed I have done all I could to get them but have not been able to do it. I expect you will say I am a right American, but do n't be angry.

EDWARD SHIPPEN (CH. J.) TO JOSEPH SHIPPEN (COL.)

London, Feb. 25*th*, 1748.

DEAR JOE :—Yours per Child I received, and am pleased with its contents. I hope you will never neglect any opportunity of writing, and expect that you will from time to time acquaint me with every thing worth noticing which occurs. You desire that I should give you a particular account of my voyage ; which I shall do with the greatest pleasure, though the narration may not be altogether so agreeable as you could wish. For eight days after we left the capes, we had as fine winds and pleasant weather as one could possibly desire ; in which time we had run to the outermost part of the Banks of Newfoundland, something above a third part of our passage; the eighth night, about nine o'clock, we had a storm come on from the north-west so suddenly, that we could not possibly get our sails furled time enough to prevent the violence of the wind from tearing our mainsail and foresail all to pieces. The maintop yard was lowered and the sail furled, but the fury of the wind drove the yard from its proper place quite up to the head of the maintopmast, blew the sail loose, and made it stand abroad like a vane. We continued in this situation for about an hour, without any further damage, when the gale increased to such a degree, that we could not by any means keep the ship before the wind, but she violently broached to, and we must have inevitably gone to the bottom, had not the captain very seasonably cut away the mizenmast, which brought her to rights. Some time after this, the wind raged still more, and obliged the ship, notwithstanding the loss of our mizenmast, to broach to a second time. And now, we had lost all hopes, and thought that nothing less than a miracle could save us from the impending ruin. The ship lay on her beam-ends, so that one could sit strait up on her side, and we expected every moment to perish. The sailors were so disheartened that they would not work a stroke, but quitted the deck, every man but one, and retired to their cabins to pray. After laying some time in this melancholy posture, we had the good fortune to have our maintopmast, with the head of our mainmast, blown away; which took away so much of the power of the wind over us, that we righted once more, and got before the wind. And thus we continued, exposed to the mercy of the winds and seas, till about six o'clock in the morning, when we found the storm something abating, and, in about two hours afterwards, we had but a very moderate gale. But to have seen the havoc that was made upon deck, and the miserable plight we were reduced to from the loss of our sails and masts, and the shattered condition of every thing about us, would have made men of more philosophy than any of us, feel concerned, even after the abatement of the wind. But, thank God! this terrible storm was succeeded by three or four days of very fine weather, which gave us time to mend our sails, and put ourselves in as good a posture for proceeding with the voyage as could possibly be expected from people in our condition; yet, we thought ourselves so unfit to venture into the English channel, that we consulted several times whether it was not most proper to put into Lisbon to refit. But the captain's opinion prevailed, that we should stand for the channel, and put into the first harbor in England, in case it should be thick or stormy weather. So we proceeded, and arrived safe in the Downs the twenty-seventh day after we left the capes. We landed at Deal, and took coaches for London, where we have had the pleasure of congratulating one another upon our deliverance. I heartily wish, dear brother, that you may never meet with any thing like what I have been relating. You cannot, from reading this or any description of our calamity, be any sort of a judge of the horror of it.

Since I have been in London, I have enjoyed a very good state of health, and have spent some time in seeing all the curiosities of this populous city, which I shall forbear to particularize at present. The relation will serve to pass away an hour or two of our winter evenings when we get together again, if ever it please God to bring about that happiness.

Give my love to mammy,* and tell her I have her often in my mind, and wish she could mention any thing that would be agreeable to her from hence. I should take great pleasure in supplying her.

Remember me kindly to Uncle Billy and his family, Mr. Willing and his family, Billy and Jemmy Logan, Tommy Smith, and all other friends; and, dear Joe, accept my hearty love to yourself, and believe me, your very loving and affectionate brother.

JOHN SWIFT TO JOHN WHITE, PENN'A COFFEE HOUSE, LONDON.

Philadelphia, April 12th, 1748.

DEAR UNCLE:—The association for the militia goes on very well here, there are upwards of eight hundred men in this city, that bear arms, and are already become pretty expert

* The second wife of Edward Shippen, of Lancaster.

in the exercise; and in the province there are near twenty thousand associators, and more daily coming in. The platform for a battery is begun by the swamp below the Swedes' church, and we have cannon coming to us from New York, viz: twelve twelve-pounders, and two eighteen-pounders, which are to serve till we can be better provided. With these we shall be able to make some resistance in case of an attack. There is another lottery going to be set on foot, to raise six thousand pounds, which is to be applied for defending the city.

JOHN SWIFT TO JOHN WHITE, AT CROYDON, IN SURRY, ENGLAND.

Philadelphia, July 22d, 1748.

DEAR UNCLE:—We have had an account of a cessation of arms between England and France, which I hope will be the forerunner of a peace, but I fear it will not be a very advantageous one for the English. The giving up of Cape Breton will be a great mortification to the people of New England, and indeed to all North America.

RICHARD PETERS (SECRETARY) TO JAMES LOGAN.

Philadelphia, Nov. 26th, 1748.

HON'D SIR:—I was going on Thursday afternoon to write to you, to tell you that I had given the Governor your congratulations, in the most affectionate manner I could express myself, which was but doing you justice, and that there was no reason in the world to imagine that there would be a general * * * * * But, on his asking me if he could not steal a visit to you before he went to New Castle, I thought it better he should give you the first account of present affairs. *England is a most debauched place.* If the weather permits he will see you this afternoon; if not, you must excuse him till his return from the lower counties.

EDWARD SHIPPEN (CH. J.) TO HIS FATHER, AT LANCASTER.

London, Jan. 23*d*, 1749.

DEAR AND HON'D SIR:—With regard to a journeyman from a sugar-house, I am afraid it will be difficult to procure one to go over, for a man who understands the business well, can get £50 stg. per an. in London, and an indifferent hand would not, I suppose, suit your purpose.

I have, according to your desire, visited Mr. Rich'd Penn, who made me very welcome, and yesterday I had the honor of dining with him.

I shall send mammy the Mantua silk per Mesnard, who sails in a month. You will find that article is very high, the ships from India not having brought any this fall, so that silk has risen 25 to 30 per cent. within these three months.

I am sorry that I have to inform you that I am disappointed in my expectations of being called to the Bar at this term: the occasion of it, I could not possibly prevent. Every student, before he comes to the Bar, is obliged to perform six vacation exercises, three candlelight exercises, and two new-inn exercises; which he is not allowed to do alone, but must be joined with another student. I had calculated matters so as to have performed them all before the end of this term; but, unluckily for me, the gentleman who was my companion in the exercises, having some engagements in the country, could not attend at the time appointed for the performance of one of the vacation exercises, which obliged me to defer that duty until next vacation. So that it will be Easter Term before I can be possibly called, unless I consent to compound for vacation exercises, which would cost me near twenty pounds. I know, sir, that you expect me to leave England in March or February, which makes me at a loss how to act. But I am reduced to the necessity of either returning home without being made a barrister, and so making all my expenses at the Temple useless, or of prolonging my stay in England two or three months. The former, I am sensible, would not be so agreeable to you, and, since I have gone so far at the Temple, I believe I must stay and see it out, and depend on your goodness to send me about £30 upon my coming away. According to my calculation, that amount, together with the money you have already favored me with, and the £20 you order Storke to let me have, will suffice, with frugality, to maintain me till my departure and defray the expenses of my being called to the bar. All that I shall then want further will be some £30 or £40 for my gown and tie-wig, a suit of clothes, my sea-stores and passage. Easter Term is in May, but I cannot take the oaths until about the middle of June; after which I shall leave in the first vessel. In the meantime, I hope you will furnish me with the money necessary to complete my affairs with advantage, and to quit England with credit.

I mentioned in my last, that Mr. Leybourne had desired his nephew, Mr. Taylor, in Lisbon, to send you some of his best vine-cuttings, with directions about planting them. He is now advised that they were shipt to you in the "Entwistle," Capt. Smith, from Lisbon to Phil'a. I hope they will get safe to hand, and in good time.

JOHN SWIFT TO GROSVENOR BEDFORD, ESQ., GENERAL EXCISE OFFICE, LONDON.

April 27th, 1749.

DEAR SIR:—Your writing to me when in so painful a condition, is an unquestionable proof of your good nature and sincerity. I am very sorry to hear of your being so often visited by that vile, troublesome gout, and sincerely wish you could fall upon some method to get clear of it, before it is too strongly fixed upon your constitution. Why should you be placed in such a manner, when there are people enough in the world that are much better able to bear it than you are? Drinking tar water is found in this part of the world to be a remedy against it, I have heard of several that have kept it off by that means, particularly one Mr. Alexander, of New York, who used to have it every year very violently, and since he has used tar water, has had but very slight fits, and not so often as before.

CH. J. SHIPPEN TO COL. SHIPPEN.

London, August 2d, 1749.

DEAR JOE:—I received your letters via Ireland, and per Arthur, and perceive the great sympathy you have in every thing that happens to your brother, which, if it were possible, would endear me to you more than ever: your kind concern on hearing of my danger at sea, and your joy on my deliverance, are marks of a sincere esteem and regard for me. And I am also as sensible of and grateful for mammy's interesting herself so much in my welfare: I charge you, give her my sincere thanks.

You tell me you have been to school the last winter, to improve yourself in Latin and to prepare you for the College. I would take the liberty to press you to pursue learning with a great deal of assiduity. You are now in a time of life the most proper to lay a foundation for being a man of consequence. You have nothing to perplex you or take your mind from study: all the conveniences and blessings of life are provided for you in great plenty. If ever you travel, you'll find how men of letters are everywhere respected; you'll see the ascendancy the knowing man has over the blockhead; you'll have a friend in your learning which you can never be deprived of, a friend which will stand by you when all others fail. Be a man of learning, and you'll be a man of consequence wherever you go. Take this advice, dear Joe, as from a brother who loves you dearly, and has your future well-being in life greatly at heart.

As I am busy writing several other letters, you'll excuse this short one from, dear Joe, your loving brother.

CH. J. SHIPPEN TO COL. SHIPPEN.

London, September 14th, 1749.

DEAR JOE:—I have received your acceptable letter of the 22d July, per Child, enclosing invoice and bill of lading for a box of skins, per Clark, and covering copy of your favor per that vessel. I am afraid your first adventure will prove unfortunate, as we have had an account of Clark's springing aleak and being obliged to put into Rhode Island. So that possibly the skins may be damaged by the sea; or, if not, their being kept so long a time packed in the summer season, may be a means of their breeding worms. But, however, let us hope for the best.

I am extremely pleased to hear of your fondness for books, and shall take care to furnish you with such as will be of real service to you; for two-thirds of the books in the world had much better be burnt than read, as they only serve to fill the minds of young people with wrong prejudices.

EDWARD SHIPPEN (CH. J.) TO JOSEPH SHIPPEN (COL.) AT NASSAU HALL.

Philadelphia, June 13th, 1751.

DEAR BROTHER:—I received yours by the hands of Mr. Dove, and am thankful for your description of Passaic Falls, which upon examination I find very accurate, and hope ere long to have the pleasure of viewing them. I find you make the perpendicular fall to be but 60 feet, yet it has been generally called 70. But these things are often exaggerated by travelers, who have a greater itch for telling strange things, than candor to describe them justly. I observe you mention nothing of the rent in the rock, of which I have frequently heard very pompous accounts. If you remember anything of that sort, do mention it in your next.

I could wish you would inform me what books you are reading; I mean in ethics or philosophy. As to logic, it is well enough to make that a small part of your study, but don't rely much on it. It has misled many, and instead of aiding in the investigation of truth, has been mostly used to support the greatest sophistry. The great Mr. Locke is of opinion, that syllogism is far from being the usefullest way of exercising our reasoning faculties: that we can observe the connection of proofs in their plain and natural order, much better than in the perplexed repetitions of a number of syllogisms. But this only by the way, as I would not have you neglect the schoolmen's knowledge, though you may never have occasion to use it. It may enable you to detect falsehood when disguised in syllogism.

I have no news to acquaint you with. Your father is at Susquehanna. All are well at home, and desire to be remembered. Yesterday died old Mrs. Gray, your mammy's aunt. Remember me to Mr. Burr.*

EDWARD SHIPPEN, OF LANCASTER, TO COL. BURD, AT SHIPPENSBURG.

Philadelphia, Nov. 8th, 1752.

DEAR MR. BURD :—After speaking of some sheep and farm affairs, he says :—" Tell Sally, her Aunt Robeson went off like a lamb. I attended her funeral last night. Captain Stirling† arrived yesterday in five weeks from London, but did not bring over Mr. John Penn as was expected. Mr. Thomas Penn is certainly to be here next spring, with his lady and family. Josey‡ sets off next Monday for the Col-

* President of the college.

† m. Mr. Shippen's niece, Miss Willing. He was afterwards Sir Walter Stirling, &c.—*Burke's Peerage.*

‡ Afterwards Col. Shippen.

lege. To-morrow all the principal gentlemen of the town are to drink his majesty's health at Bush Hill; and after dinner, they are to wait upon the ladies in town, and conduct them to the State-House to a ball in the Assembly Room, and after a dance or two all hands are to go up stairs.

EDWARD SHIPPEN (CH. J.) TO HIS FATHER, AT LANCASTER.

Philadelphia, September 15th, 1753.

HON'D SIR:—Mr. Allen returned a few days ago from the sea-side, and has brought Mrs. Allen pretty much in the same condition he carried her away, in much danger.

We begin to be apprehensive that General Forbes does not mean to go on with the Expedition, as he talks of not being able to get wagons, and of laying the fault of the failure of the expedition to the Province.

Bradstreet, your countryman, has done bravely. Saying Provincials are worthless troops, won't go down, now; and the story that the repulse at Cavillon was owing to the backwardness of the irregulars, won't be believed in England when they hear that an American, with about 3000 Provincials, marched into the very heart of the enemy's country, and took a fortress which is the very key to all the French settlements on the Lakes.

EDW'D SHIPPEN TO MR. AND MRS. BURD, AT SHIPPENSBURG.

Lancaster, Sept. 24th, 1753.

DEAR CHILDREN:—I hope to find myself better in the

morning, so as to be fit for traveling to Carlisle to the treaty, as the Governor cannot attend. Mr. Weiser* wrote to me yesterday, that he expected Mr. Peters to be at his house to-night, by a letter which the Governor had sent him. But Mr. James Foley says, that Messrs. Isaac Norris, the Speaker of the Assembly, Richard Peters, and Benjamin Franklin, were appointed to go to Carlisle, and that they said they should be here this evening. Mr. Weiser hopes to have my company at the treaty; but as the Governor thought I should be setting out for Newark,† he did not write, lest it should baulk me, but waited for my return until yesterday's express. I, however, had outrun my time. If I am well, and Mr. Peters presses me to go, I shall not refuse; and, even if I don't see him, I don't know but that I may go, for, without vanity, I imagine I may be very useful on that important occasion.

If I should build a mill, or mills, at Shippensburg, I shall let you have the management and benefit of it, or them, until further orders, or until I should live there, which may not be impossible. Yet don't hint such a word for the world. If I were ever to set up a grist-mill, I could not bear the thoughts of paying through the nose to Findley for joists and boards; so I think I had better erect a saw-mill, without a cover, first of all, which will work for itself and the grist-mill too, and the same dam and race will answer for both mills. If there should be but water enough

* Col. Conrad Weiser, so well and deservedly known in the provincial history of Pennsylvania. For an extended notice of him, see *History of Berks and Lebanon, by J. Daniel Rupp;* (*Lancaster,* 1844), *p.* 195, *et. seq.; also p.* 40, *&c.*

† Mr. Shippen took an active interest in the removal of "the College of New Jersey," from Newark to Princeton.

for one at a time, I am for going on with the project, so I can only see my way clear. Perhaps Ben. Chambers can build saw-mills as well as any man; but I intend soon, please God, to consult Moses Dickey, who lives near John Harris. I would have an overshot wheel. It is only going to a little more expense in the race, and then at the end of it to place troughs about 100 feet long. As you go along the road to Virginia, you may take notice of Ben. Chambers' saw-mill, where he does without any dam at all: a glorious thing! formed by nature.

I am, with love to yourselves and the ducky children, your loving father.

P. S.—Since the above, Mr. Peters came here, and I shall carry this letter to Carlisle.

EDW'D SHIPPEN TO HIS SON EDWARD (CH. J.) AT PHILAD'A.

Lancaster, March 20th, 1754.

My Dear Son:—My son Joe and myself get up every morning at about sunrise, having prepared over night some dry hickory for a good fire. We then sit close to our business till 9 o'clock, and find we can do more in that time than all the rest of the day, as we are afterwards often interrupted. Neither do we receive visits, nor return any, until it is near sunset, and we eat so moderately, without tasting a drop of strong liquor, that the whole day seems like a long morning to us; and if a best friend should happen to come to saunter away an hour or two with us, we make it a fixed rule plainly to tell him that we are so engaged that we cannot possibly wait upon him. And then, that we may be sufficiently refreshed with sleep, we have agreed upon ten o'clock at night for going to bed; and so, after eating a light supper, and drinking a little wine, we lay ourselves down with light stomachs, cool heads, and quiet consciences. Now this practice I most affectionately recommend to you. Your promotion and happiness in this vexatious world will depend principally upon your own conduct, and the more the world sees you are able to do for yourself, the more ready it will be to offer you its best services. It is too common a thing for young men, when they first appear upon the stage of action, to aim at grandeur and politeness. They delight to see their friends (often falsely so called) frequently at their houses, and to entertain them in a genteel manner. The friends are pleased with this, and bring other acquaintances with them to dine, &c. Then afterwards they sit at table two or three hours, tippling of wine and punch, which, rendering the company unfit for any business, a walk to the bowling-green, or to the billiard-table, is proposed and consented to, and on their return from thence in the evening, instead of being calm and cool, and having the pleasure of reflecting upon a well-spent day, either for the advantage of their family or the public, or both, they are become so stupid that they don't know what to do with themselves, but either go to tavern or to one or other of their houses, to drink away care till the clock strikes twelve; and then being quite devils and quite beasts, they stagger away home to snore and groan by the sides of their poor innocent young wives, who deserve ten thousand better things at their hands. And all this after the poor young things have been moping at home and bemoaning themselves of their hard fate, and crying out a hundred times in an evening—"Well, if these be the pleasures of matrimony, would to heaven we had remained under our parents' roofs!" But to return. When they have wallowed in their beds till about eleven o'clock next morning, then they raise their unclean bodies in order to act the same part over again. Can any rational creature excuse such a behaviour to God, his wife and family, or even to himself? Will not the practice of these things bring a man into contempt, and soon reduce him to penury and want, by destroying his constitution, and of course his capacity for his employment? A young married man should be very diligent, frugal, and careful, that he may not only be able to always support himself, his wife, and a houseful of children, but also to lay up a hundred or two pounds for every one of them when they go out into the wide, wide world. Young folks ought never to begin where their industrious, saving parents left off. I have almost gone through the world, and have gained a little experience by my own mistakes and blunders, having had no friends to advise me, as you and your brother and sister have; and therefore I hope you will all three of you be always ready and willing to obey my instructions. You are not able to conceive, without great consideration, the unspeakable advantage of having a bosom friend, who always has and always will make your happiness his study; and, whilst others will behave and speak to you as suits their interests, he will never tell you anything but the truth. But of counsel, as valuable as this is, you are soon to be deprived; for, according to the course of nature, I cannot stay long here, even if I lived beyond the usual age of a man. However, we must all wait till the change comes; and were I sure it was very near at hand, I hope it would not be grievous but joyous; and, as I know that I then must hold up my hand at the bar of God, I am resolved, by Divine assistance, to work out my salvation with fear and trembling.

But I have made a digression. I am not able to express the great anxiety with which I have supported and educated my children; so I say no more on that head. Avoid what the world calls pleasure. Pleasure is only for crowned heads, and the great, who have their incomes, sleeping and waking. But young men, who are just beginning the world, ought to shudder at the thought of spending their youthful days in idleness. Not that I would refuse young people innocent diversons, provided they are well timed and not too frequent. If you seek pleasure, you will find it in temperance and sobriety, charity and virtue, and in the diligent and honest pursuits of your concerns. Will it not yield a man the greatest satisfaction in the evening, to think he has been closely employed all day for the support of the friend of his bosom and his little babes, all hovering about him? How sweet and refreshing is it for man and wife often to spend their evenings together at home, without any other company? For my own part, rather than be deprived by my very best friends of such a pleasure sometimes, I should choose to retire into our chambers, so that even our own servants should not know where to find us out. But I have not done with our own method of husbanding our precious time. Go to your cousin Allen. Opulent as he is, you will find him up early, and busily employed until coffee-house hours; and, when he invites any number of gentlemen to dinner, (which he can so well afford,) he soon desires the favor of being excused from drinking, and this without blushing. Visit Mr. Francis, Mr. Turner, Mr. Willing, and other temperate, industrious gentlemen,—I mean in the day time,—and you will presently see by their countenances that they would rather have your room than your company. I desire you will never go a fishing to the capes or any other dangerous place, nor keep company with any ruinous set of companions.

Remember, if a man should spend 3*s.* in liquor, necessarily or otherwise, in his own house, every day, and 3*s.* 6*d.* at club every night, and £3 at the assembly, and £4 per annum for the concert, it will require £125 12*s.* 6*d.* to support such proceedings. And remember, if a man rises from the breakfast table at eleven, dines alone and sits till three, goes to the coffee-house at the end of the day; I say, if a man is guilty of such practices, then he will only have three hours a day for his business, and no time at all for his studies.

This letter I write, God knows, with my heart full of love and affection, for your instruction as far as you may stand in need of it; and I desire you will lock it up in your drawer, for my sake. I have a copy in my own hand-writing, which I shall keep. Consider! Consider it; and may God bless and preserve you, for Jesus Christ's sake.

EDWARD SHIPPEN TO DR. WM. SHIPPEN.

Lancaster, March 27th, 1754.

DEAR DOCTOR:—Yesterday I was favored with yours of the 13th of February, perfumed with drugs and herbs as if it had been an apothecary's advertisement, just taken out of a box newly arrived from England. And to-day at one o'clock, I received yours of the 25th instant, enclosing a deed for me to sign, for the benefit of poor Joe; and, if it had not been to serve a brother, I will assure him I would not have done it to alienate the one foot whereon his kitchen stands.

I have not had a good opportunity since the last adjournment of our assembly, to speak with any of our members except Cowpland Cowper, (a friend,) about their not allowing a handsome salary to the King's attorney. I fancy it is the man that stands in the way, and that they would be glad for an opportunity to say to one another—'Come, since his 'Honor, the Governor, has appointed to that high station 'of prosecuting for the Crown, a young gentleman born among 'us, and educated at the Inn's Court, let us, for his encourage-'ment, vote him an hundred pounds sterling per annum.'

Neddy tells me that Mr. Francis would resign to him immediately, if he would accept the commission; nay, he is amazed he should hesitate a moment about it, even should he never get a salary. I believe Mr. Allen has the matter under consideration. We all think that now is the time for the change, for if the new Governor should favor us with a commission, yet we would rather be obliged to the Hon. James Hamilton for it; and if the clerk's place of the Supreme Court should fall to Johnny Lawrence's share, his mouth would be quite made up, considering he is Clerk of the Quarter Sessions already; and these things would be so pleasing to Mr. Lawrence's family, that they would not be so jealous of Neddy's running away with too many favors from Mr. Francis. I don't suppose that when Mr. Francis did all the business, he received more than one hundred pounds a year for all the Courts in the Province. He has more influence on the Speaker than any man in the world. Messrs. John and James Wright are also his great favorites; and as to Bennie Franklin, Esq., if he did but know how Mr. Allen stands affected to Ned, he would for a weighty reason turn some wheel to get a salary fixed upon the officer before mentioned. However, I am in hopes there will be a harmony between the Governor and the Assembly, at the next Convention, and if our friends should advise Ned to accept of the commission before mentioned, perhaps a petition for an allowance to the King's attorney may be encouraged.

JOSEPH SHIPPEN (COL.) TO JAMES BURD (COL.) AT SHIPPENSBURG.

Lancaster, April 2d, 1754.

DEAR BROTHER :—In the course of my reading I happened, the other day, to meet with a very beautiful poem, entitled "The Hop-Garden,"* lately composed by the ingenious Mr. Smart; from which I collected the substance of what he says with regard to the raising of hops; which, I think, very good, so I have, therefore, now enclosed them to you, that they may not lay eternally buried in theory, (as many excellent mechanical and other inventions do,) without being reduced to practice, especially as I am sensible you have not been negligent in exercising your thoughts on the rational science of agriculture. I hope you will excuse my presumption in giving you any rules on this head, since I don't pretend to even a smattering knowledge of husbandry. Indeed, I acknowledge myself an entire novice in it. However, this confession won't debar me from being Mr. Smart's amanuensis.

The other day there was a rumor throughout the city of Philadelphia of a French war, and it filled up the whole conversation of the town for a day or two, when it was ridiculed

* The Hop-Garden, an English Georgic, &c., by Christopher Smart. London, 1752.

as false, the report being occasioned by the arrival of one of his majesty's ships at New York. However, it is imagined she may have brought some instructions relating to the French encroachments upon our frontiers. But of this, I suppose, we shall be satisfied soon.

The Freemasons in Philadelphia are now erecting in Second street, somewhere behind Billy Logan's new house, a noble and spacious building for their Lodge, which they will so contrive as to serve the purpose of a fine assembly room; and they intend to receive a rent per annum for that use of it.

CHARLES THOMSON TO JOSEPH SHIPPEN, JR., (COL.)

Philadelphia, January 31*st,* 1755.

DEAR SIR:—Were I to give you, for news, the conjectures with which our town now abounds, I might fill a sheet; I shall therefore confine myself to truth.

We have had Mr. Shirley here for some time, recruiting. He has got pretty near one hundred men. On Sunday or Monday, they are to be shipped off for Boston or Rhode Island. The Lieutenant Colonels Mercer and Elisson, left town Tuesday.

We have now in town several officers, among which I hear is the Commissary General.

Our accounts from Boston are various, none certainly to be depended on, except that they seem intent on something of importance. Letters from London, advise that the affairs of the colonies are under the consideration of the parliament; that the union of the colonies has for some time been deliberated on, and 'tis thought will soon be brought to bear, an event much to be desired, since it effectually will secure us from the insults of our haughty aspiring neighbors, the French, and make our security independent of the fickle humor of our Indian allies.

Whatever news occurs worth mentioning, you may expect in my next, in the mean time, let me conclude with assuring you,

I am, with much esteem, your hearty
well-wisher and humble servant,
CHARLES THOMSON.*

P. S.—Please to make my compliments to Mr. and Mrs. Shippen.

I should be glad you would inform Mr. Shippen, that as the five years for which the subscriptions were made to the academy† are now expired, and as the disbursements have been great, the trustees desire that the gentlemen who have subscribed would, as soon as possible, send in to me what remains due.

In the list of outstandings given to me, is marked: Mr. Edward Shippen, at £10, his fourth and fifth payment, £20.

EDWARD SHIPPEN, (CH. J.,) TO EDWARD SHIPPEN, AT LANCASTER.

Philadelphia, February 21*st*, 1755.

HON'D SIR:—I was pleasing myself with the thoughts of your eating some of our fine Rhode Island oysters. I had prepared a barrel of them to go in Spore's wagon. He told

* Afterwards the Secretary to Congress.

† Since grown into the University of Pennsylvania.—"*History of the University*," *by Dr. Geo. B. Wood.* Pub. by order, &c.

Sammy, he should not set off till this afternoon, but, to my great disappointment, on sending at 8 o'clock this morning, I found that his, and all the other wagons were gone. I had also packed up all the books you desired in a little bundle, to send you by the same opportunity. I believe the oysters will keep, so they shall remain in the barrel till the next opportunity. They are the first Rhode Island oysters we have had this year, or you should not have been without some so long. But I thought it hardly worth while to send you our common bay oysters, which have been remarkably bad this year.

EDWARD SHIPPEN, (CH. J ,) TO HIS FATHER, AT LANCASTER.

Philadelphia, March 13*th*, 1755.

Hon'd Sir:—You desire to know the reason of the Assembly's being called together. You will see, by the papers, that General Braddock is arrived in Virginia, and our Governor has directions to get the Assembly to cut a road of one hundred feet from Conogocheague to Will's Creek, for the troops. The Governor is also to get provisions for the New England troops, that are to march through the Province. Governor Shirley has raised five thousand men for a secret expedition. The design has been concealed from all the world, except the Council and Assembly of Massachusetts Bay, and every member has taken the oath of secrecy. The New England men are now esteemed the champions of the American world.

Tommy Willing has still some of the old wine, but no doubt the best pipes have been culled out.

EDWARD SHIPPEN, (CH. J.,) TO HIS FATHER, AT SHIPPENSBURG.

Philadelphia, March 19th, 1755.

HON'D SIR:—The Governor has laid before the Assembly a most alarming letter, from General Braddock, which charges them in strong terms with faction and disaffection, and assures them, that, as the assigning quarters for the army is his province, he shall take due care to burthen those colonies the most, that show the least loyalty to his Majesty; and lets them know that he is determined to obtain, by unpleasant methods, what it is their duty to contribute with the utmost cheerfulness. The Assembly know not how to stomach this military address, but 'tis thought it will frighten them into some reasonable measures, as it must be a vain thing to contend with a General at the head of an army, though he should act an arbitrary part; especially as in all probability he will be supported in everything at home.

Please to tell Josey that Riley has lost two hundred dollars, by insuring tickets in the lottery. It seems, he insured but six hundred instead of eight hundred tickets.

EDWARD SHIPPEN, (CH. J.,) TO HIS FATHER, AT LANCASTER.

Philadelphia, March 21st, 1755.

HON'D SIR:—Agreeably to your directions, I have sent you the early peas and a collection of garden seeds, which I hope will prove to your satisfaction; radish seeds I can get from nobody but Duberry. If the bearer should not set off very early in the morning, I will send some by him, otherwise, by the next safe hand.

States Morris* has been in the country several days, I cannot learn when he is to be at Lancaster.

Thomas Riley, who so burnt his fingers with the last lottery, has a scheme to make money by the next, by purchasing the blanks in the first, second and third classes.

Two Commissioners are arrived from Boston, viz: Mr. Oliver and Mr. Quincy.

LETTER FROM THE COMMISSIONERS TO THE GOVERNOR OF PENNSYLVANIA.

Fort Cumberland, April 16th, 1755.

HON'D SIR:—In pursuance of your commission, we set out on the road from Carlisle on the 29th of March, and with the greatest industry reached the waters of the Yohiogain on the 11th inst. We stopped at about eighteen miles on this side of the forks, and would have proceeded further, had we not had certain intelligence of great numbers of French and Indians hunting and scouting, &c. Our Indians all fled from us: some at Reastown, some on the Alleghany hills, save one Delaware.

We were very fortunate in finding a good road all the way, and particularly through the Alleghany hills, considering how mountainous that country is.

From Barnall's Knob to McDowell's Mill, is about sixty miles, and, were it not for the interposition of mountains,

* A brother of Lewis and Gouverneur Morris. He went to England and became a M. P. and a Lieut. General in the British army. He married the Duchess of Gordon. See *Sabine's Loyalists*, s. v. Wilkins.

would not be so far by ten or fifteen miles. The expense of making a road thirteen feet wide, in the principal places twenty feet, will be about eight hundred pounds.

Last Saturday evening we came to the camp, and were kindly received by the officers, particularly Captain Rutherford. We waited for Sir John's coming to the camp, from the road towards Winchester. He came this day at three o'clock, but treated us in a very disagreeable manner. He is extremely warm and angry at our Province. He would not look at our draughts, nor suffer any representations to be made to him, in regard to our Province, but stormed like a lion rampant. He said our commission to lay out the roads should have issued in January last, upon the receipt of his first letter, that it is now mere doing of nothing; that the troops must march on the 1st of May; that the want of this road, and of the provisions promised by the Pennsylvanians, has retarded the expedition, which may cost them their lives, because of the fresh numbers of French which are like to be suddenly poured into the country; that, instead of marching to the Ohio, he would, in nine days, march his army into Cumberland county, to cut roads, press wagons, horses, &c.; that he would not allow a soldier to handle an axe, but would, by the sword, compel the inhabitants to do it, and take every man that refused, to the Ohio; that yesterday he told some of the Virginians, that he would kill all kinds of cattle, carry away horses, burn houses, &c., and that if the French defeated them in consequence of the delays of this Province, he would, with his sword drawn, pass through it, and treat the inhabitants as traitors to his master; that he would, to-morrow, write to England by a man-of-war, shake Mr. Penn's proprietaryship, and represent Pennsylvania as a disaffected province; that he would not hesitate to impress* our Assembly, for his hands were not tied, and that we should find. He ordered us to take notice of these warnings, and instantly to publish them to our Governor and Assembly, and tell them he did not value anything they did, seeing that they were dilatory, and retarded the march of the troops.† He told us to go to the General if we pleased, who would give us ten bad words, where he had given us one.

At length he allowed us to speak, which we did in favor of the Province, to the best of our ability. Capt. Rutherford and Col. Ennis assisted us. All in vain. Our delays were unpardonable. He said he would do our duty for us himself, and never trust to us, but that we should pay dearly for it. To every sentence he solemnly swore, and desired that we would believe him to be in earnest.

In these circumstances, Sir, and especially as we have not yet run the camp-road, we cannot send you a draught, but thought it best to send forthwith this express, that your Honor might take the most speedy measures for opening the road. In the meantime, we have taken the liberty of writing to the representatives of our county, to inquire whether the Assembly had made provision for opening the road, and in such case, to encourage the people to set about it immediately; also, to send the flour without delay to the mouth of the Connogocheague, as being the only thing left to avert the mischiefs threatened by Sir John. We acquainted Capt. Rutherford with our design, who highly approved of it.

* For soldiers.

† I omit Sir John's Hudibrastic expression, which, though rendered classic by the genius of Butler, is still forbidden to ears and eyes polite.

We expect to be at home in six days. Please to excuse the blunders of this letter, written, as it is, after one o'clock at night.

We are, Sir,

Your most obed't and humble servants,

GEORGE CROGHAN,
JAMES BURD,
WILLIAM BUCHANAN.
ADAM HOOPES.*

REV. RICHARD PETERS TO JAS. BURD, (COL.,) AT SIDELING HILL, ON THE NEW PROVINCIAL ROAD.

Mr. Maxwell's, May 27th, 1755.

SIR:—I laid down the road you are opening, to the General† and Sir John St. Clair, and they all mightily approve of it. The General, in particular, expressed his acknowledgments to you and the workmen, and said that he would not march one foot to the northward, until you came up to him, and assured him of a good wagon-road to the Yhioagany, he would, I might depend upon it, stay until this road was finished at or near the place of its intersection with the road of the army from Wills' Creek to Monongahela mouth. It is a road of the utmost consequence, as he expects his provisions by this road, and has ordered a magazine of stores to be laid in at Shippensburgh, and to be carried to him in July through this road.

* On the 19th of April, 3 days after date of foregoing, Col. Burd, Mr. Buchanan and Mr. Hoopes, issued "an advertisement," offering large pay for laborers on the roads laid out in Cumberland county, to the Yoyhiogain, and camp at Will's creek.

† Braddock.

You are not to proceed on the road to the camp at Wills' Creek now, but make all despatch possible with this road to the Crowfoot or Yhiogany. In case of any danger when you are over the Alleghany hills, apply by express to the General; and, whether danger or no, as soon as you are over the Alleghany hills, send an express to him with the news, tell him your numbers, any accidents that may have happened, and the time when you think you shall meet him. Do me the honor to write me an account of your progress, and Mr. Maxwell, or others in this neighborhood, will get it to my hands. The General, the officers, the whole army place their account on this road, and the offsets that may be made from it. I am, &c., &c.

This work will redound to your glory, and the advantage of Shippensburgh.

It is the General's orders that the road be brought up to the very place through which the army passes to the fort, on the Ohio; but as you approach him within ten, fifteen, twenty, or thirty miles, he will, on your application, cover you and assist you likewise. You will be pleased to make the road good and easy for wagons, in every low, stony, or hilly place. Twenty feet wide is enough in any place, and fifteen where it is very difficult. The change from thirty to twenty feet was judged right and reasonable.

SECRETARY PETERS TO COL. BURD AND THE COMMISSIONERS AT THE NEW ROAD.

Philadelphia, June 19th, 1755.

SIR:—I have the favor of yours. To-day is the fast-day. To-morrow Mr. Armstrong (the Assembly man,) will be dispatched by the Assembly, and, I make no doubt, will bring a sufficient sum of money with him to buy the necessary provisions. So keep up your spirits, and I hope your provisions will not fail hereafter.

Your conduct is agreeable, and deserves our thanks.

I am, Sir,

Your affectionate, humble, &c.

The Governor says he will come to you, as soon as the Assembly rises.

ROBERT H. MORRIS, GOVERNOR OF PENNSYLVANIA, TO COL. JAMES BURD, CUMBERLAND CO.

Philadelphia, July 3d, 1755.

SIR:—I have, by this post, the honor of a letter from General Braddock, who desires, 'that as it is not pefectly 'understood in what part your road is to communicate 'through that to which he is now proceeding to Fort Du-'quesne, this may be immediately settled by me: and an 'express sent after him, with the most exact description of 'it, that there may be no mistake in a matter of so much 'importance.' I could have wished the General had enquired this of you by a special messenger, but as he has thought proper to write to me upon the subject, I must refer him to your judgment, not being able to form any of my own, for want of information. I took it for granted, by the reports that the Commissioners made on their return from examining the country, and laying out a road to Mononghiale, in the most convenient places that the waters and mountains would admit, 'that such road must pass by the 'Turkey Fork, or three Forks of Yohiogany, and that there 'could be no road got to the northward.' If I am right in this, then it should seem to me that as the General's road passes through to the Great Crossings of Yohiogany, which is but three miles from the junction of the three branches that form the Turkey Fork, the place where the two roads can best meet is at the Great Crossings, and that you must open and clear your road so far as that water. But if I am mistaken, and your own experience can find a better place, then, after consulting with all the persons of judgment along with you, you are to name some other place to the General, and give him a draught and oral description of it, and send it to him by express, for which purpose I have wrote a letter to Captain Hog, to dispatch away one of his officers, who may at the same time give a verbal account to the General, and explain all matters that may remain doubtful, or want explanation. I approve of your maintaining the General's detachment, and hope you make everything as agreeable to Captain Hog and his officers, as the place you are in will allow.

The Commissioners have a discretionary power in all matters respecting either the price of wagons or provisions, which I must desire they will make use of in such a manner as that there may be no loss or hindrance to the King's business, or to the clearing of the road, which I expect will be finished time enough for it to be used by the army as a road of communication between it and this Province. And you will likewise take care that the Province be not imposed upon by unreasonable and extravagant bills. I propose to be at Shippensburg next week, and there you may write to me on any subject, in which you shall think my advice and acquaintance necessary. Pray, consult together immediately, and let the General be informed by express, with all possible expedition, of the place where you will enter into his road, with draughts and an exact description, and be sure mention the time that you think you shall be there, to the General.

Sir, your most humble servant,

ROBERT H. MORRIS.

RICHARD PETERS, (SECRETARY,) TO COL. JAMES BURD, CUMBERLAND CO.

Philadelphia, July 3d, 1755.

SIR:—Yours, of the 19th ultimo, came by the post yesterday, and, as twelve days have intervened, it is hoped that the price of wagons is fixed to mutual satisfaction, and that you are well provided with all necessaries, and not far from the general road; the Commissioners surely have in themselves the power of giving reasonable prices as well for wagons as for provisions, and will take care that none go from them for want of paying, or agreeing to pay them an higher price if it cannot be done for less. The work must be finished at all events, and if one price is objected to another must be fixed on, so that there be no obstruction to the work. It proves, indeed, heavier than was at first imagined, but what then? It is not the less necessary on that account, and as you have had more trouble and are likely to have the weight of all upon you, I am instructed to tell you that all reasonable expenses will be paid, and all moneys or victuals, or necessaries advanced, will be honorably allowed for. Public faith will not admit of any one doubting this.

The Commissioners will, I am sure, from the method

taken when I was there, be always able to certify, at the foot of each account, the quantity and quality of everything used, and Joseph Armstrong or John Smith, or whoever has made the contract, will likewise certify it; and when this is done, who can doubt but all will be paid to entire satisfaction. On all differences about this, the Commissioners (to whom the work is committed,) must be judges, and take effectual care that the best be done that the nature of the case will admit of, but always so as that no obstruction be put to the finishing the road. The General desires the Governor will send an express to him, to settle the exact place where your road is to come into the general road. Now this cannot well be done by the Governor, at this distance, he therefore writes to you on this subject. I take it that your intentions are to carry the road to the Turkey Fork, or Forks of Yohiogany, where there are three branches. I am told that the General's road passes within three miles of these branches, and if so, it should seem best to carry the road over one of these branches to the General's road. But as that part of the country is entirely unknown to us, it is judged proper that one of the officers, on receipt of the Governor's letters, go to the General's with your account of the place, where our road may be brought to intersect the road taken by him. I believe the Province will not scruple to pay for the provisions necessary to support the escort, and think you did well to undertake it till further order. I shall be always ready to do justice to the zeal and industry with which you have prosecuted this necessary work. I have not heard a word from Mr. Samuel Smith, or Mr. Joseph Armstrong, or Mr. John Smith, of any obstruction or difficulty, either in point of wagonage or provisions, or whiskey, whence I am confirmed in my opinion that all is well hitherto. I am the friend and well-wisher of the Commissioners, to whom this is written, as well as to you.

(AN EXACT COPY OF THE PRINTED PAPERS, LETTERS, &C.)*

Pennsylvania, July 7th, 1755.

Last night arrived here from Halifax, (via Boston,) in fourteen days, and proceeded this morn to General Braddock; by him we have the following important intelligence, viz:

Boston, June 30th.

On Tuesday last, arrived here, Major Bourne, who left the English camp, near Chigneck, the 18th instant, charged with dispatches from the Honorable Col. Monckton, to his Excellency, Gov. Shirley, and brings the agreeable news, that on the first day of this inst., in the evening, his Excellency, Gov. Shirley's two regiments arrived at Chigneck, in the Bay of Fundy, and on the 2d, landed and joined his Majesty's regular forces there, near Fort Lawrence; that the English troops marched the 4th, and invested the French Fort of Beau Séjour, (now called Fort Cumberland,) in the evening, and in their way took possession of Fort du Buott, where the French had a battery of four small pieces of cannon, &c., block-house, and had posted four hundred men to oppose their passage, who soon returned, when closely attacked, and left their block-house and the sundry adjacent houses in flames. Our forces began bombarding the French Fort from batteries, advanced within five hun-

* It appears to have been a copy made for his father by Ch. J. Shippen, from letters, broadsides, &c., received in Philadelphia.

dred yards of it, on the 13th, which, by a continued firing, obliged the French to surrender before our batteries were finished, on the 16th inst. The fort is a regular built pentagon, with 26 pieces of cannon, mounted chiefly of twelve, nine and six-pounders, and one ten-inch mortar, was garrisoned by one hundred and fifty regular troops, and four hundred peasants, commanded by Mons. du Chamleon,* was plentifully furnished with provisions, as well as all other kind of stores; the regular troops are to be transported to Louisbourg, and under a prohibition of bearing arms in North America for six months. The fort the French had on the side of the bay, where they had requested the same terms of capitulation, and Col. Winslow marched with five hundred men the same morning that Major Bourne came away, in order to take possession of it, and that the [troops] were soon to sail for St. John's river, where it is not doubted they would have the like success.

Extract of a letter from an officer in our army, in Nova Scotia, from the camp before Beau S'jour.

June 11*th*, 1755.

We had a very pleasant passage of four days, from Boston to Annapolis, where we all arrived safe on Monday, 6th of May. We remained there till Sunday, the 1st of June, when we all sailed and got up here the same night, but did not land till morning.

We were not a little pleased to learn, on our arrival, that the French had received no reinforcement from Louisburg, as we heard at Boston, nor were they apprised of our design till we got here; the troops were quartered, the night we arrived upon the settlers and inhabitants, and Tuesday even-

* A mistake. It was De Vergor.—*Bancroft*, IV. 197.

ing, near our fort, which day was employed in preparing to march to the French side, on the next day. Accordingly, on the 4th of June, (being the Prince of Wales' birthday,) at break of day, the troops were under arms, and joined by all the regulars of our garrison, both officers and soldiers, except Capt. Hamilton, who was left to command Fort Lawrence, with whom we left Capt. Brintnal, and about sixty New England troops. At 7 o'clock, the whole army being two thousand four hundred and fifty men, marched with four fold persons in the front. As soon as they arrived at the carrying-place, where was a log house with some several guns and a detachment of twenty troops, they fired upon us, which was soon returned, and they driven from their post, which they set fire to, as they did to all the houses in their retreat, between them and the French Fort; and before night almost every house at Beau Séjour, together with their new large mass houses, the priest's house, hospital, barns, &c., to the number of about sixty, were burnt to the ground. We had only one man killed, (a Sergeant of our garrison,) and eleven wounded, one of which is since dead; the French had five or six killed, and we suppose more, how many wounded we can 't tell. Our troops traversed the ground on their side, and reconnoitered the fort pretty near without being fired on; their people were employed in protecting their fort by a glacis and covered way, as if they did not intend to surrender without a dispute, but turned their defence chiefly against an assault, sword in hand, expecting we would storm the garrison, as they did not apprehend we had any artillery except our * * * * * *

They have since taken off the roofs of their houses, and pulled down the chimneys to prevent the ill consequences of our cannonading, as they are now satisfied we have battering cannon and thirteen-inch shells. We have landed our cannon and mortars, and the troops have been employed in clearing a road for transporting them to the place where we designed to open our battery, which we hope will be effected this night, (within three hundred yards of their ramparts.) We had reconnoitering parties frequently out, within half musket shot of the fort, which they frequently fired at, but have as yet not hurt us a man. They have in the fort about one hundred and fifty regulars, and as many of the inhabitants; the remainder, with the women and children, are gone off to the Bay Verde and other distant places. We have not lost one of the men we brought from New England, either by enemy or sickness, and have only three slightly wounded; our men are in high spirits, and perform their fatigues (which are not a few,) with great cheerfulness.

Fort Cumberland, June 18*th,* 1755.

I have now the pleasure to congratulate you on the surrender of the French Fort, (which we have named as above.) I have not time to write you the particulars, the Fork and Bay Verde, and Gasperau, have surrendered upon terms. Col. Winslow is gone there this morning, to take possession. We have lost but one of our New England troops, killed on opening the trenches, and about twelve wounded, who are like to do well. We began to fire some small shells the 13th, some larger ones the 14th, the 15th with a few thirteen-inch, and the 16th they desired to capitulate, the terms being agreed upon. Col. Scot, who commanded in the trenches, marched in the same evening in one procession, and struck the colors yesterday, the memorable 17th of June, the same day that Louisburg surrendered to us. The English flag was hoisted and saluted by all the guns in the fort. We found twenty cannon, the largest twelve-pounders, one ten-inch mortar, plenty of ammunition, and provisions enough to have held out a long siege. I heartily wish our army at the south-east may meet with the same success as we have. I believe there never was so considerable a conquest with so little loss. We had not a man hurt by all their cannon and shells, and I suppose at a moderate computation, they fired five hundred shot, and sixty or eighty shells.

Extract from Another Letter.

We did not expect, by their preparations, they would have surrendered so soon, and it was chiefly occasioned by a shell which broke through one of their case-mates, whereby four officers were killed and several wounded. Among those killed, was Mr. Hay, an ensign of ours, in Warburton's regiment, who had been taken a week before by some skulking Indians, as he was passing from our fort to the camp; and we learn, by other letters, that the New England men behaved to the satisfaction of everybody; that the only New England man killed was Joseph Pille; that the French have lost, in all, eight officers, and fifty-one private men and three Indians.

Halifax, June 21st.

Yesterday arrived Capt. Spry, in Majesty's ship, Tongeers, who brought with him here the Alcides, a French ship of war, of sixty-four guns, taken by Admiral Boscawen's squadron, cruising off Louisburg. The English fleet have also taken the Lys, a French seventy-four gun ship, with eight companies of French troops on board, several officers and engineers, and the military chest. It is hoped, by this time, the Admiral has fallen in with the rest of the squadron. Capt. Spry has also taken a brigantine and schooner.

Besides the above, we were informed, by letters and passengers, that the French were designed for Louisburg, there to refit and put themselves in a condition to attack Halifax, and reduce all Nova Scotia; that the Lys had eleven hundred men on board, and a General, who was to command all the French troops on the Ohio, and elsewhere in these parts; that the French fleet had a large train of artillery on board, and thirty engineers, the chief of whom was killed the first broadside; that the Lys lost seventy men in the engagement, and the ship that took her, thirty; and that Capt. Taggart was arrived at Halifax, from England, with cannon and other military stores, and that another store ship is daily expected.

EDWARD SHIPPEN TO COL. BURD.

Lancaster, December 17th, 1755.

DEAR MR. BURD:—I just now received a letter from Mr. Hamilton, informing me, that he and Mr. Franklin should set out to-morrow on a journey to the frontiers on the Delaware, and from there all along to the Susquehanna, and perhaps over that river, in order to get the Province put into the best posture of defence they are able. Neddy writes me that there is to be an Indian treaty held at Harris's,* on the 1st of January, but does not say who are to go

* Now Harrisburg.

in it from Philadelphia. The Governor went to New York on the 8th instant, and is not yet returned, but I expect he will be at the treaty, and it is very probable I shall accompany him.*

I hope you are going on briskly with the fort, for you may expect the Governor will be there before he returns.

CHIEF JUSTICE SHIPPEN, TO HIS FATHER, AT LANCASTER.

Philadelphia, February 18th, 1756.

HON'D SIR:—If my brother Jo. has an inclination to go into the army, there never was a better opportunity, and perhaps never will be so good an one as now. He might get recommendatory letters to General Shirley, who will admit him as a volunteer, and upon the first vacancy give him a commission. Young fellows of less merit and much fewer friends, are continually promoting. What inclines me to give this hint is, the consideration of Joseph having nothing to do in the world, at a time of life when activity would be of the greatest use.

If it suits your circumstances to put him into trade, the prospect of an approaching war would be very discouraging, and without some scheme of life he will probably spend his youth in idleness.

This thought occurred to me since my return home, I thought it more proper to mention it to you than to Josey himself, who will unquestionably follow your advice in this as well as everything else.

* A treaty was certainly very desirable on many accounts; for I find in a letter from Ch. J. Shippen to his father, (Dec. 8th): 'Our 'Commissioners set every day, and I understand will offer rewards 'of £40 or £50 for every scalp.'

DR. WILLIAM SHIPPEN TO HIS BROTHER, AT LANCASTER.

Philadelphia, March 8th, 1756.

DEAR BROTHER:—Upon the receipt of your last favor I went to Peter Chevalier's farm, where I met with young Hopkins with a few scions from Point-no-Point of the Priest apple. He says it is a fine apple to look at, and that the tree grows very handsome, but that the apple won't keep; and for that reason they have cut all the trees down save one. Will. Peters has promised to bring me those he promised you, but he has not as yet done it. I thank you for your kindness to my son Jo. He has finished his Ledger to pretty good purpose, and has gone over Euclid again, and I think can raise a proportion secundum artem.

I would write you a long letter about our late politics, but I take it for granted you have had it already.

His Excellency Gov. Belcher is cheerful and well. I just now received another very complaisant, religious letter from him.

EDWARD SHIPPEN TO COL. BURD, AT FORT GRENVILLE.

Lancaster, March 24th, 1756.

DEAR MR. BURD:—This gives you a copy of a joyful letter, which I received just now from Mr. Peters, and to let you know that we are all well. You have heard, no doubt, of William's Fort, lying on the Virginia side of Potomoc, being taken by the Indians, and thirty-three of the men killed; only two men made their escape out of thirty-five. It seems the fort had little or no ammunition, and as soon as the enemy perceived a slack firing, they immediately took advantage of it. I hope our forts are better provided.

If the Six Nations should stop the Delawares and Shawanoes from giving us any more uneasiness, you are then to apprehend your danger from the French and their own Indians, who have had such a bad example set them, and seen so much success attend our perfidious Delawares, in getting about two hundred scalps. I suppose that you have heard that Mr. Croghan threw up his commission. He is expected here every day. I shall endeavor to persuade him to something, before he goes to General Shirley.

(COPY.)

'DEAR SIR:—Scarroyady and Montour are returned, with 'an agreeable account of the treaty, and say, positively, that 'a party of warriors of every nation were to set out before 'they left Colonel Johnston, for Susquehanna, to call off the 'Delawares and Shawnese, or, in case of refusal, to cut them 'off. Pray inform the people at Harris's, and in every part 'of the frontiers, with this account of the return of our two 'friends, and the hearty disposition of the Six Nations.'

REV. MR. PETERS (SECRETARY) TO EDWARD SHIPPEN, OF LANCASTER.

Friday, April 16th, 1756.

SIR:—I thank you for your kind letters, and hope your son will return with laurels and scalps. I very heartily wish him all kinds of prosperity.

Please to inform Mr. Chew and the other gentlemen,

that the Assembly is adjourned to the 24th May, so that I shall have some respite.

I am, &c.

COL. SHIPPEN TO CAPT. THOMAS M'KEE.

Fort at Hunter's Mill, April 16th, 1756.

Sir:—Be pleased to enlist for me some young, active men, of no less a size than five feet six inches high, agreeable to the terms in the advertisement I herewith give you. As fast as you enlist them, I beg you will send them to Mr. John Harris, who will entertain them, till I send him further directions.

After they have taken the oath of fidelity and signed it, let the Justice of Peace sign a certificate of it, setting down the day of the month. I leave with you five dollars, to give to the men, each one dollar for their advance money. Let the articles of war be read to each man, before he enlists.

Your compliance will much oblige, dear sir, &c.

P. S.—They must be enlisted for not less than twelve months.

REVEREND JOHN BLAIR TO COL. BURD, AT CARLISLE.

Shippensburg, April 17th, 1756.

Dear Sir:—I am sorry we can't have the pleasure of seeing you here at this time,—as to news, I scarcely ever expect to hear any that are good, respecting our public affairs, until our land confesses the hand of God in his judgments that are upon us, and our governments alter their maxims.

You have sustained your share of loss in the late melancholy action. That affair has given us the greatest damp we have yet met with, and the loss of our men has weakened this neighborhood. I have been trying, since, to prevail on our people to form into larger bodies, but without success. I think this valley will soon be waste, and indeed all about Rockey-firing is almost so already. I can say little or nothing about your domestic affairs, except that the cattle are brought this far, and there is yet a good deal of hay.

COL. CLAPHAM TO CAPT. JOS. SHIPPEN, AT LANCASTER, OR ELSEWHERE, BY SERGT. BRADDOCK.

Philadelphia, April 18*th*, 1756.

SIR :—Yours I received, and hope your recruiting is attended with success. I have herewith sent a detachment from the regiment, consisting of thirty-one men, under the command of Serg't Braddock, to be disposed of in any manner you shall think most conducive to the good of the service. I have seventy more in town, almost ready to march, which I intend to dispatch with all possible expedition to the place of rendezvous; as some provision for their coming may be necessary, I thought proper to give you previous notice of it, and assure myself you will omit nothing in your power necessary for that purpose. I have sent forty-six supernumerary bullet-moulders by this party, which you will distribute as you think proper, and am, sir,

Your most obedient humble servant,

WILLIAM CLAPHAM.

EDWARD SHIPPEN, OF LANCASTER, TO COL. JOSEPH SHIPPEN, AT SHAMOKIN.

Lancaster, August 5th, 1756.

DEAR SON:—Last Saturday night I received your affectionate favor of the 25th and 28th ult., in one sheet, very agreeable, except what you say concerning the unkind treatment which your brother-in-law has had. But we will sing an opera song, and so forget it. I am glad to hear Col. Clapham deserved no blame, respecting his march and management of his regiment. I am very well pleased to see you go on so briskly with your barracks and stockadoes, and that you are likely to be quite secured from the attacks of your enemies.

If you find, on examination, that the hill on your opposite side, has an easy ascent for an enemy, no doubt the Colonel will represent it in a proper light to the Governor, that he may order a small fort to be immediately erected there. Your present situation must be very pleasant, but remember now is coming fast on fevers and agues, and intermittent fevers, and pleurisies. I have been credibly informed, that in August and September, it is always so very sickly at Shamokin, that the Indians endeavored as much as possible to be absent in these months. My advice to you and Mr. Burd is, immediately to provide yourselves each with a dozen doses of the bark, taking one every morning, fasting; and after you have done this, you should rest a week, and then take six doses apiece of Æthiops' minerals,* every morning, and these cordials, under God, will preserve you in health, that you may be able to assist others, who will

* Now better known as 'Blue Pill.'

not be advised until they get sick, and indeed, were I the commanding officer, I would send to Philadelphia for Jesuit's bark, enough for the whole regiment, for a twelfth part of what would cure them when sick, would be enough to prevent disease. Pray, give the Colonel a hint of this. I told you his honor, the Governor, was gone to Bethlehem, to hold a treaty with the Delawares, &c., but I did not know, at that time, that Israel Pemberton and fifty more of the Quakers, were gone to attend the treaty, and to inform the Indians that their people throughout the continent, were using their utmost endeavors to raise £15,000, to be put out to interest for them forever. The last papers are not come to hand, nor indeed have I received any from Franklin these two weeks; I imagine somebody takes them up at our Post Office. I am very much of your opinion concerning the Delawares and Shawnese, taking up the hatchet at Col. Johnson's, against the French, except a few scattering ones, who went from the Susquehanna to the treaty at Onondago; but, I hope that Col. Clapham has desired Ogaghiadauha to come back, and bring him an exact account of that treaty. I wrote a congratulatory letter this morning, to your cousin Allen, on the recovery of little Peggy and Billy from their innoculation, and took that opportunity to say a good deal to him, of the great importance of keeping up our forts at the frontiers, and more particularly that at Shamokin; not that I think it just upon wealthy men, (who have raised their fortunes by trade, to the great encouragement of all the tradesmen, such as ship-carpenters, smiths, sailmakers, and many others,) to issue an inundation of paper money. But, I propose that the Assembly shall borrow thirty or forty thousand pounds, and pay six per cent. interest for it, till we know my Lord Loudon's determination about these forts, though I think he will have matters stated to him in such a light, as he will put you all on the establishment, and keep all there, and that he will not look upon the other forts as vain things. He is gone to Albany, and it is not known when he will be in Philadelphia. He came in the Nightingale, and took a prize, bound from Martinico to old France, worth £20,000, and sent her into New York. I am very glad your detachment of a hundred men were prevented from proceeding as far as was intended, because they might possibly have brought in some scalps, which would have been difficult to make up with the Delawares and Shawnese, should they now have entered into any agreement with us about a peace; though, as I said before, I see no likelihood of it.

Mr. Burd mentions your and his intention to apply for a furlough, to come to see us a little, but, although you will always be very welcome guests, yet as everything stands on a very ticklish foundation, I can't now advise you to such a step. You tell me the Colonel* frequently says he will soon resign and go to Philadelphia, if he intends to do it, I suppose he is not to be persuaded against it, but I imagine he will stay with you till Capt. Lloyd returns; nay, he is obliged in honor to wait for an answer to the letters, he and all officers have sent to his honor, the Governor; for, if your requests are all granted, you are bound, in justice to your King and country, to remain there until the time of your enlistment is over; and if your demands are not all complied with, you are not obliged to resign, while you have a good store of provisions, and ammunition found you for this month, and at the latter end of it, a full stock

* Clapham.

laid in to last till April, (I speak of yourself and Mr. Burd,) unless the men should desert you for want of their pay, which I hope will not be the case. As to your own pay, you will be sure of it sometime or other, and so will Mr. Burd, of his, either as major or captain, if not for both. However, be that as it may respecting his pay, I advise you both to stand your ground, while ever the men will stand by you, provided you have necessaries as just mentioned. You received your commission from the Governor, and if Mr. Burd is not paid for two services it will not be his fault. He intended it should be so, and would fulfil his intentions; poor gentleman, had he but the command of the purse strings, for he is certainly a fast friend to you both, and for that you are greatly obliged to him, as it has never been in your power to merit anything more at his hands, than your cheerful acceptance of the commissions for the present service, at too low a pay. Col. Clapham is a stranger to him, and so is Capt. Lloyd. I say they are strangers to him, and to all your friends at Philadelphia, and so its no matter how they act. But as to yourself and Mr. Burd, their eyes and whole dependence will be on you both, and on nobody else.

We are apprehensive that Port Mahon is taken by the French, if so, it is a bad beginning for the English. Our troops have marched for Crown Point. It seems Gen. Winslow, who commands the seven thousand New Englandmen, let Major General Abercrombie know that he would be under no command, nor march with him and the English troops, but was resolved to try that fortress with his own strength, to which the General consented rather than to suffer such a number of fine fellows to return home again. Then the Major General said, he had a request to make to

Gen. Winslow, and that was, that he might be suffered to follow with his regulars and artillery, that in case of a repulse, he might in his retreat have some protection. This was also agreed to, and Abercrombie is to keep exactly two miles behind Winslow's army.

P. S.—The best physicians in the world, agree that a man at forty should chew a little piece of Jesuit's bark, and swallow the spittle, two months, fall and spring, every morning, and should take a few doses every year of Æthiop's mineral. This last is a great sweetener of the blood, and frequently given to children for that purpose. Doctor Chew is the most lavish in the praise of these medicines.

EDWARD SHIPPEN TO COL. SHIPPEN.

Lancaster, August 31*st*, 1756.

DEAR SON:—I wrote you very fully by Capt. Lloyd, and whether he forwarded my letters and the papers by the express that was killed, I am at a great loss to know. However, I send you a copy of cousin Allen's letters to me, and told you what Mr. Hamilton said, too, concerning the menacing letter sent by the officers to his Honor. Neddy writes me that Mr. Morris also was of opinion that you were all punishable, but added,—'that although he could 'not account for your and Mr. Burd joining in such a 'mutinous manner with the Colonel, yet he intended to do 'you both all the service in his power.' Mr. Hamilton makes great allowance for your youth, but cannot excuse Mr. Burd. We were lately alarmed here, with a story as if our Fort Oswego, on Lake Ontario, was taken by the French and Indians, an army said to consist of six thousand. Neither have we much reason to think it otherwise. Here is what we have heard since. An officer came here two days ago, from New York, and says Oswego is besieged only, and that my Lord Loudon has detached a thousand men to its assistance. And what Dr. Shippen says to me of the 28th inst.,—'my Lord Loudon writes that he hears 'at Albany, from Oswego, that it is taken by the French, 'and apprehends it is true, but I imagine it must only be 'one or two of our out forts, and not Oswego, which I think 'cannot be given up under four or five weeks to any force 'at all.'

My Lord Loudon has sent up here for Capt. Herbert, (a genteel Switzer,) to bring away his one hundred and fifty men as soon as possible.

Our Assembly is in town. Stand your ground, and sign no more papers to the Governor, of such a tenor. Capt. Lloyd showed me all which you had signed, and I objected to the menacing part of it, but he said you were all resolved to show spirit.

I would have you and Mr. Burd to be very cautious of venturing to come to see us, lest you should both be way-laid. How you will get this letter I cannot tell or imagine, the Indians are said to be so thick about.

SIR JOHN ST. CLAIR TO COL. BURD.

Belvil, September 29th, 11 *at night,* [1756.]

DEAR SIR:—I received yours at nine this evening, and have lost no time in answering it. I am sorry that the Post Master here is above his business.

I transfer you Sir Jeffry Amherst's letter to me, as much as relates to provisions, viz:—

'I have wrote particularly to Col. Bouquet, regarding 'the provisions that are to be allowed to the provincial 'troops, inhabitants, &c., and whatever he may approve of, 'will be allowed of in the provision account, and passed ac-'cordingly, in certificates to be granted on the treasury. 'But I do not suppose the account you sent to me was pre-'sented to you, to be paid for in cash here.'

These were the accounts of Fort Cumberland, of the same value as part of yours, so that you see I can do nothing in them. Had it been in my power, no man should be readier to serve you.

If Doctor Græme is in Philadelphia, pray send him out to Betsey, (I mean lady St. Clair.) I have just dispatched a messenger to Græme Park for him, as my dear girl continues very bad.

I am, with much truth,

Dear Colonel, &c.

CHIEF JUSTICE SHIPPEN TO HIS FATHER, AT LANCASTER.

Philadelphia, September 14th, 1756.

HON'D SIR:—Enclosed you have two letters from Mr. Allen on the subject of my last, which, after perusing, please to seal up and forward by some very safe hand. Mr. Cross has wrote to several of the ministers. How the thing will take I cannot tell. It is proposed that Mr. Stedman and myself should be up at Lancaster on the election day. It is a very disagreeable task to appear to solicit for one's self, but if it is necessary, I must submit. You'll please to speak to George Ross, Dr. Kuhn, and what others you think have interest, and let me know how the thing is thought of. What two members we must be put in the room of, must be left to the people; but I should think if Jimmy Wright inclines to stay in, it would be wrong to leave him out of the ticket. The chief thing is to split the Dutch, how that can be managed I do n't know till I hear your sentiments. We are pushing for a change in all the counties, and shall certainly carry it in some.

The militia and associations are about making a junction in this town. What will be the event I cannot yet tell, but we shall very probably carry two or three good men for this county.

The conduct of the Assembly, with regard to this excise bill, is universally condemned: first, to request the Governor to show them his instructions, that they might avoid offering any bill that should interfere with them; and as soon as the Governor had gratified them, to send immediately a bill directly in the teeth of one of the positive instructions, is a behaviour utterly indefensible. If the Governor's amendments should not be acceded to, and so the bill should drop, it will forever ruin the credit of the present members. I impatiently expect to hear from you.

EDWARD SHIPPEN (CH. J.) TO HIS FATHER, AT LANCASTER.

Philadelphia, Sept. 19th, 1756.

HON. SIR:—I received your favors of the 15th and 17th inst. and am very sorry to hear that the prejudices of the people are so strong against Mr. Stedman. What to do we cannot tell. Mr. Hamilton declares positively he will never sit in Assembly after filling the station he has; and we can think of no other proper man here that is known in the county. The thing must be left to the people. For my part I am not anxious to be in the House. A seat there would give me much trouble, take up a great deal of my time, and yield no advantage to my family, whose good I am bound first to consult. And really, in these times, it is no easy matter to provide as one would wish for an increasing family. However, as our friends thought it was necessary I should stand for Lancaster, I gave my consent, and am still willing to stand if there is any chance of succeeding.

No ticket is yet settled for this county, nor can any be until the result of the yearly meeting at Burlington is known. Galloway and Baynton are talked of by some: Jacob Duché and Coleman by others. Nothing fixed.

CAPT. DAVID JAMESON TO WILLIAM ALLEN, ESQ., AT PHILADELPHIA.

Fort Augusta, December 4th, 1756.

HONORED SIR:—The great concern I am under for the irregularities in our regiment, and the sincere desire I have for the provincial service to go on well, have caused me to break through the diffidence under which I have labored for some time, as to representing the bad state of our regiment, and complaining of the injuries which I have received from Col. Clapham. The character you bear of exerting yourself for the public good has induced me to exhibit them first to you, for your consideration; in the hope that, if they appear to you likely to obstruct the service of his Majesty or the Province, you will deliver the enclosed complaint to his honor, Governor Denny, and at the same time make mention of those things I write concerning the regiment: if you think otherwise, then I beg you to excuse my presumption, for I act from a mistaken notion of my duty.

The men of the regiment are not yet trained, and therefore of no more service to the Province than a number of men, gathered together in a hurry, would be.

The Col. often damning the service, pointing out the disadvantages of serving in this Province, and threatening to leave it and go to the Indian country, whereby many officers and men are prejudiced.

Officers frequently arrested, and sometimes kept in confinement longer than the express words in the act of Parliament permit. Capt. Salter and Captain Miles (the latter tricked out of his commission) were confined some weeks, when there could not be the least pretence for it, there being a sufficient number of officers to hold a general court martial at the time of their confinement.

An exclusive license given to one Taaffe to sell dry goods, and all other persons prevented, (Mr. Hunter, who sells liquors, only excepted,) by the Col.'s orders, from bringing any goods whatever to this fort or fort Halifax, whereby both officers and men, that before this prohibition used to get their things at reasonable rates, are imposed upon, and obliged to pay extravagant rates.

Officers frequently used ill by the Col.; the whole body of them often called by him a pack of rascals; officers and men prejudiced against the Commissioners by crafty insinuations. Some of the former had nearly been drawn by the Col. into what (I think) was mutiny; for that remonstrance, which was sent to the late Governor Morris, as it was first drawn up and assented to by the Colonel, instead of having in it, "beg liberty," had "insist." This was objected to by several persons, and, contrary to the Col.'s desire, was altered.

Thus far, sir, the duty which, as I think, I owe to my king and country, has made me venture. I say venture, because I know not but what I have done may be looked upon as ill, because Col. Clapham is my commanding officer. You may depend that all, or at least the most of what I assert, can be sufficiently proved. Now, sir, I submit to your wise judgment, whether the complaint and the things mentioned in this letter ought to be made known to the Governor.

I am, honored sir, &c.

CAPT. THOMAS LLOYD TO COL. JAMES BURD.

Philadelphia, February, 1757.

SIR:—Your favor of 16th inst. and that of January 9th, came both to hand; since the receipt of which the Colonel has done himself the pleasure to write to you by Capt. Trump. I am directed by the Colonel to inform you, that he desires no person may be admitted to lodge in his quarters except the Doctor and Ensign McKee. Enclosed is a list of the men whom the Colonel would have to hold themselves in readiness to march down to Philadelphia at a minute's warning and be employed in recruiting. Since my last we have undoubted assurances of the embarkation of twelve regiments for America, to be made on the 10th of January last. Four of the officers' transports are yet missing. The first batallion of Royal Americans ordered to take the field the first of March. Lord Loudon hourly expected here to preside at a conference of all the Governors to westward of

York, in order to which Governors Sharpe* and Dinwyddie† arrived last night. It is said a fleet has sailed from Brest with a force sufficient to storm Hell. Whither they direct their course is unknown, but it is imagined that Jamaica or the American continent will taste the fruits of their labors. May continual tempests and everlasting rain whelm them all!

A bill for 60,000 pounds, including Proprietary estate, and since, another, excepting that estate, have been rejected, upon which two of the venerable sages of Pennsylvania are going home with their fingers in their eyes. Boscawen convoys the twelve regiments with seventeen sail of the line, and we promise ourselves fair winds and prosperous gales to waft him over.

I have exhausted all my subjects and have nothing more to add, except that I hope the pleasure of seeing you in a few days, and am, &c.

COL. JOHN ARMSTRONG TO MAJOR JAMES BURD, AT FORT AUGUSTA.

Carlisle, February 22d, 1757.

DEAR SIR:—Your favor of the 17th instant for John Lee is just come to hand, and the readiness on your part, in regard to the two companies from that regiment, is very satisfactory. I have not yet received an answer to the letter referred to in yours, but look for it early next week. Soon after the receipt of it, if the orders are not countermanded, I shall write you per express. Let me inform you, in strict confidence, that my designs are not to march to the enemy's

* Of Maryland.

† Of Virginia.

country, but only to waylay and endeavor to intercept their descent upon us. This is all that can possibly be done before grass grows and proper numbers unite, except it were agreed to fortify at Reastown, of which I yet know nothing.

I think the route for your men, in case we rendezvous at Littletown, will be as straight a course as the woods will permit from Augusta to Aughwick—Juniatta to be crossed by a raft. As to the horses you mention, they are a principal part of the instructions I now wait for, which, if not granted, I don't see how we can leave the forts or inhabited parts, but if your people can carry four days' provisions, it will fetch them to Littletown. Next week, by a general court martial, we are to try the conduct of English Dick. The Commissioners and we are at great odds. It seems to me as if the devil had got possession of Bennie Franklin. We hear the money bill is not yet passed—that Franklin and Morris are to go to England.

This week his Lordship, with sundry of the neighboring Governors, are expected in Philadelphia. May God preside in that Congress for his glory and the British interest. Not less than 8000 more troops are daily expected in Halifax. A report is going that a York privateer on their own coast has lately discovered fourteen sail of French ships, upon which the privateer returned to York, and an express was immediately dispatched to his Lordship at Boston; but this story we hope will not prove true.

Mr. Thompson has obtained furlough to Philadelphia with expectation of obtaining a pair of colors, and it is not improbable that others, from the conduct of the Commissioners, will resign the service. His Royal Highness, the Duke, has been pleased to express great satisfaction on the news of the destruction of the Kittanning and death of Capt.

Jacobs. The Proprietaries send a general letter of thanks, and I believe some presents. Capt. Callender has lain by the chief part of this winter with the rheumatism. You'll doubtless have the news-folio by the return of your officers now in town.

My wife joins in our good wishes to you, and I am, with friendly compliments to Captain Shippen, Doctor Morgan, &c., sir, your real well-wisher and very humble serv't.

P. S.—I am sorry for your indisposition, and think the reasons of it are justly accounted for. If we should have a set of damp heavy weather I fear it may impede the service in sundry places. I doubt a scurvy next summer from the constant use of salt meat.

CAPT. DANIEL CLARK TO COL. BURD, AT FORT AUGUSTA.

Harris's, February 22d, 1757.

Dear Major:—This minute I arrived here from Philadelphia. Matters stand in so great a confusion there that I cannot give you any news of moment.

The Governor has rejected the money bill, the tenor of which was that by the tax of one shilling the pound one hundred thousand pounds was to be of all estates, real and personal, in the province, the proprietary only excepted, and to be sunk in four years. Lord Loudon was expected in Philadelphia last Saturday; the Governors of Virginia and Maryland were arrived there before I left it. The Royal Americans I heard were commanded to prepare for a march to Halifax, which is to be the place of general rendezvous, and the Halifax brigade ordered to Philadelphia, by which some imagine there will be an expedition carried on from these parts. I am afraid we Pennsylvanians shall have no share in it; the Assembly will never give any sum or sums for its use until Mr. Franklin returns from England, who is immediately setting off. Colonel Clapham had received his beating orders. He went to the Commissioners for the money; told them the consequence of delays at this time, when this regiment was so near being free, &c. They told him they could not be free in a better time. He sent his boys for his horses. For my part, I don't think that Fort Augusta will ever be ornamented with his presence. Captain Jameson's grievances will be inquired into by Colonel Armstrong's officers. It was reported in town that Captain Jackson was a lunatic. This policy was a heavy slap on the face of the author. It gave the gentlemen a worse opinion of him,* (if it were possible for them to conceive a worse,) as they were all convinced it was only made use of as a plea of defence.

I am extremely ill with the pain in my breast. I am under a necessity of taking some medicines to prevent its growth. Dr. Shirley advised me strongly to it lest it turn to consumption; so I must stay in Carlisle until I get better. I have no leave from my commanding officer for this. I beg you will excuse me if the Colonel should come before I am able to return to the regiment. The Assembly prepared another bill, but of the same tenor with the former, desiring the Governor may either pass the bill or discharge the troops. My compliments to Captain Shippen. I am your most obedient, &c.

P. S.—I have sent you the last news and three magazines.

* Col. Clapham.

EDWARD SHIPPEN TO MAJOR JAMES BURD.

Lancaster, March 24th, 1757.

DEAR MR. BURD :—Captain Shippen wrote me lately that you had encouraged your good gentlemen soldiers to stay with you till the 1st of April, to defend your fine Fort Augusta, which they had labored so hard to build for one of the most glorious and most gracious kings in the whole world : they know whom I mean, George the Second, of Great Britain, France and Ireland, King, Defender of the Faith, &c., who, I hope, will one day reward them very well for their fidelity and loyalty; and if he should not live to do it himself, as he is now grown very ancient, yet there is no doubt but the noble Duke of Cumberland, who always inquires after his trusty and well beloved gentlemen soldiers, as well in America as in other places, will requite them for their extraordinary services, as he did all the gentlemen soldiers who fought so courageously and beat the rebels, taking great numbers of them prisoners, at the time of the last rebellion in Scotland. I am very sensible your corps has been kept too long out of their pay, but I have great reason to believe they will not only very soon be paid all their arrears, but paid most punctually for the future, for since my Lord Loudon has arrived at Philadelphia, I am informed that the Governor and Assembly have agreed to raise a hundred thousand pounds and to pass a militia act, the sweets of which I hope you will feel, and expect before the tenth day of April, Capt. Young will carry every farthing that is due to them. Wherefore I shall only beg my compliments to all the worthy officers and gentlemen soldiers at Fort Augusta, and so conclude,

Your affectionate father, &c.

EDWARD SHIPPEN TO MAJOR JAMES BURD, AT FORT AUGUSTA.

Lancaster, March 26*th*, 1757,
Saturday, 5 *o'clock P. M.*

DEAR MR. BURD:—Though I had not heard that Captain Young was going up to Shamokin yet, I ventured to tell you I made no doubt of his being sent up with the men's pay as well as the officers', and the £100,000 money bill was also passed according to my expectation. I congratulate you on the good news. Col. Clapham has resigned, (so Doctor Shippen says,) and if he is pleased you have no cause to be displeased, I am sure. I never doubted his skill in fighting Indians, nor his natural disposition to quarrel with and abuse all mankind. It was always my opinion, that if a man had the natural abilities and education of an Indian or a Negro Prince, and if he were never so famous a General among them, yet until he changed his manner and savage nature and became like one of us, and had had the advantage of keeping gentlemen's company; I say, unless those changes had been wrought in him, he was as unfit to command a batallion belonging to the king of England as ever Shengar or Jacobs were.

RICHARD PETERS (SECRETARY) TO JOSEPH SHIPPEN, (COL.)

April, 1757.

The Governor inclines to send six twelve, or eighteen-pounders to Fort Augusta, and with them, attairil.

The General and Sir John St. Clair say, they will be of

no use. Pray contrive some way of satisfying these great men of their mistakes.

Yours, &c.

I dine at Willing's.

GEORGE CROGHAN (COL.) TO MAJOR JAS. BURD, AT FORT AUGUSTA.

Harris's Ferry, April 3d, 1757.

DEAR SIR:—After a long silence I beg leave to acknowledge the receipt of your several favors. To-morrow I set off for Lancaster with the Indians; but have not been able to fix the time the treaty will hold, as there is a great number of Indians yet to come in. Some, I suppose, will come in by the way of the fort, and others by Easton.

I left Philadelphia the 29th of March. Lord Loudon had been there ten days, and was to set off for York the next day. He had a Congress with the several Governors, which ended before I left town, but he is so capable of keeping secrets that nothing has yet transpired. A packet arrived in York the 24th of March with express to his Lordship, by which it is considered that Mr. Byng was condemned to be shot for cowardice, but recommended to the mercy of his Majesty by the Council.

'Tis said there is a fleet of twenty odd sail of men-of-war, with seventy transports, sailed from England with ten regiments on board for North America, two of which are Highland regiments: young Lord Lovatt has one of them. 'Tis generally thought this great embarkation is designed for Cape Breton or Quebec, or perhaps both. There is little talk of an expedition against Ohio, but I believe there will be a number of Provincial troops rendezvoused at South Carolina, though this is kept a secret. The New England government has engaged fifty companies of dragoons to join his Lordship and the King's troops; no field officers, and 'tis said there will be no field officers in the Provincial troops in those Provinces. This is perhaps only talk.

I need not inform you that Colonel Clapham has resigned. I suppose Captain Young has informed you of that; and I believe he is in great disgrace with his Lordship, as well as with most gentlemen in Philadelphia.

EDWARD SHIPPEN TO COL. BURD.

Lancaster, April 5th, 1757.

DEAR MR. BURD:—I am glad you have got so well rid of Clapham as your Colonel, and if the poor fellow should desire a license to set up his trade at your camp, I hope you will grant him the favor; for though he did not understand the business of a commandant, yet he can bring credentials from the Carbuncle, alias Rednosed Club, in Boston, of his skill in *hat making;* and as he was well recommended by my countrymen as a good *wood-ranger,* he can never be at a loss for materials to make up. But if there are no sheep in the wilderness to fleece for wool, perhaps there are wolves and buffaloes to be found to answer his purpose; for a man, who had not cunning enough to keep a ball at his foot which turned him £365 per annum, could not be expected to outwit foxes, beavers, and such other sagacious creatures.*

The behaviour of Capt. Shippen and yourself to the officer

* As proposed, this is quite a specimen of Mohammedan ups-and-downs. See Edinburgh Review, Jan. 1854, p. 290.

who refused to mount guard in his turn, reflects honor on you both; and, as he is a gentleman of good parts and of pretty school education, he will improve that act of indulgence to his own advantage. First of all, the thought will fill him with shame, as you had no regard to lex talionis, and then, if he has any ingenuousness, he will naturally make the proper concessions, and behave, as Captain Staats Morris says, 'excessively well for the future.' I don't wonder in the least that he is afflicted with the gripes. How could he, as he is a physician, expect that the Colonel's poultry, fine as it was, could set well on his stomach, when he and his two companions devoured them all without the sanction of Major Burd and Captain Shippen; or I should rather say without the favor and enjoyment of their company at the banquets. However, Providence has made it up to you, and I congratulate you too on the addition of your turnips, &c. Your poor sick man will be all the better for them.

RICHARD PETERS (SECRETARY) TO COL. BURD, AT FORT AUGUSTA.

Philadelphia, April 7th, 1757.

SIR :—I am obliged to you for your kind favor. As Col. Clapham declines further service, my duty, as well as the particular attachment which I have to your person and family, will lead me to serve you, inform you, correspond with you, and promote your interest, ease and satisfaction, all I can. At present you stand well with the Governor.

Could you preserve the soldiers from leaving the service all would do well, and I should not doubt of your making a gallant defence. I will write you by Peter Bard, as I shall then know in what temper the garrison is, after Capt. Young's visit.

I am in the greatest haste. I wish you everything your heart can desire. God bless you.

SECRETARY PETERS TO MAJOR BURD, AT FORT AUGUSTA.

Philadelphia, May 1*st*, 1757.

DEAR SIR:—I am favored with two of yours. The Governor expressed great satisfaction in your conduct. Pray write to him by all opportunities. It is not here that the intelligence given you by the Six Nation Indians would have any foundation in it; but as our accounts agree that there are seven hundred men more at Fort Du Quesne and four hundred at Venango, it is not improbable but parties of fifty or sixty French and Indians, perhaps more French to a party, will drive a final stroke on our back inhabitants this spring and in harvest. The two main points are to screen your numbers, and to obtain intelligence, in which I am sure you will do all in your power, as you know the country would think you could convey letters to Colonel Armstrong, who may post his men so as to cut off those parties in their retreat, though I believe the routes will be from above Drahaye through the country east of Susquehanna to the Minnicks and Northampton county, where murders are daily committed, and new parties expected.

Dr. Morgan's business very much requires his waiting here, and particularly his attendance at the commencement, and I would fain have persuaded the General to order him down, but he did not choose to do it, on receipt of your letters. I think if you would so far favor him as immediately to order him on service with the recruits here, it would, at this time, be particularly kind and agreeable to him. You can judge best of the circumstances of your command; but if those will admit, his friends here, who are all yours, desire much that he may not let slip the taking his degrees at the commencement. No news, no packet, no fleet, no trade—all are embargoed. I am, sir, yours affectionately.

COL. SHIPPEN TO MAJOR JAMES BURD, FORT AUGUSTA.

Lancaster, May 19th, 1757.

DEAR BROTHER:—I have the pleasure to inform you that we all arrived here Tuesday night, except Capt. Lloyd, whom we left at Harris' ferry, too much indisposed to ride; he therefore gave me your letter to the Governor, and desired me to wait upon him, with the other Captains, agreeably to your instructions. When I came here, I found the Governor, Col. Stanwix, with other Royal American officers, and Mr. Hamilton, at our house drinking tea, and as soon as I came into the parlor, Mr. Hamilton introduced me to them. We all waited upon the Governor yesterday morning, but his hurry in the public affairs on his hands, prevented him from finishing our business with him.

This morning I waited upon him myself, and had a long conversation with him in regard to recruiting the regiment, when he told me, he had recommended it to the Commissioners to allow the officers £4 for every man they enlisted for 3 or 4 years, and £5 for any enlisted during life. But they say they cannot consent to allow us any recruiting expenses without a full board, and they assure us, when they go to

Philadelphia, they will take that matter into consideration, and I believe they will allow us something, the Governor having recommended it to them very strongly. They have given us £25 each to recruit with for the present, as they have but little cash with them, and they will supply us with more money whenever we shall draw upon them. They insist that all the troops (except 300 in garrison), shall be employed for the future in scouting and ranging, as the Act of Assembly directs, because they say they cannot otherwise pay them agreeable to law. The small pox continues amongst the Indians; 14 of them died of it. The treaty, I believe, will be over to-morrow. As soon as I know the purport of it, I will inform you. The Indians have lately killed a great many of the inhabitants about Swatara Gap, four of whom were yesterday brought in town scalped, as a spectacle for a number of Quakers now in town. The officers are to set off this afternoon for their different homes to recruit. I am therefore in a great hurry. The Governor has summoned the Assembly to meet in Philadelphia soon, in consequence of the late murders.

EDWARD SHIPPEN TO MAJ. JAMES BURD, AT FORT AUGUSTA.

Lancaster, May 22d, 1757.

Dear Maj. Burd:—Captain Shippen, a most welcome guest, brought in your agreeable favor of the 14th instant, and found Col. Stanwix, the Governor, Mr. Hamilton, and Captain Munster (a German Baron,) and several other officers of the first rank, drinking tea with us; to every one of whom Mr. Hamilton immediately introduced him.

I have engaged nine wagons at the Col's request, to go to Winchester for powder and lead, (being the remains of General Braddock's cargo,) to be all bought and left there, excepting as much as he shall deem necessary for his army of two hundred or three hundred men at Carlisle, or Shippensburg, whither he is going next week, and if I can possibly spare the time, I have promised to go with him to show him the country, and the best place of encampment. We have had May meetings of the Indians here, to whom valuable presents have been given by the Governor and the Quakers; but as Tedyescung and the Indians who were expected along with him, were not come, a very handsome part is reserved for them. The Governor went off this morning very privately by way of Reading, leaving the Speaker of the Assembly and some other members, besides a majority of the Commissioners, except Mr. Lardner, who is gone home. You will see by the enclosed papers, that the savages have been committing more murders near Swatara, and it appears to me that unless the Militia Act be passed, with the Governor's amendments, we of this borough shall, in less than a month, become the frontiers. The Quakers want to have the choosing of officers. Several Quaker preachers, with all the principal men of that Society, attended the treaty. The Indians assisted this government to send a message to the Senecas and to Tedyescung, to come down with the Shawanese and the Delawares, to hold a treaty with their brothers the English, hinting at the same time, that it would be very prudent in us to give up some points respecting some late purchases, rather than not to bring about an accommodation of matters, especially considering that we either would not, or could not fight, and they made no doubt but a peace might, by such means, be concluded between us. And according to their judgments, Mr. Jacob Gary, an Indian trader, is employed to go to Diaboga, to invite these Indians down, and Mr. M. Lee, I hear, is to escort some of those Indians (who are here) up to your fort, where they are to plant Indian corn this spring, for their subsistence, as they are to settle near the fort. You will see by the papers, that Admiral Byng was shot the 24th of March, 1757, on board the Monarque, which belonged formerly to the French. The Governor has issued his warrants to all of the Assembly, on the 30th instant.

I was absent from the 8th ultimo to the 7th instant. I spent two weeks of my time at Philadelphia, almost one with good Mr. Morris, (who sent you his compliments,) and another with Governor Belcher, and riding about the Jerseys, and coming home. And as to your savage black Colonel, (for you know the natives of Guinea have countenances as black as their diabolical hearts, and our Indians blacken their faces that they may be of the same color with their hearts also,) I can only say if he knows what humility* is, that he has had enough of it, ever since he came to this borough. He appeared, it's very true, with the crowd at the court house, once or twice at the time of the treaty, but was so totally neglected by the Governor and the officers and the gentlemen present, that he seemed to be sitting upon needles the whole time. Nay, I would not pretend to affirm that even one of his sad colored brothers took the least notice of him, so that it seemed to me that he was condemned by the universal consent of the whole human race, except the pity that Captains Croghan and McKee took on him, for they visited him pretty often at his lodgings at Frederick Yesser's, upon the score of mere charity; so

* Humiliation.

that with their good company and a little good punch, he has been able to survive the mortification of seeing himself lowered from the state of a colonel to the condition of a nobody. Israel Pemberton has reported about, that you are a useless member, and of no service in your station, but your happiness is that nobody except the Quakers believe his report, (nor they neither,) for the Governor and Mr. Hamilton, Mr. Peters and Mr. Lardner, and many other deserving gentlemen take your part, and speak very respectfully of you. I had this story from the several gentlemen above mentioned. Capt. Young has done justice to your character, and to Capt. Shippen's, so that said Israel Pemberton may snarl, but will never be able to bite you.

I have good reason to believe said Black a mere colonel, who goes about, I doubt not, like a lion, not a roaring one, for that he durst not do, but a whispering one, seeking whom he may devour.

Write very respectfully to the Commissioners, who, I hope, have a regard for you. Captain Shippen is not returned from Reading.

CAPTAIN JOSEPH SHIPPEN TO MAJOR JAMES BURD.

Lancaster, May 31st, 1757.

DEAR BROTHER :—I wrote you on the 19th or 20th inst., since which, I have not had the pleasure of an opportunity to write till now. On Sunday, the 22d inst., the Governor ordered me to attend him to Reading and Fort Henry. The Governor took this small excursion on the frontiers to spirit up the people to act for their own defence, and in these troublesome times he would have visited all the forts on the eastern frontiers, if he had not been obliged to meet the Assembly in Philadelphia yesterday. There are eleven forts garrisoned by Col. Weiser's battalion. The Governor intends to evacuate them all but Fort Henry, Fort Allen, and Fort Hamilton, between which all that battalion, consisting of 450 men, will be continually ranging, so as to leave always a garrison of 50 men in each fort. The Governor has, with the consent of the Commissioners, ordered the Colonels to raise 150 men for the immediate defence of the Eastern Frontiers, and they are to be discharged when our regiment is complete, and the three companies of his battalion can be recalled from fort Augusta. I was absent from hence eight days with the Governor, which retarded my recruiting so long, in which I have found little success, having enlisted as yet but five men. Captain Jameson writes me he has got but six. Captain Hambright has had better success; the day when all the Captains came to town to wait on the Governor he enlisted twelve or thirteen of our discharged Dutchmen, by assuring them that they were not to go to Shamokin, nor do any kind of work, but to range and scour the woods continually. This pleased them so much that they have been endeavoring to persuade all their countrymen they meet with to enlist with Captain Hambright, by which means I believe he has now thirty recruits. He himself left this town ten days ago, since which I have not heard from him, but his brother, (together with ten or twelve of his men,) recruits here, and gives every man a dollar, besides a pistol, which I can't afford to do unless the Commissioners would allow it, so that nobody recruits upon the same footing with Captain Hambright, and so can't expect equal success. I enclose you the original beating orders by Mr. Peters' desire, as he had not time when here to write to you.

Captain Lloyd, (from whom I have not yet heard,) did not come by way of Lancaster. Perhaps the Governor, Commissioners and a number of gentlemen and Quakers being here, prevented him. They continued here four days after I arrived. He desired me to apologize to the Governor for his not coming, that he was sick at Harris'. Christian Vertz behaves himself extremely well, and takes a vast deal of pains to persuade men to enlist, and if we have not much success it is not for the want of efforts. I should be glad if you'd send me Vertz' discharge, with a blank for the date, that I may have it ready for him when he chooses to go, though he says he will continue with me while I have occasion for him. I think he should be paid as Sergeant while he is recruiting with me, he deserves it as well as Bane, who assists Captain Work in recruiting. If you think proper I would be glad if you'd mention him as a Sergeant in his discharge, and then he can receive Sergeant's pay from Captain Young. I have not learned yet whether the Commissioners have come to a determination about an allowance for our recruiting expenses. I told them that unless they did something for us in that respect the recruiting service would necessarily go on very slowly, &c. I am informed that my lord Loudon sailed last week from New York, that a day or two before he ordered a general press there, by which means he got 1100 men very quickly. It is imagined from thence that the English fleet and transports are arrived which every body is impatient to hear. Jemmy Pike who came to town yesterday, asserts that Major Lewis, of Virginia, with fifty soldiers and one hundred and seventy Cherokees, has destroyed some Indian town on the Ohio below Du Quesne, taken nineteen Indians prisoners and brought home five scalps. I hope this may be true; most people believe it.

I shall write to my brother for your sword and one for Mr. Scott, as I am disappointed in going to Philadelphia by meeting the Governor here. Enclosed are the papers; my compliments to the gentlemen.

The Governor told me he could not tell me whether our regimentals were to be changed till he should see Captain Young in Philadelphia. He seems to like green, trimmed up with red.

EDWARD SHIPPEN TO MAJOR JAMES BURD.

Lancaster, June 16th, 1757.

DEAR MR. BURD:—And now I have begun this letter, I have little else to say than to tell you we are all well, except that just as Allen Burd begins to find the use of his feet,* poor Polly's heels are tripped up. She was taken with the small pox four days ago, and as her fever is not high, we have as great reason to think she will be as favorably dealt with as her brother. She lodges with her mammy Shippen, and will not be contented any otherwise.

Perhaps it may not be improper to inform you that I have here under my care, seven wagon-loads of powder and musket-shot, 50 six-pound balls, and plenty of flints, which Col. Washington sent me from Winchester (Fort Loudoun) by Col. Stanwix's orders, (being some of the remains of poor General Braddock's ammunition.) There were nine loads at first, but the Colonel ordered me to send him two of them to Carlisle, which I took care immediately to do. I refer you

* After an attack of small pox.

to Captain Shippen for information in relation to your recruits, &c., and for the newspapers; but I must observe, that the officers have been very diligent, and that Captain Hambright seems to have had the most success; and if he has not been too cunning in his business, he will have reason to rejoice at the thoughts of filling his company so soon. I hope he has promised his men nothing more than he is able to perform; I wish him very well, I am sure. However, I might relate you a little story of him, which caused me to smile last night at Gibson's, where I was with Doctor Thompson, hearing the complaint of a married woman against Clinch. Observing Clinch to sit while she was giving in her evidence; (we took notice of the same thing, but we said nothing;) but by-and-by he took occasion to speak to the prisoner again, at which I gave a gentle reproof, and desired him not to speak another word in an affair he could not possibly have anything to do with. He seemed a little crumpled at first, but presently came to himself again, yet I could perceive by his countenance he would not account more of us than a couple of wooden Justices; but, notwithstanding all I have said about him, I believe him to be a good officer when put upon the right scent, and kept within due bounds.

We wait now with great impatience to learn whether Lord Loudon is going against Louisbourg or Quebec. Various are the opinions about it; but be it against one or both, may God be pleased to give him success. I understand that Mr. Lee was confined by the Indians he was sent to accompany to Shamokin. I should be glad to know the truth of that story. I don't approve of your crossing the river with parties to attack any impudent Indians who may show themselves there in a small number, when a majority of them might be lying in ambush, resolving beforehand to attack your men or not, according to their number. No, no; let the dogs and their brothers, the French, come over to your shore, and try to decoy you if they dare, and then I think you will know how to deal with them, with all their stratagems. But don't misunderstand me; I am very sensible I am speaking upon a subject I don't understand, and must insist upon it that you take your own advice.

Captain Davis, belonging to Col. Stanwix's regiment, from Fort William Henry, and last from New York, tells us all is well, but that Lord Loudon has not yet sailed with his Government transports, for as he has but three men-of-war with him, and has heard from Halifax that five French men-of-war have been seen hovering off and on thereabouts, he does not care to venture till he receives certain advice of the arrival of our seventeen line-of-battle ships, with the transports from England.

CAPT. THOS. LLOYD TO MAJ. JAMES BURD.

Philadelphia, July 5th, 1757.

SIR:—His honor, the Governor, has ordered me to acquaint you, that Captain Jameson has his permission to be absent from Fort Augusta till he finds himself reinstated in his health; on which account you will be pleased to send down one subaltern the less, till he shall signify to you the recovery of his health. We have no news, of any consequence, but ill news—that the Fleet from Ireland is not yet arrived, though we flattered ourselves, from some accounts from the northward, (since contradicted,) that it was arrived; nor hear we a word of Lord Loudon. The nation at home is in the greatest ferment ever known, insomuch that almost a civil war is apprehended. Secretary Fox is reinstated at Westminster, and Mr. Pitt obliged to resign his place in his favor. 'Tis said, that Pitt was for confining the war totally to America, that Fox was opposide in his sentiments, and for carrying it into Flanders, with the very forces destined and embarked for America; which opinion pleased the Duke and Court best. The former was most popular and agreeable to the nation: in short, the Court espouse one, and the people the other, and nobody knows where 'twill end. I beg leave for Boon Penny, one of my recruits, to stay at Halifax till I come up, as I promised him at the time of his enlistment that he should not go to Fort Augusta before I did. He writes a very good hand, and will be an assistance to Captain Work in the store, and has borne commissions as Lieutenant and Ensign in his majesty's service. I hope you will have no objection to my keeping my promise with him,

And am, sir, &c.

P. S. I have leave to detain Knipp beyond the extent of his furlough on the recruiting service, and am, &c.

7th. We have now certain intelligence of the Fleet sailing, by a vessel which left Cork in company with them; 17 sail of the line, 2 ketches, 2 fire-ships and 150 transports, and parted from them 200 leagues off the land.

CAPT. THOS. LLOYD TO MAJOR JAMES BURD, AT FORT AUGUSTA.

Philadelphia, July 26th, 1757.

SIR:—I was disappointed in my expectation of a conveyance of the enclosed, and shall take the opportunity to let you know that I fear some difficulty will arise on account of the defective blankets and arms, &c., as the Governor told me, in a conversation on that subject, wherein I proposed their being given to the recruits, to save the expense of carriage, that the Commissioners being pressed on that subject, had refused, in a manner, to grant them, until informed what was become of those already given, for they had once completed the battalion, and expected no more such demands; (I don't know that the Governor meant this as an answer on that head;) but you must know they intended, I suppose, to pass an act that arms should never perish through time, age, and blankets never decay—in short, that everything which had the honor to pass through their hands, should acquire a sort of immortality. I have purchased, at my own expense, knapsacks for my men, and don't doubt the rest of the captains will think them necessary, as it is a much better way to carry their provisions and their clothes free from the effects of the bad weather, than osnaburg sacks, or any other kind of bags they can procure.

I have enlisted one Theobold Scheibel, a very decent and well-behaved fellow, who has been long in the German service, whom I would desire to recommend as a sergeant in our company, to which, from the regard I have for the fellow and his merit, I flatter myself you will have no objection. You observe, I remember, in a former letter, that some of the recruits are bad and unfit for service, insomuch as to oblige you to discharge them, for which I am sorry, and hope I shall not be a sufferer by it, as every one of mine have been examined and approved by the Governor. But, after all, it happens that the proof of the pudding is in the eating; and a man who looks very well, may prove, when tried, quite otherwise. Indeed, I can't say much for the looks of mine, and in a court of justice would advise some of them myself not to have great dependence thereon. However, I hope you will not conclude to discharge any till the regiment is complete, and the officers reimbursed what they may have advanced their men; some of mine are many pounds in debt to me—three of whom I purchased of their masters, and one at £14 expense.* The Duke of Cumberland is now at the head of 60,000 men in Westphalia—an army of observation—to be shortly joined by a body of Prussians. I suppose the good old man, his sire, is a little apprehensive for the safety of his electoral dominions. God guard him and all belonging to him, even Hanover.

I am, sir, with the utmost esteem, yours, &c.

This party of mine are a set of damned fine fellows.

JAMES READ TO EDWARD SHIPPEN, AT LANCASTER.

Reading, July 31*st*, 1757.

Dear Sir :—I am exceedingly obliged to you, for your very kind letter by Henry Hahn. There is much matter in it for my serious consideration; but there is nothing more pleasing than your giving me hopes of seeing you. I am sorry you so quickly returned Ozinde; and I must, when I see you, give my reasons why. The Grammar was published in 1736, and the Dialogues which I mention, not till 1749; that is the reason, in the former, he makes no mention of the latter. I know two grammars of the Greek language written in English. You shall hear of them, and

* Redemptioners; persons brought out and sold to pay for their passage-money.

of some other things, which, by your letter, I see you inclined to hear from me about. I am just now going to get together our night-watch, and must leave off. If I am not exceedingly hurried, (which, having no clerk who understands business, I expect to be,) I will write you pretty fully by Mr. G. Ross, when he returns from our court. I have not much fear about my Lord Loudon. I expect good news from him soon. Let us not despond. It is my request *now*, that when I write to you next, you would read my whole letter over, and consider what I write, before you mention anything contained in it; you will, *then*, know my reasons for this caution. What a terrible prospect have *we* in this quarter! I will soon let you know what reason I have to expect sad desolation! Strange officers! — surprising inactivity! I am of opinion, that, except in the regiment at Shamokin, there is no discipline on this side Susquehanna. I should, too, except the discipline observed by Dr. Busse.

I am, dear sir, your most obliged,
affectionate, humble servant.

P. S.—I beg you would put me in a way to get a supply of powder and lead of Colonel Stanwix. It would be a very great service done us.

CHIEF JUSTICE SHIPPEN TO HIS FATHER, AT LANCASTER.

Philadelphia, August, 1757.

HONORED SIR:—I suppose you must, before now, have heard the melancholy news of the loss of Fort William Henry, an event which has thrown us into the utmost confusion. We have no regular account of particulars: but, as well as I can collect them, I will relate them to you. On the news of the approach of the French army, General Webb, then at Fort Edward, despatched Col. Young, with 1300 men, to the assistance of William Henry, whose garrison consisted of about 2200. Col. Young seized an advantageous post near the fort, and awaited the arrival of the enemy, who appeared (about 11,000 strong) on Thursday, the 4th instant, and invested the fort. They were repulsed several times, both by the fort and by Col. Young, whom they attempted to dislodge three several times, but without success. We know nothing more of the action, but that on Monday following the garrison capitulated, by which 3000 men, together with a very considerable quantity of artillery, fell into the hands of the enemy.

The next morning the enemy appeared before Fort Edward. What has happened since, we know not—but it is the opinion of everybody that Fort Edward could not hold out long. We are in hope General Webb has not suffered himself to be taken. Should that be the case, we have lost an able general, and the only train of artillery left in North America. Where the victorious army will stop, we know not; not short of Albany certainly, perhaps New York. We hear that there is an embargo at New York, and not a boat suffered to cross the water, that they may be as full-handed as possible. Part of the Jersey militia is marched; more are going.

Pennsylvania does nothing. To complete our misfortunes, there is news of sixteen sail of French line of battle-ships in Louisbourg, expecting the arrival of my Lord; well prepared, no doubt, to receive him. Should he be destroyed, I'm afraid America is gone.

August 17*th*.

Since writing the above, Mr. Allen has received a letter from Mr. Jno. Watts, of New York, giving an account that Fort William Henry surrendered on the 9th instant, after a very vigorous defence, having expended all their ammunition, and split their largest cannon and mortars by quick firing. The forms of capitulation were, that the garrison should march out with all the honors of war, (that is, with their arms, drums, and colors,) and that they should not bear arms against the French in America, for eighteen months. After the articles of capitulation were signed, and the enemy admitted into the fort, our people were told they must leave their guns behind them, and they were accordingly escorted, unarmed, by a French guard, about a mile from the fort, and there left to the mercy of a large body of Indians, who scalped and slaughtered all they could. Out of eighty women and children, but ten escaped. Col. Munroe got into Fort Edward in his shirt, having been stripped, but not murdered. Good Col. Young was wounded in the head, his brain so affected that he is run mad. Capts. Ord, Furnace, Collins, with, I know not how many more, killed. What number of soldiers escaped their fury, is not yet known. The thoughts of such a horrid massacre chill my blood. Nothing but French perfidy and Indian barbarity, could have planned or executed so hellish a villany. Fort Edward was not attacked the 10th. Great numbers of men have marched from New York and Jersey; New England is all in motion. We are not without hopes that there will be so considerable a body collected, as at least to frighten the French from pursuing their victory.

As none but posts and expresses are permitted to leave New York, we do not hear how matters go, as often as we wish. This affair concerns us all so nearly, that, for my own part, I can think of nothing else.

EDWARD SHIPPEN TO MAJOR JAMES BURD, AT FORT AUGUSTA.

Lancaster, Monday, August 23d, 1757.

DEAR MR. BURD:—This covers a scheme of Mr.——for driving away the French; but this I am sure of, let it be ever so good an one, that unless we put it in execution very soon, they will drive us away. We have heard nothing since the post (which always comes on Saturday,) from Fort Edward, so that we are in hopes it has not been attacked, or if it has, that the enemy has not prevailed, or cannot prevail against it. We have all the reason in the world to hope for Lord Loudon's success against Louisbourg, and should that place fall into our hands, it will moderate the very great joy which possesses Monsieur's heart at this day, for having taken Port Mahon, Oswego and Fort William Henry from us. The English Lion is opening his eyes and ears, and I hope will roar first, and then tear up all before him. Let us hope that every demi-century will produce a Marlborough or an Eugene, (Generals,) for the land service, and as noble Admirals for that of the sea, as ever the English nation were blessed withal. May God be pleased to give us success against all our copper-colored cannibals and French savages, equally cruel and perfidious in their natures and the truth of what they say and promise, just as much to be depended upon as every thing which the old serpent said to our first parents in Paradise. I write by this conveyance to Captain Shippen, my love to him and compliments to the Rev. Mr. Steele, to Mr. Bard and the other officers of the corps.

The Indians rage, scalp, cut, and slash more and more at Swatara, and have lately began upon Paxtang, so that unless Hunter's Fort be kept open, all Paxtang will be obliged to move away with their families. And this day, Justice Galbraith has carried a petition from Paxtang to the Governor and Assembly, to remove the garrison from Fort Halifax, down to Hunter's Fort, as it cannot be supported by the Province.

I hope you both take bark every day by way of prevention of the intermittent fever, which rages almost throughout the whole Province. I mentioned this before.

CAPT. T. LLOYD TO MAJOR JAMES BURD.

Philadelphia, Sept. 4th, 1757.

SIR :—I have herewith sent —— recruits, the names of whom you will see in the roll. I am greatly obliged to you for the appointment of Sheibel and Gotlib, as Sergeants in my company, and am fully convinced that you will take no step prejudicial to the interests of the Captains of the regiment, who have never yet had any just cause of complaint against your conduct, and are fully persuaded never will. I am extremely sorry to hear of the [state] of your hospital, and believe nothing will be more effectual in preventing disorders in the garrison than the plenty of vegetables which your care has furnished them. My Lord Loudon has returned to New York, with ten regiments, prevented in his expedition by the arrival of a superior force of twenty-three sail of the line and 15,000 land forces at Louisbourg. His lordship is honest, brave and wise, and yet there is no character so sacred which envy and malignant obloquy will not attempt, no merit so great which ill-nature will not sacrifice. 'Tis for this reason that his lordship is censured, but 'tis only by the bad—and scoundrels who are themselves incapable either of acting or judging. Scandal is a tribute which all great men pay the public, yet, if amongst my Lord's enemies there should appear but one person worthy our notice, would'nt you be surprised to hear that my Lord Chas. Hay was he. My Lord, in order to discipline his men, exercised them in sham sieges and feign battles; and 'tis said that, in council, Lord Charles Hay asked Admiral Holborne why he did not divert his folks with sham fights as well as Lord Loudon. For this and other freedoms of speech he was arrested, though the third in command and a Major General. I told you, in my last, of the unhappy loss of Fort Henry, but Fort Edward is ours yet.

'Tis rumored, and we fear from too good authority, that the Duke's army in Flanders is routed, and himself slain. Avert it, heaven! though there is, from circumstances, room to apprehend its truth.

We have yet no Militia Bill, nor any likelihood of one shortly. Governor Denny's lady is arrived; he writes you by this opportunity. Barracks are to be built for the regulars in this city. Recruits are very scarce. Prague is not yet taken, though reduced to the utmost distress; and, except the report of the Duke's defeat, we have no European news, unless the taking of Bengal from the East India Company by the Indians themselves, together with the loss of more than two millions of treasure, is news to you. By ——! I think we meet with nothing but losses, and am tired with reciting them. I believe you think me like Job's messenger. I am sorry the comparison is just. Unhappy times! I hope, in return, you'll send me better news from Augusta. You can't conceive the low ebb our service is at. Colonel Munroe, in his capitulation with the Montcalm, has deprived himself of the whole of his garrison, which was 3000 regulars, for eighteen months. Men are wanted, and very scarce. Perhaps his lordship, for the want of them, may find himself under the necessity of establishing us. I wish he may; and am sure he'll find the benefit of it. 'Tis thought he'll dispose of some of his men in garrison, and lead his recruits into winter quarters, without attempting anything more this season. Give me leave, before I conclude, to observe one thing worth your notice: which is, that both lawyers and magistrates unite in asserting that we have no right to the same privileges with the King's soldiers, in regard to enlisting and desertions, and in every other respect. If a man enlists and recruits, we have no right to smart money, (which I never took in my life,) but a man may play the fool or the devil with us with impunity; if a man deserts, he may and welcome, for them; in short, they make such damned distinctions, that the recruiting work is a heavy burthen. Immunity from prosecution for a debt if less than £10 sterling, has been peremptorily refused. Nay, my drummer was cast into jail for 7*s.* 6*d.* currency, and I forced to pay it. I wish you would solicit this matter, by a letter to be laid before the House, in order to obtain a law in our favor. Some of the members told me it would be easily carried. I wish you would write to his Honor on that head, and he will lay it before them. I am sure 'tis necessary, and I know he thinks so, and if you apply for it, he will countenance it.

RICHARD PETERS (SECRETARY) TO EDWARD SHIPPEN, AT LANCASTER.

Lancaster, Sept. 12th, 1757.

Dear Sir :—The Governor is very importunate for the tavern fees. Pray enable me to quiet his demands. He expects much from your diligence, but says he never saw any return of fines, or a stated account for the Gov. from 10th August, 1756, to 10th August, 1757, from Lancaster, which he expects.

RICHARD PETERS (SECRETARY) TO COL. JAMES BURD, FORT AUGUSTA.

September 12th, 1757.

Sir :—John Young will tell you how difficult it is for me to get one moment for my friends; you give great satisfaction to the Governor and every one else. If a new regulation is made, throwing the three battalions into two regiments; one will, I think, be in your power. The second battalion of Royal Americans is now on its march to reinforce Colonel Stanwix, and one to Carlisle. All your friends are well. The continuance of Captain Lloyd in this city so long, had been taken notice of by some people who do not wish him well, and the Governor is blamed for performing unequal duty. If the Duke of Cumberland holds his ground and Prague falls into the hands of Prussia, all will do well; but if any accident happens to either, we shall be obliged to patch up a bad peace. I thank you for your favors. I deserve no more, being so bad a correspondent, but affection and readiness to serve you are not wanting.

CAPT. DANIEL CLARK TO COL. BURD, AT FORT AUGUSTA.

Lancaster, September 27th, 1757.

DEAR MAJOR:—I have this day sent off six men, which I hope, with the command, will arrive safe at Fort Augusta. I have kept them to assist at the election which is next Saturday. Captain Bosomworth's lady arrived here last night from New York, and informs, that his lordship has marched toward Lake George, and is determined to rebuild Fort William Henry this winter. Enclosed are the last papers. Our Assembly is now sitting. The people hope a militia law will be made at this sitting. Last week no less than twenty-two were killed and captivated in Hanover township. Lord Charles Hay is still at Halifax under an arrest, and will be sent home with the fleet.

Barracks for five thousand troops are building in Philadelphia. It was proposed they should be built at the head of Arch street, on one of the proprietors' lots, but Mr. Hockley forewarned them of erecting any buildings on the proprietors' lots, else they must expect to have forfeited them. They have since purchased lots and are going on very fast with the works. Colonel Weiser is now in Philadelphia, and I hear will resign. Captain Bosomworth, a Lieutenant and thirty men are stationed here, two companies in Reading, an ensign and thirty men at York.

CAPT. SHIPPEN TO MAJ. BURD, AT FORT AUGUSTA.

Harris', Sunday, at 12 *o'clock, October* 23*d,* 1757.

DEAR BROTHER:—The Governor (agreeable to the promises made the Indians at Easton,) has appointed John

Hughes, Edward Shippen, James Galbraith and Henry Pawling, Esqrs., Commissioners for constructing a stockade fort, and building a number of houses for the accommodation of the Indians, at Wyoming, which is an affair of great consequence, to be done immediately. The Governor has ordered a party of three companies to be detached from the Western battalion, to escort the above Commissioners to Wyoming, and to accomplish the work there, and he has appointed Capt. Mercer and myself to be two of the officers upon this service. The batteaux are to be employed in carrying provisions and tools, &c., for this expedition to Wyoming. The Commissioners will be here on Friday, and are to make no delay: therefore I am sent up with orders from the Governor to detain all the batteaux at Hunter's, till they come up. But upon consulting with Capts. Hambright and Mercer, I have concluded it is most prudent to suffer the batteaux to go up to Augusta with the present loading, as you will be in great want of salt, and the cattle for the garrison's winter provisions. This and other considerations have prevailed on me to suspend, in some measure, my orders from the Governor. I therefore beg it as a favor and as a thing of the greatest necessity, that you will, immediately upon the arrival of the batteaux at Augusta, dispatch them off again for Hunter's, that the Commissioners and the detachment may not wait there. I expect them up on Friday next, at furthest. If they are detained at Hunter's any time, all the blame will be laid at my door. Everything else I have to say, I must leave till I have the pleasure of seeing you, which can't be till the Commissioners go up. I've given the Governor's letters to you in Capt. Hambright's care, and the last news. I have something to say in excuse of Capt. Lloyd's not coming up now.

CAPT. THOS. LLOYD TO MAJ. JAS. BURD.

Philadelphia, November 15th, 1757.

SIR:—Ever since the loss of Mrs. Lloyd, I have been so indisposed as not to relish writing at all, or even able to write, for the most part, having been in a very bad state of health, which still continues. I wrote you some time past his Honor's answer when I waited on him for his commands to Fort Augusta, which, least the letter may have miscarried, I here repeat, namely, to make his compliments, and tell you he had ordered me to stay for some time. I have great reason to be tired of Philadelphia, and if it is agreeable to you, would be glad you would write to me with orders to return to my duty, in such manner that I may show your letter to his Honor.

SECRETARY PETERS TO MAJ. JAS. BURD, AT FORT AUGUSTA.

Philadelphia, November 18th, 1757.

DEAR SIR:—I am ashamed that the Governor has not given you leave of absence. The length of time and severity of your duty make it also of late necessary, as I observe by the return, there are only sixty-seven wanting to complete the regiment. All the officers now recruiting, may be ordered to their posts, and then you may be spared to meet your family. This shall be my endeavor to obtain for you from the Governor, who is afraid of leaving the command to any other person, lest accidents should happen, and therefore postpones answering this part of your letter. I have here no news of a public nature different from that you see in the newspapers. Poor Captain Lyon was taken lately by the English, and retaken by the French, and is now in a French post. It appears to me that the Commissioners will send no more things of any sort to Fort Augusta, till a new supply bill passes. All the sum of £100,000 is entirely expended, and a new debt incurred. Your conduct is highly approved. It is not, I assure you, for want of reminding the Governor, that there is anything wanting in the regiment. Lieut. Clark resigned, because he was not justly paid, and had no prospect of preferment. This is to yourself, as well as what I say above. My prayers attend the Commissioners at Wyoming. Col. Stanwix marches with five companies this day, from Carlisle towards Lancaster, where he takes his quarters.

COL. BURD TO THE GOVERNOR, GIVING THE CHARACTER OF THE OFFICERS OF THE AUGUSTA REGIMENT.

Captain Lloyd, a young gentleman of a pretty education and a good scholar; he has acted always as aid-de-camp to Col. Clapham, and has done no duty in this regiment, only mounted two guards since he came last from Philadelphia. He is a gentleman of a hasty temper, and his understanding entirely subservient to his extravagant passion, which is greatly prejudicial to himself and troublesome to all around him.

Captain Shippen.—My near connection with this gentleman, I hope, will apologize for me to the Governor for not doing justice to his merit. I beg leave to refer his Honor to Mr. Young, the Paymaster, or to Wm. Allen, Esq., and James Hamilton, Esq., for his character, and will only say that he does his duty with great punctuality.

Captain Work, a gentleman of good nature, does his duty with cheerfulness, and of good spirit.

Captain Jameson, a gentleman of education; does his duty well, and is an exceeding good officer.

Captain Hambright, a good soldier, and indefatigable in the service of his country.

Captain Trump, does his duty with freedom, and has shown a good spirit upon all occasions.

Captain-Lieutenant Davis, does his duty well, and a good officer.

Lieut. Garraway, a gentleman of some education, strictly punctual in the observance of duty, a good soldier, and ready to exert himself at all times in the service of his country.

Lieut. Clark, a young gentleman of education, a very good officer, does his duty well, and has a great deal of spirit and merit.

Lieut. Clayton, Adjutant, an exceeding good soldier, very active, and extremely assiduous in the discharge of his duty.

Lieut. Clapham, Jr., I can say very little about.

Lieut. Miles, Sen., does his duty pretty well.

Lieut. Atlee, a young gentleman of some education, a sprightly young man, has good spirit, and does his duty well.

Ensign Broadhead, a gentleman of little education but a very good soldier; does his duty well and cheerfully.

Ensign Patterson, a gentleman of little education, a very good soldier, and does his duty well.

Ensign Scott, does his duty pretty well.

Morgan, Surgeon, a gentleman of education, and does his duty very well.

Miles, Jr., a sprightly young man, does his duty very well; will make a very good officer.

Rev. Mr. Steele, Chaplain, acts in his station to the general satisfaction of all the officers, and claims their respect.

CHIEF JUSTICE SHIPPEN TO HIS FATHER, AT LANCASTER.

Philadelphia, Dec. 9th, 1757.

HON'D SIR :—I have spoke to two of the master chimney sweepers, about sending a boy or two to Lancaster, but they say they are at present so busy in town that they can by no means stir as yet. I hope to prevail on one to go in a short time.

The Governor has been prevailed upon at last to give his consent that Mr. Burd shall come down to Philadelphia, and I believe orders have gone up accordingly.

Morning Report of the Main and Quarter Guards of the Garrison of Fort Augusta, commanded by Capt. Joseph Shippen, Esq., December 31st, 1757.

COUNTIES.	MAIN GUARDS.	QUARTER GUARDS.		ARTILLERY.	
Chester.	1 Sergeant, 1 Corporal, 1 Drum, 18 Privates, 2 Patrols, 2 Matresses, Flocks, etc. 6 Sentries.	1 Sergeant, 1 Corporal, 12 Privates, 2 Patrols, 16 Total. 4 Sentinels.	2 Prisoners, etc.	6 Cannon, 2 Swivels, 3 Blunderbusses, 4 Muskets, in good order. 104 Cannon Balls.	IA Watch Coats, in good order, 19 Tomahawks, 15 Wheelbarrows, 6 Batteaux, 10 Canoes.

Officers round every two hours, Sergeants round every hour.

McKEE,

Officer of the Guards.

COL. SHIPPEN TO HIS FATHER, AT LANCASTER.

Fort Augusta, January 2d, 1758.

DEAR AND HONORED SIR :—I was favored with several of your affectionate letters two nights before the Major* left us.

I am sorry for the unfortunate accident in the accademy, between Mr. Smith and Mr. Allen's son. I hope the consequence of the quarrel will teach that gentlemen to practice more philosophy in his discipline for the future.

I believe Captain Jameson has lost the small book on fortification, you desired me to borrow for you from Captain Mercer. However, I will ask him when he comes up with the batteaux. I should have been glad to have had the pleasure of testing some of mammy's good minced pies, and enjoying all your companies with the Major at Christmas, but I must content myself with only having had the honor of feasting on a few *whortleberry pies,* made by the famous quondam cook of the brave old General Blakeny. Plain, wholesome repast.

CH. J. SHIPPEN TO HIS FATHER, AT LANCASTER.

Philadelphia, January 8th, 1758.

HON. SIR :—Conrad Weiser has resigned, and a commission is making out for Mr. Burd as Lieutenant Colonel.

Our Assembly have taken up William Moore and the Provost, and put them into custody for writing a libel against the former assembly. Thomas Bond and Phineas

* Colonel Burd.

(Bond,) were on the point of being committed on the same account. The latter was actually in the custody of the Sergeant-at-arms, but afterwards discharged. How the matter will end is yet uncertain.

Samuel Rhodes, William Griffiths, and Jacob Lewis, have purchased of the proprietors, all that piece of ground adjoining the house where the Governor lives, together with the ground on the opposite side of the way down to the dock, for which they have given a bill of exchange for two thousand guineas. They design to lay it out in lots for sale. Thomas Willing has almost agreed for the piece of ground adjoining his house for £900 sterling.

Mr. Burd is not certain when he shall leave town. The Governor is so dilatory, that no business can be done with him.

Mr. Burd has an account of Johnny Burd's death at Jamaica, and also of the death of another brother at Surinam.

JOSEPH SHIPPEN (COL.) TO MAJOR JAMES BURD, AT LANCASTER.

Fort Augusta, January 20th, 1758.

Dear Brother:—I had the pleasure to write you the 2d inst., per Mr. Bard, when I enclosed you the returns, &c., for the 1st January, 1758; since which several small parties of Delaware Indians have arrived here with skins to trade, at the store; among the rest came old King Neutimus, Joseph, and all their family; and we have now forty-three present, including women and children.

Job Chilloway (brother to Bill Chilloway,) came here

t'other day from the Munsey country, at the heads of the Cuyuga Branch, above Diatoga. He was born and bred at Egg-Harbor, is a very sensible fellow, and speaks the English language perfectly well. From all the circumstances of his conversation and behaviour, he appears to be a strict friend to the English interest. His releasing Armstrong's wife from the enemy Indians last summer, and the prudent precautions he used in sending her here, is a confirmation of my good opinion of him. He assures me that the only Indians on the Susquehanna who are our enemies, are those of the Munsey nation, and they are determined to continue the war against the English. He says, he understood from some of the Indians, when he came away, that a small party of French were expected next month from Niagara, to join a Munsey captain and some of his warriors; and their intention is to go towards the settlements near Delaware, and to take an English fort, situated at a place called by the Indians the Bending Hill, which we suppose to be Fort Allen. He further informs me, that last March he carried a parcel of skins to the French at Niagara, to purchase clothing for his family, which sheer necessity obliged him to do, much contrary to his inclination, observing that the unhappy Indian war had put an end to English trade; that while he was at that fort there were but five officers, and he computed the number of soldiers not to exceed 150, who by his description of their appearance and dress are regulars; that they mounted in the fort 45 pieces of cannon, some of which were the brass field pieces taken from General Braddock, which they intended in the summer to send to Fort Frontenac; that the fort was strong and pretty large, having in it a great stone house, three stories high, where the officers lived. He intends to return to the Munsey country in a few days, in order to bring away his things, and in the spring is determined to live among his brethren the English, with whom he has always enjoyed peace and friendship. I have the pleasure to inform you, that Captain Jameson and Lieutenant Garraway arrived here yesterday, with 12 batteaux, containing 6000 pounds of flour, 2 hogsheads of whiskey, 3 barrels of salt, and 20 bushels of Indian corn for the garrison, beside a quantity for Mr. Carson's store.

In the morning, I shall dispatch off Captain ———, Lieutenant Davis and Ensign McKee, with a party of fifty men in the batteaux, to make another trip, if possible, while the river is open and favorable. I have restricted the garrison to an allowance of one pound of flour per man since the first of January, and shall think it necessary to continue the same till Captain Davis' return with an additional supply. We have now in store 17,390 pounds of flour, and 91,481 pounds of beef.

Enclosed you have a list of prisoners here for desertion.

EDWARD SHIPPEN (CH. J.) TO HIS FATHER, AT LANCASTER.

Philadelphia, January 28th, 1758.

HON. SIR:—The affair of Will. Moore and Mr. Smith has put everything into a flame. Moore, upon being called upon, acknowledged himself the author, so that he was committed without any trouble. Smith denied the charge, which was against him, for aiding and abetting the writing, and publishing the libel; so a solemn trial came on, which lasted two or three days, and at last ended in the conviction of Smith. After his condemnation, he made a very eloquent and pathetic speech, which had such an effect upon the auditory, that about a hundred people joined in a general clapping of hands, in the face of the House. This, you may believe, gave great offence. The members started from their seats, and called upon their friends for assistance. The doors were immediately shut to, and, after the confusion was pretty well over, there was an inquiry set on foot for the discovery of the clappers; several were charged and committed to the sergeant-at-arms; the rest of the evening was spent in long harangues on the heinousness of the insult. The next morning, people were invited in to make discoveries, but, in so general and sudden affairs, few particulars could be fixed upon. However, the following persons were at last charged upon oath, viz: John Bell, James Young, Thomas Lawrence, William Peters, Richard Hockley, Charles Osborne, and William Vanderspiegel. They were sent accordingly to make their defence; some asked pardon, others were more stout, and would make little or no confession. The House has the matter still under consideration, and the above gentlemen are in the custody of the sergeant-at-arms, but permitted by him to remain at their own houses. Thomas Willing, apprehensive that he likewise should be charged, went voluntarily into the House, and acknowledged himself guilty, and made proper concessions; upon which he was excused, as having behaved with manliness and candor.

Mr. Lardner was charged, but was acquitted, upon proving he was not out of his own house all that evening. I make no comments on this affair till I see you. I shall only say that people are more equally divided in their sentiments of the Assembly, than has been usual. I have only told you the general part of the story; the particulars are so numerous and so circumstantial, that I will not attempt a relation by letter.

EXTRACT FROM MR. FRANKLIN'S LETTER,

Dated January 14*th*, 1758.

Benjamin Franklin insisted, in a conference with the Proprietaries, that when commissioners were named in a bill, the Governor might not strike out or change them at his pleasure, as none but his own creatures might be admitted, and the Assembly might as well trust him with the whole; and that it was an undoubted right of the House of Commons to name commissioners in bills, in all cases, where they thought it necessary and proper; and to have such commissioners so named, stand without alteration and amendment, and therefore our Assembly claimed the said privileges. To which he was answered, that, in such cases, before the House of Commons inserted the names of commissioners in bills, the rest was privately settled with the ministry by the committees, but, though it must be a privilege of the House of Commons, it did not follow that it was the privilege of a Pennsylvania Assembly; that we were only a kind of corporation acting by a charter from the crown, and could have no privileges or rights but what was granted by that charter, in which no such privilege as we now claim, was anywhere mentioned. *But*, says *I*,* your father's charter expressly says that the Assembly of Pennsylvania shall have all the power and privileges of an assembly, according to the rights of the free-born subjects

* Franklin.

of England, and as is usual in any of the British Plantations in America.

'*Yes*,' says *he*, 'but if my father granted privileges, he 'was not by the royal charter empowered to grant; nothing can be claimed by such grant.' I said, if then your father had no right to grant the privileges he pretended to grant, and published all over Europe as granted, those who came to settle in the province, on the faith of that grant, and in expectation of enjoying the privileges contained in it, were deceived, cheated, and betrayed. He answered they should have themselves looked to that, that the royal charter was no secret; they who came into the province, on my father's offer of privileges, if they were deceived, it was their own faults, and that he said with a kind of triumphing, laughing insolence, such as a low jockey might do, when a purchaser complained that he had cheated him in a horse. I was astonished to see him thus meanly give up his father's character, and conceived at that moment a more cordial and thorough contempt for him, than I ever before felt for any man living, a contempt that I cannot express in words, but I believed my countenance expressed it strongly, and that his brother, who was looking at me, must have observed it. However, finding myself grow warm, I made no other answer to this, than that the poor people were no lawyers themselves, and confiding in his father, did not think it necessary to consult any.

CH. J. SHIPPEN TO HIS FATHER, AT LANCASTER.

Philadelphia, *February* 16*th*, 1758.

HON. SIR:—I observe your rule for discounting, and think it much better than my own, which, however, I shall give you as what occurred to me from the reason of the thing.

Suppose I owe £100, payable six months hence. It is agreed I shall pay it now upon a proper discount. What is the sum to be paid? First, I consider it shall be that sum, which with its interest, will amount to £100 in six months.

Then from	£100	Then calculate the interest on £3 for six months, which is 1*s*. 9*d*.
Deduct half per ct. interest,	3	
	£97	Which added to £97 0*s*. 0*d*.
		Makes the sum £97 1*s*. 9*d*.

EDWARD SHIPPEN (CH. J.) TO HIS FATHER, AT LANCASTER.

Philadelphia February 21*st*, 1758.

HON. SIR:—I this day saw a letter from Colonel Gage,* giving a very discouraging account of the intended expedition to Ticonderoga. He writes from Albany that the forces would not be assembled at that place till the 14th instant; that things were not in that state of readiness which he expected, and that everything appeared to be conducted in a loose manner; that the snow upon level grounds was four feet deep, so that till a rain and thaw should come to settle it, they could not expect to make much head in marching; or if they should get before the place, that it would be impracticable to storm it while so deep a snow remained; that in short their success would much depend upon being favored with weather and some lucky accidents. He seems to intimate, that there might have been much better management in making preparation for this expedi-

* Afterwards commander of the British troops at Boston.

tion, of which he does not seem to have very sanguine expectations. He writes this to a friend in confidence, so that you'll please to be careful about mentioning it. There seems as if some kind of fatality attended all our affairs; what with cross-accidents, our inattention and the bad conduct of our superiors, nothing succeeds. Our Assembly sent an Indian trade bill up to the Governor, in which they appointed nine commissioners, most of whom the Governor struck out, and named others in their room.

Commissioners named in the Assembly, were:

Joseph Fox,	Abel James,
John Hughes,	Edw'd Pennington,
Jos. Galloway,	Sam'l Wharton,
John Baynton,	William Fisher,

Isaac Zane.

Commissioners named by the Governor, were:

Edw'd Pennington,	Samuel Smith,
William Fisher,	Tho's Willing,
William Coleman,	Will'm West,
Henry Harrison,	John Wilcocks,

Evan Morgan.

The Assembly sent up the bill again, with the following new Commissioners.

James Pemberton,	Thomas Wharton,
Joseph Richardson,	Enoch Story,
John Reynell,	Daniel Rundle,
Thomas Combs,	Plunkett Fleeson,

Peter Chevalier, Jr.

The bill is now with the Governor, but I believe will not pass. In that case, it is said there is a number of gentlemen who will apply to the Governor for his license, to carry on the trade in much the same manner as is proposed by the bill. They are to furnish the whole stock themselves, draw six per cent interest for their money, and five per cent commissions for managing the business.

Lord Loudon has applied to this province for eight hundred men, to be under his command the ensuing campaign, to be paid by us, and victualled by the King. What our Assembly will do I know not. A report prevails that the eastern battalion will be destined for that service, and that a guard of fifty men only is to be left at Fort Augusta. But this is only town talk, and therefore I cannot say how far to be relied on.

Mr. Hamilton sailed last Sunday from New York, and my Lord Loudon has set off for Connecticut.

I write you all our news, because you seemed to desire it when I last saw you.

JOSEPH SHIPPEN (COL.) TO LIEUT. COL. BURD, AT FORT AUGUSTA.

Philadelphia, April 19th, 1758.

DEAR BROTHER:—I have been here now a week, with Capt. Jameson, waiting till the money bill should pass, before I could safely purchase clothing and other necessaries for my company. The Assembly adjourned themselves from the 8th to the 18th inst., and now they are sitting to prepare another bill, laying aside the clause for taxing the Proprietary Estate, which must certainly be assented to by the Governor to-morrow or next day, unless he still insists to have new Commissioners. I waited with Capt. Jameson on the Governor when he came from New Castle, and acquainted him with your orders to us about our companies, but that we could do nothing without money. He told us there was no money yet, but perhaps there would be some in a short time. As soon as the bill is passed, I shall proceed to get everything in readiness for my company immediately.

General Forbes arrived in town with Major Walker last night, but nothing yet transpires from him about the expedition. We hear, by express from New York, that Admiral Boscawen is actually arrived at Halifax with a large fleet, and, after landing the troops there, proceeded immediately to join Admiral Hardy to block up Louisbourg. The 2d battalion Royal American regiment, and Otway's regiment, have embarked here on board of transports, and to sail for Halifax to-morrow to join the troops there. The troops, which the several colonies have agreed to raise for his Majesty's general service, the ensuing campaigns, are:

In the Province of		Men.
Massachusetts Bay, - - - - .		7,000
Rhode Island, - - - - - -		1,000
New Hampshire, - - - - -		1,000
Connecticut, - - - - - -		5,000
New York, - - - - - -		2,600
New Jersey, - - - - - -		1,000
Pennsylvania, - - - -	2,700	3,000
3 (Lower Counties) - - -	300	
Maryland, (suppose) - - - -		1,000
Virginia, (suppose) - - - -		2,000
		23,600

The Army under General Forbes will be composed of Montgomery's Highlanders, 13 companies, - - - - - - -	1,300
4 companies of 1st Batt. Royal Am's., under Col. Bouquet, - - - - - -	400
3 Carolina Independent Companies, - -	300
Regulars,	2,000

To be joined by the Provincials of Pennsylvania, Maryland, and Virginia, and a large number of Cherokees, now at Winchester. Mr. Allen has released Smith and Moore from prison, by a habeas corpus; and, as soon as the money bill is passed, the House will resume the consideration of that affair, to support their dignity.* I shall endeavor to return to Augusta as soon as possible, with the Paymaster, who says he will pay the companies there first.

EDWARD SHIPPEN TO LIEUT. COL. JAMES BURD, AT FORT AUGUSTA.

Lancaster, May 2d, 1758.

DEAR MR. BURD :—Enclosed is a few lines from Captain Shippen, whom, with Mr. Allen and family, and all our friends, I left well in Philadelphia last Saturday. I know no news but what you will find in the papers, except that a Liverpool man tells us that the King of Prussia has obtained more victories over the French, and particularly beaten the Marshal De Richelieu, and all his troops, from Hanover. I expect Sir John St. Clair, with Tommy Willing and his

* See *Gordon's History of Pennsylvania*, p. 353. Smith appealed to the Council in England, which sustained his appeal.

sister Nancy, here to-night. I can't tell you, of a certainty, of any promotions of our Provincial officers. Capt. Allen thinks Capt. Shippen ought to stay behind to command Fort Augusta, as you (it is supposed) will go on an expedition. But he will not agree to this. We have three companies of Highlanders in Lancaster, in exchange for Colonel or rather General Stanwix's battalion, which is now near Albany.

P. S.—Mr. Coleman, at a Common Council held last Saturday, resigned his office of Clerk of the Mayor's Court and of the Common Council to Neddy's hundred a-year.* My compliments to the Major and all the officers. Colonel Armstrong is in town (I mean Philadelphia) and Mr. Peters told Captain Shippen that Colonel Burd ought to have come down too, to have been present while General Forbes and Sir John St. Clair were in their consultations. I and Capt. Shippen made answer that the Colonel would have readily come if he had had any intimation of it. I would advise you to consider whether it may not be proper for you, now you hear the General is in town, to wait upon him. I can't say yes or no. Do what you please; but if you should resolve to come, you ought to lose no time.

ORDER OF GOVERNOR DENNY TO JOHN HUGHES AND OTHERS RESPECTING WYOMING.

Philadelphia, May 4th, 1758.

Gentlemen:—Tedyescung having demanded the performance of the engagements made by this government in building houses, clearing ground and making some other

* Mr. Shippen, according to the fashion of the day, paid an annuity to his predecessor.

improvements at Wyoming, and having fixed the time for doing it to be within three weeks after this date, and the Assembly having very much approved of my intention to employ the gentlemen already commissionated, and recommended it to me to use the utmost dispatch in forwarding this work, I make you acquainted therewith, and desire you would once more undertake the journey to Wyoming, and superintend the finishing of the buildings and other works to be done there in consequence of my promises. I must particularly desire of Mr. Hughes, as he is in town, and one of the Provincial Commissioners to settle everything with them respecting the number of carpenters and workmen, as well as the sums of money necessary to be engaged and provided for this service; and further, that he will confer with Tedyescung, and fix with him such matters as he shall think proper should be previously agreed upon, and to give notice thereof to the other Commissioners, that they may conform thereto, so as not to miss of one another, or to suffer anything necessary for the work to be left behind; I understand that the provisions for the Commissioners and their company must be sent from Fort Augusta, together with the tools, and many other things which were left there. The Commissioners who go by Augusta, will take them with them; and if no Commissioners go by the way of Fort Augusta, they are nevertheless to give directions that the provisions be sent in batteaux to Wyoming; and the commanding officer at that fort, is hereby ordered to yield obedience to the directions of the Commissioners, and send them up with a proper escort, to consist of an officer and twenty men, which is to return to the garrison immediately on delivering the provisions, &c., to the Commissioners at Wyoming. You are to act agreeable to my commission of the fifth day of October last. If it shall happen that only one Commissioner can attend, the person attending is hereby invested with the same power and authority as if the whole were present, at the same time requesting that all may attend this important work, if possible.

If Mr. Hughes should choose to go by way of Fort Allen, and a convoy be wanted for him and his attendants, Capt. Orndt, or the officer commanding there, is hereby ordered to send along with them fifteen or twenty of his men, with an officer, for a guard, and who are to conduct them to Wyoming, make no stay there, and return forthwith to the Governor.

I recommend it to you to take care that everything be done in the premises that the Government stands engaged to do, as far as in your power. You will consult the Indians in the course of the work, and act to their satisfaction. I most heartily wish you health and a safe return.

Gentlemen,

Your most humble servant,

WILLIAM DENNY.

JOHN HUGHES,
EDWARD SHIPPEN,
JAMES GALBREATH,
FRANCIS TOMLIN, } *Esquires.*

CAPT. JOSEPH SHIPPEN (COL.) TO LIEUT. COL. JAMES BURD, AT FORT AUGUSTA.

Philadelphia, May 8th, 1758.

DEAR BROTHER:—When I shall take my departure from hence I can't yet tell, as the Governor, with General

Forbes and Sir John St. Clair's approbation, has been pleased to appoint me Brigade Major to the Provincial troops; wherefore, the Governor keeps me in town a little longer. The money bill is now making, but it will not be finished and signed these ten days. The Government is therefore borrowing money, that the Paymaster may immediately pay off the companies westward of Susquehanna, it being thought they will march first in order to take post at Reastown. How this will be I can't tell.

The Commissioners are ordered to take another journey to Wyoming, agreeably to Tedyescung's request; Mr. Hughes to go by the way of Fort Allen, the others via Fort Augusta, and to take with them the tools, provisions, &c., in batteaux, to be escorted by only twenty men; but I believe neither my father nor Jemmy Galbreath will consent to go. General Forbes is a sensible and prudent gentleman; I wish you had been here to have enjoyed his acquaintance; however, you will have that happiness this summer.

The Highland regiment of 1100 men is to be embarked at Carolina the 12th inst., and I suppose will be here the latter end of this month.

Please to tell Lieut. Scott, that in two days I shall send off the clothes for my company, viz., coats, waistcoats, leather breeches, stockings, hats, (my shirts are making at Lancaster).

CAPT T. LLOYD TO MAJ. JOS. SHIPPEN.

Fort Henry, May 15th, 1758.

DEAR SIR:—I had the pleasure to receive at Fort Henry his Honor, the Governor's, orders of the 11th of May, transmitted by you, to which I have paid a proper obedience. I sincerely congratulate you on your promotion, which I hope will prove an introduction to something more considerable, and that I shall have the pleasure of saluting you Imperator before I die. It gives me unspeakable satisfaction to observe the order of your regiment in general for this campaign, as I take it to be a happy omen of their future good behaviour, and perhaps the surest foundation of victory, should not anything unhappily check this generous spirit. You'll see the Pennsylvania phalanx sacrifice myriads of enemies to the Manes of their butchered friends, and thunder with irresistible fury at the gates of Fort Duquesne. You may perhaps mistake this last effort of my genius for a quotation from some modern tragedy, but I'll assure you upon honor 'tis all my own, and that I would as much despise to steal a quotation as I would a victory. If it should sound a little tragical you know 'tis a tragical subject—to the French, I mean. I intend to halt here, for want of breath; but do you go on and prosper, and believe me to be,

Most sincerely and affectionately yours,

T. LLOYD.

'Tis odd, but certainly true, that the company at Fort Henry, who before used to sing psalms fervently every day, have, ever since the news of the expedition, sang nothing but songs of mirth, and seem to have certainly forgot their psalms. One fellow, on being told that he would have two hundred acres of rich land on the Ohio, swore he would have no lands, for he never intended to work any more. The same fellow, being apprehensive that he should be left behind in garrison, damned himself if he did not desert, and follow the regiment, if they left open, one minute, the back gate of the Fort.

The following story of Dudley Dougherty, I think ought never to be forgot:

Dudley, on his passage from Augusta, fell into the river in a d——d deep hole, and would have been drowned if Captain Hambright had not pulled him out. On being asked by Hambright if he could not swim, he answered, very well. Why the devil, then, did not you do it? By my soul, answered he, I never once thought of it.

EDWARD SHIPPEN TO MAJOR JOSEPH SHIPPEN, AT PHILADELPHIA.

Lancaster, May 28th, 1758.

DEAR SON:—Yesterday arrived twelve Cherokees and one Mohawk from Winchester, recommended by magistrates there to Sir John St. Clair. They are going to Col. Johnston's, and I have employed Mr. John Head to go to Philadelphia with them, as he understands the principal man of the Cherokees, who speaks the Shawnees tongue well; and I hope the General or the Commissioners will pay Mr.

Head handsomely for his trouble. The expenses will, I hope, be paid; for if the charges of sending Indians backwards and forwards are to be borne by me, without a reimbursement, I must let them travel as well as they can for the future. I paid £4.10 last fall, for a man and horse, conducting Indians down to Philadelphia, and wrote to Mr. Peters to get me the money, but he sent me no answer. I look upon the safety of these Indians of some consequence to the continent, and that I would have gone myself, and so would the Sheriff, down to Park's with them, were we not engaged to send off at six o'clock, A. M. on Tuesday morning, sixty wagons to Colonel Bouquet, at Carlisle, which we shall be a little puzzled to do, as drivers are very scarce and saucy, since the late enlistment.

MAJOR SHIPPEN TO COLONEL BURD, AT FORT AUGUSTA.

Philadelphia, May 31st, 1758.

DEAR BROTHER :—I have been to Doctor Gream's place at Horsham, where Mrs. Young show'd me a letter of thanks from the Proprietary, Mr. T. Penn, to Captain Young, for his care and diligence, &c., in executing the duties of his station as Commissary of Musters and Pay Master, desiring him also, when he should see you, to pay his (the Proprietary's) compliments to you, and his hearty thanks for your care and good conduct in the government of the forces under your command at Fort Augusta, &c. This is only the purport of the Proprietary's letter; I cannot remember his words, nor the genteel manner of his expressions; he says he shall have occasion to write to you and Colonel Armstrong. Yesterday, arrived here two ships from New York, with ammunition and military stores for our expedition, which we were fearful would be taken in coming round, as they sailed without a convoy, and we had heard that several French privateers were on our coast. A parcel of blankets, arms, cartridge boxes, &c., are to be sent up by the commissioners to day for the 1st and 2d battalions, Pennsylvania Regiment, at Carlisle. Captain Armstrong sets off, too, with the horses for the two troops of Light Horse.

The General told me two days ago to get myself in readiness to go out of town, for that he must hurry me off very soon. I know not when I shall leave town, as he has not said anything to me about it since. The Governor intends to go up himself as soon as it is possible.

It was first determined to divide the Pennsylvania Troops into four battalions, but it seems probable now they will consist only of three; this matter nor the number of field officers is not yet settled.

CAPT. PETER BARD TO LIEUTENANT COLONEL JAMES BURD, AT RAYSTOWN.

Fort Augusta, July 20th, 1758.

DEAR SIR:—I could not omit this opportunity of letting you hear from me. I arrived hear the 20th past, in company with Captains Eastburn and Jackson, and sixty-five men, being a detachment from each of their companies and four officers, and found one hundred and twenty-one men in garrison, the leavings of the battalion; some dragging their legs after them, others with their arms in slings, several sick. The garrison cuts a droll figure to what it formerly did. The 17th instant came here one Captain Montgomery with sixty-two men to relieve Eastburn and Jackson's companies. I think they exceed anything of men-kind I ever saw. They look more like a detachment from the dead than the living. I would have given five pounds to have had Hogarth here when they were drawn up upon the parade, to have taken them off that I might have had the pleasure of giving you a view of them. Major Shippen wrote to the Captain,* upon some complaint of the inhabitants, for his not going in quest of some Indians of whom they had discovered the tracks. It's my opinion that six Indian warriors would have scalped them all. They had six bullocks in charge for this garrison, and a mile from Hunter's they lost them all, they did not bring one to the fort. This day, march the Captains Eastburn and Jackson with their companies, to join you and forty picked men of your battalion, so I leave you to judge what a blessed corps we have got left. Captain Trump and Ensign Henry are all of the old officers here. The garden is the only thing that looks like itself, and that in a great measure has lost its relish with me for want of your good company. I saunter in it now and then like a lost sheep. We have great quantities of almost everything that is good in it, and I often wish you and the gentlemen at Raystown could partake of them. Our soldiers, who have their share, find great comfort from it. I believe we

* Montgomery.

shall have no occasion to trouble our friends next year for seeds, I shall take care to save a sufficient quantity.

Our young nursery grows charmingly. I can't forbear smiling as I am walking in the garden, to observe the great quantities of marigolds you have planted, there is enough to make soup for your whole army.

Jem Cottes and his brother, two Indians, went from here some time since hunting, and opposite Captain McKee's, they being on an island, discovered about thirty Indian warriors going down towards the inhabitants; upon which they made the best of their way to the fort, and informed Captain Trump that evening, he sent them and one of our men down in a canoe to acquaint Lieutenant Brodhead, whom we expect up with the party, and to alarm the inhabitants; and at Hunter's, Hambus and Jem Cottes quarrelled, and the former killed the latter. My compliments to the gentlemen in general, and I do most sincerely wish you all the success your heart can wish, and a safe return to your family and friends. I hope I shall have the pleasure of hearing from you.

CH. J. SHIPPEN TO HIS FATHER, AT LANCASTER.

Philadelphia, July 20th, 1758.

HONORED SIR:—The account I wrote you of the taking of Ticonderoga, proved a false one. It proceeded from a letter received by Townsend White, said to come from New York, but we have great reason to believe it was forged in this town. We have since heard the melancholy news of the defeat of our army, owing, as it is generally thought, to the rashness of our troops, animated with the success they had on landing. They expected to force the French entrenchments sword in hand, without the help of a single cannon, and so were cut to pieces. Three times over, the brave Highlanders mounted the ramparts, and were as often repelled. Our whole loss amounts to about 1500 regulars and 500 provincials; the newspapers make the number smaller, I suppose, with design. The army is returned to Fort William Henry, but, it is said, preparing to go back and renew the attack. God send them success. Lord Howe is certainly killed, and his body brought to Fort Edward. Major Rutherford is also killed; Major Fulliken is said, in some letters, to be killed; Cochran and Mather wounded. Complete lists of killed and wounded are not yet come to hand.

Our affairs at Louisbourg are in a very prosperous way, and we are in daily expectation of hearing of the reduction of that valuable fortress.

EDWARD SHIPPEN TO MAJOR SHIPPEN, RAYSTOWN.

Lancaster, Saturday, Aug. 5th, 1758.

DEAR SON: — Having just run over the enclosed papers, I thought I could not begin the evening more agreeably, than by writing you a line or two on the present situation of affairs. I hope, by this time, Louisbourg is adorned with

English colors, and, if so, will Mr. Pitt listen to the solicitations of the English merchants, who, for want of knowledge, will naturally be pressing him to give it up, in exchange for Port Mahon? The loss of Port Mahon, I own, is great; but, if our sea-officers will but do their duty in the Mediterranean, our trade will not be much affected by its remaining in the hands of the French. But, while the island of Cape Breton remains in the hands of the English, the French not only lose a million sterling per annum in the fish trade, but must be forced to buy it of us at a dear price. And this is a trifling argument to what follows, for if the French can get the island into their hands again, and are suffered to keep it, they will, one day or other, be able to drive us off the continent, (which, otherwise, they can never do,) and this will give them a power over our West India islands. Pray let me then ask the English merchants what they will do with their manufactures, if they can't find markets for them abroad? The answer is, that no more will be made; and then we may say, O poor England, thou must soon become a province of France! to say no worse about the matter. It is now England's business, it is her only resort to fight; and, if she cannot conquer, it will not be her fault—for Cape Breton must never be ceded again to France, nor must we ever make a peace with the Grand Monarque, but upon our own terms. If we do it on any other conditions, it must be on his terms, which has been the case too often already, but I hope will never be the case again. Did not the mighty Marlborough open a door almost into Paris, by his grand conquests; and did not a devilish ministry give up everything he had taken, for nothing, at the treaty of

Utrecht in 1713? After that, the French king was in a better situation, than he was before that war.

As to our late slaughter at Ticonderoga, I could think of it but with the deepest concern. The papers say, that our General intercepted a letter from the Marquis de Montcalm, calling back 3,000 men, whom he had sent towards the German flats. I believe there was such a letter, and that the express was ordered to fall in our way, in order to deceive us, and so we shall find it will turn out,—for that general knew some weeks beforehand, of our design against Ticonderoga, and therefore it ought not be once imagined that he would weaken his garrison at such a time, upon any consideration in the world. Besides, if the story could be supposed to be true, that they had that number of men to spare, for the purpose mentioned, we should have brought our cannon against the place, as we had an army of 15,000—a certain number of men who were obliged to invest that fortress, containing an uncertain number. But it is easy talking about matters we don't understand; however, if anything I here say, in relation to the affair, should appear to you ever so just, yet, *ne dites rien,* because it might give offence to some gentleman of your army, for as Cato says—*Nulli tacuisse nocet, nocet esse locutum.* We have heard nothing of General Abercombie this week, but it is thought he is reinforced by this time with three or four thousand New England men. As soon as I have any intelligence from that quarter, or Cape Breton, I shall write you again.

Your brother, who left us yesterday morning, desired me, when I wrote again, to give his kind love to you and Mr. Burd. I long to know whether Col. Bouquet has resolved to try for a road towards Loyal Hannon: in short, I shall remain impatient, till I hear from you how the army is to march. If, therefore, you can get a leisure hour, I would desire you to gratify me in this. I hope your wine is got up safe to Raystown. It is accounted not only by physicians, but by other experienced persons, the most wholesome liquor (diluted sometimes with water), in the world. Mr. Allen has put Andrew out to Mr. Chew, and he has a great mind to make Jemmy a lawyer, too. He has spoke to your brother about it, and it is to be determined when he and his wife return from Shrewsbury, where, I am sorry to tell you, she has found no alteration for the better. I am really afraid it is almost over with that most valuable lady. Doctor Shippen has made application for Jack, (I said, as to this, we all know the turn of the family, and especially Jack's,) and he has been spoke to by some others, — but I advised him, that, as much as he stood in need of an apprentice, by all means to wait for Col. Allen's determination. Take care of your health. Be not poisoning your stomach with meat-suppers, and pray press my doctrine on Mr. Burd. Your mammy is come to call me to my crust of bread, and gill of wine and water for my supper. My kind love to you and Mr. Burd. God bless you both.

A Copy of the Rates and Prices for Sutlers' Liquors and Goods; settled at Raystown, August 10th, 1758, by order of Col. Bouquet, Commanding Officer.

PRICES AND RATES.	At Rays Town.			At Loyal Hannon.			At Ohio.		
	£.	s.	d.	£.	s.	d.	£.	s.	d.
Madeira Wine, per gallon, - -	0	10	0	0	17	0	1	2	0
Vidonia,* do - -	0	11	0	0	11	0	0	12	0
West India Rum, do - -	0	10	0	0	11	6	0	13	0
Spirits, do - -	0	12	0	0	13	6	0	15	0
Shrubb, do - -	1	7	0	1	10	0	1	13	0
Shrubb Punch, per 3 pints, - -	0	2	3	0	2	3	0	3	0
Fruit do do - -	0	2	3	0	2	3	0	3	0
Sangaree, do - -	0	2	3	0	2	3	0	3	0
Wine, do - -	0	1	3	0	1	6	0	1	10
Single Fine Sugar, per ℔, - -	0	2	0	0	2	3	0	2	6
Brown Sugar, do - -	0	1	3	0	1	6	0	1	9
Hard Soap, do - -	0	1	4	0	1	7	0	1	10
Tamarinds, do - -	0	2	0	0	2	3	0	2	6
Candles, do - -	0	1	6	0	1	9	0	2	0
Shoes, per pair, - - - -	0	8	0	0	9	0	0	10	0
English Cheese, per lb., - - -	0	1	6	0	1	9	0	2	0
Chocolate, do - - -	0	2	6	0	2	10	0	3	2
Coffee, do - - -	0	1	0	0	1	11	0	2	2
Bohea Tea, do - - -	0	12	0	0	13	0	0	14	0
Writing Paper, per quire, - -	0	2	0	0	2	3	0	2	6
Mustard, per bottle, - - -	0	1	9	0	2	0	0	2	3
Pepper, per lb., - - - -	0	5	0	0	5	6	0	6	0
Wine Vinegar, per gallon, - -	0	10	0	0	12	0	0	15	0
Cider Vinegar, do - -	0	3	0	0	4	0	0	5	0
Salad Oil, do - -	0	5	0	0	6	0	0	7	0
Indian Blankets, each, - - -	1	0	0	1	2	6	1	5	0
Pigtail Tobacco, per lb., - - -	0	1	6	0	1	9	0	2	0
Leaf Tobacco, do - - -	0	0	9	0	1	0	0	1	3
Pricked Tobacco, do - - -	0	0	9	0	1	0	0	1	3
Butter, do - - -	0	1	3	0	1	6	0	2	0
Gammons, do - - -	0	1	1	0	1	3	0	1	6
Smoked Beef, do - - -	0	1	0	0	1	0	0	1	2
Dried Meat and Tongues, per lb., -	0	1	0	0	1	3	0	1	6
American Cheese, do -	0	0	10	0	1	0	0	1	3
Whiskey, per gallon, - - -	0	5	0	0	6	6	0	8	0
American Rum, per gallon, - -	0	5	0	0	6	6	0	8	0

* Vidonia was a Spanish wine, something like Malaga.

A Daily Return of the Second Battalion of the Penna.

COMPANIES.	OFFICERS PRESENT.													
	COMMISSIONED.						STAFF.					NON COMMISS'N'D.		
	Colonel.	Lieut. Colonels.	Majors.	Captains.	Lieutenants.	Ensigns.	Chaplains.	Adjutants.	Quarter Masters.	Surgeons.	Mates.	Sergeants.	Drummers.	Fifers.
Colonel James Burd, - - - - - - - - -	1	0	0	0	0	1	1	0	0	0	1	2	1	0
Lieut. Col. Lloyd, - - - - - - - - -	0	1	0	0	0	0	0	0	0	0	0	2	1	0
Lieut. Col. Work, - - - - - - - - -	0	1	0	0	0	0	0	0	0	0	0	1	0	0
Major Shippen, - - - - - - - - -	0	0	1	0	1	1	0	0	0	0	0	1	1	0
Major Jameson, - - - - - - - - -	0	0	0	0	0	1	1	0	0	0	0	2	1	0
Major Orndt, - - - - - - - - -	0	0	0	0	1	0	0	0	0	0	0	1	1	0
Capt. Bussec, - - - - - - - - -	0	0	0	0	0	1	0	1	0	0	0	2	1	1
Capt. Hambright, - - - - - - - - -	0	0	0	0	0	1	0	0	0	1	0	1	1	0
Capt. Morgan, - - - - - - - - -	0	0	0	1	1	0	0	0	0	0	0	1	0	0
Capt. Weiser, - - - - - - - - -	0	0	0	0	0	1	0	0	0	0	0	2	1	1
Capt. Clayton, - - - - - - - - -	0	0	0	0	1	0	0	0	1	0	0	2	1	0
Capt. Haselet, - - - - - - - - -	0	0	0	0	1	1	0	0	0	0	1	2	0	0
Capt. Singleton, - - - - - - - - -	0	0	0	1	1	1	0	0	0	0	0	2	1	0
Capt. Hassler, - - - - - - - - -	0	0	0	1	0	1	0	0	0	0	0	2	0	0
Capt. Eastburn, - - - - - - - - -	0	0	0	0	1	1	0	0	0	0	0	2	1	0
	1	2	1	3	7	10	2	1	1	1	2	25	11	2

Orderly Officer, Ensign Haller.

OFFICERS ABSENT, DRAWING PROVISIONS.					OFFICERS ABSENT, NOT DRAWING PROVISIONS.				
Captains.	Lieutenants.	Ensigns.	Sergeants.	Drummers.	Captains.	Lieutenants.	Ensigns.	Sergeants.	Drummers.
Total. 12			5		Total. 4			6	1

Regiment, Camp at Rays Town, August 19*th,* 1758.

EFFECTIVE RANK AND FILE.													WANTING TO COMPLETE THE ESTABLISHMENT.			SINCE LAST RETURN.				JOINED.				
			ON COMMAND.																					
Present for Duty.	Sick in the Camp.	Sick absent in the Hospital.	Drawing Provisions here.	Not Drawing Provisions here.	Artificers and Artillery.	Light Horse present.	Light Horse on Command.	Hatchet Men.	Bow Men	Camp Colored Men.	On Furlough.	TOTAL.	Sergeants.	Drummers.	Rank and File.	Recruited.	Dead.	Deserted.	Discharged.	Sergeants.	Drummers.	Rank and File.	Women.	Rations Drawn.
8	9	0	18	3	4	0	0	1	1	0		45		0	5								1	17
11	1	1	13	12	3	1	0	1	1	1		45		0	5								0	36
10	2	0	9	10	1	0	0	1	1	1		35		0	16								1	26
9	4	2	20	2	3	2	0	1	1	1		45		0	6								1	46
6	2	0	6	14	4	0	0	1	1	1		35		0	15								0	26
13	1	0	10	21	2	0	1	1	1	1		51		0	0								1	33
13	0	0	14	7	8	3	1	1	1	1		44		0	5								1	42
12	1	0	10	1	6	6	0	1	1	1		39		0	11								1	43
4	6	0	12	7	3	1	0	0	1	0		34		0	17								0	31
13	1	0	18	1	7	3	1	1	1	1		47		0	2								1	52
6	3	0	15	8	2	1	0	1	2	1		39		0	11								1	37
11	4	0	11	11	7	0	3	1	1	1		50		0	0								1	42
17	6	0	4	9	8	1	2	1	1	1		50		0	0								1	46
13	2	0	15	5	5	0	3	1	1	1		48		1	2								1	35
12	2	0	4	22	6	0	0	1	1	1		49		0	1								1	34
160	44	3	179	134	64	18	11	14	16	13		656		1	96									580

Officers absent, drawing Provisions, . . . 12
Sergeants absent, drawing Provisions, . . 5

597

JACOB KERN,

Adjutaut.

CHIEF JUSTICE SHIPPEN TO HIS FATHER, AT LANCASTER.

Philadelphia August 24th, 1758.

HON. SIR:—We have at last received the joyful news of the surrender of Louisbourg, which, with the account of the Duke of Marlborough's destroying such a number of French ships in the harbor of St. Maloes, has given this town great spirits. An application to the Assembly for barracks would be a vain thing. In the first place, they have no money to dispose of, and in the next, they would tell you Lancaster is no more burthened than the other towns in the province, in proportion to its size. And if you should have barracks it is a question whether you would be relieved, for a commanding officer might think Lancaster the most proper place to quarter a number of men, and after filling the barracks, might put as many men on the tavern keepers as they could conveniently take; so that in fact, barracks in Lancaster, might turn out only a relief to some other smaller towns, not so conveniently situated for quartering soldiers.

If, notwithstanding, the people will petition the Assembly, they had better get Johnny Mather or George Ross to draw their petition, than I, who am not sufficiently acquainted with the nature of the distress they would complain of. The numerous petitions against William Moore for mal-administration as a justice of peace, are now under examination before the Governor and Council at the state house. I understand they have gone through five already, all which turn out most villainously vicious.

RICHARD PETERS, (SECRETARY,) TO EDWARD SHIPPEN, AT LANCASTER.

Philadelphia, August 24th, 1758.

SIR :—The Governor, on examining his cash, received with his list of tavern licenses, finds that he has only received for sixty, whereas by the list there are eighty-four; therefore desires you will send him the names of the delinquents, that they may be prosecuted, and in the mean time, that you would not give out licenses, till they have paid their arrears. Mr. Morse gave me a list of delinquents, but it is some how mislaid, so please to order him to make out a new one. But the Governor, who is responsible for each, every year finds great fault that the townships, where people live, are not mentioned in the list. Pray send me by the next post a complete list, with townships, and keep the people up to their pay within the first quarters. If two or three examples were made, it would be better for you and the Governor. He is really angry, and I give you this information without his knowing it, that you may write to him on the subject.

Field Return of the Second Division, First Battalion, of the Royal American Regiment; in Camp, on the March, August 24th, 1758.

COMPANIES.		SERGEANTS.			DRUMMERS.		RANK AND FILE.					
		Present.	Left at Reastown.	Total.	Present.	Total.	Present.	Left Sick at Reastown.	Sick Absent in Hospital.	Artificers left at Reastown.	On Furlough.	Total.
Col. Henry Bouquet's, - -		3	1	4	2	2	81	0	7	1	3	92
Captains	Ralph Harding's, - -	4	0	4	2	2	80	1	4	0	0	85
	Frans. Lander's, - - -	3	1	4	2	2	81	2	7	2	0	92
	Thos. Jocelyn's, - - -	4	0	4	2	2	83	5	5	0	1	94
Totals, - - - - - - - -		14	2	16	8	8	325	8	23	3	4	363

RUDOLPH BENTINCK,

Adjutant.

A Field Return of the Maryland Forces encamped near Reas Town, August the 26th, 1758.

COMPANIES.	OFFICERS PRESENT.						EFFECTIVE RANK AND FILE.										Wanting to complete establishment.				
	COMMISSIONED.			STAFF.	NON COMMISS'ND.					ON COMMAND.											
	Captains.	Lieutenants.	Ensigns.	Surgeons.	Serjeants.	Drummers.	Present for Duty.	Sick in Camp.	Sick, absent, in Hospital.	Drawing Provisions here.	Not Drawing here.	Artificers and Artillery.	Hatchet Men.	Camp Colormen.	Batmen.	TOTAL.	Serjeants.	Drummers.	Rank and File.	Women.	Rations drawn.
Captain Dagworthy's, . . .	1	2	1	1	4	1	45	2	1	24	0	0	0	0	0	72	0	0	19	3	84
Do Alexander Beall's,* .	0	1	1	0	1	0	96		0	63	0	0	0	0	2	71	0	0	20	2	76
Do Joshua Beall's,* . .	0	0	1	0	1	0	9	5	0	48	0	1	0	0	0	63	1	0	28	2	66
Do Ware's, ...	1	2	0	0	3	1	56	2	0	12	0	0	0	0	0	70	0	0	21	3	80
Total, ...	2	5	3	1	9	2	116	9	1	147	0	1	0	0	2	276	1	0	88	10	306

Officers absent, drawing here, ... 6
Serjeants absent, drawing here, ... 5
Drummers, ... 2

319

JNO. DAGWORTHY.

OFFICERS ON COMMAND.									
DRAWING PROVISIONS HERE.					NOT DRAWING HERE.				
COMMISSIONED.		NON COMMISSIONED.			COMMISSIONED.		NON COMMISSIONED.		
Captains.	Subalterns.	Sergeants.	Drummers.	TOTAL.	Captains.	Subalterns.	Sergeants.	Drummers.	TOTAL.
2	4	5	2	13	0	0	1	0	1

* These Captains Beall were the grandsons, I believe, of Col. Ninian Beall, for whose services against the Indians, "*An Act of Gratitude*" was passed by the Maryland Assembly. (*Bacon's Laws of Maryland.*) The "gratitude" was not confined to mere words, but 'material' proofs of the esteem of the Legislature were given, in addition to others previously bestowed. His services certainly deserved high consideration. The defeat of 'the Susquehannocks" by him, was the blow which broke their power. (*Lewis Evans' Middle British Colonies.* Phil'a. 1755. pp. 12–14, 2d Ed.)

A Field Return of the Maryland Forces, Encamped near Reas Town, Sept. 11th, 1758.

	OFFICERS PRESENT.							EFFECTIVE RANK AND FILE.												
	COMMISSIONED.				STAFF.	NON COMM'D.						ON COMMAND.				WANTING TO COMPLETE THE ESTABLISHMENT.				
									SICK.											
COMPANIES.	Lieutenant Colonels.	Captains.	Lieutenants.	Ensigns.	Surgeons.	Sergeants.	Drummers.	Present for Duty.	In Camp.	Present in Hospital.	Absent in Hospital.	Drawing Provisions here.	Not Drawing here.	Artillery.	TOTAL.	Sergeants.	Drummers.	Rank and File.	Women.	Rations Drawn.
Lieut. Col. Dagworthy's,			1			2		2		2	1	63			68			23	2	72
Captain Alexander Beall's,								2				69			71			20	2	73
Captain Joshua Beall's,				1				2		3		57		1	63			28	2	62
Captain Ware's,						1		1	1	4		62			68	1		23	4	67
Total,			1	1		3		7	1	9	1	251		1	270	1		94	10	274

N. B.—The three Sergeants sick.

Officers on command and drawing Rations here,	15
Sergeants,	12
Drummers,	4
Total Rations,	305

WM. LINN.

OFFICERS ON COMMAND.												RANK AND FILE ON COMMAND.		
DRAWING PROVISIONS HERE.						NOT DRAWING HERE.								
COMMMISSIONED.			NON COMM'ND.			COMMISSIONED.			NON COMMISS'D.					
Lieutenant Colonels.	Captains.	Subalterns.	Sergeants.	Drummers.	TOTAL.	Lieutenant Colonels.	Captains.	Subalterns.	Sergeants.	Drummers.	TOTAL.	With Lieutenant Col. John Dagworthy.	On the Grass Guard.	TOTAL.
1	3	12	12	4	31							210	41	251

List of Officers and Soldiers Killed, Missing, and Returned from the action near Fort Duquesne, September 14th, 1758.

DIFFERENT TROOPS.	KILLED OR MISSING.		RETURNED.	Soldiers not Wounded.	Soldiers Wounded.	
	OFFICERS.	No. of Soldiers.	OFFICERS.			
Royal Americans,	Lieut. Billings, Lieut. Ryders, Ensign Rhor, Ensign Jenkins,	35	Captain Lander, - Lieut. Bentinck.	70	3	
Highlanders,	Major Grant, Captain Munro, Captain A. McKenzie, Captain McDonald, Lt. Alex. McKenzie, Lieut. Colin Campbell, Lieut. Wm. McKenzie. Lieut. Rod'k McKenzie, Lieut. Alex. McDonald, Ensign John McDonald,	131	Lt. Arch'd Robinson, Lieut. Hen. Mann. Ensign Alex. Grant. Lieut. McDonald. Surgeon McDunit, - Surgeon Harriss, -	162	24	Wounded, Wounded.
1st Virginia Reg't,	Major Lewis, Lieut. Baker, Lieut. Campbell, Ensign Allen, Ensign Chew, Ensign Guest,	61	Capt. Walter Stuart, Captain Bullitt.	103	2	Wounded.
Carolinians, - -		4		7	2	
Marylanders, - -	Lieut. McCrea, - -	27	Captain Ware, - Lieut. Ripley. Ensign Harrison, -	46	4	Wounded.
Lower Counties of Pennsylvania,		2		12		
2d Battalion of Pennsylvanians,	Ensign Haller, - -	18	Captain Clayton, - Lieut. Hayes. Lieut. Renolds.	85	5	
		278		483	40	

A Field Return of the Division of the Sixty-second Regiment, or First Highland Battalion, commanded by the Hon. Col. Archibald Montgomery, Camp at Raystown, September 15th, 1758.

COMPANIES.	OFFICERS PRESENT. Commissions.			Non Commissions.		EFFECTIVE RANK AND FILE.	Sick.			Command.						WANTING TO COMPLETE.				
	Captains.	Lieutenants.	Ensigns.	Sergeants.	Drummers.	Present, fit for Duty.	In Camp.	In Hospital.	Left Behind.	Drawing Rations here.	Not Drawing here.	Ball Men.	Camp Colormen.	Hall. Men.	TOTAL.	Sergeants.	Drummers.	Rank and File	Women.	Rations Drawn here.
Captain Sir Allan MacLean's,	1	1	1	4	2	71	3	6	2	10		1	1	1	95			9	3	89
Captain Robertson's,	1	2	1	3	1	58	2	5	6	16		1	1	1	90		1	14	3	74
Captain Cameron's	1	2	1	3	2	42	6	13	1	19		1	1	1	84			20	3	63
Detachments,		1	2	5	4	134	9	8		34					185				5	160
Total,	3	6	5	15	9	305	20	32	9	79		3	3	3	454		1	43	14	386
																				500

N. B.—One Servant with Col. Montgomery, no rations drawn for.

JOHN M'LACHLAN,
As Adjutant.

COMPANIES.	ON COMMAND, AND WHERE. At the Alleghenies. Subalterns.	Sergeants.	Rank & File.	TOTAL.
Captain Sir Allan MacLean's,			10	10
Do Robertson's,		1	16	16
Do Cameron's,		1	19	19
Detachments,	1		34	34
Total,	1	2	79	79

N. B.—All on command, 1 Lieut.; 2 Serg'ts; 79 Rank and File.

A Daily Return of the Lower County Companies, Commanded by Major Wells, encamped near Reas Town, Sept. 17*th*, 1758.

COMPANIES.	OFFICERS PRESENT.											RANK AND FILE.			
	COMMISSIONED.				STAFF.					NON COMMISS'NED.					
	Majors.	Captains.	Lieutenants.	Ensigns.	Chaplains.	Adjutants.	Quarter Masters.	Surgeons.	Mates.	Sergeants.	Drummers.	Fit for Duty.	Sick.	On Command.	TOTAL.
Major Wells', - - -	1	0	0	1	0	0	0	1	0	2	1	8	9	17	34
Capt. M'Clughan's, -	0	0	0	0	0	0	0	0	0	0	0	0	4	3	7
Capt. Gooding's, - -	0	0	0	1	0	0	0	0	0	0	0	3	5	13	21
Total, - - - -	1	0	0	2	0	0	0	1	0	2	1	11	18	33	62

RICH'D WELLS,

Major.

Return of the Killed, Wounded, and Missing, in the Action at Loyal Hannon, October 12th, 1758.

REGIMENT.	OFFICERS.									WAGONERS.	
	COMMISSIONED.			NON COMMISSIONED.			RANK AND FILE.				
	Killed.	Wounded.	Missing.	Killed.	Wounded.	Missing.	Killed.	Wounded.	Missing.		
Highland, - - - - - - -	0	0	0	0	0	0	1	1	0		
1st Virginia, - - - - - -	0	1	0	0	1	0	4	4	0		Lt. James Duncanson, wounded.
North Carolina, - - - - -	0	0	0	0	0	0	0	0	3		
Maryland, - - - - - -	1	1	1	0	0	1	0	0	10		Lt. Thos. Prater, killed; Ens. Bell, wounded; [Lt. Matthews, missing.
1st Pennsylvania Battalion,	0	0	0	0	0	1	4	4	11		
Lower Counties, - - - - -	0	0	0	0	0	0	1	1	4		
2d Pennsylvania Battalion,	0	0	0	0	0	0	0	0	1		
Total, - - - - - - -	1	2	1	0	1	1	10	15	29		

Lieut. Wright, of the Royal Train of Artillery, wounded slightly in the head.

COL. BOUQUET TO COL. JAMES BURD.

Stony Creek, October 12th, 1758.

DEAR SIR :—I deferred answering your several letters, in expectation of joining you every day. The rains, broken roads, and several other contingent causes, have kept me back. To-morrow I hope to dine with you; but don't retard your dinner for me. The Laurel being impassable, I sent Captains Callender and Shelby to look for another ascent, and they have had the good luck to find one greatly preferable. We cut quite a new road from this post to the top of Laurel Hill, which will be four miles shorter, and eight miles better. I set out this moment to reconnoitre, and shall encamp at the foot of the hill, to have sufficient time to view it to-morrow morning (nothing out even in the night) upon pack-horses, with two-inch augers, one-inch chisel, and another two inches, and one handsaw, to build a bridge over Queenatong Creek. Your horse-driver will find at the top of the hill a branch cut across the road, and the blazes at his right hand, which blazes he is to follow to the foot of the mountain, where he will see an encampment and deliver his tools. The second division of the artillery will stay here until the new road is cut, and the last division set out from Reastown, to say which fifty wagons. I beg you will get an exact return ready of all the troops on the west of the Laurel Hill, that we may make the necessary dispositions to move immediately forward. I am impatient to see you. My compliments to Capt. Gordon and friends. I hope the General's hut is ready, as he will soon be with us. He mends apace.

Dear Sir,

Your humble servant,

HENRY BOUQUET.

Room must be made and ground cleared for the fifty wagons of the artillery.

If you have no falling axes well ground, or no time to grind them, pray let it be done to-morrow morning. As we have no grindstone, the work would not go on.

H. B.

HARRY GORDON TO LIEUT. COL. JAMES BURD.

Loyal Hannon, October 14th, 1758.

SIR:—The following is what happened between the French prisoner, who was brought in wounded, and who made the answers to the following questions, put down in the same words:

Q. Quelle force aviez vous aujourdhui, que nous attaquoit.

R. Nous etions mille Hommes.

Q. Outre Les Sauvages.

R. Non: entre huit et neuf cens Francois et le reste des Sauvages.

Q. Et quelle etoit votre dessein et comment et ce que vous avez osez nous attaquer dans les Retrenchmens?

Le prisonier me disoit que au commencement je lui avois promis de ne lui pas demander beaucoup des questions et que il lui falloit du temps pour me repondre. Te l'assurois que ce n'etoit que un seul question de plus, et seulement pour voir si ce qu'il diroit, s'accordoit avec les reponses des autres prisoniers que nous avions fait, que j'avois dit au commencement aussi.

The answer was to the last question in these words, as follows:

Que leur dessunetoit d'attaquer toutes nos gardes avances et de les survive s'ils pourroient dans les retrenchmens.

The above are the words that happened between the said prisoner and myself, which upon account of the ingenuity, I have put in the same words as they were pronounced.

HARRY GORDON.

To Colonel Burd,

Commanding at Loyal Hannon.

COL. HENRY BOUQUET TO LIEUT. COL. JAMES BURD, AT LOYAL HANNON.

Stoney Creek, October 16*th,* 1758.

Dear Sir:—I received yesterday morning your last of the 14th, and transmitted to the General all the intelligence you sent me. I am very sorry you could not make a prisoner. I suppose you have ordered some parties out to endeavor to get some straggler. I don't believe a word of their pretended reinforcement in provisions and men, but to know the truth, be pleased to send two small parties to spy on the opposite sides of Monongahela and Ohio, if there are more batteaux than before.

The General desires that all the parties sent out do reconnoitre the country betwixt the old path and Braddock's road, to know where we could fall in said road. The path discovered by Captain Funk seems to be the best, but as he could not go to the end of it, there is little depending upon it.

Col. Washington will be here this day with the rest of his regiment. The new road will be cut in three days (if good weather) to the top of the Laurel. All our wagons, provisions, &c., are coming up, and nothing I hope will prevent our marching forward immediately. The General grows better and better; he has fired a *feu de joie* for your affair. The Little Carpenter is there, with thirty Cherokees and thirty Catawbas. King Hegler is expected every day, and the General hopes to engage them to come up with us. The news of the King of Prussia beating Marshal Davon, is confirmed by all the vessels. I have forwarded all your letters. As soon as I can, I shall be with you.

I am, Dear Sir, your most obedient, humble serv't,

HENRY BOUQUET.

A Daily Return of the Virginia Regiment Encamped at Loyal Hannon, under the Command of Col. Washington, October 21*st*, 1758.

COMPANIES.	OFFICERS PRESENT.											EFFECTIVE RANK AND FILE.							SINCE LAST RETURN.			
	COMMISSIONED.						STAFF.		NON COMMISSIONED.													
	Colonels.	Lieutenant Colonels.	Majors.	Captains.	Lieutenants.	Ensigns.	Surgeons.	Mate.	Sergeants.	Fife.	Drummers.	Pesent fit for service.	Sick pesent.		On Command with Maj. Sh'd.	Artificers.	Camp Colormen.	TOTAL.	Joined.	Dead.	Deserted.	Discharged.
Col. Washington's,	1	0	0	1	1	1	1	1	3	1	1	24	11	7	12	16	6	78				
Lt. Col. Stephen's,	0	1	0	0	2	0	0	0	3	1	1	36	3	6	14	7	6	72				
Maj. Lewis's, - -	0	0	0	0	2	1	0	0	2	0	0	29	14	8	16	7	6	80				
	0	0	0	0	2	0	0	0	2	1	2	33	6	6	17	8	6	76				
Capt. Bullitt's, -	0	0	0	1	1	0	0	0	3	0	2	30	11	11	15	8	6	81				
	0	0	0	0	1	0	0	0	3	1	2	33	9	2	18	8	6	76				
Total, - - -	1	1	0	2	9	2	1	1	16	4	8	185	54	40	92	54	36	461				

G°. WASHINGTON,

Colonel.

Wanting Necessaries to Equip each Man for the March, in the 2d Division, 1st Battalion, of the Royal American Regiment, Loyal Hannon, October 25th, 1758.

COMPANIES.		Shirts.	Stockings.	Breeches or Trowsers.	Shoes.	Blankets.	Small Hatchets.	Haths.
Colonel Henry Bouquet, -		20	24	6	54	20	12	3
Captains.	Ralph Harding, - - -	19	35	5	18	16	7	2
	Francis Lander, - - -	6	40	19	48	17	4	2
	Thos. Jocelyn, - - - -	3	21	12	24	14	14	0
Total, - - - - - -		48	120	42	144	67	37	7

R. HARDING.

A Return of the Maryland Troops under the Command of Lt. Col. Dagworthy, Wanting Necessaries, at Loyal Hannon, Oct. 25th, 1758.

The Whole wants Blankets, but they are sent for.
The Whole wants Clothes, but they are making.

JNO. DAGWORTHY,
Lt. Col. Maryland Forces.

GENERAL FORBES TO COLONEL BURD.

New Camp, 20 *miles west of Loyal Hannon,*
November 19*th,* 1758.

Sir :—

astonished and amazed upon
and villainous desertion of
of the methods he had used
from our assistance at so very
He has often told us in public
that his nation were going to make war against the Virginians and His Majesty's subjects. I therefore thought him a good pledge in our hands to prevent that, and consequently the whole of them were indulged in every extravagant, avaricious demand they made; but seeing that those who have thus deserted and abandoned us, with all the aggravating circumstances attending their desertion, now preludes to what we may expect from them. I therefore desire, that upon receipt of this, you will instantly dispatch an express to the commanding officer at Raystown, who is to send one to Winchester and Fort Cumberland, in case that he, the Carpenter* and his followers, should have already past Raystown, and notice ought to be sent to Fort Loudon likewise with my orders, which are that having under the cloak of friendship robbed us these several months, but now having discovered themselves our private enemies, and having turned the arms, put in their hands by us, against his Majesty's subjects, which the former parties have already done, that, therefore prudence and self preservation obliged us, to require of them the returning of their arms and ammunition directly, as likewise the horses that were furnished them to accompany us to war; that as their

* The Cherokee Chief.

blankets, shirts, silver truck, &c., are not of that consequence, therefore the peremptory stripping of them need not I insist upon the inhabitants
Chester making them
and horses, which is but
fellow subjects of the parts of Virginia
borough, where no doubt they would commit all sorts of outrage, so that it will be necessary to send a sufficient escort along with them, allowing of them a sufficiency of provisions and no more, so that the Cherokee nation may see plainly they will have nothing to complain of but the baseness and perfidy of those, whom they have sent amongst us as friends for these seven months past. The garrison of Fort Cumberland is strong enough to compel them to deliver up their arms, so let a copy of this my letter be sent to the commanding officer, who is to make use of all the fair means in his power before he takes their arms from them. At Raystown they are to do the same.

But as the garrison of Fort Loudon is perhaps too weak either to refuse them their presents, or make them deliver up their arms, I desire, therefore, that in case they take that way, that Major Wells marches directly himself with a sufficient force from Raystown to Fort Loudon to execute this, which you and all concerned, are always first to try by gentle methods, before that rougher ones be made use of; as it is impossible any of your garrison can overtake them before they reach Raystown, I therefore desire no time may be lost in sending copies of my letter and directions to Raystown, to be forthwith transmitted by expresses to Fort Loudon, Cumberland and Winchester. * * * Mr. Smith the interpreter ought to be sent after them to serve to explain matters, and to prevent as far as can be, the bad consequences of their going home through Virginia and North Carolina, armed, for which purpose this letter is wrote, as Virginia has always suffered.

I am, sir,
Your obedient, humble servant,
JNO. FORBES.

CHIEF JUSTICE SHIPPEN TO HIS FATHER, AT LANCASTER.

Philadelphia, December 14th, 1758.

HONORED SIR:—Your account of our army getting possession of Fort Duquesne, you may be sure gave us a great deal of pleasure. The reduction of the fort by driving the French away, though it will not make such an eclat in the world as obtaining it by a regular siege or a pitched battle would have done, is nevertheless equally beneficial in its consequences, and General Forbes' prudence and good conduct will establish his character with thinking people, as effectually as if he had obtained his conquest through blood and slaughter. I had the pleasure, on Monday last, of rejoicing on a double occasion, for amidst the ringing of bells and firing off guns for the above mentioned glorious event, my Peggy was safely delivered of a fine, lusty *boy;* so that you may be sure I was very sincere in illuminating my house for joy. The Governor tells me General Forbes expects to have quarters provided for 1800 men, and he (the Governor) thinks Lancaster can take 500, as formerly; Reading 300, and York 200. The remainder will be fixed at Germantown and other places near Philadelphia; the Governor desired me to mention this to you. I shall take a proper opportunity of mentioning Mr. Burd for the office in Cumberland, though I cannot help thinking with you, he acts more in character as a soldier, and perhaps his present office is the most profitable, and will be not less durable, for though a peace should come on, we shall always keep up one or two troops for the protection of our Indian trade, and the commander of a fort in time of peace, earns his money very easily, for as no danger is apprehended, the absence of an officer from his post would be in a great measure winked at. This, however, I only mean as a hint to you, for I would not have Mr. Burd think me slow in doing him a kindness.

I will look out for a good quarter cask of wine for you; my kind love to mammy, &c.

SIR JOHN ST. CLAIR TO COL. BURD.

Four miles west of Kikoney Parolings,
Tuesday morning.

SIR:—The fifty men of your battalion which began to work on the road yesterday at 12 o'clock, cut one mile of it, so that there remains three quarters of a mile to finish of what I expected, which I shall immediately set about, with the two companies of carpenters; it may take them two or three hours. I dare not camp at the foot of the ridge, as I could wish, for it is full of laurels, but shall encamp a little on this side of the clear fields. The food for horses all along, from this to the clear fields, is very good. From the clear fields to the foot of the hill is cut, but several stones are to be broken or removed. I shall keep working on the hill all this day, and if after you come up, you choose to see the descent of the hill, I shall accompany you. I enclose you the return of the men that I have here, that you may make your disposition accordingly. In case I should be obliged to blow rocks, pray send me a piece of brimstone; the artillery have some; you'll not forget the wagon cloths which are in the redout.

I am, sir, your most humble serv't,

JNO. ST. CLAIR.

CH. J. SHIPPEN TO HIS FATHER, AT LANCASTER.

Philadelphia, March 3d, 1759.

HONORED SIR:—I give you joy of the taking of the Island of Guadaloupe. The enclosed was the first account, which is since confirmed. The engagement mentioned by Gaine was on the Island of Martinique, between 7000 English and 5000 French. The latter were soon put into confusion, which the Highlanders did not fail to improve by rushing in, sword in hand. But the cause is not yet known, why our troops should hasten to reimbark without attempting anything further. Some accounts intimate, that the landing on Martinique was only a feint to cover the real design, which was the reducing Guadaloupe. The account of the action in the Bay of Biscay is corroborated by an account from Barbadoes, that says, a master of a vessel has taken his oath that he actually saw the French and British fleets engaged, the former consisting of fourteen sail of the line, and the latter of twenty-one sail.

CH. J. SHIPPEN TO HIS FATHER, AT LANCASTER.

Philadelphia, March 14th, 1759.

HONORED SIR:—General Forbes is to be interred this afternoon, with great pomp. Mr. Burd got safe down, and sends his love. We are in some apprehension that the yellow fever will be imported this summer from Guadaloupe.

COL. JAMES BURD TO HIS WIFE, AT HER FATHER'S, LANCASTER.

Philadelphia, March 24th, 1759.

My Dearest:—I am sorry to hear of the distresses of your family; the more so, as I cannot at present come up to see you all. I hope, however, the children are all doing well.

There is great disturbance here, occasioned by General Amherst's giving the command to the westward to my namesake, Colonel Burd,* of Virginia. The Assembly are determined that they will grant neither men nor money, unless the commander is changed; and I believe a deputation from the Council and Assembly of this Province is to be sent on to New York to General Amherst.

These disturbances prevent my receiving my money, for which I am sorry. If you want any, I shall be obliged to your father for lending you some, until I can receive my own.

Since writing the above, I hear General Stanwix commands. He arrived last night. This will remove all objections. I am, my dearest,

With the greatest regard,

Your most affectionate husband,

JAMES BURD.

EDWARD SHIPPEN TO COL. JAS. BURD, AT PHILADELPHIA.

Lancaster, March 27th, 1759.

Dear Mr. Burd:—I am very sorry that General Amherst ever thought of commissioning Col. William Byrd,

* Colonel Byrd, of Westover.

as fine a gentleman and soldier as he is, since it proves so very disagreeable to our wisdoms. Sally received yours of the 24th, wherein you mention General Stanwix as your commander to the westward, but I think your information as to him will prove wrong.

Point d'argent, Point de suisse, so that I say nothing more to you of your buying Mr. Ross' negro girl, who is a very fine one by all accounts, and I wish with all my heart Sally had her. The price will be fifty or sixty pounds at most, and I hope, as the girl is not yet sold, that in a week or two you will be able to pay for her; and if otherwise, we must be contented.

THOMAS LLOYD (MAJOR) TO COL. JAMES BURD.

Ligonier, April 14th, 1759.

DEAR COLONEL:—Yours of the 9th of March I had the pleasure to receive by Ensign Biddle, and was extremely glad to have that satisfaction. I have wrote you frequently relativé to the battalion, but conclude that my letters have been intercepted and you have not received any. I am extremely sorry to tell you, what now remains of your unfortunate battalion is hardly worth writing about. The graveyard has most of them. Exhausted as they were, with the fatigues of a most unmerciful campaign, 'twas impossible they should stand the united effects of sickness and hard duty. I have, agreeably to the dictates of humanity and duty, afforded them all the relief in my power, and contracted great debts in doing it; how I shall be paid, is a matter of some doubt. At any rate, the satisfaction that accompanied it will in some measure repay me. I have urged their distressed situation with all the eloquence I was master of, to the commanding officer; I am sorry with so little success.

The hurry has been fatal to them, and that I think might have been in some measure prevented. There are none of the second battalion at this post. Captain, one; Lieutenants, two; Ensigns, two; rank and file fit for duty, thirty-two.

Intelligence says that there are at Venango forty French and subalterns; at Le Bœuf a hundred; at Presque Isle a hundred; at Niagara a thousand. As to Indian affairs, they don't seem to be at present on the best footing—many treaties but little sincerity. I believe their friendship is like that of the rest of the world, and will attend those who stand the least in need of it; and, in order to gain it, we must first convince them that it can be of no use to us; after which, perhaps we may obtain it. I am extremely tired of this place, and should be extremely obliged to you if you can by any means procure me relief. For further particulars I refer you to Mr. Atlee. Being, sir, &c.

HUGH MERCER, (LIEUT. COL.,) TO COL. JAMES BURD.

Pittsburg, April 23d, 1759.

DEAR SIR:—Your favor of the 10th, I had the pleasure to receive yesterday, and should undoubtedly have had great satisfaction of hearing of your and Mrs. Burd's welfare long ago. It is very different with one who lives in exile, and has little entertainment, besides calling to mind past scenes of happiness in the society of his friends, from what it is with you who have fresh objects of delight hourly crowding in. We have endeavored to pass through the gloom of this winter as easily as possible; and, what with public work, and frequent perusal of the history of the four kings, are at length happily arrived among shady groves, blushing blossoms, and verdant fields.

This place becomes now very agreeable to most of us, and, excepting the sick and the lazy, 'tis my opinion that few of the soldiers, and not one of the officers, of a grain of sense or spirit, would take it of choice to go down the country. For what purpose are we to be ordered down, to have the additional fatigue of making some hundred miles, starving all the way, and, during the campaign, become the rear of the army, to be tormented with escorts? I propose writing on this subject to Colonel Armstrong, and hope you will agree not to harrass your people, after what they have already suffered. The subject might become too tedious, was I to describe to you the miseries of the Pennsylvania troops here, and much more so at Ligonier, for want of surgeons; your battalions have lost immensely this way. I have, 'tis true, been in Dr. Johnston, who, purely to oblige me, has attended our people at this post; but, to take proper care of such numbers, is beyond the power even of his industry. Will our surgeons agree to indemnify me and Dr. Johnston, or will they acknowledge that their pay is granted by the government to be frolicked away in quarters, when the lives entrusted to their care, demand their attendance upon the frontiers. In the event of an attack on this post, a scene of tumult must have ensued, too shocking for imagination.

The enemy keeps peppering away up in the communication—the particulars of which, I take for granted you have, before this reaches you. Hitherto we have escaped their parties, excepting the batteau-men. It is with no small pleasure I find that Col. Bouquet is to command here, who will be a proper balance between the provincial troops, besides many other advantages arising from a gentleman whom every man must esteem. Your namesake on

, sent his orders to Col. Lloyd, to remit to him the roll of his garrison, and that of Pellsby, without writing me a single line. How far this fire missed in the military way, you may judge. We are extremely obliged to your endeavors and Colonel Armstrong's, before the Assembly; for my part, I have no expectations, and therefore can suffer no disappointment. I wish the insisting on augmentation of pay may not disconcert the other view as to bet-money, &c., for you know our people have weak constitutions, and won't bear a great deal at once. I tell you a word in your ear, "your battalion and Colonel Armstrong's will never be in character, till half a-dozen officers are broke from the service with disgrace. Another nuisance, almost equal to the scoundrel behavior of too many of the officers, is such as quit the service, following the army as pedlars, &c. To-day I made an excursion to Charles old town, one of the finest places for a strong post to be found perhaps in America, besides a view infinitely superior to any about Pittsburg, and the river equally commanded. I begin to think your patience has suffered sufficiently, and therefore shall beg leave to present my kind regards to Mrs. Burd and your young family.

JOSEPH SHIPPEN, (COL.,) TO COL. JAMES BURD, AT LANCASTER.

Philadelphia, May 23d, 1759.

DEAR BROTHER:—Captain Jones' Company marched on Monday for Carlisle, where he is to encamp, having an order on the keeper of the king's store, from Capt. Hay, to receive nine tents, and fifty-three stands of arms.

Since you left town, the Governor has peremptorily told Mr. Peters, Young, and myself, that he will have a third battalion, and that he had settled it with the General the day before, telling us that otherwise the two battalions would be too large.

I have enclosed you a copy of the new exercise, which the Royal Americans performed very well when received last Monday. I hear they are to leave this town next week with the artillery, etc.

Yesterday the General gave a public breakfast at the Assembly Room; there were forty-two ladies there, and many more gentlemen; all danced after breakfast till near 2 o'clock, and then formed parties with the ladies to Schuylkill and Springettsberry. The man whom you enlisted before you left town, for three years, is extremely troubled with fits; I am of opinion he will be of very little service; I saw him the other day, and he appeared very sickly and weak. What shall be done with him? I give you joy of the surrender of Guadaloupe.

P. S.—The Governor says he will be paid for the commissions he has already signed since he has been in the Government and those he is yet to give out, exclusive of the secretary's fees; he has settled his own thus:

£	s.	
5		from a Colonel.
4		do a Lieutenant.
3		do a Major.
2		do a Captain.
1	10	do a Lieutenant.
1		do an Ensign.

And he has ordered Mr. Young to collect them.

HUGH MERCER, (LT. COL.,) TO COL. JAMES BURD, AT LANCASTER.

Pittsburgh, May 23d, 1759.

DEAR SIR :—Yours of the 30th April and 3d inst., I had the pleasure to receive yesterday, and am extremely pleased to find that your young family have happily got over the distemper which has raged even here, and among our neighbors at . Since my last, having occasion to write to Col. Armstrong, I enclosed him lists of the dead of your battalion, to the 1st instant, desiring he should send you that of the Second Battalion. But few have dropped off since, and I flatter myself that your people will not appear despicable on your arrival here. They mend every day, and will be fit for any service required of them, before the army arrives, if that should even happen some time before next fall.

My opinion as to their going to the settlement, you shall have with all the freedom in life. I never knew any other advantage accruing to soldiers (I mean ours) from being in town on the frontier than blacked eyes and eternal floggings, and unless Carlisle and Shippensburgh are of late more closely altered in point of morals, the old game at either of these seats of virtue and good manners would undoubtedly be played over; especially if N. has intended the men should receive their pay there, to enable them to indulge more and more, besides having their pockets picked by tavernkeepers. Then this garrison is to march (on the intended scheme) four hundred miles; but for what? Why to give the finishing stroke to their health and spirits, too much exhausted by severe duty and hard labor, experienced here through the winter. The battalions will be assembled complete on the

Ohio, and I am convinced even the common men will choose rather to pay the expense of transporting the articles intended them, to this place, than carry them some hundred miles themselves. But I hope better things from the Government, than that such a tax will be laid on us. On Monday last, a skirmish happened between a party of a Corporal and ten Provincials, and about twenty Indians. Poor Swails, to the great comfort of Molly and Tommy, was killed, off a hunting from the party. Our men behaved well, killed one and wounded another of the enemy; but were obliged to return, on an attempt to surround them. We endeavored to come up with them afterwards, but in vain; they had made off in great haste with two Vermont soldiers, prisoners. Two officers and some Indians from Venango have hovered about us some days, but carefully avoid all the traps we can lay for them. There is no coming up with them, but by a fox hunt to Venango, where we may possibly catch old Le Narie in his hole, unless he has timely notice of our desire. The only news is, that we are all well, and have no reason to dread a sudden reverse of fortune.

COL. BURD TO COL. BOUQUET.

Camp at the Little Meadows, Sept. 7th, 1759.

Dear Sir :—I came to this ground last night, where late in the evening I had the pleasure to receive your favors of the 4th instant. It is very lucky you did not attempt to send your wagons to Fort Cumberland, as they certainly could not get along that road; after so much rain it must be a perfect swamp. I last night received a horse-load of the oats you were so good to send to Cumberland.

The road from my last encampment to this is really excessively bad; the Alleghany Hill is by no means the worst of it; there are two hills extremely bad and long. From Martin's place to this they esteem it eleven miles, and I think it very bad for wagons. There has been nothing done upon it by Finney. If the road is all along as I have found it hither, I think wagons can carry one-third more on the other roads than this, and with more ease to the horses; and I would strongly advise that a party from Fort Cumberland may be ordered upon this road from thence to Guest's; I'll answer from thence to the mouth of Redstone Creek. The commanding officer of the party should not hurry, but make the road good, and take time. It seems to me that Mr. Braddock was in a hurry to get along, and so did not allow time to make the road as it ought or easily could be made. It is not more than ten feet wide, and carried right up every hill almost without a turn, and the hills almost perpendicular; however, if the officer who is sent on it from Cumberland has any understanding and regard for the service, he may make it a good communication, as it is very capable of improvement; and I know I could make it a good road for the part of the country, but as it now stands it is too bad. You know Mr. Avery weighed the loads of my wagons, and they were 12 cwt.[each.] I found they could not get along even with this moderate load; and I took out about 14 cwt. and loaded upon the officers' horses, and at the hill I put six soldiers to each wagon to hoist them up. I hope to march from hence twelve miles to-day; if I make out this march I will be very happy at night.

I observe you have some thought of sending the three wagons this way. I hope they will do very well after the road is mended; as the hills must be turned up by winding, and not left as they are now, straight up. The stones must be thrown out of the road, all new bridges, and old ones tossed on one side, and I think the road should be widened; but this might be dispensed with. I am very glad the General will find a conveyance to meet me at the Monongahela. I will immediately upon my arrival ascertain the situation of the water, and then we can proceed accordingly with the transportation from Cumberland. The weather has been very severe upon my people, and not a little so upon myself, as I have had a fever; but now we are all in good spirits and no complaints.

I conclude, my dear Colonel,

Your sincere friend and humble servant,

JAMES BURD.

Col. Shippen's compliments to you.

COL. BOUQUET TO COL. BURD.

Fort Duefoir, Sept. 13*th*, 1759.

DEAR SIR:—We have had an account from St. Lawrence, that General Wolf attacked the lines the 31st July, with all the grenadiers and two hundred R. A., but was repelled with loss of four hundred men, partly wounded. People begin to think that he will not succeed, but will ruin the country in his retreat. I hope better; he has beaten the Canadians and Indians everywhere, killed great numbers, and got five hundred prisoners. No news from Europe. Callender has arrived with his men's horses, but Hambright is yet at Lancaster.

COL. BURD TO GENERAL STANWIX.

Camp at the mouth of Nemoraling's Creek, on the Monongahela, about one mile above the mouth of Redstone Creek, Sept. 30th, 1759.

SIR :—I have cut the road from Guest's, and came to this ground the twenty-third inst. I would have wrote your excellency ere now, but have been hourly expecting the arrival of a batteau at Pittsburgh. I think this will be a very fine post, it is situated upon a hill in the fork of the river and creek, commands both, and is not commanded by anything; the hill is almost fifty yards from the river, and joins the creek. I have kept the people constantly employed on the works since my arrival, although we have been for eight days past upon the small allowance of one pound of beef and half a pound of flour per man a day, and this day we begin upon one pound of beef, not having one ounce of flour left, and only three bullocks, I am therefore obliged to give over working till I receive some supplies. I have expected Captain Poaris with a quantity of provisions for some time, and know nothing of the reason of the delay. I wrote five days ago on this subject, and shall find an express to Cumberland this day. I shall measure the road from Guest's thither, and make a return of it; I compute the distance seven miles. Enclosed is a return of the troops under my command.

I am with esteem, your excellency's
most obedient, humble servant,
JAMES BURD.

His Excellency, General Stanwix.

EDWARD SHIPPEN TO COL. JAMES BURD, AT PITTSBURGH.

New York, October 11th, 1759.

This evening the Brig Seahorse, Capt. Williams, arrived here in nine days from Louisbourg, by whom we have the following extract of a letter containing the particulars undermentioned:

Louisbourg, Oct. 2d, 1759.

* * * Yesterday a vessel arrived at this place from Quebec, which brings us the agreeable news of the fall of that place the 17th of last month; the only letter is from Captain Brea, of the Princess Amelia, who says that on the 13th, as General Wolfe landed on the north side above the town, that Montcalm opposed him, when a most bloody engagement commenced, in which poor General Wolfe was killed, much lamented; but he died gloriously, and I think rather to be envied than pitied. General Monckton is wounded through the lungs; Captain Millbanks, of Bragg's, killed; Lord Seymore, Lt. Col. Fletcher, Col. Barney, Col. Carlton, Major Spittle, Captain Cazneau, his officers and many more wounded, in all on our side, above 500. On that of the French, Montcalm and Levy both killed; the third in command both taken prisoners, and the fourth killed, in all, about 1600. We pursued them to their sally ports; Brigadier Townsend, the then commander, made a battery within 300 yards of the citadel, and by the 16th it was finished. The 17th he summoned the town to surrender, and in case of refusal, they should have no quarters, when they immediately sent him a carte blanche.

This is all I know.

DAVID HALL.

Lancaster, 3 *o'clock P. M., Oct.* 14*th*, 1759.

DEAR SON,—Mr. BURD :—Just as we were setting out for Church, Byerly, the General's express, brought in a paper of which the above is a copy, I hope the news is true, and so I heartily congratulate you on the occasion. Your wife and children are all well. Your mammy joins with me in our kind love to yourself and your Lieut. Colonel. I should not be so brief, but for two reasons, that the bell is ringing for prayers, and Byerly can't stay.

I am your affectionate and loving father,

EDWD. SHIPPEN.

COL. SHIPPEN, JR., TO HIS FATHER, AT LANCASTER.

Philadelphia, Oct. 11*th*, 1759.

HONORED SIR :—It is the most difficult thing imaginable, to get pieces of eight changed for paper, so that I can send you up no money by Ennis.* There are generally some shopkeepers from Lancaster, coming to this town, can't you get their money and draw orders on me? Doctor Smith has brought with him the resolution of the King and Council in his favor, in which our Governor is required to signify his Majesty's high displeasure to the Assembly of Pennsylvania for their unjust, illegal and arbitrary proceedings in the affair of Mr. Smith, for their bold invasion of the prerogative of the Crown and unwarrantable attack upon the liberties of the subject.† He is also required to take especial care that no such measure be suffered for the

* Things have changed now-a-days. The difficulty is now to get money for paper.

† Ante page 108, 116.

future, and that the King's writs do issue freely, and that all officers of justice be protected in the execution of them. This will be laid before the Assembly on their next meeting, and will no doubt create a great ferment in the house; some hot heads still talk of imprisoning Smith.

You ought to be well paid for all the trouble you take in the King's affairs. Col. Bouquet told Mr. Allen, you should either have 2½ per cent. commission, or a guinea per day, which you pleased, I suppose the commission would mount highest.

CH. J. SHIPPEN TO HIS FATHER AT LANCASTER.

Philadelphia, November 26th, 1759.

Honored Sir :—Governor Hamilton is very hearty, and will not run the risk of becoming otherwise by living at Bush Hill. He is to have Denny's house—Swaine is to be turned out, and Lewis Gordon to succeed him. Things in the government begin to wear a pleasant aspect, and the late administration is looked upon with a proper contempt. Denny, it is said, carries pocket pistols for fear of insults. I don't wonder at his apprehensions, since if his conscience be awake, he must tremble at the sight of every honest man.

Disposition of the Pennsylvania Troops stationed at the Posts on the communication from Pittsburgh to Carlisle, and at Fort Augusta and Fort Allen, on the frontiers of the Province of Pennsylvania, Nov. 13th, 1759.

WHERE STATIONED	BATTALION.	FIELD OFFICERS.	CAPTAINS.	SUBALTERNS.	SERGEANTS.	DRUMMERS.	RANK AND FILE.
	F. B.,	Maj. Armstrong,	Clapham,	Hutchings, Anderson,	3	2	92
	S. B.,		Broadhead,	Price, Wackerberg,	2	1	58
					5	3	150
Bush Run, -	F. B.,				1		12
Ligonier, - -	F. B.,	Maj. Jameson,	Hyndshaw,	Craighead, Piper,	2	2	61
	S. B.,			Humphries, Bond,	2	1	39
					4	3	100
Stony Creek, -	S. B.,			Curched,	1		20
Bedford, - -	F. B.,	Lt. Col. Shippen,	Potter,	Lytell, Stetler,	2	2	61
	S. B.,	Maj. Orndt,		Miles, Hunter,	2	1	39
					4	3	100
Juniatta, - - -	F. B.,			Wilkes,	1		20
Fort Lyttleton, -	S. B.,			McKee,	1		20
Loudon, - - -	F. B.,			Blyth,	1		20
Shippensburg,	F. B.,						8
	S. B.,			Scott,	1		12
					1		20
Carlisle, - - -	F. B.,			Lyttle,	1		20
Fort Augusta, -	S. B.,		Trump Atlee.	4	4	3	100
Fort Allen, - -	S. B.,			1	1		20
TOTAL, - - -	F. B.,	1	3	9	11	6	294
	S. B.,	3	3	14	14	6	308
		4	6	23	25	12	602

N. B.—Lieut. McKee, by the General's orders, remains here for a particular department; therefore, Lieut. Anderson, who, in the former disposition, was appointed to Bush Run, or some other officer of the First Battalion, ought to be at Shippensburg.

CH. J. SHIPPEN TO HIS FATHER, AT LANCASTER.

Philadelphia, Dec. 4th, 1759.

HONORED SIR:—We are very much surprised to hear that three of the Lancaster Judges are qualified; especially as it must have been so long ago as in Mr. Denny's time, and we never heard of it before. No new dedimus has been issued since Mr. Hamilton's time, and I hope they have not been qualified under Mr. Denny's dedimus after he was out of the government, because it must be clear that his power died with his administration; and if, after the supersedeas to his commission, he could not have qualified the judges himself, it is very evident no person under a delegated power from him could do it. A dedimus potestatem is of the same nature with a power of attorney, it dies with the party giving it. However, if the case had been so, it is all a mistake, and they can have no power till they are properly qualified by the present Governor, or by some person to whom he shall give a power for that purpose. Upon a supposition that the Judges are or soon will be properly qualified, then in answer to the queries in the little paper enclosed to me, I am of opinion that all the writs to be issued before next Court must be tested, and may be signed by you in the same manner as heretofore, because they bear test on the last day of the last term, when no new judges were in being, and the writs are supposed in law to have issued on the day they bear test. Whether, after next Court, the writs may be signed by you as prothonotary, or must be signed by a judge, I shall have sufficient time between this and then to consider of. As to the entering judgments, they must certainly be done before a judge of the court; and where judgments confessed are sent up from Philadelphia, the usual entry must be made in the docket, and signed by a judge upon his seeing the confession of the judgment under the attorney's hand. My fingers are numbed with cold.

CH. J. SHIPPEN TO HIS FATHER, AT LANCASTER.

Philadelphia, Dec. 13*th*, 1759.

HONORED SIR :—I returned last night from Bucks, when I received Josey's letter; but as the news he mentions has not yet been confirmed, I conclude there is nothing in it. We shall probably have frequent alarms this winter, and perhaps more people will be cut off on the frontiers, but I have no notion that any body of Indians will venture into the thick settled part of the country. Their cowardly disposition, and the difficulty they would have in returning, will be our security. The treaty with the Indians is to be held at Harris' Ferry, the 1st of January. I enclose you a party paper for your amusement; the authors are said to be Wm. Franklin, Jos. Galloway, and George Bryan, but I know not with what justice. The introduction, and the letter from Montreal, are said to be wrote by an older hand. The difference between them and the other parts of the paper is very apparent. If a superlative degree of scurrility is wit, I think the piece has merit. Read and judge.

COLONEL SHIPPEN TO GENERAL STANWIX.

Fort Bedford, January 4*th*, 1760.

SIR:—I had the honor to receive your Excellency's letter of the 24th ultimo, directing me, as soon as I am relieved by a party of the Royal Americans, to march all the Pennsylvanians under my command to Lancaster, leaving garrisons of twenty-five men at Loudon and Lyttleton. Colonel Burd now informs me, it is the Governor's intention to dispose of the one hundred and fifty Pennsylvanians remaining in pay, thus: a hundred at Augusta, twenty at Fort Allen, and thirty at Lyttleton; nevertheless, I shall execute the orders I have received from your Excellency.

Major Jameson, with his detachment from Ligonier, left this yesterday morning, and Captain Brodhead's division marched to-day.

I enclose a return of the Pennsylvania troops remaining here, by which your Excellency will observe, there are twenty-four men more than was destined for this post: but this was occasioned by a number of sick and lame, left here by the different parties, marching downwards; and I was under a necessity of detaining a few artificers, in order to finish a large bridge across the Juniata, two miles up the road.

Your Excellency may depend upon my using my best endeavors to promote the recruiting service for the Royal Americans; as I shall be proud, at all times, to execute any of your commands,—and beg you will believe me to be, with the greatest esteem,

Your Excellency's, &c.

COL. SHIPPEN TO COL. BURD, AT CARLISLE.

Fort Bedford, January 21*st,* 1760.

Dear Brother: — Your favor of the 17th instant, I received last night, by which I unexpectedly find that

Mr. Young is come to Carlisle for the two old battalions, though it was the General's peremptory orders to Major Jameson, Captain Broadhead and myself, to march them to Lancaster for that purpose. But, while I continue in the army under his command, I think myself obliged to obey his instructions. You ask me, if I can send down your company immediately. I am sorry it is not in my power to oblige you, as I cannot dispense with any part of this garrison, till the Royals arrive, without the General's permission, which, if I had, I could not possibly spare an officer to march with it at present, having sent down Lieut. Graydon last week, agreeable to your former desire, and only Lieut. Miles and Mr. Curched left to do the duty here; Ensign Price acting as Adjutant and Quartermaster.

And I am sorry to tell you of another material reason, that would prevent me from sending away any part of the garrison—which is, a violent general mutiny that broke out this morning among the men, in consequence of their having heard that they were to receive no pay after the 15th instant. They almost, to a man, refused to do their duty, and I having confined a sergeant to begin with, all the men run out of their barracks and rescued him, and took him under their protection. I was obliged to march at the head of the guard, with my sword drawn among them, and swear that I was determined to run the first man through, that attempted to detain the prisoner, or do any kind of violence. With difficulty, I took the prisoner. The whole of them swore they would follow him—the consequences of which I dreaded—and therefore prevented it, by standing with my sword at the door of the barrack, and assuring them I was resolved to put to death the first man that moved a step. I cannot now mention any more particulars, as the express waits. But, with storming and threatening death, and forfeiture of pay, and by setting their disgraceful, infamous behavior and rebellion, in their proper light, I have, in a great measure, appeased the violent spirit of most of them, and I hope that the orders that I have this moment given out, (it is now about twelve o'clock,) with what I shall say to them on the parade, will be the means of putting an end to all disturbances.

Copy of the Orders given at Fort Bedford.

Fort Bedford, January 21*st*, 1760.
12 *o'clock*, (*M.*)

The whole detachment to parade with their arms at one o'clock, when every man that does not attend, as well as those that refuse to do their duty, shall be looked upon as ringleaders of mutiny and rebellion against his Majesty, and will be punished as such by the sentence of a general court-martial, and forfeit all his pay; and the commanding officer takes this opportunity to inform them, that he has received certain intelligence by letters to Capt. Oury and himself, that the Royal Americans arrived at Carlisle the 17th instant, and are marching up with all expedition to relieve this garrison, and will undoubtedly be here this week; and Colonel Shippen hereby acquaints those that will cheerfully do their duty as good soldiers till that relief arrives, that he will do everything in his power to have justice done to them in every respect.

Monday, 1½ *o'clock, P. M.*

I have just returned from the parade, and have the satisfaction to tell you that the men have all agreed to do their duty, and I beg you will use your interest to get an order from the commissioners, that all the men be paid to the day of their discharge, if Mr. Young is not already empowered to do this. I shall march down with all the expedition I can. My compliments to Colonels Armstrong and Mercer, and Messrs. Young and Bard, and the gentlemen with you.

I am, dear colonel,

Your very affectionate brother,

JOSEPH SHIPPEN, Jr.

CH. J. SHIPPEN TO HIS FATHER, AT LANCASTER.

Philadelphia, January 28th, 1760.

Honored Sir:—I received your favor by Col. Bouquet's express. As to your question, whether you ought to refuse granting writs for masters against servants enlisted, I have considered it, and think you have no power to refuse the writs.

The contract between master and servant is for servitude, which the master can get enforced by the Court of Quarter Sessions. You know there is an Act of Parliament to oblige officers enlisting servants to pay for them, and it is my opinion, that the master ought to pursue the steps directed by that Act, and that no other remedy is in his power. Mr. John Ross declares he never advised such a step.

CH. J. SHIPPEN TO HIS FATHER, AT LANCASTER.

Philadelphia, March 28th, 1760.

Honored Sir:—There is a petition going to the Assembly to erect the land southward of the south bounds of this city into a borough, which, it is said, will be the means of drawing a great number of people there, and of course will improve the value of the lands. I have been looking over a rough sketch of the plan of division between you and Uncle Joe of the square where Logan's house now stands, and observe that your lots on Second street are all bounded on the east by lots belonging to him, and those of his in the same manner by yours, which I cannot help thinking a great detriment to both of you. The houses building on Mrs. Jekyl's ground, and other ground thereabout, are in a very good fashion, and will be inhabited by people of circumstances. Many others will be daily looking out for good lots to build on. The improvement of the water lots will draw many of the merchants there, and it will in a little time be a very reputable part of the town; in which case, there will be many customers for lots of a good front, 130 feet deep, who would never think of a lot only sixty feet deep. I should think, if your brother and yourself were to release to each other the several lots on Vernon street that tail upon the lots on Second street, it would unquestionably raise the value of both your estates. At the time the division was made, there was no reason to expect any but the lower sort of people would build on lots so remote from the centre of business, and such shallow lots might suit them well enough. But the case is now altered, and we see good houses daily building where formerly nobody would have thought of such a thing. Lots are grown very scarce. There are few vacant ones, and people of business will not retire to the upper end of Market street while they can get lots near the water. You'll excuse my hinting this matter to you; I really think it of consequence.

CH. J. SHIPPEN, TO HIS FATHER, AT LANCASTER.

March, 1760.

HON. SIR:—General Amherst favored us with his company but two days. He would not interfere between the Governor and Assembly about passing the money bill. But they all seem determined not to give it up, so that it is yet doubtful whether any money will be granted. I have heard that General Amherst left orders with General Stanwix, that if the bill should pass, to give him immediate notice of it, that he might order the battalion destined to the westward, to some other quarter. If so, we shall be left in as bad a plight on our frontiers as ever. However, I am not without hopes that some means may still be found out to reconcile, at least for the present, the contending parties.

CH. J. SHIPPEN TO HIS FATHER, AT LANCASTER.

Philadelphia, April 11*th,* 1760.

HON. SIR:—I accompanied poor Joe last Sunday as far as Gloucester, when he embarked for Leghorn, but from the winds I imagined he could not get out of the cape till to-day; he is in a good vessel and has a cheerful and obliging captain. I give my prayers with yours for his safe and prosperous voyage. Mr. Burd has had some kind offers of being employed in the room of Adam Hoopes this campaign. He seems very fond of the thing and asked my advice. I have great doubts and therefore consulted Mr. Allen, who is clearly of opinion he had better continue Colonel. He thinks the gentlemen who at present are agents for the contractors, viz: Moss, Plumsted and Franks, are greatly unequal to the task, and will not be able to raise money enough to supply the under agents as they call for it, in which case Mr. Burd would lose his credit, and perhaps have a number of writs clapped on his back.

Joshua Howell, who had as much management and address as any man among us, was frequently under the greatest difficulties, and could never have carried on the business, but for the assistance the whole body of Quakers from time to time afforded him. The present people have neither address, industry, friends, nor money. Mr. Burd listens to this advice, and I believe will not be obstinate, though the prospect is tempting.

CH. J. SHIPPEN TO COL. SHIPPEN, AT LEGHORN.

Philadelphia, May 12th, 1760.

DEAR BROTHER:—Though I date my letter from Philadelphia, I am in fact at Reading, on my Western Circuit, and write at this time lest Captain Ritchie should sail before I got to town. Nothing very material has happened since you left us. We are still in a state of uncertainty as to the continuance of the war; however, we think at all events you must have come to a tolerable market. If you should not return in the vessel, you will write me very particularly your sentiments concerning the trade in the Mediterranean, and what commodities would answer from hence in time of peace, and also what houses you think best of in the several ports. This knowledge will be very useful, as few people here are in the least acquainted with it. Cousin Johnny Allen will have heard of the death of his good old grandmamma: if the most remarkable virtue and piety is proportionably rewarded in the other world, this good aunt of ours must now possess an excellent place in heaven.

The last article that was inserted in your list of goods was 500 dozen of Leghorn hats. I hope you will not mistake our meaning as to the quality of this article; it must be a very cheap kind—not higher than two, three or four shillings per dozen.

In my private list of things I mentioned a marble slab; if you have not already purchased it, let it be a few inches longer and an inch or two wider than I directed. If you can conveniently get a small Italian greyhound, I would be glad you would send me one; and Col. Burd desires, if pointers are plenty where you are, that you would send him one.

The expedition to the westward is going on under General Monckton. It is thought the army will proceed to Fort Detroit. Our two Provincial regiments, under Col. Burd and Col. Mercer, are in a fair way of being completed.

All our families are well. My father is now in Philadelphia, and will no doubt write to you by this opportunity.

I mentioned two Turkey carpets, one about 16 or 17 feet by 12 or 13, the other 14 or 15 by 11. I am afraid they will be too narrow; so that, if not already shipped, let the first be about 14 and the other 12.

CH. J. SHIPPEN TO HIS FATHER, AT LANCASTER.

Philadelphia, June 9th, 1760.

HON'D SIR:—I give you joy of our having raised the siege of Quebec, after the enemy had actually made a breach in the walls and were preparing to enter, sword in hand. It does not yet, I think, clearly appear from the accounts, whether the flight of the enemy proceeded from the appearance of Lord Colville's fleet, or from an actual drubbing they got from our people in a sally from the town. After the account which we had ten days ago, most people here and at New York gave up the place; so that this account affords double joy.

A List of Officers in First Battalion of the Pennsylvania Regiment, June, 1760.

OFFICERS.	RANK.	DATES OF COMMISSION.
The Governor,	Colonel.	
John Armstrong,	Colonel Command't,	Dec. 2, 1757
Hugh Mercer,	Lieut. Colonel,	Dec. 4, 1757
Patrick Work,	Major,	Mch 23, 1759–60
George Armstrong,	Captain,	Dec. 12, 1757
Edward Ward,	do	Dec. 13, 1757
Robert Callender,	Captain,	Dec. 15, 1757
James Patterson,	do	Dec. 16, 1757
John N. Weatherholt,	do	Dec. 19, 1757
Patrick Davis,	do	Dec. 22, 1757
William Armstrong,	do	Dec. 24, 1757
James Potter,	do	Feb. 17, 1759
John Prentice,	do	May 12, 1759–60
James Hynd Shaw,	Captain Lieutenant,	May 15, 1759–60
Thomas Hutchins,	L't. and Q'rmaster,	Dec. 18, 1757
Henry Griger,	Lieutenant,	Dec. 21, 1757
Nicholas Conrad,	do	Dec. 22, 1757
William Blyth,	do	Dec. 24, 1757
James Hughes,	do	Mch 17, 1759–60

OFFICERS.	RANK.	DATES OF COMMISSION.
Robert Anderson,	Lieutenant,	Mch 18, 1759–60
Joseph Halkner,	do	May 14, 1759–60
George Craighead,	do	May 15, 1759–60
Joseph Quicksale,	do	May 16, 1759–60
John Lytle,	do	May 27, 1759–60
John Philip DeHaas,	do	May 19, 1759–60
Edmond Matthews,	do	May 20, 1759–60
Thomas Haip,	Ensign,	Dec. 2, 1757
John Kennedy,	do	Dec. 13, 1757
Hugh Crawford,	do	Mch 11, 1758–9
Fred'k Von Homback,	do	Ap'l 2, 1758–9
Conrad Butcher,	do	Ap'l 11, 1758–9
Samuel Montgomery,	do	Jan'y 1, 1759
James Pyper,	do	Mch 18, 1759–60
Caspar Stadler,	do	Mch 20, 1759–60
——— Orndt,	do	May 10, 1759–60
Andrew Wilker,	do	May 11, 1759–60

A List of the Officers of the Second Battalion of the Pennsylvania Regiment, June, 1760.

OFFICERS' NAMES.	RANK.	DATES OF COMMISSION.
James Burd,	Col. Command't,	Jan'y 2, 1758
Thomas Lloyd,	Lieut. Colonel,	Feb'y 22, 1758
Joseph Shippen,	Major,	May 28, 1758
Jacob Orndt,	Captain,	Dec'r 10, 1757
David Jameson,	do	Dec'r 11, 1757
John Hambright,	do	Dec'r 14, 1757
Levi Trump,	do	Dec'r 17, 1757
Jacob Morgan,	do	Dec'r 18, 1757
Asher Clayton,	do	Jan'y 9, 1758

OFFICERS' NAMES.	RANK.	DATES OF COMMISSION.
Thomas Smallman,	Captain,	M'ch 23, 1759–60
Samuel Atlee,	do	May 13, 1759–60
Charles Broadhead,	do	May 14, 1759–60
Jacob Thearn,	Lieutenant,	Dec'r 11, 1757
Samuel Humphreys,	do	Dec'r 11, 1757
William Patterson,	do	Dec'r 12, 1757
Samuel Miles,	do	Dec'r 14, 1757
Joseph Scott,	do	Dec'r 15, 1757
Patrick Allison,	do	Dec'r 16, 1757
Alexander McKee,	do	Dec'r 17, 1757
William Clapham,	do	Jan'y 9, 1758
John Morgan,	do	April 1, 1758
Caleb Graydon,	do	Nov'r 23, 1758
Edward Biddle,	do	Feb'y 1, 1758–60
Henry Haller,	do	May 18, 1759–60
Adam Henry,	Ensign,	Dec'r 6, 1757
Francis Johnson,	do	M'ch 10, 1758
Jacob Morgan,	do	M'ch 12, 1758
John Baird,	do	M'ch 13, 1758
Martin Heister,	do	M'ch 16, 1758
George Price,	do	Nov'r 23, 1758
David Clayton,	do	Feb'y 1, 1758
Andrew Wackerberg,	do	M'ch 19, 1759–60
—— Courshod,	do	May 12, 1759–60

CH. J. SHIPPEN TO HIS FATHER, AT LANCASTER.

Philadelphia, July 10th, 1760.

Hon'd Sir:—I now send you by Hinzelman the 12 lbs. chocolate, and the silk gown for my sister. The doctor says he has sent the court-plaster. I shall look out for a quarter cask of good Madeira wine, and another of Lisbon, and send them up to you by the first good opportunity.

As to carpets, I would have you stay till the fall, when there will be plenty of them imported, either in Snead or Charles Coxe's vessels, from Italy, and they will be much better and cheaper than any other sort.

As to the emphasis. I find fault with the question that is made for an example. "May a man walk in at the door now," because it is nonsense unless the emphasis is laid on the word "*now*," at least that word is useless, and vain, unless the emphasis was meant to be laid on it.

EDWARD SHIPPEN, OF LANCASTER, TO COLONEL BURD, AT FORT PITT.

Lancaster, July 25th, 1760.

DEAR MR. BURD :—Last night I had the pleasure to receive your very agreeable favor of the 15th instant, which is the only one that is come to my hands since you left Carlisle, but Sally received a letter last week, and you may be sure it gives us joy to hear of the regards paid you by the General in appointing you an Assistant Deputy Quarter Master General, &c. I hope you will be allowed something for the years 1758 and 1759. Good Colonel Bouquet, I make no doubt of it, has been a good spoke in your wheel. I am glad to hear that he is gone to Presque Isle, but why such an amount for that small place, which was deserted last winter? but may-be it is for a general rendezvous, and that Fort I suppose of the Royal Americans. I have wrote you three or four letters since you sat off from Carlisle for Fort Pitt, and always enclosed the newspapers, and shall continue to send them according to my wonted custom ever since you have been in the army. Neddy is just gone over to York Court, he thinks there will be no Spanish war: our connoisseurs have concluded that our noble sovereign, King George, will not take part with the King of Sardinia.

Neddy,* has taken my great house at Thomas Lane's, price sixty pounds per annum, because he cannot put up with Billy Bingham's† house, and under the sound of Bow Bell; though as to the latter he is not like to be much better off, for our parson Jemmy and the vestry turning out McClanahan for saying that Jemmy preached nonsense and false doctrine. The Quakers have sold McClanahan's friends a lot opposite to Thomas Willing's for a church, and they must have *bells* too, or things won't *chime* well. T. Willing was so disturbed at this that he talks of moving away.

CH. J. SHIPPEN TO HIS FATHER, AT LANCASTER.

Philadelphia, Sept. 15th, 1760.

HONORED SIR:—There is an Act of Parliament passed in England, to authorize the sale of the London Company's land in this and the neighboring provinces, the money is to be lodged in the Bank of England, and three years time given for those that claim shares to make their claim. Then they will receive their shares, and the unclaimed

* His son Edward.

† Father of Mr. Wm. Bingham, who was afterwards United States Senator.

shares are to remain in the Bank until the year 1770, and then if no persons can make out a title to them, they are directly to be paid for the benefit of the Pennsylvania Hospital. There is a list annexed to the Act of Parliament, (which now lies before me,) of the names of the persons who appear to have shares in the Company books, and I observe, Thomas Story is set down as the owner of 102 shares. The whole number of shares are 5119, so that computing the estate to be worth £200,000, (a moderate calculation,) the residuary legatees of Thomas Story will get about £1,000 each, and our hospital, by the computation of unclaimed shares, will get about £16,000.

CH. J. SHIPPEN TO HIS FATHER, AT LANCASTER.

Philadelphia, Sept. 17th, 1760.

HONORED SIR:—I think damning the re-emitting Act was quite right, notwithstanding the wincing of our people, who would rather that bill should have been saved, than all the rest put together. The reason is plain: it gives them the sole disposition of so much public money, without being accountable to the Governor or anybody else. The reason assigned by the Board of Trade for advising his Majesty against passing that Act, is principally this: that at this time there appeared no necessity for such a re-issue, as there was rather too large a quantity of paper currency emitted by the supply bills, which would be current for some years to come, and this additional quantity, instead of being of any use as a medium in commerce, would only tend to depreciate that already current. Beside, it is insinuated that they have not made the most honest use of the sole power of disposing of public money, and corrupting the Governor is mentioned as one instance.

For my part, I think a medium ought to be observed in these cases, the Assembly should not have the disposal of all the public money, and yet they should not be without a proper sum to enable them to repel any attacks that may be made against their just rights. I don't wish to see the day that we shall be at the mercy of the proprietor. This puts me in mind of a rap over the knuckles that this great man has got in the report above mentioned, in which, after reproving our Assembly for their daring attempts to wrest the prerogatives of the crown, out of the hand of the the government; it is charged upon the proprietor that he has shamefully suffered their people from time to time, to succeed in these attempts, and notwithstanding he was trusted by the crown with the powers of government in the country, and was accountable to the crown for the infringement of any of its rights, yet he has acted so narrow and contracted a part, as never once to complain of these people to his Majesty, till his own private property and interest was struck at.

I shall send the tea by the stage.

I hope you received my letter, containing a copy of Joe's letter from Leghorn.

Mr. Allen has just received a letter from Messrs. Jackson & Rutherford, merchants, in Leghorn, to whom Joe and Johnny Allen were recommended. They let him know our cargo of sugars is come to a good market, that the ship is obliged to perform quarantine for a fortnight on account of her having called at Gibraltar, but that on another account the calling there has been of great use, as it gave her the benefit of a convoy, without which, in all likelihood, she would have been taken, the French privateers at that time swarming in the Mediterranean. This last circumstance, however, we kept a secret, because the underwriters would exact an unreasonable premium on the voyage back if they knew it. I have wrote to New York to know their premium; when I get an answer, I shall either insure there or here immediately. The gentlemen further write, that as soon as the confinement of the young gentlemen is over, they shall take them to their own house, and take a pleasure in entertaining them to the best of their power; they will likewise introduce or recommend them to the English Ambassador, and other persons of distinction in the several places they are to visit in Italy.

About forty recruits at Germantown, having broke open a house to recover some of their brethren, and done some other mischief, the militia got together and siezed and brought them all together, with their Captain, Kennedy Farrell, to our prison.

CH. J. SHIPPEN TO HIS FATHER, AT LANCASTER.

Philadelphia December 3d, 1760.

Hon. Sir:—I shall forward to you, by the first careful wagoner, the things sent by my brother Joe, for Mrs. Burd and Mammy, viz; one box of Vermicelli, one box of flowers (at the bottom of which I have put the garden seeds for yourself) and two Bologna saussages. I have got a Turkey carpet, which comes very high, but there is no more for sale, so that if you have a mind for a handsome Scotch carpet, please to send me an account of the size you would have it, and I will buy one and send it up. Those are the sorts most used here.

CH. J. SHIPPEN TO HIS FATHER, AT LANCASTER.

Philadelphia, January 1st, 1761.

HON. SIR:—I received your favor of the 29th ult. I was at a loss about sending your letter to Mr. Logan, as it was accompanied with newspapers, for which he would be obliged to pay a most heavy postage from the Downs to London, as all letters are put into the Post-office, in whatever part of England the vessel first stops at, and I did not care to send the letter without the papers, as I did not know the purpose of sending them; so I detained both till another opportunity offered, that I might in the mean time know your mind.

The wine we sell for £6 10*s*. is a generous Malaga, some sweet, some dry. Mr. Allen and Mr. Turner are both so fond of this kind of wine that they have each taken several casks for their own use, and say they shall use no other sort (in common) in their families. If you choose to have a cask, I will send you one by the first wagon; but at the same time, not to raise your expectations too high, I must inform you I do not think so highly of it as these gentlemen, but it will mend by age. As we have a good deal of this wine on hand, I would be glad of your opinion, whether, if we should send forty or fifty quarter casks to Lancaster, we should be able to get them off at the above price with charges of carriage.

You desire to know whether this sort of wine is commonly to be had so cheap as I mentioned. I suppose you mean at the place we bought them from. I believe the price we gave is as high as ever they are, either in war or peace: but the difficulty of the trade lies in this, that we have no commodity of this country's growth that will answer to send to that part of the world, except once in five or six years, there should be a scarcity of grain in Europe.

We have an account by a vessel from Bristol into New York, that our good old King died of an apoplexy, on the 25th October, and that King George the Third was proclaimed at Bristol, the 27th. Though this account does not come authoritatively, and so is not mentioned in the newspapers, yet there is no doubt of the truth of it. The roads have been so bad that no wagons have offered, by which I could send the things I mentioned to you in a former letter, among which is some citron from Miss Betsy Anderson.

RICHARD PETERS (SECRETARY) TO EDWARD SHIPPEN, ESQ., AT LANCASTER.

Philadelphia, March 19th, 1761.

DEAR SIR:—You will see a proclamation in the paper for raising three hundred men, of which Colonel Burd is to have the command. Yesterday arrived dispatches from Secretary Pitt, with orders to raise more men, for a certain expedition which does not transpire. The Assembly is called on in these despatches to meet the 2d of April. Send this letter and the one enclosed to Colonel Burd, wherever he is, that he may come here and receive his commission. In the meantime, he will beat up for volunteers, and get all he can. The Governor, Mr. Allen, Mr. Chew and myself are going, on Saturday, to Newtown, in Maryland. We shall return the 31st inst., or as soon as the weather will permit after that day. On the 2d of April, I would have Col. Burd in town. One packet is taken, another missing, above three hundred privateers of the enemy on our English coast. This accounts for your not hearing from your son, nor I from Mr. Allen.

All is war, and the most violent war, in Europe.

RICHARD PETERS (SECRETARY) TO COL. BURD, OF THE PENNSYLVANIA FORCES.

Philadelphia, June 5th, 1761.

DEAR SIR:—The Governor strictly charges and commands you, to give it in order, that every officer do duty according to the seniority of his rank last year. He desires you will settle the dates of the commissions, and with the strictest regard to each officer's rank. If this be not agreed to, he will issue new commissions, according to the dates you shall send.

Enclosed are four commissions; two to you, a colonel's and a captain's commission, and two blank ones for your lieutenant and ensign; for the fees whereof you will be accountable. I heartily wish you health and happiness.

EDWARD SHIPPEN TO COL. JAS. BURD, AT FORT PITT.

Lancaster, Saturday, October 3d, 1761.

DEAR MR. BURD:—This acknowledges the receipt of your kind letter, per *nôtre bon ami,* Capt. Young, both which inform us of your good health and of Col. Bouquet's, and the rest of our good friends at Fort Pitt, to whom I beg my respectful compliments.

No other news stirring, than that everybody thinks we are at the eve of peace. All Canada, and the country down as far as Louisiana, but not Louisiana itself, to be ceded to the English, as also Minorca; and we are to release Guadaloupe, and all other conquests, to the French.

Mr. Peters (who is now at York, settling accounts with Mr. Galloway, who kindly inquired for you,) says he thinks Capt. Friend, in whose ship Col. Shippen is expected, waits for a convoy.

Mr. Peters says we are to have twelve battalions kept up, to garrison the Forts at Halifax, Quebec, Oswego, Niagara, Presqu' Isle, Venango, Detroit, and Fort Pitt, &c., &c. The Governor and the Assembly broke up in a very friendly manner; and of the £50,000 or £60,000 sterling in Mr. Franklin's hands, given us by the Government, £3,000 currency is given to the Hospital; £1,300 currency to be paid to Mr. John Hughes for copying the proprietor's papers, which that scribe says is too little, by a great deal; and the remainder is to be drawn for in bills of exchange, and the paper money received for them to be immediately burnt; which will not only keep up the credit of our paper money, but ease the people much in their taxes. I desire, God willing, to set out next Monday for the Jerseys, which will cost me a week, if not ten days.

I hear nothing as yet of the Governor and Assembly's determination as to Fort Augusta, but imagine they will not let it drop.

I am sorry to hear the French privateers have been so thick on our coast, and also on the banks of Newfoundland. Col. Byrd* is in Philadelphia. Enclosed are both the newspapers.

COL. SHIPPEN TO COL. BURD, AT LANCASTER.

Philadelphia, Feb. 17*th*, 1762.

DEAR BROTHER:—I received your kind congratulatory letter, upon my arrival among my friends, with pleasure, and return you my sincere thanks. Permit me, in my turn, to give you joy on your safe return from the wilderness to your family, after so long an absence. I have no reason to doubt that you found both our good families in the midst of health and plenty; it would give me great satisfaction, if I was able to participate with you in the happiness you enjoy in their good company.

I am too much engaged with the Governor and Assembly now,† to write you at length; I have only time to tell you that the Governor has just received letters from the Earl of Egremont, (the principal Secretary,) from Mr. Pitt, and Sir Jeffrey Amherst, making a requisition of 1800 troops to be raised by the Province, for the ensuing year; and his Honor has in consequence made that demand of the Assembly; but as several of the country members have leave of

* Of Westover.

† January 2, 1762, Col. Shippen was appointed Secretary to the Province. *Gordon*, 394.

absence, and are gone home, the House has proposed to make a short adjournment before they proceed upon that business; though this is not agreeable to the Governor's mind.

We have a very straight account from Antigua, told us by Capt. Phœnix, who is an honest, intelligent man, that the King of Prussia and Prince Henry had gained a complete victory over Marshal Daun's army, in which the latter lost about 20,000 men, killed and taken, 180 pieces of cannon, and 300 wagons, &c. &c. This he assures us he read in the Gazette, brought in a packet to Antigua, and that Governor Thomas had ordered rejoicings to be made on that account, which he was present at.

Cousin Nancy was married to Mr. Francis on Monday, the 8th instant.

P. S. The Assembly have adjourned till the 8th of March.

WM. ALLEN, ESQ., TO COL. BURD, IN LANCASTER.

Philadelphia, July 10th, 1762.

DEAR SIR:—Your letter, with the piece of ore, together with that of the 5th instant, I have had the pleasure to receive. The ore is not copper, but iron, consequently of little value. I had a good deal of conversation with Job Chelloway, the Indian, at Easton. He seems confident that there is a good lead mine between Tulpehockon and Augusta, and that he can procure the Indians to discover it. I wish you would speak to him on that subject, in order to have the discovery made, and should be glad, if you think there is any truth in the Dutch woman's account of the lead mine near Augusta, that you would, at your leisure, take some steps to find it out. If you will send me down some pieces of the crystal, I shall inquire about the value; except it is clear of flaws, it is of little worth.

I presume you will be desired by the merchants of this place, to examine the west branch of the Susquehanna, having heard that they have applied to the Governor to procure it to be done.

COL. SHIPPEN TO COL. BURD, AT LANCASTER.

Philadelphia, Friday, Sept. 24th, 1762.

DEAR BROTHER:—I am now to inform you, by the Governor's desire, (who is himself sick and keeps his bed,) that you are appointed (with Mr. Davenport, at Fort Pitt) by the Governor and Commissioners, to go up to Pittsburg to receive the prisoners, &c. I give you this information now by the post, that you may begin immediately to prepare for your journey. Mr. Peters, by the Governor's desire, is to draw up this day such instructions as will be necessary for you in the management of the business upon which you go, and he will forward them to you without delay. In the meantime, he desires that you will write to some person near Fort Loudon, cr about Shippensburg, to provide a good wagon and team to transport all goods, &c., which lie at Fort Loudon, to Pittsburg. This wagon should be ready by the time you arrive there, that you may see the goods carefully put in it.

Mr. Peters desires me to tell you that he is ashamed he has neglected to send you the £50 he borrowed of you; he thought Mr. Hockley would have sent it to you while he was at New Castle last week; however, he says he will send it to you with your instructions. The Governor and Commissioners will put £500 into your hands at first, to defray the expenses, &c. attending the department you are appointed to.

COL. SHIPPEN TO COL. BURD, AT LANCASTER.

Philadelphia, September 9th, 1762.

DEAR BROTHER :—I have now the pleasure to congratulate you on the most agreeable news of a victory gained by Prince Ferdinand over the French army, commanded by the Marshals D'Estrees and Soubize, the particulars of which you will see in this day's paper. May God grant a continuance of such glorious successes, with which the British nation has been so remarkably blessed, till France and Spain shall be convinced that it is their interest to give us an honorable and good peace.

The Governor had a meeting to-day with the commissioners, to agree upon the persons to go to Pittsburgh to receive the prisoners, and they all unanimously chose yourself as one, but have not been able to fix yet upon the other to accompany you, as Mr. Logan finds that his business and family will not permit him to go. I suppose they will conclude upon some gentleman, to-morrow or next day, that will be agreeable and proper for the purpose. I mention this because I understood from you, that you intended to set out for Augusta next Monday.

But if you are to go to Pittsburgh and are to be there by the second day of October next, which was the day fixed upon by the Governor at the treaty, I think your journey to Augusta must be deferred, as you cannot be back from thence in time for the other purpose.

I am pleased you have so good an opportunity of sending Neddy down. I shall be very glad to see him, and to receive him into my house. I shall take particular care of him in every respect, and it will be a pleasure to me if I can be of use to him in forwarding his education.

JOHN SWIFT TO LYNFORD LARDNER,* ESQ., LONDON.

Philadelphia, December 6th, 1762.

DEAR SIR:—Mr. Duché,† who arrived here about a week ago, brought us the news of your safe arrival in London, upon which I heartily congratulate you. Mr.

* As Mr. Lardner's name occurs several times in these pages, it may not be amiss to insert the following letter:

JOHN PENN TO LYNFORD LARDNER, ESQ.

DEAR SIR: I have yours of the 6th November before me, and am glad you approve of my brother's agreement with you. I heartily wish the country may agree with your health, and everything answer your expectation. I assure you, all that you can reasonably desire in my power, shall be done to accomplish it; both for the great regard I have for you, and the expectation I have of your discharging whatever post you may be put in, with honor and justice.

I am sorry to find the great differences that have been stirred up in the Province, and hope they may soon be determined.

The Assembly have acted a part that every body here, of common sense, is ashamed of.

Your natural temper is very happy; but if you'll let me advise you, it is to meddle or make with either party as little as you can; for nothing can make a man more uneasy than party. It robs him of all his quiet, and makes him go all lengths without reflection or judgment. He hardly ever thinks for himself, but forms his opinions on the sentiments of others, who have ends to serve he knows not of. So that in all his actions, he is like a puppet, that's play'd with wires we do not see.

I shall be always glad to hear from you, and am, with best wishes,

Your sincere friend and kinsman,

JOHN PENN.

London, 18*th March*, 1740-41.

My brother, sister, Miss Fanny, and all the family at Stanwell, are very well; he, I suppose, will write you by this ship, unless you had letters by Capt. Wright.

† The Rev. Jacob Duché, author of the well known, perhaps I ought to say, notorious letter to General Washington.

Bedford* informed me by the same opportunity, that he saw you the night of your arrival, and that you went into the country the next day, not very well. I hope you did not continue long so. I trust that your native air will be a means of restoring you to a better state of health than that which you enjoyed on this side the water. I assure you I sincerely wish for your happiness and welfare in every respect, and you may depend, if occasion offers, I shall not be unmindful of the trust you have reposed in me here. Mr. Edwards has not yet had occasion to consult much with me in regard to any of your affairs, but should he do it, he will at all times find me very ready to give my best assistance. I doubt not you will hear from other hands that your friend Mr. Peters† was unanimously chosen rector of Christ Church a few days ago. I don't recollect anything very remarkable that has happened to any of our friends since you left us. We are waiting just now with great impatience for the post coming in from New York, as we have heard another packet is arrived there from Falmouth, by whom we expect great news, and I flatter myself I shall be favored with a line from you which will be very agreeable. Mr. Bedford informs me he has had great offers made him for the office, but has so good an opinion of me as to believe I shall do him as much justice as any other person, in which I shall not deceive him. If he should say anything to you on the subject, I doubt not but you will be kind enough to say what you think you justly can, to confirm him in the good opinion he has of

Your affectionate, &c.

Maggy desires her compliments to you.

This is the second epistle I have troubled you with.

* Grosvenor Bedford of London.

† The Secretary to the Province.

JOHN SWIFT TO LYNFORD LARDNER, ESQ., LONDON.

Philadelphia, Feb. 26th, 1763.

DEAR SIR:—I am now to acknowledge and thank you for your kind favor of 12th October, per Burden, (which I received about a fortnight ago,) though the vessel has not yet got up to town, being prevented by the ice. Our winter was very moderate till the last of December, since which time the river navigation has been stopped. In January there fell the largest quantity of hail I ever knew, after which there was a little rain, and then a hard frost, which made a solid body of ice, with which the country has been and is covered to this day.

How can you talk of being under obligations to me? I shall think myself very happy if it would be in my power to render you any service during your absence; but the most I can do will, in my estimation, be but a drop in the sea, compared to what I owe you for so cheerfully and kindly taking upon you to answer for my good conduct in the office I now enjoy.

I received a letter from Mr. Bedford, dated 9th of October last, which lays me under the necessity of asking a further favor of you, which I flatter myself you will comply with. The bonds you were so kind as to join with me in, were made out from those given by Mr. Alexander when he had the deputation, in one of which I made the penalty double what it was in his time, and it seems the other should have been so too. What Mr. Bedford says relating to it is as follows:—'When I wrote to you the 12th ultimo, by the 'packet, I had not received your bonds to the office and to 'myself, but having now got them, I find that the bond to me 'is only for £500, which should have been double, in con-'sideration of the increased engagement and the possible 'chance of a seizure to the value. I do not mention this 'from the least imagination that you are only to be bound 'by the penalties, but because both you and I are to have 'executors.' This I think seems very reasonable, and therefore have sent him by this opportunity another bond, which, if you will be kind enough to put your name to, and see the first cancelled, I shall esteem it as a great addition to the favors you have already done me. I have told Mr. Bedford that I thought you would be kind enough to call on him for this purpose. I must likewise inform you, that in this bond, I have made an addition to the sum I was to allow Mr. Bedford, and have now made it three hundred pounds per annum, which I think will not be too much, as I find it turns out better than I expected. I hope the freedom I take with you on this occasion, will induce you to believe that you cannot give me a greater pleasure than by laying your commands on me, if you should ever have occasion for any services that I can do you. Your family are all well; I often call in to inquire after them. I think you were very lucky in meeting with two persons, so suitable for taking care of your affairs in your absence, as Mr. Edwards and Mr. Hall.

My wife desires her compliments to you. I hope you will keep your resolution of returning hither this spring, because I shall be extremely glad to see you, and am

Your affectionate, &c.

JOHN SWIFT TO LYNFORD LARDNER, LONDON.

Philadelphia, April 29*th*, 1763.

DEAR SIR:—I did myself the pleasure of writing you a long letter the 26th February, per the Ann, Capt. McClure, via Liverpool, since which I have been favored with yours of 7th January, from the "land of pleasure," as you call it, for which I am much obliged to you, and cannot omit this opportunity of letting you know it; because, notwithstanding you say you intend embarking in March or April, I am persuaded this will find you there in June or July. The appearance of a new spring will have such ravishing charms, that I prophecy you will not have power to stir one step till you have had a full enjoyment of them; and for twenty reasons that I could give, I think it will be impossible for you to leave England till the fall. And why would you hurry yourself? Your children are all in good health and well taken care of. Indeed, if your presence here be necessary on any account, it is that as to which a few months can make no great difference.

So much for business. Now let me surprise you with a little piece of news. Our friend, John Bell, was married last Wednesday night to a sister of Mrs. Geo. Smith, who lately became a widow. What else shall I say? I can think of nothing strange that would give you pleasure, and therefore will conclude with telling you that all your old friends and acquaintances are well, and will be very glad to see you here again. My good wishes you may be assured will ever attend you, because I am

Your affectionate, &c.

GOVERNOR JAMES HAMILTON TO COLONEL BURD, AT LANCASTER.

Philadelphia, June 2d, 1763.

SIR: — I was favored with your letter of the 19th of May, enclosing your returns, and the state of the garrison at Augusta, and also informing me of the arrival and settlement of ten or twelve families of New England people at Wyoming, and that a great number of others are shortly expected to come thither on the same design.

As it is of great consequence to the Proprietary, as well as to the peace of the Province, to prevent, as much as possible, all jealousies and suspicions taking root in the minds of the Indians, that the English intend to take possession of their lands against their consent, and without having first purchased and paid them for the same, of which they have, from time to time, expressed their apprehensions to us, I am very desirous to do everything in my power to quiet their minds in that regard, at least so far as regards these provinces, and consequently find myself under a necessity of endeavoring to remove these intruders, before they are too firmly established.

And as I have a very good opinion of your prudence and discretion, in the conduct of anything committed to your care, I earnestly desire that you will, with Mr. Thomas McKee, (who, from his knowledge of the Indians, may be useful to you,) repair forthwith to Wyoming, and pursue the instructions herein enclosed, with regard to the conduct you are to use to any persons you shall find settled there; and that you may be fully armed with all the civil power necessary for that purpose, I herewith send you a comission, appointing you and Mr. McKee justices of the peace, for the counties of Northampton, Berks, and Lancaster, with a blank dedimus for qualifying you, to be filled up with the names of Mr. Shippen, and of any other person you please; and as perhaps this may not find you at Lancaster, Mr. McKee is directed to call on Mr. Shippen, to furnish him with a copy of the oaths which you both will take care to subscribe, and transmit the same to me, attested by the person who shall qualify you. I have had much discourse upon this affair with Mr. Croghan, who, being deputy agent for Indian affairs, gives his directions to Thos. McKee, and also writes to Sir William Johnson these opinions; and as very probably you will see Mr. Croghan, you may, in conference with him, obtain much useful knowledge with regard to the transaction of this affair.

I should observe to you, that, Sir William Johnson having represented to his Majesty the dangerous tendency of this Connecticut intrusion, his Majesty has been pleased to signify to Sir Jeffrey Amherst and the Governor of Connecticut his high displeasure at the intended proceedings of these intruders, and to order them to forbear, till a statement of the case can be laid before him,—and the government of Connecticut, on receiving these orders here, publicly [proclaimed the same,] as appears in an article in the New York papers enclosed to you, which you will show to those people, and make the best use of, to convince them that their own government disallows their proceedings. Be pleased to advance or take up, on my credit, as much money as you shall judge necessary for the hire and subsistence of such persons as you shall employ on this occasion, which I shall cheerfully pay, upon its being made known to me. I have only further to recommend to you prudence and dispatch, in the execution of my written instructions, and to assure you that, in so doing, you will very sensibly oblige one who is, sir, &c.

COL. SHIPPEN TO COL. BURD, AT FORT AUGUSTA.

Lancaster, June 14th, 1763.

DEAR BROTHER:—I am this moment arrived here from Philadelphia, with instructions from the Governor to raise a number of volunteers, to reinforce Fort Augusta without delay, in consequence of the intelligence you sent to his Honor by the express. I am furnished for that purpose with blank commissions and beating orders, which I am to fill up with the names of such persons as I shall judge best capable of raising the recruits in the most expeditious manner. Your company is to be completed to sixty men, including officers; and another company of the same number of men and officers is to be raised immediately, so as to make the garrison at Augusta one hundred and twenty men strong. Arms, ammunition, and three months provisions, will be sent off from Philadelphia this day for Harris's, where I expect to be to-morrow night, after I have called upon Colonel Work, to propose to him to undertake this recruiting service, and to commence the second company. I cannot think of any person so proper for this purpose. He is a good officer, and well-known and esteemed, and I believe his influence will be of good use in raising recruits expeditiously. I am provided with money and authority to raise a number of the frontier inhabitants, to send to the relief of Augusta, if I find that, by the intelligence I receive, to be absolutely necessary till the recruits can be raised. I shall send you the express this evening, or early in the morning, with a letter and belt from the Governor.

THOMAS PENN TO COL. SHIPPEN, AT PHILADELPHIA.

MR. SHIPPEN :—As Mr. Richard Peters has resigned the offices he held under us in order to apply his time principally to the duties of his function as a minister, we cannot any longer desire him to receive and disburse the money necessary for the service of the commissioners and surveyors, appointed for running the lines between Maryland and Pennsylvania, and we desire, in his stead, that you will undertake this service.

We have written to Mr. Hockley to supply you with what money you shall want for that purpose, and desire you will apply it in such manner as shall be most for our service, and send us the accounts of your disbursements whenever we shall order them.

You will observe any orders you shall receive from the commissioners, and confer with Mr. John Penn on all occasions relating to this business.

I am,

Your affectionate friend.

THOS. PENN.

London, August 10*th*, 1763.

TO THE HONORABLE JOHN PENN, ESQ., LIEUTENANT GOVERNOR, &C.

The humble address of the missionaries of the Church of England in the province of Pennsylvania.

MAY IT PLEASE YOUR HONOR :—Animated with sentiments of duty and respect, we, the missionaries of the Church of England, in the province of Pennsylvania, beg leave to embrace this first opportunity our dispersed situation would allow of, to be admitted with our compliments of congratulation upon your appointment to the administration of this government, and your safe arrival among us. Submission to civil authority being essentially necessary for the support of good government, the Church of England hath always manifested her loyalty to the king, and all those in authority under him. Upon these principles it is our duty as well as inclination to form our conduct; and we assure your honor, that we will as far as our influence extends, contribute with cheerfulness and zeal to impress them upon the minds of the people committed to our care, and to make them sensible of the many invaluable blessings they enjoy in the free exercise of their religion, and the advantage of civil government under the benign and auspicious religion of a protestant and patriot king. By these means we hope to render ourselves acceptable to your honor, and to enjoy the continuance of that favor, which we happily experienced under your worthy and benevolent predecessor.

Permit us, sir, to recommend the mission in this Province to your honor's protection and countenance, and we pray that the Supreme Governor of the universe may support and direct you through all the weighty duties of your high station, and render your administration an honor to yourself, and a permanent felicity to the people of Pennsylvania.

Signed by order and on behalf of the said missionaries.

HUGH NEILE, *Missionary,*

Oxford.

December 16th, 1763.

COL. SHIPPEN TO COL. BURD, AT FORT AUGUSTA.

Philadelphia, February 9th, 1764.

DEAR BROTHER:—In the beginning of last March, I received your favor of the 19th ultimo, enclosing the receipts of the bullock-drivers and batteau-men. I should have returned an answer before now, but was prevented by the great disturbances made here by the approach of seven hundren armed men, near to this city, with a design to destroy' the Indians in the barracks. The whole city was under arms three days, with a determination to support Government, and defend their liberties and laws. The rioters rendezvoused at Germantown, where Mr. Chew, Mr. Franklin, Mr. Galloway and Mr. Willing went to confer with them, and demand their reasons for assembling in arms and approaching. They continued with them several hours, and happily settled the affair, so that they agreed to return peaceably to their homes, leaving three of their principals behind, to lay an humble petition of their grievances before the Governor and Assembly. I intended to give you all the particulars of these affairs, but have not time, and refer you to my letter to my father, when you see him. I mentioned the substance of your letter to the Governor, and he readily granted you liberty to come down to settle your private affairs as soon as you please, and desired me to write you this, but says Capt. Graydon must command at Augusta in your absence.

SAMUEL PURVIANCE, JR., TO COL. BURD, AT LANCASTER.

Philadelphia, September 10th, 1764.

DEAR SIR:—The news, which I brought from Lancaster, of the Quakers and Mennonists having made a powerful party to thwart the steps your friends have so vigorously pursued of late for thrusting out of the Assembly those members, who have lately endangered our happy constitution by their precipitate measures, has given great concern to all your friends here, and very much damped our hopes, which were very sanguine, that there could be no danger of carrying the election in the county to our wishes. This unfavorable prospect has induced several gentlemen here to think that, in order to prevent our being defeated at so critical a time, when measures are taken to bring about a general change through the whole Province, it will be expedient to fall on some alteration of the ticket lately proposed by a few leading friends, and submitted to consideration, for alteration or amendment, against the borough election, viz., to put in Ernani Carpenter, Dr. Adam Kuhn, or Jacob Carpenter and Isaac Saunders, and John Hays, or Andrew Work. The design is, by putting in two Germans, to draw such a party of them as will turn the scale in our favor; and though by such a measure we must reject Mr. Ross, yet I'm persuaded he has too much regard for the public good to be offended at such a measure, when taken purely to defeat the views of our antagonists, and not through any disrepect to him. It would be equally agreeable, if Mr. Ross came in place of any of the Irish, but as their interest must be much stronger than his, it would be imprudent to offend them by rejecting one of their proposing. I wish the unhappy contests about Sheriff could be reduced to two competitors, on our side (suppose Colonel Work and Samuel Anderson); it would unite our friends to act with more spirit, and prevent their hurting the public cause. Our friends in Chester county are very sanguine in hopes of carrying the election, and we scarce admit a doubt of it here. We are this day taking measures for Bucks county, and hope to make a strong interest. Franklin and Galloway, or at least one of them, will be run in Bucks, it is said.

Last night, Jno. Hunt, a famous Quaker preacher, arrived from London, in order, it is believed, to give Friends a rap on the knuckles for their late proceedings; and, it is said, a brother of the famous Fothergill will immediately follow on the same errand, though their great sticklers have, by numberless falsehoods, propagated a belief that their friends at home highly approve their measures. You may communicate this to any of your friends.

I am, &c.

COL. SHIPPEN TO COL. BURD, AT LANCASTER.

Philadelphia, October 6th, 1764.

DEAR BROTHER:—I received your favor by Mr. Hay, and am extremely pleased to find that you have succeeded so far with your election as to keep in Mr. Saunders, having heard there was a great probability of his being left out.

I am in great hopes Wright and Carpenter will acquiesce in the measures of our new assembly, since we have had the good fortune to exclude Franklin, Galloway, Rhodes, and Evans; and in their room have put in Messrs. Willing, Bryan, Stretle, and Keppele.

This change, in our representatives here, has caused the greatest dejection of spirits in those of the Quaker party and their friends.

Thos. Barr and Slough may have acted a political part in the election, that they might succeed themselves, yet the

Governor has been well assured by several gentlemen, that they privately pushed Saunders in the tickets of many of their friends, by which means alone he was kept in. However this may be, the Governor could not possibly think of appointing the son of a Quaker to be Sheriff, who had taken infinite pains in riding about the country to secure the interest of the Germans, in favor of the violent measures of the late assembly against his own family and government. Barr indeed has a better pretence to the Sheriff's office, from his having been on the return twice before, and now highest in votes, and if any objections are made against him, on account of his favoring the old ticket, the same are to be made against the other in a greater degree, so that the appointment of Barr is approved of by all the Governor's friends here without exception.

EDWARD BURD TO HIS FATHER, COL. BURD, AT LANCASTER.

Philadelphia, September 18th, 1765.

Dear and Hon'd Sir:—We have had advice lately of a joyful change in the ministry, for which last night the mob made a bon-fire and burnt an effigy for our stamper,* and surrounded his house, whooping and hallooing, which caused him to load his arms. I heartily wish that you may be successful in the ensuing election. I believe the Quakers will leave out Hughes and Galloway this time. Some think that Bucks will do something, but that is uncertain. The Dutch express a great detestation to Hughes' party.

* John Hughes, the stamp-tax collector.

SAMUEL PURVIANCE, JR., OF PHILADELPHIA, TO COL. BURD, AT LANCASTER.

Philadelphia, Sept. 20th, 1765.

DEAR SIR :—You may possibly imagine, from the general silence with which our political affairs have been conducted this year, that perhaps we are relapsed again into the old passive humor of submitting the conduct of public affairs to our former State Pilots; and that, if we at the fountain-head observe such a conduct, you at a distance should follow the same non-resisting plan of your friends in town. Be assured, that nothing is less thought of by us than such a scheme; though matters go on very quietly, yet everything is preparing for making a vigorous stand at the ensuing election, and every possible pains have been taken to strengthen and cement our interest in such a manner as to afford us good hopes of carrying every man for both city and county. Our interest is greatly increased amongst several societies who last year were divided in their views, and particularly strengthened by the opposition lately made by John Hughes and his friends, against sending commissioners to attend the Congress at New York, in order to remonstrate home against the Stamp Act. This unpopular action has greatly damped the Faction, turned many of their warm friends out of doors against them, and even brought over some of their members in the House to our party, by which means they carried the vote. There's great reason to hope this affair will produce the same effects through the country, and open the eyes of many, who, blindly attached to them through party, must now see what destructive measures these pretended defenders of liberty and privilege are capable of pursuing. I met some of our friends at Chester

Court, and there concerted some measures for dividing the Quaker interest in that county, that our friends may join one party of them. This scheme promises good success, and will, I hope, be warmly pushed by our friends there. I went lately up to Bucks Court, in order to concert measures for their election, in pursuance of which we have appointed a considerable meeting of the Germans, Baptists and Presbyterians, to be held next Monday at Neshaminy, where some of us, some Germans and Baptists of this place, have appointed to attend, in order to attempt a general confederacy of the three societies in opposition to the ruling party. We have sent up emissaries among the Germans, which I hope will bring them into this measure, and if it can be effected, will give us a great chance for carrying matters in that county. Could that be carried, it would infallibly secure our friends a majority in the House, and consequently enable them to recal our dangerous enemy, Franklin, with his petitions, which is the great object we have now in view, and which should engage the endeavors of all our friends at the approaching election to make a spirited push for a majority in the Assembly, without which all our struggles here will prove of little service to the public interest. The general committee of our society meet this day, and on Tuesday next shall finally settle our ticket, which is now all fixed but one man. Few of your friends here entertain any hopes of being able to change any of your members this year, after failing last year in your spirited attempt; however, I think it mean to submit tamely, or without bearing the testimony against bad men and bad measures, and was I to stand alone, I would vote against the enemies of my country. If you knew thoroughly the methods Mr. Franklin is taking at home to blacken and stigmatise our society, you would perhaps judge with me that you never had more reason to exert yourselves in order to overset him, which we can only do by commanding a majority in the Assembly. I have seen a letter lately from a person of character, that advises his wicked designs against us. The little hopes of success, as well as the difficulty of engaging proper persons for the purpose, has discouraged me from attempting a project recommended by some friends, of sending up some Germans to work upon their countrymen. But that no probable means may fail, have sent up some copies of a piece lately printed by Sowers, of Germantown, to be dispersed, and which may possibly have some effect.

I have just received certain advice of a project laid by the Mennonists to turn Mr. Saunders out of your ticket—the only good member you have. I hope it will inspire our people with more industry to keep him in. The only plan I would recommend to you, to run Dr. Kuhn, or some other popular Lutheran or Calvinist, in Webb's place. You'll please to make a discreet use of this to any of our friends. I am, with best wishes for a successful election,

Dear sir, your and the public's sincere well wisher,

SAM'L PURVIANCE, Jr.

Shall be glad to know what measures you resolve on as soon as possible.

I beg no mention may be made of the author of the enclosed.

Paper enclosed in the foregoing Letter.

As I understand the Mennonists have certainly resolved to turn out Isaac Saunders this year, though the only good member your county has, I would beg leave to offer to you and other friends the following scheme, as the only probable chance, I think, you have to carry the election and keep Mr. Saunders. If the scheme is properly executed, and can be conducted without danger of a riot, I think you could infallibly carry your ticket by it.

Don't attempt to change any of your members save Webb. If you can run Dr. Kuhn, or any other popular German, and can keep Mr. Saunders, you will do great things. As soon as your ticket is agreed on, let it be spread through the country, that your party intend to come well armed to the election, and that you intend, if there's the least partiality in either sheriff, inspectors, or managers of the election, that you will thrash the sheriff, every inspector, Quaker and Mennonist to a jelly; and further, I would report it, that not a Mennonist nor German should be admitted to give in a ticket without being sworn that he is naturalized and worth £50, and that he has not voted already; and further, that if you discovered any person attempting to give in a vote without being naturalized, or voting twice, you would that moment deliver him up to the mob to chastise him. Let this report be industriously spread before the election, which will certainly keep great numbers of the Mennonists at home. I would at the same time have all our friends warned to put on a bold face, to be every man provided with a good shillelah, as if determined to put their threats in execution, though at the same time let them be solemnly charged to keep the greatest order and peace. Let our friends choose about two dozen of the most reputable men, magistrates, &c., who shall attend the inspectors, sheriff and clerks during the whole election, to mount guard half at a time, and relieve one another in spells, to prevent all cheating and administer the oath to every suspicious person, and to commit to immediate punishment every one who offers to vote twice. I'll engage, if you conduct the election in that manner, and our people turn out with spirit, you can't fail of carrying every man on your ticket, as I am well assured not a third of the Mennonists are naturalized. I would submit this to your consideration. If it's well thought of, take your measures immediately. I beg no mention may be made of the author of this. I see no danger in the scheme but that of a riot, which would require great prudence to avoid.

EDWARD SHIPPEN TO COL. SHIPPEN, AT PHILADELPHIA.

Lancaster, Christmas, 1765.

DEAR SON: — Your favor of the 10th instant I received last Thursday morning, enclosing the pamphlets, which were very acceptable. I had only seen a little of that published by Mr. Dulaney, which I have gone over once, but shall give it another reading or two, it appearing to me a masterly performance. I am also pleased with the other, of which Mr. Dickinson is the reputed author. Our Americans certainly are extremely obliged to them and the others, who have endeavored to serve their country in those respects. Colonel Burd received your letter on the subject of rum, and I think all you said about it very right. I am glad to understand that our custom-house offices are open; but, what will become of our vessels and their cargoes, if they should any of them be forced by any stress of bad weather to run to Barbadoes?—for as to the port of London, as madly as matters are managed there, they will not be suffered by the manufacturers to clap the broad arrow* on

* The Custom House mark.

their masts, because such a step would stagnate all their business at once, and at the same time ruin themselves and our factories. The people in England, no doubt, pay large taxes; and the only reason they don't take our part is, because they have been made to believe that we are not only able, but the Stamp Act is so wisely framed, that will force us to bear at least one-half of their burthen. But when those people come to be very sensible that the act is defective, and that if we are to be forced, it must be done by a mighty army raised from among themselves, for the levying of which they must be *forced* to open their own purse-strings, and this, too, before they have recovered themselves from the difficulty from which they had to struggle with, in the last expensive wars with France and Spain; I say, if they should find this to be their forlorn hope, they will (one would think), turn their backs upon the ministry, and cry aloud for the stamping of the Stamp Act to death. Our mother country should consider us at least as their hunters and slaves, as we in fact are. They ought to suffer us to dig and delve in the ground, and not only encourage us in raising wheat and other grain, and making iron, &c., but give us leave to send it to any people in the world who will give us gold and silver for it, because they know, by long experience, it will finally centre in the city of London.

Mr. Dulaney remarks, and very justly, too, that the British manufactures come dearer, and not so good in quality to America, as formerly. He might, with equal justice, have gone further and said, (and to Great Britain's everlasting shame and reproach,) that, for these twenty or thirty years past, they neither held out their just measures in width or length—according to justice. Duroys, for instance, are usually sold in England by the piece—which used to contain twenty-one yards in length, and of a certain breadth; but, every year since, they have been pinched gradatim, so that they have been reduced at least to sixteen or seventeen yards in length, and at least three or four inches narrower. The linens, too, whether made in England, or imported thither from Ireland this year, hold out generally in length, yet are very deficient in breadth. These deceitful methods are very prejudicial to our shopkeepers, who sell them out, the Duroys and the like, by the yard—a piece falling short sometimes a yard or half a yard of the quantity mentioned by the merchants; and as to the linens, when they are asked for a yard wide, if the customer, on measuring it, finds it a nail or two short, and takes notice of it, then the poor shopkeepers answer that it comes for yard wide; and pieces marked seven-eighths or three-quarters of a yard wide, are commonly wanting in proportion. The merchants at home are blamed for this—some of them wanting to send Duroys and other stuffs at a lower rate by the piece than their neighbors. Honesty is certainly the best policy. The French, our great rival in trade and everything else, are so very exact in their weights and measures, that they have made very severe laws against frauds of that kind. Our Indian traders have often assured me that they could never sell their half-thicks, &c., in any Indian town where Jean Cœur, a great trader from Canada, was, because his half-thicks were always kept up to their original width and goodness, whereas ours were deficient in both.

Agreeable to his Honor, the Governor's, instructions to the magistrates, suitable provision for the troops from the westward was made, of which it certainly was my duty and my design to write him; but his letter was delivered to Mr. Webb, the barrack-master, and I could not get it back in time, and so I beg you will tell his Honor the reason, if he should *wonder* at my silence. As to the tavern licences, you see by the money and accounts sent you down by the post, that I managed that business tolerably well: but, as to the marriage licences, I find the people had taken up a mistaken notion about them, believing they would cost them four or five pounds sterling a piece, till last Sunday, when Mr. Gates inquiring of me concerning the affair, I set the matter right, and he has undertaken to undeceive his own congregation, and I am writing to the same purpose to the rest of the ministers in this county. I am pleased with your instruction of Neddy Burd; I sent him my old navigation book, (which I am choice of, as it is mere gold almost,) for him to copy at his leisure, a little at a time, every morning or every other morning, as you shall judge best. I want a small octavo, intituled "Instructions for the education of daughters," (as proper, I think, for sons,) by Monsieur Fenelon, Archbishop of Cainbray, (he was the author of Telemaque,) translated from the French, and revised by George Hick, D. D., Glasgow, printed and sold by R. & A. Foulis, 1750. Mr. Yeates is to inquire among the gentlemen of St. Andrew's Club for it, either in French or English. If he fails in all these searches, I must beg the favor of Mr. Luman, or Mr. Bell, to send to Scotland for it in each language, but let Mr. Hall send for them both to London,—for I should not dislike it, if they should succeed at London and Glasgow too.

GROSVENOR BEDFORD, ESQ., TO JOHN SWIFT, PHILADELPHIA.

London, February 16*th*, 1767.

DEAR SWIFT:—I am now possessed of all your favors by Davidson. The rum is so smooth that it will swiftly slide away. Mark that! The ginger is the best I ever tasted. You have my best thanks for them.

Captain Beers has delivered your "make-shift" box, which, besides the Michaelmas accounts, contains newspapers which I am at a loss what to do with.

By your bill of mortality for the year '65, which I presume slipt into your package, I find that you are subject to surprising casualities. *Two* people choked with *one* bean; and that not in the parish of St. Patrick! One died by a *dead* palsy! Pray, how long had he been dead before he died? Twenty-two of *decay!* This surely is *poverty,* for there is besides the deaths from *consumption.* What *new buildings* are those of which so many people die? Your papers appear to me very comical upon so melancholy a subject.

Heaven preserve you from all casualities, new or old.

Mr. Francis' bill on Hagen to me is accepted.

I am your affectionate,

humble servant,

GROSV'R BEDFORD.

Love to yours.

JUDGE YEATES TO COL. BURD, AT TINIAN.

Lancaster September 8th, 1768.

HON'D SIR:—Mr. Shippen informing us of a conveyance to you, I sit down to let you know the politics of the town. Strange events have happened amongst us, which I dare pronounce, ere now have caused no small speculation in Paxton. Brother Porter, it seems, is in the vocative. A few weeks ago, he headed a party of yellow wigs, between twenty and thirty in number, and notoriously attacked the house of one William Reynolds, a broad brim, in West Nottingham township, Chester county. This large corps he summoned together, on being repulsed with a smaller party, the same day that he was trying to take away by force some negroes claimed by his brother, Robert Porter, in Reynolds' possession. After committing some outrages, (among which Friends say may be reckoned a burglary,) they went off in triumph, being disguised with handkerchiefs about their heads, having no hats on. Mr. Saunders issued a warrant against Mr. Porter, on a complaint made to him of the Taits, which the latter satisfied by giving bail for his appearance at the next court. A few days afterwards Reynolds took an affirmation before him, that his wife's life was despaired of in consequence of the hurt received from Porter. On this, a writ was issued to put poor Porter in limbo, until the matter of Reynolds' wife's life or death could be ascertained. The sheriff, at Mr. Ross' importunity, did not carry his prisoner, after he was arrested, to jail, but detained him until Dr. Boyd could view the dying woman and make report of her condition. Boyd went immediately off, and on his return gave his opinion, that he thought Porter's wife, so far from being dangerously ill had every appearance of health. Porter was then bailed by the justices, greatly against the judgment of Friends, who still insist there was an actual burglary, though none could be proved. The same evening Robert Porter attacked, overcame and beat Reynolds, the prosecutor, on his return home, for his unjust charge against his brother, who then took out a warrant for him also.

After he had eluded the sheriff's search, by a stratagem, the sheriff took him about eight miles off, where he was rescued by Stephen Porter and some others, as Webb says. If such be the case Porter has forfeited his recognizance for good behavior, which he entered into; on being discharged from the sheriff's custody himself in £500, and two sureties in £250 each; and now the parties are both gone to the Chief Justice to seek redress for their mutual complaints. When Robert Porter was rescued, the sheriff brought off his own and two other horses, though I don't know he had any writ against the latter.

A replevin has been sued out by the owner of one of the beasts, which the sheriff refuses to serve, alleging what he did was clearly his duty.

I brought the action at the party's entreaty, which the sheriff takes in high [dudgeon,] and he [says,] God knows what, against my practice.

Of this, however, I am perfectly innocent, as I used him with more kindness and delicacy than he deserved, by repeated notices, peaceably to give up the creature. On the whole, Mr. Porter, I think, has acted a most weak and imprudent part, Mr. Webb as warm and foolish a one, and both Presbyterians and Quakers are as hot as party feuds and disappointed rage can make them. Mr. Wright has just told us he will serve no longer in the Assembly, and will put his intentions in print. Mr. Saunders and Ross will then become candidates, and try their strength at the next election. I make no doubt but your department will unanimously declare in favor of the former, as having by far the most right to represent the country. I barely give you this hint that you may solicit his interest, if you judge proper, though Saunders never mentioned the matter plainly to me.

COL. SHIPPEN TO COL. BURD, AT TINIAM.

Philadelphia, Feb'y 23d, 1769.

DEAR BROTHER:—I am now to acknowledge the receipt of your favor of the 6th instant, enclosing a list of officers who paid you 10*s*. each, (they have all signed the articles,) and Captain Patterson's and Killbuck's letters, both which I herewith return you.

With respect to the subject of our application for lands,* I refer you to the joint letter of Dr. Morgan and myself to you of this day.

I have shown Killbuck's complaint to the Governor and Mr. Allen, as well as the paragraph of your letter relative to it, and they look upon John Mitcheltree to have acted in a very villainous manner; and this his attempt on the Indian Killbuck, and his threats expressed to you of putting him to death whenever it shall be in his power, have so dangerous a tendency to involve the whole country in an Indian war, that they think it absolutely incumbent on the civil authority to take strict notice of such alarming villainy. They therefore desire you will bind John Mitcheltree over to the next Court of Quarter Sessions, for his good behavior, in £400, and oblige him to give two sufficient sureties in £200 each; and they are of opinion that this should be continued from Court to Court.

COL. TURBUTT FRANCIS TO COL. JAS. BURD.

Harris's, May 10th, 1769.

DEAR SIR:—I would not have passed your house without calling on you, but had very particular business which

* Bounty lands for their services.

pressed me. There are now here five or six New Englanders from Wyoming, who are come down to purchase provisions for their friends, and perhaps have some other plan in view. If you could lay hold of them with propriety I fancy it might be of service, as they are in want of provisions at Wyoming. It would prevent these provisions from going up to them, and would deter others from coming down on the same errand. They talk of going from hence on Monday next. All our friends at Philadelphia are well. Pray, present my best respects, if you please, to Mrs. and Miss Burd.

I shall start for Augusta this afternoon, to spend my summer. If you come within reach of me, I hope you will give me an opportunity to show you how much

I am, sir,

Your most humble servant,

TURBUTT FRANCIS.

CH. J. SHIPPEN TO COLONEL BURD, AT TINIAN.

Philadelphia, June 25th, 1769.

DEAR SIR:—I received your letters of the 23d of May and 11th inst., and have communicated to the Governor what you say concerning the New England people, who will, I believe, now give us no more trouble, 120 of them having been last week, at Easton Court, indicted for riots and forcible entries, which proceeding has so intimidated them, that Major Dyer and their other principal abettors have agreed to remove immediately from the Susquehanna lands, and give the Government no more trouble about their claims, unless they shall be able to obtain a determination in their favor in England. On this consideration the Government will forbear any rigor in the prosecutions on these indictments; which, however, are to hang over their heads till they have given up the possession of the lands. Wherefore, unless you hear something more of this affair hereafter, you need not give yourself any further trouble concerning the apprehending any of these people.

JUDGE YEATES TO COL. BURD, AT TINIAN.

Lancaster, September 17*th,* 1769.

HONORED SIR:—The deputies from the upper part of the country, attended here on Friday last, to give their assistance in forming a ticket for the ensuing election. In what manner that assistance was given I know not, nor whether their [presence] was required by Myer and Bachman at the settlement of measures [or not]. Wallace informs me they were not consulted, and seemed delighted, [but was unable] to determine whether this might not proceed from other [motives].

In the evening of the Congress, Dr. Boyd and myself called at Little's to see how matters went on, and after I had spoke with Wallace, I mentioned to Martin Myer that I feared the proper steps had not been taken to secure unanimity. Mr. Atlee tartly replied, that a ticket had been framed, and if Paxton, Hannover, &c., did not agree to it, they might e'en stay at home. After some little altercation, we parted, not very well satisfied, I believe, with each other.

The current objections to the ticket, (herewith sent,) are that no leading men among the politicians are introduced therein, which might be a lure to others of the same persuasion to join the party, and that the intended alteration stands not sufficiently on the broad-bottom, but regards those chiefly to the northward of Lancaster. I am told by the knowing ones, that the last omission will knock up the ticket, as the other parts of the county will look on themselves as slighted, and consequently, if they do turn out, will do it in favor of the other side, unless there is a speedy change. In fact, the same thing may be now urged to the present measure, as was formerly made a capital [objection]. * * * * * * I fancy no attempt will be made to displace James Webb, as the struggle seems to be chiefly about the board, and they will not weaken their interests on either side to remove a man, merely to please the favorite schemes of an ambitious, restless, and fighting brother. So much for electioneering.

I had forgot to tell you, that the Board have thought proper to return yesterday unto the office, an abstract of their accounts for the last year; so far that point is carried.

WM. ATLEE TO COL. BURD, AT TINIAN.

Lancaster, September 19th, 1769.

SIR:—I wrote you the other day by Christian Bachman and enclosed you a ticket. Since that there has been another meeting, some objections having been made by persons in town, with respect to some of the assessors, and upon a fresh consultation between Bachman, Myer, Early, and a great many of the reputable people in town, the enclosed ticket is now fixed on, and determined to be carried, if possible. Bachman and Myer requested me to give you the earliest advice of this alteration, &c. I hope you will encourage the upper people to turn out. There will be warm work I assure you, the lower side still keep their ticket private. 'Tis thought they only waited for this to be finished, that they might include some other persons of the town in theirs, and so divide us. So you see the town, since the late regulations, has become of some consequence, and stands a chance of being courted by both sides.

I am sir, &c.

JUDGE YEATES TO COL. BURD, AT TINIAN.

Lancaster, September 19th, 1769.

HON'D SIR :—Once more I address you on the affairs of the nation. Since my last, a new set of assessors has been fixed on by Messrs. Myers and Bachman, to obviate one of the objections mentioned in my last, which they hope will prove satisfactory. A number of persons of weight assisted in the framing this new ticket, who, I think, will try their utmost efforts, that it shall not miscarry. Wallace, I believe, represented the former mutiny in the worst point of light to me, so that I am tempted to forget brother Atlee's stroke at Paxtang, &c, and sincerely wish the people round you may show activity and alertness at the ensuing push. Bachman told me last night he places great dependence on you, in which I assured him he will not be disappointed.

After all, if the point aimed at by the minority should not be carried, the township round you will at least show themselves to be of some consequence, and not to be —— on. 'Tis thought by some that an attempt will be made to the eastward of Connistoga to displace Webb, and that Moses Brinton or James Old will be opposed by him. I conceive this will be one great means of running their ticket, which we hear is not to be settled till Friday next. An impertinent scrawl was delivered to Martin Myers from Dav. Wister, of Philadelphia, informing him, that as the sheriff's father had behaved very unworthily, it would be most eligible to desert him. The letter was treated with the contempt it deserved.

The Assessors in the new ticket stand thus:

Asher Shaffner, Jr.,	Samuel Barr,
Alexander Martin,	Thomas Clarke, (Dromore,)
Frederick Hummell,	Thomas Clarke, (Hannover.)

COL. JOSEPH SHIPPEN TO HON. JOHN PENN, AT NEW YORK.

Philadelphia, November 13th, 1769.

SIR:—I herewith send you a bond of security for your observance of the acts of trade as Governor of this Province, which was executed this morning by Mr. Allen and Mr. Chew. And as they both thought it most regular for you to join in the bond also, I have inserted your name, and a blank is left above their names that you may sign, seal, and deliver it before two witnesses at New York, when you receive your commission. I also enclose you a copy of Governor Sharpe's certificate, to serve as a precedent to draw one by, for the Governor of New York to execute. I showed Col. Francis your letter from Sir William Johnson, and he says he has relinquished his design of taking up the two salt springs, as he found, on examination, that they were not within the Proprietary purchase. He intends to write to Sir William on the subject, to satisfy him that there are no grounds for any complaint from the Indians respecting that matter.

I hope you and the ladies had an agreeable journey. Jenny joins with me in compliments to them.

I am, with sincere esteem, sir, &c.

EDWARD BURD* TO COL. BURD.

Philadelphia, October 4th, 1770.

DEAR AND HON'D SIR :—On the arrival of a Dutch ship, I informed uncle Edward Shippen of it, who ordered me to purchase for you a servant, which I have done accordingly, and send to grandpapa's care. He cost £19 17*s.* or 18*s.*, I am not certain which, and staid two or three days in town. His indenture cost 4*s.* 6*d.*, and I gave him 7*s.* 6*d.* earnest money, according to custom. I would not get an assignment of his indenture, which is enclosed, as it would only be an additional expense without necessity. The young man has been used to farming, so that he will be of immediate service to you. He is to wear his own clothes so long as they will last, and then have provision from you. This was by particular agreement.

Mr. Galloway is turned out of the Assemby, (if not elected at Bucks,) and Mr. Taylor put in his room. This was principally owing to a pamphlet written by Goddard, which I have sent to grandpapa for his perusal, and desired him afterwards to forward it to you.

* Afterwards Major Burd.

GROSVENOR BEDFORD, ESQ. TO JOHN SWIFT, PHILADELPHIA.

London, June 1st, 1771.

DEAR SWIFT: — I hope that, before now, you have been made easy as to the whisper about my death. I have frequently desired you not to regard such reports. Don't you think that, whenever it happens, my sons will give you an account of it?

I have often informed you of proposals being made to me for your deputation.* I can now tell you of offers to me for the resignation of my patent, which, I do assure you, nothing but my regard for you has made me decline: for I would very gladly be quit of such a set of arbitrary and unreasonable commissioners. Suppose you were to die, how am I to settle my accounts, when there will always be a year's rent in arrear? Is it that their sense and judgment are only annual, that they cannot tell, when an account is laid before them quarterly, what incidents they ought to allow; or do they only study to embarrass and distress their officers, to show their newly-acquired power? I am sure they have no reason to complain of the arbitrary proceedings of the people against them, when they must feel the same principles at work in themselves. But, to return to my accounts. If your death should happen, they will be transmitted to the custom-house here, without the year's incidents due upon them appearing, but with a large sum of money apparently in your hands—money which they have not suffered you to remit to them—and so my account will be made up, and I called upon immediately for the balance. Their superseding Mr. Lardner was extremely ungenteel; and, I think, their appointment of a controller very

* The collectorship, or "deputy-surveyorship," as it was officially called.

absurd. He ought to be a check upon the collector, and is not supposed to proceed from the same creation.

As they treat you, a man may be ruined by his industry in collecting. They will neither indemnify you against the money which they oblige you to keep in your own hands, nor suffer you to remit it, but in such a manner as shall subject you to their objection and cavil, if an accident happen. Every ship is declared to be "a good ship" by the bills of lading; and how are you to know otherwise? Can they suppose that a ship, in which people venture their lives, is not "good" enough to convey their money? They must have other reasons for keeping a bank in an officer's hands, giving no indemnity, and holding themselves not accountable, till they have received the money. You should be allowed to remit here, and not be compelled to keep it there.

I hope Mr. Barkly has left his widow in easy circumstances. Captain Stainforth's bill is accepted.

I have desired you not to expect me to be constant in writing. Many ships depart without my knowledge. Captain Osborne was going weekly, for six weeks, and he slipped me at last. I write to you by the packets.

You made me happy, by agreeing with me about Madeira. I dared not, for fear of offence, declare my opinion before; but now, I fear not to say that it has not, for some years, been like that of former years.* The sweetness is artificial: and, when it goes off, there is no flavor left of old wine. Therefore, no more of that, 'an you love me.

* It is perhaps needless to say, that Mr. Bedford was advanced in years when he penned this letter. The handwriting is tremulous, and proves the truth of his assurance, that its composition tired him. But, though the days had come, when 'the keepers of the house' had begun 'to tremble,' yet his heart was still warm with the feelings of generous, early friendship. The last sentence of this letter, the last received (so far as is now known) from him, glows with the most unselfish affection.

I believe you will think I have given you enough. I do assure you I am tired, and so rest.

Your truly affectionate, humble servant,

GROSV'R BEDFORD.

Love to yours and Joe.

Commissioner Robinson and my son Dick are become very well acquainted. They are both very gay men, and meet in all polite assemblies. I have seen him but once.

I have been offered security to pay me my present income during life, and a handsome premium besides. But, then, what must have become of you?

CH. J. SHIPPEN TO HIS FATHER, AT LANCASTER.

Philadelphia, August 24th, 1771.

HONORED SIR: -- I shall take the proper steps to obtain your share of the Perquiomen lands. I find an act of Assembly is to be first passed, which I shall of course have the inspecting of, before passing.

Relfe and Shriver must have their accounts presented to the Assembly, at their next sitting, at which time the accounts of the whole year will be settled. We shall, however, canvass the matter in Council first.

As to Neddy Burd, I am glad you approve of my proposal of settling him at Northampton, as I am certain there is the best opening for a young fellow at this time. He will be free* some time about Christmas, and may then take a ride up to see the place, and make known his intentions of settling there; but it will not be amiss that he should return, and stay in my office till the Spring. As to survey-

* From his "apprenticeship" to the law.

ing, it is very well he should understand it, but I would by no means have him undertake practical surveying; he has a better profession, and, by applying himself to that, may soon get into a good way of business; but, if he should get at all into the surveying business, it will take him off his studies, and give him a habit of riding through the country upon every trifling occasion, much to the injury of his proper business. Peggy Allen has had a sly private wedding at Black Point. The family are all pleased.

JASPER YEATES TO COL. BURD, AT TINIAN.

Lancaster, March 28th, 1772.

HON'D SIR:— * * As to the laws passed this session, the newspapers will inform you of their titles. Brother George* blames himself exceedingly about the Excise Acts approved of by the Governor. It seems his Honor at first rejected the bill, but finding it had reference to another bill, which granted supplies for his majesty's troops, his Honor was under the necessity of SWALLOWING it. We are told the introduction of Mr. Hickes into the party gives great uneasiness. He is distinguished as the favorite, and his advice is generally received in preference to those of another standing, who are better acquainted with the constitution. Many anecdotes are current of Mr. Chew, showing his sense of matters and his opinion of that citizen's abilities. Mr. Penn will involve himself in innumerable difficulties, should he persist in the strong attachment to Hicks, and in his resolution of acting the part of an independent man.

* George Yeates.

EDWARD SHIPPEN TO COL. BURD, AT TINIAN.

Lancaster, July 25th, 1772.

DEAR MR. BURD:—I have your agreeable favor of yesterday before me, and we are glad to hear you are all well. I was well pleased with Junius' letter to Lord North. As to Goddard's letter directed to the public, I can only say he is a severe fellow. But for all the stripes he lays upon Galloway's back, let that gentleman blame himself. A man ought to consider, that although a speech in the House of Commons may oftentimes carry all before him, by a majority of voices, which answer perhaps the present purposes, as if the votes were *nem. con.*, yet a Junius or a Goddard may pay them off through the press, and if some of our statesmen and clergymen are callous, as some speakers and preachers, both abroad and at home undoubtedly are, (as old Sir Robert in England, and a nameless gentleman in the province were, one Doctor Smith,) yet, when the stamp act was damned and Junius' letters came out respecting it, a Grenville broke his heart, and is now gone off the stage of action; and now Goddard's letters penetrate so deeply into the heart of our Galloway, that it is thought that he will soon give up the ghost, too.* How do you like the spirited paper of my countrymen, the Bostonians, respecting the independency of their Governor?

* For a full account of Mr. Galloway and Mr. Goddard, and also for the dispute, to which reference is here had, see *Sabine's Loyalists*, s. v. Galloway and Goddard.

JUDGE YEATES TO COL. BURD, AT TINIAN.

Lancaster, September 20th, 1773.

HON. SIR:—I have just received your favor of the 18th instant. The friends of Mr. Atlee were not a little alarmed during the election for Burgesses, to find him so warmly pressed by the late Justice Hamilton, insomuch that it was generally thought the latter would be the highest on the poll. The event, however, was contrary, as Mr. Atlee exceeded him by nineteen votes, and the other remains under-Burgess.

This being finished, the Board of Commissioners and Assessors, with Myers and Bachman, and several leading men from different townships, proceeded to Stophel Reigart's, where a ticket was to be formed.

The result of their deliberations was, that Mr. Curtis Grubb should run in the place of Isaac Whitelock as a representative, and that John Ferru, and Andrew Graeff, should be inserted in their ticket as Sheriffs. The removal of friend Whitelock gives no small uneasiness to the brethren, and is indeed censured by very many of the county. He came in without any kind of solicitation on his part, and has attended the house constantly; behaving with credit during his year of probation. The impetuosity also of Curtis fortifies their argument, and it is commonly thought the proposal of his remaining in is to prove the Lebanon interest in the new county scheme. Thus matters rest at present. What other turn they may take it is impossible to say. Mr. Ross went down yesterday to the house to attend the debate, with respect to the petition of the city about their taxes, and the questioning of the several back counties, but I don't apprehend there is any kind of danger of this measure taking place.

JUDGE YEATES TO COL. BURD, AT TINIAN.

Lancaster, October 6th, 1773.

Hon'd Sir:—Our election being over, the borough is restored to its former quiet, and the inhabitants have again resumed their senses. Many people are much pleased at the defeat of Bachman and Myers, who have taken the lead for this three years past, as they consider it an indignity to the county. The displacing of friend Whitelock has given umbrage to some, who think him very undeserving of the treatment shown him.

By this conveyance I send you a parcel of peach-stones, chiefly of the best kind, for your nursery, and a few flower roots procured of Mr. Adam Reigart; they should be planted this fall, or as soon as possible. The accounts from Philadelphia tell us, there is no connection between the present and late Governors, though they have dined together twice in public. Mr. Richard Penn takes no notice whatever of his brother, nor even speaks to him. The consequence of such conduct need not be animadverted on.*

EDWARD SHIPPEN TO COL. BURD, AT TINIAN.

Lancaster, December 13th, 1773.

Dear Mr. Burd:—Mr. Whitfield,† Annno Domini 1770, gave us the sacrament in Mr. Barton's church, and,

* The quarrel between the two Penns is also mentioned in a letter from Edward Shippen to Col. Burd: "*Lancaster, October 7th,* 1773, 'Mr. Bob. Morris, the head man at the Merchants' feast, placed 'Governor Penn on his right hand, and his brother, the late Gover- 'nor, on his left hand; but not a word passed between the two broth- 'ers.'

† The celebrated Preacher.

observing that he broke the bread into pieces as small as a hazlenut, it brought into my mind some passages which I had formerly taken notice of in his journal, wherein he mentions his giving bread and wine to a thousand at a time, in commemoration of the dying love of our Crucified Lord. I suppose, poor gentleman, he thought he was at Lady Huntingdon's tabernacle.

Mr. Yeates writes me to-night from Philadelphia, that the English Company's tea ship arrived at Boston, and that notwithstanding all that Gov. Hutchinson, and the consignees could do to land that exotic plant, the Captain was obliged immediately to return to England with it; and printed accounts of all their proceedings herein, are sent by express to Rhode Island, New York and Philadelphia, and they have unanimously agreed, that, if any of their own merchants shall presume again to send for any tea, they will oblige them to return it to England again; and this cause in which they are (I may say) universally agreed, they will endeavor to support at the risk of their lives and fortunes. Mr. Yeates says, that they heard the Philadelphia tea ship was seen off Cape May last week. I suppose an express will be sent to meet her at Red Bank, commanding (I dont say advising,) the Captain of her to tack about and make the best of his way home again, for that this Continent is as much surfeited with the smell of her old, rotten tea, as ever a Spanish cook was with dressing *Porco de como*, at his Catholic Majesty's kitchen.

JUDGE YEATES TO COL. BURD, AT TINIAN.

Lancaster, February 28th, 1774.

HONORED SIR:—I waited upon Mr. Barton agreeable to your desire, respecting the point of conscience. He informs me that a deputation lately came down from Middletown to Mr. Hilmuth, for his sentiments on the subject, and that Mr. Hilmuth called upon him on the occasion, so that he was fully acquainted with the matter, which is like to occasion a schism in the church.

In consequence of the request of the people who were just here, Mr. Barton and Mr. Hilmuth both wrote to Mr. Illing their opinions: that as he ministered among persons who were not strictly in communion with the church of England, it would be highly proper to admit of some relaxation of the mere forms of the Liturgy, in cases of necessity, and that too, more particularly, when the persons made it a matter of conscience to refuse those forms; that a contrary conduct would, in pursuit of things unessential, miss the substance and thereby introduce a total dislike of the discipline of the church; that such relaxations had been heretofore allowed by missionaries of the first character, such as suffering communicants to receive the sacraments standing, administering baptism where only one sponsor could be conveniently procured &c., &c. Mr. Barton is now quite sick, but promises to write to you with Mr. Hilmuth, when his health and leisure will permit, fully on this subject. For my own part, I look on the dispute as the most trifling one imaginable. It seems to me equally absurd, with the ridiculous deliberations of the Doctors of the Sorbonne, on a question proposed to them, whether an unborn child might not be baptized?

Doctor Sterne, in his 1st Vol. of Tristram Shandy, treats their determinations of this knotty point with great humor and just ridicule. If your parson had used me as he has poor Wofley, I would convince him, by every means offered me, of my resentment; though perhaps, contempt would be proper to a person of his narrow and illiberal sentiments.

COL. SHIPPEN TO COL. BURD, AT TINIAN.

Philadelphia, March 21st, 1774.

Dear Brother:—On Monday last, I wrote you a few lines enclosing you a copy of a letter from Dr. Morgan, at Fredericksburg, since which I have been favored with your letter of the 5th inst.; in answer to which, I am sorry to inform you, that the hopes we had entertained of obtaining a grant of lands from the Government of Virginia, are now entirely vanished. This appears by a letter I this moment received from Doctor Morgan, dated at Williamsburg, March 11th, 1774. An extract thereof is as follows:

"The resolutions of the Governor and Council of Virginia have lately taken an unfavorable turn in respect to the Pennsylvania officers who might think of applying for land in this colony. About a fortnight ago, a Council was called, when the affair of granting lands to Pennsylvania officers was debated; and it was resolved upon, that no such officer should obtain any warrant for land in Virginia in virtue of the King's proclamation of 1763, without personal application at Williamsburg, and without being furnished (each officer) with a certificate from Gen. Haldemand, of his service during the war.

"The Governor declares this to be agreeable to his instructions, from which he cannot deviate, alleging that the former minutes of Council only respected Virginia officers and soldiers."

"On acquainting Lord Dunmore that it was in vain to expect Gen. Haldemand to give the officers certificates, and asking him whether we could not obtain warrants without, he answered, the only means the Pennsylvania officers had left was to apply at home,* and promised, that if they would

* England.

set forth their grievances and claims, &c., in a memorial or petition to him, he would transmit the same to England, and write himself for further instructions. I write this in haste, that you may, by a line to Cols. Armstrong and Burd, and Capt. Thompson, acquaint them with this resolution, as well as other officers, who might otherwise be preparing to come to Virginia."

As to an application at home, after the disappointment we have already met with, I am of opinion it can have no other effect than to involve us in further trouble and expense; and as I am unwilling to risk anything more on such an uncertainty, I am determined to remain as contented as I can, under the trouble, loss of money and time, I have hitherto experienced in this *Ohio bubble.* As I know not who will be the bearer of this letter, I propose to return your commission by some future opportunity; one I can depend on as safe.

EDWARD SHIPPEN TO COL. BURD, AT TINIAN.

Lancaster, Monday evening, April 11*th*, 1774.

DEAR MR. BURD:—Presbyterians love Churchmen as well as they love Presbyterians.* For my own part, I hope I hate nobody. We have a gentleman in town who condemns the Bostonians for destroying the tea, though at the same time the Governor, Collector and Consignees, were solicited to send it to the place from whence it came. The same gentleman finds great fault, too, with the Assembly there for impeaching their Chief Justice. When the Act of

* This refers to 'the point of conscience' spoken of in Judge Yeates' letter to Col. Burd, *ante*, p. 233.

Parliament for laying a duty upon cider in England was published, the farmers rose in a large body and declared publicly, that although this Act was passed by their own representatives, yet if they did not immediately get it repealed, they would vote for other men as soon as they had it in their power; and this menacing had so good an effect, that the wicked Act was soon repealed. Lord North says that the English Parliament virtually represents us, but he can prove it no other way than by swords and guns and implements of war. Three men of war may be sent to Boston to enforce the payment for the tea, but I don't believe that any Admiral of England, who really deserves such a title, will ever draw sword or trigger against the defenders of Great Britain.

EDWARD SHIPPEN TO COL. JAMES BURD, AT TINIAN.

Lancaster, June 21st, 1774.

Dear Mr. Burd: — I am just going to wait upon the judges—so must say the less at this time. We were written to by Dr. Smith, recommending an address to the king, showing our grievances. But our answer was a disapprobation. We recommended a non-importation and non-exportation agreement. There are seventy-two Creoles who are members of Parliament — gentlemen of monstrous estates in the West Indies. They are dead votes against the colonies. What can the West Indies do without flour, starch, and hoop-poles?

EDWARD SHIPPEN TO COL. BURD, AT TINIAN.

Lancaster, June 28th, 1774.

DEAR MR. BURD:—I am just now favored with your letter of the 25th instant. I desire you will return the enclosed newspapers. The author of the political resolutions makes some grand observations, but, for want of perfection, makes some contrary ones. The merchants in England look upon us in this part of the world as their slaves, having no more regard for us than the SEVENTY WEALTHY CREOLES (who have bought themselves seats in the Parliament-house), have for their negroes on their plantations in the Western Islands. It is our duty to work for them—the merchants—and while we, the white and black servants, send them gold and silver, and the Creoles send spirits, sugar, and molasses, &c.; I say, while we supply these people with these douceurs, so that they may take their pleasure, and roll about in their coaches, they are well enough satisfied. But they must not expect to have their eggs, and eat them, too. Be it known to these Solomons and merchants, that, unless they are constantly upon their guard to serve us, we cannot enrich them, if we would. It was observed by a gentleman in town, that it would be a very imprudent step for the colonists to enter into a non-exportation agreement, however well it might be to agree to send for no goods to Great Britain; because, says he, we should then be in the same distressed condition as the people in Boston, for whose support we are making collections; and, if we should shut up our ports, the question is, who can support us? Sure the savages have it not within their power to do it, if they were so inclined; nay, as we have picked a quarrel with them, they might soon put us out of our pain with their tomahawks. But, whoever will scrutinize narrowly the late act of Parliament, may plainly discern that we are all included. The words, "Rhode Island, Connecticut, New York, East and West Jersey, Pennsylvania, Maryland, Virginia, and North and South Carolina" are included; only they are written in lime juice, and want the heat of the fire to make them legible. Well, then, seeing this is the case with us all, let us take physic when it best suits our convenience, and when it is likely to have the most salutary effect, and not wait the wicked ministerial physician's time, when it will be our death. The cursed scheme is, to let us alone until we have sent the West Indies a supply for about two or three or four months, and then to let our fate be known. But, why do we flatter ourselves? Have we not acted as rebelliously — nay, worse than the Bostonians? If we should send no provisions, nor staves and hoops to the West Indies now, the people there would not only be half-starved, (I am not for starving them entirely,) but could not be making casks for the produce of their plantations; and as soon as these resolutions should reach the ears of the Parliament, these Solomons above-mentioned must call aloud upon the Premier to open our ports, and repeal the Tea Law.

At a meeting of a very respectable body of the freeholders and other inhabitants of the county of Berks, at Reading, July 2, 1774. Edward Biddle, Esq., in the chair.

This assembly taking into their very serious consideration the present critical situation of American affairs, do unanimously resolve as follows:

1. That the inhabitants of this county do owe and will pay due allegiance to our rightful sovereign, King George the Third.

2. That the powers claimed, and now attempted to be put into execution by the British Parliament are fundamentally wrong, and cannot be admitted without the utter destruction of the liberties of America.

3. That the Boston Port-bill is unjust and tyrannical in the extreme, and that the measures pursued against Boston are intended to operate equally against the rights and liberties of the other colonies.

4. That this assembly doth concur in opinion with their respectable brethren of Philadelphia, that there is an absolute necessity for an immediate congress of deputies from the several colonies, in order to deliberate upon and pursue such measures as may radically heal our present unhappy disturbances, and settle with precision the rights and liberties of America.

5. That the inhabitants of this county, confiding in the abilities and prudence of the deputies intended to be chosen for the General Congress, will cheerfully submit to any measures which may be found by the said congress best adapted for the restoration of harmony between the mother country and the colonies, and for the security and firm establishment of the rights of America.

6. That as the people of Boston are now suffering in the grand and common cause of American liberty, *Resolved*, That it is the duty of all the inhabitants to contribute to the support of the sufferers; and that the committee hereafter named do open subscriptions for their relief; and further, that the said committee do lay out the amount of such subscriptions in the purchase of flour and other provisions, to be sent by them to our said suffering brethren.

7. That Edward Biddle, James Read, Daniel Brodhead, Henry Christ, Esqrs., and Christopher Schultz, Thomas Dundas, and Jonathan Potts, gentlemen, be and they are hereby appointed a committee to meet and correspond with the committees from the other counties in this Province.

REV. THOMAS BARTON TO COL. BURD.

Lancaster, December 2d, 1774.

DEAR SIR:—I enclose you proposals for a Pennsylvania Magazine. The publisher, Mr. Aitken, from Aberdeen, is an honest, worthy man, well esteemed, and well qualified for such an undertaking, so there is no doubt of his executing the plan he offers to the public in a manner that will give general satisfaction. I know you are a friend to merit, and as there are several persons in your neighborhood who may be inclined to encourage this work, I beg leave, in Mr. Aitken's name, to request the favor of you to assist in receiving subscriptions for it, which you will be pleased to forward before the end of the month. Mr. Illing, I hope, will lend a helping hand in getting some names. You will pardon this freedom, and believe me to be, with best compliments to Mrs. Burd, dear sir, yours affectionately,

THOS. BARTON.

JUDGE YEATES TO COL. BURD, AT TINIAN.

Lancaster, July 11th, 1775.

HON. SIR:—Yesterday Captain Smith came to town with near eighty riflemen. They chose him as Captain, Archibald Street, 1st Lieutenant, Michael Simpson, 2d Lieutenant, and William Cross, 3d Lieutenant. Our standing committee approved of their election, and sent down an express to the Congress, informing them of what had been done here, in consequence of their circular letter, and intimating to them that another company had been formed in this town chiefly through the care of ready to wait their orders. Much altercation and abuse arose on the appointment of the officers. Young Ross asserts [he was] empowered and desired by Mr. Patterson to raise men, and that those so enlisted by him were approved of by the committee of them. Patterson denies the assertion. The committee say that they can take notice of no other riflemen than such as are returned to them by the latter, to whom they had alone given orders to recruit; and that Patterson and Ross must settle that matter between themselves. Mr. Simpson in particular is much chagrined by the measures pursued, and so are very many others. Jemmy Ross set off post haste last night to Philadelphia to seek redress from the Congress, for the ill usage he thinks he has received.

Upon the whole, I cannot but sincerely lament the want of confidence and union amongst us, which so obviously retards our public deliberations. I doubt but you have heard ere now your son's determination to accept a lieutenancy amongst the Berks Riflemen. He was approved of by the committee of that county, and by the I wrote, therefore, to his grandfather, and his uncle Edward, in hopes that they would not be adverse to his going into the corps. His grandfather disapproved of his resolution, and censured him for not consulting his friends before he formed it. His uncle disliked it, and mentioning to him in a letter his want of knowledge in shooting a rifle, his unacquaintance with the manner of woodsmen, and of their hardy modes of life as capital reasons for his resignation. This was backed by another letter from Mr. Willing to the same purpose. I have heard yesterday that Mr. Patterson brings the news of Neddy's having declined in consequence of the joint opinion of all his friends, and that young Peter Grubb has got the appointment in his room; but of this we have no absolute certainty, not having received any letter from him on the subject. My sentiments are, it might have been prudent in him to have consulted his friends before he offered himself to the committee; yet his intentions were so virtuous and laudable throughout the whole proceeding, that they appear to me to palliate if not to justify the step he has taken. The qualifications necessary to form an officer amongst the riflemen he was well aware of. He knew and started every objection himself to Colonel Thompson, but he was , and encouraged, and persuaded by him to join the company. Want of due consideration therefore cannot be attributed to him, but must be charged to another account. Besides the care he had taken of his business, in writing to Jesse Ewing to come over and transact it in his absence, under certain terms, shows he was neither inattentive to his own, nor the interests of the country.

EDWARD SHIPPEN TO COL. BURD, AT TINIAN.

Lancaster, July 15th, 1775.

DEAR MR. BURD:—We are glad to hear of your recovery. Let God be praised for all his goodness. I expect every moment the account of a bloody battle at Boston. I hope HE has given us the victory in making our defence against our unnatural ministerial enemies; for should it prove otherwise, what will become of us. I have this minute received a letter from Mr. Read, wherein is the following paragraph. "I am pleased that a day of humiliation and fasting is at hand throughout the land; may our spirits be solemnized. I wish that card playing and other idle diversions were done away."

JUDGE YEATES TO COL. BURD, AT TINIAN.

Lancaster, Sept. 22d, 1775.

HON. SIR:—I received your favor of the 19th instant, and am glad to find that there is again some probability of a hearty union taking place in the remote Townships. From our united endeavors and strength alone, can we have the least prospect of success in our present glorious struggle.

Your accepting of the command of the Company, and a seat in the committee, pleased me much.

Had you declined doing so, your conduct might have been questioned by many, and your influence might have been greatly injured in your neighborhood. But I would by all means, recommend you not to sit in the County Committee, after your late refusal, until a new election takes place. This probably will soon happen. The County Committee are to fix a ticket to-day here, in consequence of a letter received from the Committee of Safety and Observation in Philadelphia. If anything happens before this scrawl is sealed up, I will communicate it to you. From what little I have seen, I cannot help observing, that this desire below* of interfering in our politics, is not generally relished amongst us. The step is viewed with jealousy and manifest dislike. It is thought some kind of control over the freedom of elections, and many do not scruple to say, that our Committee are going out of the line of their duty. I speak the sentiments of others. I carefully avoid the subject myself, in conversations.

EDWARD BURD TO EDWARD SHIPPEN, AT LANCASTER.

Prospect Hill, October 3d, 1775.

DEAR AND HON. SIR:—I have written a number of letters to you, and my other friends in Lancaster, many of which must certainly have miscarried. I find that I must not pay much regard to the cry of an engagement being likely to happen soon, as the same cry has been constantly echoed both before and since my arrival at the camp. When two armies are in sight of each other, there must be constant expectation of an engagement, no one can tell whether the opposite party will make an attack or not. I think I have acted as a volunteer at a time, and long enough to show my hearty disposition and wishes for the success of the cause we are engaged in, and have sacrificed voluntarily and freely as much, in proportion to my circumstances, as any one of them can boast. That no opportunity has offered, since my arrival, of my being in action, is not my fault. But that consideration ought not to keep me here to the ruin of my business, and longer than I can support my credit in the capacity I act. Indeed, I live as frugally as I possibly can, and would be able to continue here with what cash I have,

* At Philadelphia.

a month longer. But how must my business suffer! I am therefore determined to set off next week on my return to Pennsylvania, and be at the Lancaster Court if possible. When I shall enjoy the pleasure of seeing you and my other friends, increased by the great distance I have been from you. Gen'l Gage is going home, and Gen'l Howe will command in his stead. Dr. Church, the principal physician in our army is confined, for keeping up a very criminal correspondence with the regulars, by means of short hand writing, is and it appears that he has been as industrious as possible, in giving the enemy intelligence of our measures and situation.

JUDGE YEATES TO COL. BURD, AT TINIAN.

Lancaster, Oct. 14th, 1775.

HONORED SIR:—I wrote to you by last post, since which I sent you your new clothes, and a barrel of Newton's pippins, by one of your neighbor's wagons.

There is no late news here but what you must have heard. Kearsley's infamous conduct has drawn down on him the just resentment of the people. He, with other tories, are confined in Philadelphia gaol. It is said to be determined in Congress, that our troops shall attack Gen. Gage's line before his reinforcements arrive. How true it is, I cannot take upon me to determine. There is no doubt but Doctor Franklin, Col. Harrison, and another of the delegates, have set off for the camp about a week ago, on some public errand. By our last letters, Neddy* was to leave New England by

Edward Burd.

the middle of this month, so that we may soon expect his arrival among us. God send us a speedy peace, upon terms honorable and friendly to America.

EDWARD BURD TO COL. BURD, AT TINIAN.

Sunbury, Nov. 1st, 1775.

Dear and Honored Sir:—I arrived here, after long delays and a little missing of the road, the day before yesterday noon. We took a path that led into Plouts's valley, by which we went six miles out of our road. However, we feasted on venison all the way up, which made amends for the tediousness and length of the road.

There was a great talk here of going against the Yankees when I came up, but it has subsided a good deal. The snow and severity of the weather coming on, has made it a little discouraging. The Assembly and Governor are determined that the laws of this province shall be executed at Wyoming, the consequence of which will be a scuffle. When the attempt will be made I cannot tell, but I believe the justices are chiefly against it. At present, whether the Yankees will not by delay grow too strong to be attacked, I cannot say. I intend to set off on Saturday for Reading. I have not received a single farthing yet; bad times for us poor lawyers.

EDWARD BURD TO COL. BURD, AT TINIAN.

Reading, Feb. 25th, 1776.

Dear and Hon. Sir:—This town is divided into districts; and three companies are to be formed in it. I am placed in the lower division, quite removed from that part where I have interests, so that I suppose I shall not be among the officers. In any other part of the town I should have been chosen without dispute. I shall have the less trouble if I am not elected—though there is some talk of making me Captain. Mr. George Ross is laid up with the gout, here. We have got some tories here that were taken by Gen. Schuyler. A member of the family of Macdonald, from Scotland, had settled on the Mohawk, with great numbers of that clan. They were prevailed on by Sir John Johnston to take up arms against us in the back parts of New York, but were disarmed by Gen. Schuyler, and six of their principal men sent here as hostages.

JUDGE YEATES TO COL. BURD, AT TINIAN.

Lancaster, March 7th, 1776.

HON. SIR:—We have no news. The expected arrival of commissioners from England fills us with anxious expectation. I hope the terms which they are empowered to offer will be both just and generous, otherwise a negotiation will only serve to inflame matters.

A few warm members of committee in Philadelphia have resolved to call a provincial convention. The measure, I am told, is so much condemned by the thinking people that it is dropped for the present, until it is known what answer will be given by the house of Assembly to the numerous petitions before them. *Absolute necessity* alone should give birth to any new powers, and justify an innovation in the constitution.

COL. JAMES BURD TO THE OFFICERS OF THE THREE COMPANIES OF UPPER PAXTON.

Tinian, April 16th, 1776.

GENTLEMEN:—We received your very reasonable request* concerning an alteration in the districts of the three companies of Upper Paxton; the same was laid before the county committee by Colonel Burd, Major Cox, and Major Hummell. The committee approves of an alteration agreeable to the majority of the people, with the approbation of the field officers. We expect all the officers of the three companies will meet the officers of the battalion at Mr. John Harris', on Saturday next, at 10 o'clock before noon, where the field officers can be informed of your alteration, approve, and make report thereof to the county committee agreeable to order. You'll please bring with you the returns of your companies, that they may be made to the commissioners. Please to agree when and where we shall have the pleasure to wait upon you next week in Upper Paxton to view the three upper companies. Lieut. Col. Murray's indisposition prevented his attendance at Lancaster. We are, with much esteem, &c.

MAJOR BURD TO COL. BURD, AT TINIAN.

Reading, July 6th, 1776.

DEAR AND HON'D SIR:—I lately went to Philadelphia, expecting to find my uncle there as usual, but both houses were shut up. It made me quite melancholy; my uncle

* They had petitioned Col. Burd for leave to form a company of their own, as they "were much harrassed by crossing the mountains."

Edward Shippen has gone to the Jerseys, on a fine farm which he purchased there, about fifty miles from Philadelphia. I received a very kind invitation from him to go up to his place, but my affairs would not permit it. I will contrive before long to see them. It is not a day's ride from Easton, and if I do not turn out with the militia, it is possible I shall attend that court. But I believe, it will be expected of me to act as Major in the militia to be raised for a few months to serve in the middle colonies. If I am chosen, I am determined on going, as I have no notion of any man's refusing his service when his country calls on him. As this is a sudden emergency, I do not think I can see you before I go.

I bought a house and lot in Reading, lately, and hope what payments are left behind will not be attended with any inconvenience, as I have a good many bonds, which, together with the rent, will nearly answer it, supposing all other things to go ill with me.

EXTRACT FROM THE MINUTES OF CONGRESS.

IN CONVENTION,

Philadelphia, July 19th, 1776.

SIR :—The CONGRESS of the United States of *America*, having recommended to this Convention to hasten, with all possible expedition, the march of the associators of this province into *New Jersey*, agreeable to a former request of CONGRESS, we do earnestly recommend and require you to send forward into *New Jersey* your battalion, or as many companies as can possibly be armed, with all possible expedition, yielding a most exact obedience to the orders you may receive from this Convention, or from your superior officer, wholly disregarding all reports concerning the countermanding of orders received by you for marching the militia of this province, as such may be propagated by our enemies for wicked and destructive purposes. If you send forward only two companies, the second major is to march with them; if only three, the lieutenant-colonel, or first major; if only four, the lieutenant-colonel and second major; if only five, the colonel and both majors; if six, or the whole battalion, then all the field-officers.

Signed by Order of the CONVENTION.

BENJ. FRANKLIN.

To JAMES BURD, Esq.,
Colonel of his Battalion
of the County of Lancaster.

JUDGE YEATES TO COL. BURD, AT MIDDLETOWN.

Pittsburg, July 29th, 1776.

HONORED SIR: — I got up here safely last Saturday, having waited a week at Carlisle for Mr. Montgomery. We find that the holding of our treaty with the Indians must be deferred until the latter end of September, as it will be impracticable for any number of them to come in earlier. This will cause me a most disagreeable stay of two or three months in this place, yet it cannot be avoided. I am in hopes the treaty will be a general one, yet I sometimes fear the savages will be intimidated from siding with us, by our ill success in Canada. No step should be omitted, that may possibly prevent an Indian war; I have no expectations from the Six Nations. They are too much attached to Sir John Johnston. I am quite fatigued with writing, having been constantly engaged in that business since coming here.

EDWARD SHIPPEN TO COL. BURD, AT TINIAN.

Lancaster, November 7th, 1776.

DEAR MR. BURD:—I am this minute returned from the Committee. Mr. Yeates writes his wife of the 14th ultimo, that he had, two days before, received a letter from Neddy Burd, part of the way by water, (I suppose via Virginia, for he wrote from shipboard,) acquainting him that he was well, and very politely treated* by General Grant, Majors Leslie and Batt. But we have had no letter from him yet—for want of an opportunity. We are glad to hear of your recovery; blessed be God for all his goodness. Mr. Yeates writes that the Delawares and Shawanese were coming into the council-fire, and that he hoped the meeting would be amicable, though he was apprehensive peace would be of no long duration; some few people had been murdered about seventy miles from Fort Pitt. Some people say that Benjamin Franklin is sent to France, but this account is not confirmed. I say nothing about politics in letters. Your brother, E. S., has removed all his family back to Philadelphia. I imagine he does not like the power given to two magistrates, of calling any gentleman in that government before them, by warrant or summons, upon a bare suspicion of their being tories, and obliging him to give bail for his appearance at the next court of quarter sessions; and if he will not or cannot give bail, he must be sent to prison.

* He was a prisoner.

P. S.—I don't expect to enjoy any post in the Government two weeks longer. I have received a few shillings as Recorder of Deeds and Deputy Register, but scarcely enough to buy salt for my porridge. I must therefore be casting about for a country settlement, as well as my children, and Mr. Allen and his three sons, Johnny, Andrew, and Jemmy. But all at a proper time. I can scarce read my letters, for want of better spectacles, and there is not a pair to be had in this town.

EDWARD SHIPPEN TO COL. JAMES BURD, AT TINIAN.

Lancaster, Nov. 14th, 1776.

DEAR MR BURD:—Being just come from the Committee, I find your and my dear daughter's letters to each of us, and we thank you for your kind offer of your stone house, though so much to your own disadvantage. But out of love for yourself and family, it would be with the greatest reluctance we should accept of it. When we are obliged to move away, we shall let you know our resolutions, as we shall do to our other two children. But keep these hints to yourselves. We are daily in expectation of hearing, if not seeing, poor Neddy Burd. I must go presently to Committee again. I understand our Assembly is to meet at Philadelphia on the 20th instant, and that Lord Howe, and his brother the General, went to visit the city of Philadelphia; but I hope the season, by the kind disposition of Providence, will disappoint them.

MAJOR BURD TO COL. BURD, AT TINIAN.

Philadelphia, Dec. 12th, 1776.

DEAR AND HONORED SIR:—I am at last so fortunate as to be exchanged, though it happened not by intention, but accident. General Washington sent about ten or twelve prisoners to New York, and intended to name the persons who were to be sent in exchange; but Gen. Howe took the first Major, Captains, Lieutenants, &c., who happened to be on his list of prisoners, and sent them in exchange. I happened to be the first Major, and was therefore so lucky as to be returned. General Washington was surprised to see me. However, he was so polite as to tell me, that from the character I bore he was satisfied with my being the person, though he did not like the mode, especially as I was in a *Standing Regiment.* I do not know what he could mean by that, as the time of our regiment will expire by the first of June next, and I am sure the men will not stay a day longer.

———

CH. J. SHIPPEN, TO HIS FATHER, AT LANCASTER.

Philadelphia, January 18th, 1777.

HON'D SIR:—I send you by Mr. Adam Zantzinger, the sum of one hundred pounds, which you requested. Your condition, with regard to the income of your offices is to be lamented, and the only consolation you can have, is that everybody else is in the same situation. How long matters may thus continue, cannot be known, yet I think another summer must necessarily show us our fate. If the war should continue longer than that, we are all ruined as to our estates, whatever may be the state of our liberties. The scarcity and advanced price of every necessary of life makes it extremely difficult for those, who have large families and no share in the present measures to carry them through, and nothing but the strictest frugality will enable us to do it. I think my brother's situation a very eligible one. He is comfortably settled at a distance from the seat of war, which causes the utmost devastation and desolation wherever it comes. I thought when I purchased in Jersey, I should have been in the same situation, but it seems the country at no great distance from it, is entirely laid waste, though I have reason to think my farm is not injured at present. I live near the falls of Schuylkill, a very clever retired place, yet am in daily apprehension of every house in town being filled with soldiers, which has been the fate of all which have been left empty. In order to prevent this I now go to town almost every day, that I may be seen in and about my house; which is constantly opened every day, and has all the appearance of being inhabited, and is really lodged in by two or three women every night. By this means I hope to escape the mischief. I have lately had an affliction of another kind. My son Neddy was sent on an errand by his master into Jersey, where he staid longer than his business required. In order to avoid being pressed in the militia service, when General Howe had advanced as far as Trenton, and it was thought he was making his way to Philadelphia, Neddy was prevailed upon by Johnny, Andrew, and Billy Allen, to go in with them to the British army, which he accordingly did, and was civilly received there by General Howe and the British officers. His companions soon after went to New York, and Neddy remained at Trenton. When the attack was made on the Hessians there, he was accordingly taken prisoner by our army, and carried, with others, to General Washington, who, after examining his case, and finding he had taken no commission, nor done any act that showed him inimical, very kindly discharged him, and he is now with us. Though I highly disapprove of what he had done, yet I could not condemn him as much as I should have done, if he had not been enticed to it by those who were much older, and ought to have judged better than himself.

CH. J. SHIPPEN TO HIS FATHER, AT LANCASTER.

Philadelphia, March 11*th*, 1777.

HONORED SIR:—The complexion of the times is still bad, I know not when there will be any alteration for the better. I mean that peace (the most desirable of all human conditions,) seems at as great a distance as ever. General Howe in all probability will be in Philadelphia, in a month or two, having been reinforced, (as it is said,) at Brunswick, and General Washington's army in no condition to prevent him, but his coming to Philadelphia will only be the introduction of all the calamities of war in Pennsylvania. Philadelphia will be as a place besieged by the American army, and the country will be laid waste by the two contending parties. In this dreadful situation of affairs I am at a loss to know how to dispose of my family. Advantages and disadvantages present themselves by turns, whether I determine to remain in Philadelphia or remove to a distance. Your situation is better. You are already at a distance from the seat of war, and may remove still further if necessary. Yet no situation is actually exempt from a possibility of danger. We must make the best of it. I presume your office will get into other hands. I understand Peter Hoofnagle intends to stand candidate for it; you can certainly not expect it unless you give up the old government, and swear allegiance to the new one, together with the oath of abjuration of King George the Third. In these times I shall consider a private station as a post of honor, and if I cannot raise my fortune as high as my desires, I can bring down my desires to my fortune, "the wants of our nature are easily supplied, and the rest is but folly and care."

March 26th, 1777.

Since writing the above I am favored with yours of the 15th inst., with copies of John Hubley's letter, and your answer, which I think very proper. What plan you have formed for the future you don't mention, nor is it easy to advise. Nothing, however, should be determined with too much precipitation. At your advanced age it is a serious matter to go into a new course of life. The management of a farm is more proper for a man in the prime of life than in his decline, when nature calls for ease of body, as well as ease of mind. A little time may possibly enable you to form some resolution upon the subject, more to your satisfaction than at present. As to resigning your commision to Governor Penn there is not the least occasion for it.

JUDGE YEATES TO COL. BURD, AT TINIAN.

Lancaster, March 29th, 1777.

HON'D SIR:—I promised Henry Davis to write to you, upon the return of Mr. Baily from Philadelphia, respecting the establishment of a regular post rider here. I cannot yet find any great probability of its being done soon; every article of expense on the road is so greatly augmented that it will require treble the former sum subscribed to enable a person undertaking it to make both ends meet. If any settled plan takes place, I will acquaint you of it for Davis' information. I have just received a letter from Mr. Slough, of Philadelphia. He writes to me that 'on the 27th inst. in-'formation was given to the Board of War, that some persons 'in and about the city had prevailed on our pilots to bring 'the British fleet up the Delaware; search was immediately 'made, and the person originally concerned was soon appre-'hended and brought before the Board, when upon examina-'tion of the pilots who were so engaged, it appeared that the 'person had given each of them fifty guineas in part for 'putting this design into execution. It is apprehended that 'some people in the town furnished him with the cash; the 'person's name is Molesworth, and has served as clerk to every 'Mayor of the city, for twelve or more years past; it is 'thought examples will be made very speedily.

'There is nothing new from the camp, except that the 'enemy are preparing to move from here, and the people in 'Philadelphia are much ashamed that they should receive the 'first visit.' I find from the letter and every other account, that we probably shall have much confusion and disorder before the new constitution is fairly fixed. Many are determined to oppose it at all events, and many to support it at all hazards. I have not time nor patience to mention in how many instances the Assembly has infringed the *inviolable* frame of government, or to point out the impropriety of some late appointments; it is sufficient to say that the late steps give infinite dissatisfaction to the men of property and understanding. THE CLAMORS OF THE RED-HOT PATRIOTS HAVE SUBSIDED INTO EASY PLACES AND OFFICES OF PROFIT! The posts of mere TRUST go a begging! No one can be found to accept *them!* Whenever I reflect on the times, I am seized with the blue devils. I walk about the room in a sweat, look at my family, and wish them and myself out of the way of vexation. Sally tells me, Peggy is not to cut out her ruffles until she can send her up a pattern.

Col. Hand sets off in the morning for camp.

JUDGE YEATES TO COL. BURD, AT TINIAN.

Lancaster, Oct. 3d, 1777.

HON'D SIR:—I have received your favor of the 1st instant, with 8*s.* 9*d.* I send you the pound of chalk by the post, which cost only 9*d.* My letters to Neddy by Bakistoes, gave the most particular account of everything I could learn in the way of news. Since that time, we heard that the Delaware frigate was taken off Philadelphia, without much opposition; the ship struck to a few cannon planted on a wharf by the British troops. The chevaux-de-frize are not yet weighed; the row galleys and battery on Mud Island, having hitherto prevented the English ships coming up. The meadows opposite that Island are laid under water, by the banks being thrown down, to prevent the approaches of the enemy.

It is said that Lord Cornwallis has been appointed Governor, and Jo. Galloway, Lieutenant Governor of Philadelphia. Mr. Penn and Mr. Dulancy rode out to meet Gen'l Howe, and earnestly entreated him to save Philadelphia from plunder. The city, as we learn, escaped, but John Lawrence, near the Falls, had everything swept away by the soldiers. The truth of these things I cannot vouch for; in the nature of such things we can only look to common reports as our authority.

General Washington, we are told, is at Frankford, with his army. We expect every hour to hear of his attacking Gen'l Howe. He has received some very strong reinforcements, and large bodies of Virginians are daily passing through this town to head quarters. A general engagement will in all probability, decide the events of this campaign.

JUDGE YEATES TO COL. BURD, AT TINIAN.

Lancaster, Nov. 7, 1777.

HON. SIR:—I sent you by the boy, the bushel of salt on a little pony of my son's. There is no such thing as a waggon to be had going up the road.

Lord Sterling and his Aid-de-Camp, have been at our house these two days. There is no getting to bed at our usual hour. I am almost tired of it. His Lordship is very sanguine, that a few weeks will fully settle the fate of General Howe's Army. He speaks of those who choose to continue in Philadelphia, with pity for their situation.

Our Assembly are met,—to do great matters, I suppose. The Court bell rings as formerly, but I go not near them.

JUDGE YEATES TO COL. BURD, AT TINIAN.

Lancaster, Nov. 25th, 1777.

HON. SIR:—We have some reports in town that Fort Mercer, on Red Bank, is still in our possession. According to others, Lord Cornwallis took it on Saturday last. We know not which to believe; for my part I fear the worst. One John Brown, was confined in jail a few days ago, by orders of the Council. I have seen his examination, the purport of which is, that he came out of Philadelphia on the 5th instant, being requested thereto by Mr. Thomas Willing, who showed him a written message to him (Mr. W.,) from General Howe, that he was desirous of preventing the further effusion of human blood. Mr. Willing informed him, that in a conversation which passed between Sir William Howe and himself, the General assured him that his brother, Lord Howe and Sir William, had full power to accommodate the present matters, and for that purpose, could treat with Congress or any other person. That they were willing to put us in the same situation that we were in previous to the year 1763, and even grant us better terms. That if the Declaration of Independence was rescinded, they would withdraw their fleet and army, and would not require the disbanding of our troops, until the agreement should receive the sanction of Parliament, and that they would allow the sinking of our continental currency in our own way. Brown gave his word of honor to Mr. Willing, that he would not acquaint any one of his errand, until he had intimated it to some member of congress. He accordingly went to   when he mentioned it to Mr. Morris and Mr. Davis, when he came to   he was taken up by the Council, and the affirmation of allegiance was tendered to him, but was at length admitted to bail by the intercession of the above two gentlemen, who became surety for him. From hence he went to Yorktown, and was from thence ordered back for examination. The Council have ordered him into limbo. I would observe to you, that Brown has done business for Willing and Morris these ten years past, has the entire confidence of them both, and is universally respected, and a strictly honest man. Considering all matters, I fear we are ill disposed to an accommodation. Mr. Shippen remains very ill, every one else is in good health amongst us.

JUDGE YEATES TO COL. BURD, AT TINIAN.

Lancaster, December 19th, 1777.

HON'D SIR:—Capt. Crouch delivered your letters within this hour, so that my answers to your questions cannot be as full as I could wish. It is generally believed that the chevaux-de-frize have been raised, I do not know however that any certain news has been received on the subject, that could impede them from accomplishing it for so many weeks, when every succor of provisions depended on their exertions in this particular. There was no battle fought near Whitemarsh, the two armies were drawn up within view of each other, but our situation being exceedingly advantageous on the summit of a high hill, Gen. Howe did not think proper to risk an attack. On Thursday, Lord Cornwallis came out of Philadelphia with 4,000 men, attacked the militia under General Potts, and drove them off, and also the main body, for about eight miles, killing, and taking many prisoners. The militia, it is said, behaved in their usual way, very ill. The enemy are now all gone into Philadelphia, and our headquarters are at the light-house, about twenty-five miles from Philadelphia. In the late excursion of the enemy from Philadelphia, they committed great devastation, and were guilty of many cruelties. They stripped families of all denominations, of clothes, bedding, and everything they could lay their hands upon, making fires of the furniture.

It is told us that the assembly are busied in making a law to repeal the militia act, and proposing a commutation of money for actual service. This is done under the recommendation of Congress, who has required of each state a new quota of men for the Continental army; a law of this kind would be of infinite service to the community. A letter has this morning been received, giving an account that Lord Cornwallis, Parson Duché, and several Quakers, have lately embarked for England. Duché lately wrote a very foolish letter to General Washington, which I suppose somewhat affrights him, when he finds that America is not so easy a conquest as he once believed. If I can procure a copy of the letter I will send it to you.

JUDGE YEATES TO COL. BURD, AT TINIAN.

Lancaster, December 26th, 1777.

HON'D SIR:—I have received your favor by J. Evans, and now send you up a copy of Duché's letter to General Washington. I have just finished transcribing it. The Congress and gentlemen of the army would, I fancy, show but little mercy to the parson, if he was in their power. They are particularly reflected on with much severity, in the letter, indeed, I think, with circumstances of high aggravation. There are, however, some melancholy truths contained in it, which I ardently wish could not be told. The most exceptionable part of it to me, seems that passage wherein he exhorts the General to negotiate for America, at the head of his army, if Congress should not assent to his proposals. This is plainly advising him to commit a flagrant breach of trust. It is true, Genl. Monk, before the revolution, played the same game with success and advantage to himself. I can only reply in the words of Shakspeare, "Tho' I love the treason, yet my soul abhors the traitor." You will be able to form your own judgment of the letter. Your strictures, however, on it, should not be trusted to every conveyance. When you have perused and done with the letter be pleased to forward it to me by some safe hand, as I propose sending it up to Fort Pitt, and copies are to be had with great difficulty. I also enclose you a copy of verses on the celebrated urn of Doctor Franklin. They are, in my opinion, exceedingly well wrote, and contain the true Attic salt. The authoress, Miss Norris, acquired much political reputation by them in Philadelphia.* There is but little news stirring. We hear that a party of the enemy are gone towards Chester, to forage. Ten or twelve detachments are sent in quest of them, who are determined to give no quarters. Morgan's riflemen are determined to scalp, and the light-horse to dispatch their prisoners. It seems this resolution was taken on their being informed that a party of the British light-horse, having taken two of our soldiers, inquired of their officer what they should do with their prisoners? He answered, "Give no quarters, murder them." They accordingly dispatched one and gave the other many wounds, but he survived to tell the horrid tale to our army, who were greatly inflamed by his account. Mr. Sam. Meridith brought up this account yesterday from head-quarters, and I believe it may be depended upon as truth. Such brutalities and retaliations must aggravate in a

* Unfortunately, the verses are missing.

ten-fold degree the horrors of war. We sink from men into savages, by such inhuman conduct.

I hear our assembly have agreed on suspending the habeas corpus act for three months. If anything further occurs before Hans sets off, I will communicate it to you.

December 27th, 1777.

I have just seen the draft of a law which has just been read the second time, and is published for consideration. The purport of the law is, to direct that all persons trading in wine, rum, grain, clothes, linen, bar iron, nails, rods, shoes, whiskey, wool, cotton, (with a long etc.) or other wares or merchandise, shall take out licenses for that purpose, from commissioners to be appointed in the respective counties, for which they are to pay five shillings. That licenses are to be granted to those only who have taken the oath or affirmation of allegiance and abjuration, and are friends to freedom and independence. That previous to obtaining a license they are to give in an exact account of their goods on hand, on oath or affirmation, &c., &c. This law will probably make a great deal of confusion among us. I would send you up a copy of it, but cannot get one. Oh! tempora, Oh! mores.

EDWARD SHIPPEN TO COL. BURD, AT TINIAN.

Lancaster, June 30th, 1778.

DEAR MR. BURD:— * * * * * * I suppose there have gone to Philadelphia this week at least a dozen families, and more are removing. The president and council left the borough last week, and most of the congress passed through it yesterday. Dunlop (the printer) is now putting his furniture and press into a wagon, going off ad urbem, so that we can't expect any newspapers in less than ten days from this time.

Mr. Yeates has gone to Philadelphia, aud we shall look for him next Monday night.

CHIEF JUSTICE SHIPPEN TO HIS FATHER, AT LANCASTER.

Philadelphia, July 3d, 1778.

HON'D SIR:—I did not understand by your letters concerning Pultney's ground rent, that you meant to be paid in half joes, as no such thing is now at all expected, that commodity being merely a merchandise.

As to Galloway's expression to my brother about not selling the house on your account, it was a low, dirty pretence, as every body knows selling real estate for continental money has been avoided, though a great nominal price might be offered. When I mentioned drawing on me for two years' rent, I certainly meant continental money, as it would be utterly impossible for me to pay in gold, having been drained and put to the greatest shifts to procure sufficient to subsist my family during the residence of the British troops here, when no other money would pass, and every kind of provision a treble price. I have sent you by Mr. Yeates, half a dozen pounds of chocolate, but I am afraid it will be very difficult to procure Madeira wine at any price, the only pipe I have heard of for sale was limited at either eight or nine hundred pounds; I will keep a look out, and if possible procure you some. There is no such thing as syrup, the sugar bakers having all dropt the business a long while. It is possible after some time there may be an importation of French molasses; if so, I will try to get you some.

JUDGE YEATES TO COL. BURD, PAXTON TOWNSHIP.

Lancaster, October 10*th*, 1778.

HON'D SIR:—I have been doing little for these ten days past, but electioneering. Matters have come at length to that pass, that it becomes every good man to turn out, and endeavor to procure a proper representation for the county he lives in. The many violations of the Constitution by the late Assembly have given the people at large the most general uneasiness and disgust, and strike the most ignorant with the propriety of an exertion at the ensuing election. A ticket has been formed here this day, which will run well in the district, and if there should be a division in other districts, however small, will probably be attended with success. Will not the people about Middletown vote? Be good enough to try. We have written to Col. Cox on the subject, and enclosed him a ticket. Every moment's delay is attended with danger. In the city of Philadelphia and other counties, every nerve will be strained to effect a change of men and measures. It is very generally believed that a French and Spanish war is declared. Dominic is taken by the French, and a descent on Jamaica is meditated. It is said the Spanish have blocked up Gibraltar. A general European war seems inevitable.

The Oyer and Terminer Court will sit some weeks longer in Philadelphia. Abraham Carlyle has received sentence of death. John Roberts is convicted; Jacob Meng is convicted. Poor Billy Hamilton's trial comes on this week, and his friends are very uneasy on his account. The city is in the greatest ferment. Most good men wish for an act of oblivion. The British troops have destroyed all the salt-works and vessels at Egg Harbor.

A message was lately sent to Congress by the General and Admiral, expressing their firm determination to burn all the seaport and other accessible towns, unless the Convention of Saratoga was complied with. Congress replied, that their letter was too insolent to receive an answer, and put them at defiance. Thus stand we at present.

CH. J. SHIPPEN TO HIS FATHER, AT LANCASTER.

Philadelphia, December 21st, 1778.

HON'D SIR:—I received your favor of the 16th inst., acquainting me with the sale of Mr. Galloway's house to Mr. Yeates. I had some desire to make the purchase on my own account as well as yours, as it is not very unlikely I shall find myself under the necessity of removing from this scene of expense; and I don't know where I could more properly go than to Lancaster. The common articles of life, such as are absolutely necessary for a family, are not much higher here than at Lancaster, but the style of life my fashionable daughters have introduced into my family, and their dress, will, I fear, before long, oblige me to change the scene. The expense of supporting my family here will not fall short of four or five thousand pounds per annum, an expense insupportable without business. I have at last completed my purchase in Chester county, greatly to my satisfaction, and have sold my Jersey estate for nine thousand pounds; so that if I should live in Lancaster, I can be supplied with a variety of necessaries from my own farm, which is about twenty-four miles from thence, with a very good road all the way.

The orchard I must now defer planting till the spring; if you could in the meantime secure me the first choice of the best apple-trees in the nursery you mentioned, it would be very well. I gave my daughter Betsy to Neddy Burd last Thursday evening, and all is jollity and mirth. My youngest daughter is much solicited by a certain General, on the same subject; whether this will take place or not, depends upon circumstances. If it should, I think it will not be till spring. What other changes in my family may take place to forward or prevent my removal from Philadelphia, is still uncertain. As to the sale of Shippensburgh, I would not advise you to think of it unless you can beforehand meet with something to lay the money out in which would yield you a better income.

EDWARD SHIPPEN TO COL. BURD, AT TINIAN.

Lancaster, January 2d, 1779.

Dear Mr. Burd.—I have forwarded your letter to Neddy Burd, from whom I am in daily expectance of receiving a letter. We hear he was married the 17th instant. Allowance must be made for his not writing, as soon as expected, in these cases. The young couple are happy, and that is enough. We understand that General Arnold, a fine gentleman, lays close siege to Peggy, — and if so, there will soon be another match in the family. My son Edward has lately sold his fine house and mill and farm in the Jerseys, for

£9,000, and purchased another, within four and twenty miles of this borough, on the Horse-Shoe Road, altogether as good; and, as living in Philadelphia is so very expensive, he has some thoughts of purchasing this house, and remaining up with his family. I should not write by every post, having little to say, — but a short letter, I consider, will serve to cover the newspapers. All General Burgoyne's army are gone over Susquehanna. Happy for this borough, they were not detained by the weather all winter. Enclosed is a pretty fancy enough in French, which Neddy Burd will translate, one of these days, for his brothers and sisters.

JUDGE YEATES TO COL. BURD, AT TINIAN.

Lancaster, February 19th, 1779.

HON'D SIR: — We are told of Congress having received some dispatches of consequence from Europe, the particulars of which have not transpired. It is said that a combined fleet of France and Spain will be on the American coast next month, in order to protect our trade, and that a loan of ten millions of dollars in specie will be negotiated with Spain—the budget to be communicated to the public on Monday next. Others speak of this matter merely as a bubble, in order to assist speculation. These last think there will be a general exertion in Great Britain, in order to carry on the war, and desolate the country. They say we have not the most remote prospect of peace. In this uncertainty we must continue for some time at least.

EDWARD SHIPPEN TO COL. BURD.

Lancaster, February 24th, 1779.

Dear Mr. Burd: — I just now received your favor of the 19th instant, by the hands of Mr. Yeates. You have done very well in adding to your orchard; I wish I could get a good opportunity of sending up the young Summer apple trees which I raised on purpose for you. At your brother Edward's request, I have lately got from Hains's nursery, near Bethel, one hundred pretty apple trees of the best grafted fruit, and planted them in a nursery in my garden, to be ready whenever he sends for them, which will not be before next spring. I have advised him to plough in the stubble this fall, and to stake out the orchard with hoop-poles, and put within a foot of each stake a peck of cow-dung, or horse-dung, two or three years old; then to make a fence with posts and broad rails, five rails to a pannel, and then he may plant his trees, fall or spring. Let me observe, that even horse-dung will give the bitter rot; neither should orchards ever bear but one crop of grain, lest the ground be impoverished; for one hundred apple trees, in the course of fifteen or twenty years, in good soil, will produce more fruit than one thousand starved ones.

Mr. Bier has been three months making me a pair of shoes, and now charges me twelve dollars; whereas, last November, he would have asked but eight dollars. His excuse is, that his time was wholly taken up with making boots for strangers, which was the most profitable work. I have your letter to Mr. Yeates, about a boy which he might have in the country; but he asked me whether I would accept of him. I said no; for I will never have the trouble of another in my house. I can raise nothing in my garden, because of my neighbor's fowls; and, when I want a little wood sawed, or any other job done, I can hire a man,—and I have no horses. I enclose you a few grains of Indian corn, which General Hand has sent me from Albany, of an early sort, though small. Here follows a copy of his note about them:

'A remarkable early kind of Indian corn, brought from 'the foot of Lake Otsego, 7th November, 1778, worth 'propagating; perhaps Mr. Burd may have a curiosity 'to try it.'

The enclosed letters acknowledge the receipt of letters from Messrs. Campbell and Henderson, informing me that there is a petition sent to the Assembly for a new county, and that the struggle is between the people of Shippensburg and the environs, and those of Chambersburg, as to where the court house and prison shall be. The former have subscribed £10,000, and the latter are doing all in their power to raise as much.

Your brother Joseph writes me, that his plantation is not large enough for his family, and therefore he is looking out for another. I think I told you lately, that his brother had bought this house from Mr. Yeates; the price is £3,000.

MAJOR BURD TO COL. BURD, NEAR MIDDLETOWN, LANCASTER COUNTY.

Philadelphia, March 12th, 1779.

DEAR AND HON'D SIR:—The cat is not yet let out of the bag; the good news which it is said was so favorable to

America, is yet kept a profound secret. Thus far we are informed, that it is of a cabinet nature, and it is of the utmost importance. Amid so great a variety of conjecture, we have no ground on which we can build any opinion. We are told that we know everything, that is for our advantage at present to be informed of. Many people believe that Congress has only spread the report, with a view to keep up the spirit of the people, and raise the credit of the paper money, but I am of a far different opinion. I firmly believe that there is some news which lead to matters of the utmost consequence, but they are not yet sufficiently ripened to be asserted as facts to the public. Great Britain is preparing for a vigorous campaign, as far at least as voting in the House of Commons will make it, but there are old maxims that dictate the most vigorous exertions, in order to get the better peace, so that this circumstance does not discourage me. I expect to get to housekeeping the latter end of this month. I should be glad you would send the boy to Lancaster the last week in March — perhaps he might go behind some man—or you might possibly
to take him down, if no other mode can be used. He must come down from Lancaster in a wagon. There is a pair of candlesticks which I bought of Ab'm Wickersham, which please to send to Mr. Yeates, as early as possible. If no opportunity offers before the boy comes down, please to contrive to send them by him to Mr. Yeates.

I shall set off to-morrow with my dear Betsy, on a visit to Uncle Joseph Shipppen, in Chester county, if the weather is favorable; we have been waiting for good weather and roads some days. Mrs. Francis, Mr. Shippen, Betsy and the family, join in kind love to you all.

JUDGE YEATES TO COL. BURD, AT TINIAN.

Lancaster, June 6th, 1779.

HON'D SIR:—I returned yesterday from viewing the farm I am interested in, on the banks of Pequea, and am exceedingly pleased with my purchase. I accompanied Mr. and Mrs. Burd seven miles on their road, on Friday last, and then struck off towards my lands.

Mr. Haymaker purchased me a young negro lad while I was down, whom I think of taking into the family, and putting the lad I now have to the farming business. He is a hearty, strong, healthy boy, above twelve years old, but must know that he has a master. I will put him on the place when it comes in my possession, which will probably be in April next, but in the mean time intend sending him into the country. I have had several applications for him, but don't chose he should be too near Lancaster. If you think he will be of any service to you, I will send him to you for a few months. He can thresh somewhat, and has been used to the country.

We have many reports here that General Lincoln has defeated the British in South Carolina, and has killed or taken 1460. Should it be true, it will have amazing effects. The news gains ground daily, and a number of circumstances concur in giving it credit.

It is also said the English fleet has left the Chesapeake bay, and that all the troops landed in Virginia are embarked and gone off. Sir Henry Clinton has come out of New York to White Plains, as if he meant to do something, and General Washington has left his former camp at Bound-brook, and crossed the North river in order to be near him. It is thought Clinton's object is the taking of West Point, where a strong bomb is thrown across the North river, in order to have the same removed, that his ships may go up without interruption. I shall send your watch by Davis, if done when he goes off; it was promised to me this evening. If you do not think my negro will be useful to you, I would by no means send him up.

MAJOR BURD TO COL. BURD, AT TINIAN.

Philadelphia, June 18th, 1779.

DEAR AND HON'D SIR:—Having been much engaged since my return to the city, and expecting a full confirmation of the very important news from Charleston, I have delayed writing till this time. I am sorry it is not so well authenticated as I wished, but the accounts came through such a variety of channels, and all the same in substance, that we must give credit to it, though perhaps the truth may vary in some circumstances. We have been looking for an express every day since my arrival, but to no purpose. We are greatly at a loss to account for the neglect in the people of Charleston. Some say that they are offended at the inattention shown by congress to their defence, others attribute it to the continuance of the warlike operations before the town, which engrosses all their time and attention, notwithstanding the repulse and loss of the enemy. Their remaining force is very considerable. A sailor arrived yesterday, who says, as I am informed by some, that he was in the battle, by others, that he was within a few miles of the place, and received the information from others, but I am inclined to believe from circumstances of the relation that he was in the garrison at the time of the engagement.

The account he gives is this. That before the invasion of Carolina, an embargo had been laid on the vessels in port, that on the 7th May, the gates were shut, and martial law declared, that on the 9th the enemy advanced, and on the 10th, in the evening at five o'clock, made an assault upon the town with about 3500 British troops and as many Tory refugees, which continued till 9 o'clock. They had brought pontoons with them and attempted to cross with 1500 men, and land on another part of the town, while the main body attacked in front, but this plan was prevented by two or three vessels, and a battery, which not only hindered the execution of the design but also kept the troops from returning to the shore. They were obliged to put over to an island, called James Island, and a body of our troops are between them and their main body. The enemy were entirely repulsed, and left 653 dead on the field. They retreated to a place called the Neck, about five miles off, some say eight or nine miles off. General Williamson had got into the town, and the garrison was a very large one. General Lincoln was three days march in the rear, and the bridges were all broken by the enemy, to retard his march.

Their success is not decisive, but is nevertheless of great consequence, as it will raise the spirits of the people, and make many more join the army than perhaps otherwise would have done. I am in hopes of further good accounts from this quarter.

What is a great confirmation of the repulse is the entire silence of the New York papers, so late as the 10th instant. They pretend to know nothing of it but what they have from our papers. Such quantities of sugar have come in lately that it sells for the barrel £100 per the hundred.* We are

* Continental paper, I suppose.

in very great want of our boy; I wish it was possible to get him down soon. If he has not left Tinian before this reaches you, be pleased to send him to Mr. Yeates, at Lancaster, as I believe that will be the quickest method of getting him down. We are really at a great loss without him.

MAJOR BURD TO COL. BURD, AT TINIAN.

Philadelphia, July 9th, 1779.

Dear and Honored Sir:—I am sorry to tell you that the enemy are not in that dangerous situation at Charleston that we wished, but it is certain that they retreated suddenly from before the town, and by the help of some ferry boats got upon John and James Islands. General Lincoln writes, that the enemy's force is men that his own is 2,000. That General Moultrie has 1,500 men, Governor Rutledge 1,000, and that he can keep them from doing injury to the country, and that the town is under no apprehension. 2,000 continental troops are upon their way from Virginia, and 700 militia to join the troops, at Charleston. We have the greatest reason to expect a Spanish war. A man just from Havana says, that the harbor was ordered to be cleared for 12 sail of Spanish men-of-war while he was there, and that goods rose fifty per cent. I saw this man.

MAJOR BURD TO COL. BURD, AT TINIAN.

Philadelphia, July 25th, 1779.

Dear and Honored Sir:—You doubtless have heard of the taking the strong fort, garrisoned with near 600 men, at Stoney Point. It was a curious affair, and is no inconsiderable loss to the enemy. I suppose the enemy will soon be at Lancaster. I send you a couple of papers that mention it.

The people are to have a town meeting to-day, when it is expected that matters of some consequence will be transacted. George Ross you find is dead. He was very cheerful on his death-bed; he said he was going a long journey, and that he was almost tired before he set off, but the place was cool, and that there were most excellent wives there, and he should fare deliciously. That Mrs. Ross did not expect to see him so soon after her, &c.

JUDGE YEATES TO COL. BURD, AT TINIAN.

Lancaster, August 31*st*, 1779.

Honored Sir:—I this morning received a letter from your son, with the enclosed. At my request, he sent me two bushels of salt, and by the same wagon directed to my care, one and a half bushels of coarse salt, for you. He writes to me, that he procured the salt with the greatest difficulty, and had it not been for the friendship of Mr. John Meas, one of my clients, it would have been impossible. The bags go down to Philadelphia again, so that when you send for your salt you will please to send a bag.

I have heard that a small party of American Georgians, during the absence of General Provost, took forty-five light horse prisoners, besides killing a few of them. The account about Penobscot is is still doubtful, the attack was to be made on the 2d of August, and Sir George Collins set sail on the 3d of August. It is thought a fortnight will elapse before he arrives at that place. A vessel, part of Goodrich's fleet, has been captured by a privateer of Blair McClenachan's, with 60 brass cannons, 20 tons of powder, 40 chests of tea, and 1,000 suits of soldier clothes, and sent into Philadelphia. Another vessel of the same fleet has lately been captured, and sent into Baltimore. She had 100 soldiers on board.

Philadelphia's new jail is filled with British prisoners, and the town swarms with their officers. Every thing looks well except our money, and Congress, it is said, are busily engaged in devising some mode to retrieve its credit. I fear it will be a herculean task.

MAJOR BURD TO COL. BURD, AT TINIAN.

Lancaster, October 9th, 1779.

Dear and Honored Sir :—I received your kind letters, and intended to have wrote to you by Mr. Crouch, but the business of the court took up all my time.

To-morrow I shall off for York. The week after, I shall be at Carlisle, and understand that there will be so much business at York that I must return from Carlisle to York, but on my return to the Lancaster sessions, I must ride to Tinian and see you, if time will permit. I will spend as much at Tinian as possible; but I am determined to be there even if my time should be pinched. I shall be obliged to depend upon my island for my bread the ensuing year, and exchange corn for wheat and get it pounded into flour and sent down to me, therefore be pleased to get my share of the corn from the island. Michael owes me sixteen bushels of corn. I will speak about that when I go up to Tinian.

The troubles in Philadelphia, I dare say, you have heard. I have only time to tell you that I received a letter from Betsy, dated October 7th, which says things are tolerably quiet at Philadelphia now. You may have heard that General Arnold was in and had been in Wilson's house, but neither of these is true; he is at home with his wife. It is true he was in the street with the rest of the citizens, and even pursued by two men, but he happened to have pistols with him and prevented them from violence by threatening to fire at them. He applied to the Congress for protection, who referred him to the executive power of the state, who have provided for him.

EDWARD SHIPPEN TO COL. BURD, AT TINIAN.

Lancaster, November 24th, 1779.

DEAR MR. BURD:—Three days ago I was favored with your agreeable epistle of the 13th instant, handed to me by Mr. Yeates. But a little before I received that letter, I had wrote pretty fully by one John Tautes, of Sunbury, who promised to deliver my letter, with the newspaper concerning Captain Worke. Lest the letter should miscarry, I shall here repeat some of its contents in this. The young man who makes his addresses to Peggy, is of a good family, and that is all I know of him. The Latin phrase is, *exampla parentum bonorum est maxima dos.* The examples of good parents is a great portion. He bears a good character. I thought it advisable, as soon as prudent after the wedding, that the young couple should remove to old Mr. Worke's until they could get a place in the country to their mind. Mr. Yeates told me that he understood they were to reside in this borough. I replied that I was very sure that the profits of a sheriff's office would never admit of that, when the fees were more than double to what they are now; not to mention that it is the most dangerous office a man can undertake. A sheriff ought to have the heart of a stone to stand against the cries of women, beseeching him to take their husband's words and fair promises, and so not to put them into prison; frequently to the great loss of the sheriff. Tom Smith, the sheriff, (though he lived part of his time in the country,) was almost ruined by the office. It is indeed true, he was put in jail some time after he was out of office, but that was because he was involved in an iron work. Joseph Pugh, his successor, was so reduced by that business, that he was obliged to remove into a remote part of Virginia with his poor family. Then came in Jimmy Webb, who rented a house in town, where he must live like a gentleman, and make every leading man in the county quite welcome that came to see him. If he had not had a good estate, he would have failed. F. Stone succeeded him, who thought himself as good a gentleman as his predecessors; but he, a poor, good-natured, tender-hearted man, soon got into jail, and is at this day an object of pity. After him Johnny Ferree, of Bettellhausen, nine miles off, set up for sheriff, and carried it by a great majority of votes, and called on me for a recommendation to his honor, Governor Penn, for a commission, which I refused to give until, among other things, he promised to live very frugally, and settle his accounts with me at every court, and pay me the Governor's fees or fines, and my fees, &c. He was indulged to live at his own house at Bettel House, coming to town once or twice a week, by which means he was able to do every body justice, and save some money to himself.

The ladies and misses dress as gaily as they do in the city of Philadelphia, and loaf sugar and green tea are as plenty on our tea tables as ever they were! You shall always be as welcome as you ever were in better times.

JUDGE YEATES TO COL. BURD, AT TINIAN.

Lancaster, September 10th, 1780.

HON'D SIR:—I wrote to you on 24th ultimo, since which I have not observed anything particular respecting Mr. Shippen's health; his lowness of spirits continues, but his appetite and rest is good. I do not observe that his weakness increases, and am in hopes that the cold weather will brace him up and somewhat confirm him. Perfect sound health can hardly be expected at his time of life.

By a letter received from Mr. Parr, in Philadelphia, we have advice that old Mr. Allen is gone to his long home.

Poor gentleman! he is at length happily removed from all his troubles. His reverse of fortune is a noble lesson of morality in the most prosperous seasons of life.

The second division of the French fleet is not yet arrived, nor is it expected until the beginning of next month. General Gates' defeat near Camden, is a heavy loss; greater, I fear, than we conceive at present.

JUDGE YEATES TO COL. BURD, AT TINIAN.

Lancaster, September 18th, 1781.

HON'D SIR :—We were much pleased with Mrs. Burd's coming down, though our pleasure would have been greatly augmented by your company. We flatter ourselves that your disorder will be of no long continuance.

Mr. Shippen is very ill, though his fever is somewhat abated since yesterday. The nourishment he receives can scarcely support nature. It gives me the greatest pain to declare, that, in my opinion, he can remain but a short time among us, a very few days will probably produce the mournful event.

We expect Mr. E. Shippen here this evening, and look for Mr. J. Shippen every moment.

Some gentlemen from Philadelphia mention the arrival of Admiral Digby at New York, with ten sail of the line. But the French have a superiority of line of battle-ships on the coast. They have thirty-five ships, and the British only thirty.

J. YEATES TO JAMES BURD, AT TINIAN.

Lancaster, September 27th, 1781.

HONORED SIR :—We expect, daily, interesting news from the Southwand. Capt. Charles Stirling, a son of Captain Sir Walter Stirling, dined with me to-day. He is a sensible, agreeable young man, but rather stiff in his politics. He was lately taken in a sloop of war by the Congress, a Philadelphia privateer, after an obstinate engagement, and sent up here a prisoner on parole. It is said that Admiral

Digby is expected on the American station, with 8 or 9 ships of the line. I don't believe any such thing probable. But should he come, Sir Henry will in all likelihood, attempt succoring Lord Cornwallis, and relieving him from his difficulties.

Many are fearful of an attack on the city of Philadelphia; for my part I think there is little danger of it. It can be no object of importance to the enemy. General Clinton has been fairly taken in by General Washington. All his movements indicated an attack on New York, while his whole blow was aimed at Cornwallis.

COLONEL LAURENS AND THE SURRENDER OF CORNWALLIS AT YORKTOWN.*

Having returned from the successful accomplishment of his important mission, in which he had negotiated the co-operations of the French fleet on the American coast, Colonel Laurens assumed his military functions, and was eminently distinguished at the seige of Yorktown, where, leading the assault of one of the British redoubts, he saved the life of the officer who commanded it, and made him his prisoner.

Being appointed Commissioner for the capitulation on the part of General Washington, he met Colonel Ross, of the British Army, A. D. C. to Lord Cornwallis, and commissioner on behalf of the garrison. Having placed the terms on which a capitulation would be granted before Colonel Ross, that gentleman observed, 'This is a harsh article.' 'Which article,' said Colonel Laurens?

* From Major Jackson's MSS.

'The troops shall march out with colors cased, and 'drums beating a British or a German march.' 'Yes sir,' replied Colonel L., 'it is a harsh article.' 'Then Colonel 'Laurens, if that is your opinion, why is it here?'

'Your question, Colonel Ross, compels an observation 'which I would have gladly suppressed. You seem to forget, 'sir, that I was a capitulant at Charleston, where General 'Lincoln, after a brave defence of six weeks, open trenches 'by a very inconsiderable garrison against the British army 'and fleet under Sir Henry Clinton and Admiral Arbuthnot, 'and when your lines of approach were within pistol shot of 'our field works, was refused any other terms for his gallant 'garrison, than marching out with colors cased and drums '*not* beating a British or a German march.' 'But,' rejoined Colonel Ross, 'my Lord Cornwallis did not command at 'Charleston.' 'There, sir,' said Colonel Laurens, 'you extort 'another declaration. It is not the individual that is here considered; it is the nation. This remains an article, or I 'cease to be a Commissioner.' The result was, the British army surrendred with colors cased and drums beating a British or a German march.

The war in Virginia being closed by the capture of this army, Colonel Laurens, impelled by his ardent patriotism, hastened to the Southern army, where fresh laurels awaited his gallant exertions, and where his country was to witness his devotion, even to death in her cause.

The writer of the present article, who was then assistant Secretary at war, received his last letter, in which he says:

'I am writing to you from a sick bed; but I have just 'heard that General Greene has ordered a detachment to 'intercept a party of the British near to Cimbakee. I shall 'ask the command, and if refused, I go as a volunteer.'

General Greene, anxious for the recovery of his health, would have declined the request of Colonel Laurens, but his determination to go as a volunteer, decided him to grant it.

It would appear that, by unavoidable accident, some troops detached to the support of his party, did not arrive until he was attacked by a very superior force; and in cutting his way through it, he was mortally wounded, and fell dead from his horse into the arms of Major Smith. Such was the close, while yet in its bloom, of his illustrious life, through which he had given such proofs of devoted patriotism, heroic valor, and splendid talents, as would have secured to him the first honors of his country, as they have impressed the deepest regret for his loss, and the most heart-felt tribute of gratitude to his memory.

The following observation by Lord Cornwallis, made in conversation after the capitulation of Yorktown, attests the high estimation in which the officers, to whom it refers, were held by his Lordship:

'He said, there could be no more formidable antagonist 'in a charge, at the head of his cavalry, than Colonel 'William Washington; and that he had never taken a posi- 'tion in the vicinity of General Greene's army, that Colonel 'H. Lee did not find out his weak point, and strike at it 'before morning.'

JUDGE YEATES TO COL. BURD, AT PAXTON.

Lancaster, March 26th, 1783.

DEAR SIR:—Our prospects of a peace seem duller than ever, lately. It is reported that some dispatches have been received from France; that neither France, Spain, nor Holland, would agree to the terms which Great Britain holds out.

I can scarcely bring myself to believe that the war will continue, yet no one can form a judgment of the European Courts, nor of the views of the several belligerent powers, at present. Comparing everything, however, I am strongly of an opinion that we shall not have another American campaign.

Miss Nancy Relfe is down with us from Carlisle, paying a visit. Our winter has passed over agreeably. What with plays, cards, dances, dinners abroad and at home, we have continued to dispel all care. My daughter Molly sustained the character of Marcia, in the Tragedy of Cato, with much approbation lately, at the school-room, to a very crowded audience. The partiality of a father forbids my enlarging on this topic.

I am, &c.

Since writing the above, I have seen a hand-bill from Philadelphia, dated 24th inst., which gives the account of a peace being concluded on the 20th January last. The intelligence came in a sloop-of-war commanded by M. du Quesne, in thirty-two days from Cadiz. The outlines of the treaty are only mentioned. They are too lengthy to insert, nor would my memory serve. Great Britain retains Gibraltar; the treaties concerning the demolition of Dunkirk are vacated; the Newfoundland Fishery to be shared by Great Britain and France; Spain to enter into agreement with the former respecting the cutting of logwood in the Island of Honduras; Independence granted to us, &c., &c. Huzza! huzza!

JOHN SHIPPEN TO HIS FATHER, COL. JOSEPH SHIPPEN, AT LANCASTER.

Carlisle, March 3d, 1788.

HONORED FATHER:—I know not how to introduce the present subject, nor, indeed, do I think it is in the power of words to express fully the transactions of the people of Cumberland. However difficult it may be, I shall attempt it, hoping to give you the outlines, after a fashion, that you may complete the picture, and have some small idea of their conduct. It will not seem a credible story to people who are unacquainted with the inhabitants of the county, but when attested by the hand and name of your son, you can have no doubt of the truth of it.

I presume papa remembers the contents of a Carlisle Gazette, which I sent him, with respect to the riot of December. The sheriff of this county receiving warrants (State) from the Chief Justice, McKean, against twenty-one rioters, took said persons before Mr. Agnew and Mr. Erwin (Justices), who being in some doubt with respect to the warrants, offered them a privilege to remain on parole a month, viz., to the 25th of March, till they should have opportunity to consult the Chief Justice. The twenty-one, taking into consideration the above offer, seventeen of them insisted upon a trial, refused to give bail, though they might have obtained it, and declared they would rather go to jail than accept of a parole, as others did in the same situation. They were accordingly committed. The report of their imprisonment having spread through the country, Mr. Agnew and Mr. Erwin thought it expedient to publish in the paper the above account, which by the country people was thought to be a lie, as well as the procession in the town of Boston.

I may here remark, that whatever account favorable to the Federalists appears in the paper, it is esteemed as a lie and a falsehood by the adverse party—I mean the Anti-Federalists. Of the conduct of the latter I mean now to treat.

On Saturday, by daylight, a company from the lower settlement entered the town, singing "Federal Joy," (a song composed by one of their party, and published in the newspapers,) took possession of the Court-house, and rung the bell all the morning. (I should have mentioned, they were armed.) Several other companies came in from different parts of the country, the last of which about ten o'clock. They then marched to the jail, and demanded the prisoners; upon which, they received them, placed them in their front, and marched through town huzzaing, singing, hallooing, firing, and the like. It is thought, there was upwards of eight hundred. Such a number of dirty, rag-a-muffin-looking blackguards I never beheld.

It was feared, they would all remain (at night) in town, in order to do mischief; but their leaving it in the afternoon produced an agreeable disappointment. It may seem strange, that they should thus be permitted to do as they pleased; but for want of a sufficient number to repel them, the gentlemen of town, who are men of sense and forethought, as well as men of true courage, thought it most proper to let them alone. Not that they were afraid, for if they could but have raised two or three hundred men, well armed, they would have marched in front; but the matter would not rest here; they could have raised nearly as many more, which would have been the cause of a civil war, to prevent them, viz., the Anti-Federalists.

Thus, our Federalists acted their before-mentioned character, which, considering their situation, was, in my humble opinion, very proper and becoming.

I drank tea at Gen'l Butler's yesterday. He told me he was going to Lancaster, and is so good as to take care of this letter. I wish to be remembered with the greatest respect and love to my dear mamma, sisters and brothers, as also to Mr. Yeates, and General Hand's family, Mr. Hutchins and Miss Patty.

JOHN SHIPPEN* TO COL. BURD, AT TINIAN.

Carlisle, Oct. 19th, 1788.

HONORED SIR :—I arrived here on Sunday evening last, having dined at Harrisburg with cousin Hubley.

The Representatives, &c., chosen at our last general election for this county, for the ensuing year, are as follows :

Assemblymen—	David Mitchell,	Anti-Federal.
	Thomas Bailes,	"
	Jonathan Hoge,	"
	Thomas Kennedy,	"
Sheriff—	Charles Lieper,	Federal.
On the return—	James Wallace,	Anti-Federal.
Coroner—	John Walker.	
On the return—	John Wray,	Anti-Federal.
Commissioner—	George Logue,	"

* Son of Col. Shippen and nephew to Col. Burd.

JOSEPH BURD TO HIS FATHER, COL. BURD, AT TINIAN.

Philadelphia, April 30th, 1789.

DEAR AND HON'D SIR :—On the 20th inst. General Washington passed through this place; the whole city seemed to be rejoicing. Some of us went a little way to meet him. An elegant dinner was prepared for him at the City Tavern by the citizens, and there was a glorious spirit shown. He set off next morning for New York, to take his seat as the President.

The House of Representatives has taken up the Revenue bill, and is about laying heavy duties on many important articles.

The King of England has got over his insanity, and is recovering his health. The Prince of Wales has been appointed to the Regency.

Mrs. Burd desires her love to you. My brother I expect will return to-night from Norristown, and next Tuesday sets off for the rest of his circuit, which will take him five weeks.

Mr. Carmick, the student whom I found in the office when I came down, thinking that the business of the office interfered with his studies, has left, a circumstance which I don't like.

COL. SHIPPEN TO CH. J. SHIPPEN.

May 18, 1789.

DEAR BROTHER :—I am extremely concerned to tell you that a most unfortunate duel happened last Monday evening, between Doctor Reiger and Mr. Chambers, on a challenge of the former, for an affront received by him at a tavern. When each had fired one pistol without effect, the seconds interfered, and proposals of accommodation were made, which Reiger could not be persuaded to agree to; each then presented a second pistol; Chambers' snapped, but Reiger's discharged a ball through both his antagonist's legs. His wounds bled much, but for two days were supposed not dangerous; a mortification then ensued; its progress upwards was great and rapid till Saturday morning, when it extended to his bowels, and carried him off, to the most severe distress of the families and friends of both. The procession at his funeral, in the evening, was truly solemn and affecting. This melancholy subject has already too much agitated my mind to dwell on it longer, by relating the particular circumstances.

JAMES TILGHMAN TO COL. SHIPPEN, AT PLUMLEY, CHESTER COUNTY.

Chestertown, Maryland, Sept. 2d, 1790.

DEAR SIR:—I could not overlook the good opportunity of telling you, that I am happy to hear from Miss Shippen, whom I frequently have had the pleasure of seeing at my own house, that you retain a tolerable share of health, and are settled on a good farm. As we grow in years, we must expect to feel the natural attendants on old age. For my own part, I am weak in my sight and hearing, and have in a manner totally lost my teeth, and with them a good deal of my power of articulation. Thus hurt in my sight, hearing, and speaking, I am grown very unfit for public company; I can hear the sound of a general conversation only, but cannot distinguish what is said, which is a disagreeable circumstance. In other respects, I thank God I enjoy a good share of health. I cannot say so much for my spirits, which you may well imagine must be somewhat affected by the severe afflictions I have met with, in the loss of my good children, who were both a comfort and a credit to me; and, although I have received a very considerable addition of property, by the death of my sons Richard and Thomas, it comes through so unnatural and melancholy a channel, as to be of consequence rather to my family than myself, and I feel that wealth alone is not sufficient to constitute happiness. My farms furnish me some new employment and amusement, and are in that respect very useful to me; for having led a life of business, I should be wretched, indeed, if I had not some objects on which to employ my attention. I have lately made a purchase of a farm, about an hour's ride from town, which will not only be a hobby-horse for me, but I expect to derive some advantage from it, though I paid a great price for it, £7 10*s.* an acre, and I must lay out a good deal of money in buildings, repairs, and fences; but I expect it will soon repay me. It contains near four hundred acres, all of the first quality, and finely watered, which is not common for that part of the country. The present tenant this year makes an extraordinary crop — fifteen hundred bushels of wheat, and two thousand of Indian corn. The common crop is about twelve hundred of wheat, and fifteen hundred of corn, and to this I expect to add some tobacco, when I take it into my own hands next year. Enough of myself. Do you hear from our friend, Mr. Penn? I understand the family have fallen short of their expectations from Parliament. All things considered, they have got more than I expected, and have enough left, if it be well managed. I hear in a round-about, uncertain way, that Mrs. Penn is not so fond of England as she expected to be. She left her consequence in America, as most people do, who go to England. It is not always a portable commodity. I have had but one letter from Mr. Penn, and probably shall not have another, as I do not know that my last, written a good while ago, has been received. You know his aversion to letter-writing, even where he had subjects of business, and was urged by considerations of interest; both which motives are now wanting. I should not be surprised if they should return. I take it for granted Dick must. I am spinning out a long letter. The truth is, I have a real satisfaction with conversing, though in this imperfect way, with an old friend; I have hardly one left here. It will always give me pleasure to hear of your welfare and happiness—being,

With very sincere regard,

Your old acquaintance,

And obedient servant,

JAMES TILGHMAN.

JOHN SHIPPEN TO HIS FATHER, COL. JOSEPH SHIPPEN, AT PLUMLEY FARM, WESTON TOWNSHIP, CHESTER COUNTY, PENN'A.

Camp* at Cherry's Mill, on Jacobs' Creek, which falls into the Youghiogeny, after being the boundary line between Westmoreland and Fayette, for a considerable distance. Cherry's Mill is at the point where Jacobs' Creek begins to be the boundary line.

Mount Pleasant Township, Oct. 31st, 1794.

MY DEAR FATHER:—I am now seated in our tent, surrounded by two or three of my companions, while the re-

* For a full and careful account of this insurrection, see *Wharton's State Trials.*

mainder of the ten are finishing their suppers, composed of chocolate, bread and butter, and the remnants of a chicken or two, which gratified our palates at noon. They are supping on a little scaffold, erected by way of sunshine table, at the door, and the talking and laughing of those around, and two different songs, one from each of the neighboring tents, combined at once in my ear, would perhaps entirely incapacitate me for writing or thinking at all, but that I have been so used to it for about two weeks past, that I scarcely know that I am in the midst of it. Having begun as I have, I might add before I proceed, that, by way of table, I have placed on my lap a little board, that was yesterday morning the cover of a provision box for our mess, which had the ill fortune to be staved to pieces, among some other damage done to the property of our company, occasioned by the oversetting of our wagon yesterday. And I cannot help thanking you, sir, just in this place, for your thoughtfulness and kindness in sending me your little green waxen taper, which serves me as light on this occasion, as were it not for its aid, I should be obliged to postpone writing till morning. You will naturally inquire how I come to have nine companions as messmates. It is owing to a circumstance of which I have yet to inform you. At Carlisle there became by the arrangements, a number of supernumerary officers, from colonels to ensigns. I was one among the number, and conceived it my duty to join, as a private, some volunteer company. I accordingly proceeded from thence to Bedford, to join Captain Graham's company, of Macpherson's battalion of Blues, as a private. General Hand, with his usual kindness, assured me that if it was in his power, he would endeavor, in case of a vacancy, to get me an appointment. I overtook Graham on my way to Bedford; and proceeding on, I overtook Gen. Proctor at Hartley's. His attention and civility I cannot soon forget, especially after I had satisfied his curiosity and inquiries respecting my coming on before the troops. The General asked me to ride together with him to Bedford; which I did, where we arrived before any of the army. On our ride the General expressed his satisfaction at my determination to come forward and go on as a private, instead of returning home as some of the supernumerary officers did. And, when I think or speak of supernumerary officers, I cannot help informing you that the Governor has really very ill used the supernumerary officers, by taking no notice of them, while he gave some privates command and posts, which afterwards appeared as vacancies. The Governor is, in my opinion, an electioneering, cunning, contrary [dog,] and I know not what kind of little fellow, who has, particularly on this occasion, hurt himself so much by his conduct that it will, perhaps, be with some difficulty he will again be Governor, provided any popular man opposes him. For my part, I must have some reason for altering my opinion, if I ever vote for him as such, for I think I have found out his real character; but I will say no more on that score at present. When I found that neither Captain Graham nor myself could contrive any mode of taking on my mare, so as to draw forage for her if I joined his company; and when I found that I could procure no satisfactory quarters for her at Bedford, I then determined on joining our Chester County dragoons, under the command of Major McClellan. In this situation I now am very well, hearty, and happy, in a mess with Major Humphreys, Col. Whelen, Samuel Dennis, Dr. Kennedy, Joseph Dilworth, William Kinnard, Samuel Entriken, Willis Hemphill, &c.

What, with cooking, eating, feeding, currying and watering our horses, procuring our oats and hay, and furnishing them, attending roll, standing guard, making our beds, and riding out in the country by turns to procure such necessaries as we want and to get our clothes washed, it consumes the whole day; and when we march it requires the most indefatigable exertions to have everything go smooth. If this were not the case, we should be unhappy. This keeps our bodies, and consequently our minds, fully employed.

Things are most amazingly dear. Some have been so unconscionable as to demand 2*s.* 4*d.*, and 3*s.* 9*d.*, for a quart of whiskey, 6*s.* and 9*s.*, for a dozen of washing, counting a pair of stockings as two pieces. We have, however, reduced those prices somewhat, by declaring we would not be imposed on.

I saw bread, a small heavy rye loaf, worth 3*d.*, sold for 1*s.* 10½*d.* We have plenty of beef and flour, sometimes we are lucky enough to draw bread. Hay and oats have been the scarcest, sometimes we have not drawn more than four, sometimes six, though generally nine quarts a day. Hay has been less plenty. However, we are now getting in a more plentiful country. Our marches are excessively slow, and tiresome. We have sat on our horses, six, seven, and eight hours at a time, and in the rain; and made but eight, nine, and ten miles a day, on account of the wagons and foot, than which we must not go faster. One night, and that the worst since I left home, we slept on straw at the fire, covered by blanketing, without tents, the wagons not being able to reach us, and I believe not a single person experienced the slightest injury from it.

In what manner to give you a concise history or account of the army in general, I am at a loss. However, I may mention that the President was at Carlisle, and made some arrangements (not respecting officers,) but the modes and measures to be pursued. From there he went to Cumberland fort, where General Morgan was, with his Virginia troops at that time. Having, I supposed arranged matters there, he came to Bedford, and from thence, after two or three days' stay, returned to the city. His conduct, his appearance, his dignity, and affability of demeanor, struck admiration in a number of beholders who then saw him for the first time.

General Lee is Commander-in-chief when the army comes together, (which) I cannot say when or where it will be. We are all of us, and have been all along in the dark, as to every thing future, even our next day's march.

Governor Mifflin is second in command. Governor Howell commands the Jersey line. We, and all the county troops of horse in Pennsylvania, except the Lancaster, and three Philadelphia troops are attached to the Jersey horse, and under his command, the more immediately under the command of General White, of the horse. General Frelinghuysen commands the advanced part of the army, consisting of Macpherson's Blues, Taylor's Rifle Corps, the three Philadelphia companies of horse, and Captain Kenney's, of Jersey.

The next in advance is General Howell's command, and the last Mifflin, Irwin, and Proctor's Brigade, and park of artillery, although at present they have made a kind of junction, as we are all within the space of three miles. At Bennett's, about three or four miles from Bedford, we all turned off to the left, and left the Pennsylvania road, bending our course to the Glades and Berlin. When we had reached the top of the Alleghany mountains, the road again divided, and there we took the right, leaving Berlin on our left, while

Mifflin's command took the left, and proceeded through Berlin, which same road General Frelinghuysen had marched the day before, most terrible roads indeed: but these and other particulars I leave to relate when I have the pleasure of sitting around our happy fire-side at Plumley. Parkinson's Ferry is supposed to be the place where the whole junction of the different armies will take place. It is, I believe, a little north of west, about twenty-five miles distance.

At Carlisle, (I believe,) one or two persons were taken hold of as Whiskey-men, (for that is our term,) but at Bedford, twelve or fifteen were taken prisoners, four of whom were sent on to Philadelphia, as the most infamous and criminal of them, the others were admitted to bail. Judge Peters, and Attorney Rawle, and Attorney-General Ingersoll, are with the army.

The horse scour the country and bring in these prisoners. Harman Husbands, one of the four above, was brought by the horse forty miles to Bedford from the Glades.

I believe I am accurate when I say there are about 1300 dragoons of the Jersey and Pennsylvania lines. As to the Virginia and Maryland horse we know not, but hear they are about 5 or 600. As to the foot of the Pennsylvania line and Jersey line, they amount to about 5000. We are now about seventy miles from Bedford, and forty from Pittsburgh, at Cherry Mill, on Jacobs' creek, which I trust you will find on the map.

At Shippensburg the army parted —the horse all went by Chambersburg—the foot, by Strasburg. Capt. Rippey takes the lot at £20 per acre; as I found great necessity for it, he advanced me forty dollars, with much pleasure and readiness. I saw Major Galbraeth, who informs me he had seen James Buchanan, who promised him that he would take particular pains to search for papers, relative to your lands, among the papers of his brother John; and that he would call upon you with them, the first time he came to the city. I saw James Buchanan yesterday, by accident, about two or three miles from here, when I was out for necessaries, and he repeated the above promise; he added, he wished he had the names called for in the warrants. I referred him to Col. George Woods. I saw Judge James Webb at Bedford, who behaved with his former steadiness and kindness; he says his brother's illness prevented him from preparing his business, as soon as he otherwise would have done, for his journey to the city: but that he is perfectly recovered, and expects to go to the city in the course of some weeks, when he will certainly call on you.

P. S. We have had ten days of bad weather; every day more or less rain — sun shines one moment — rain in ten afterwards. I never saw a country like it. The boundary line between Westmoreland and Fayette, is the road from Berlin to Cherry's mill—thence Jacobs' creek to Youghiogeny — thence, a straight line, a little N. of W. to the Monongahela, south of Parkinson's ferry. I suppose your old map has not particulars on it.

JOHN SHIPPEN, TO HIS FATHER, COL. JOSEPH SHIPPEN, AT PLUMLEY FARM.

Pittsburgh, November 15th, 1794.
Camp near the town.

DEAR AND HONORED SIR:—I am sorry I have not been able to have written to you oftener than I have. You all may, however, be assured that it was not because I thought the less frequently of you. The seldomness of an opportunity, the real want of time, and sometimes the hurry and flurry of the camp, and at other times of our tent, are some circumstances that have prevented my enjoying the agreeable exercise.

I wrote you from the camp at Cherry's mill, favored by Mr. Hunt Downing, and gave you, as near as I could, the situation and motions of the army. I find I was somewhat mistaken as to some of my conjectures. The main body of the army, (I mean the Pennsylvania and Jersey lines,) is now within four miles of this place. We, and the Lancaster troops, commanded by Captain Coleman, and the Pennsylvania horse, are encamped on the Alleghany, about one mile from the town. Some of the Virginia and Maryland line yet lay, I believe, between the Youghiogeny and Monongahela, some at Parkinson's Ferry, and some at Washington; to which last place I believe, the advance of our line has marched. What regular general plan of operations is adopted, or has for some time guided the motion of the army, no inquiry, that I can with propriety make, has discovered. At Carnatan's tavern, about three miles from Burd's, and the same from Simmerel's Ferry on the Youghiogeny, we were encamped about six days. This last encampment is about thirteen miles from Cherry's mill, on the road to the above ferries. At Cherry's mill we laid about the same space of time. Our horse arrived here two or three days ago, and the foot since. When we shall return is yet not known, or what quantity of business remains yet to be done is all dark to us. Upwards of twenty prisoners, I understand, have been taken near and about Parkinson's ferry, by the Maryland and Virginia horse, and several in and about Washington by some of the troops, but which I have not learnt.

Nine prisoners were brought the other night by some of our scouring parties, from their beds in this town to the Pennsylvania camp before they reached this encampment, and are now under guard.

It is surprising and laughable, that in this country, every body tells you they were forced by threats to go to such and such place, and they talk violently against the proceedings of Tom Tinker's men, (for that is the name of the Whiskey-boys now,) and when you ask them, where are the persons that threatened them, and that were principals, "Oh! they are run off;" which is not altogether untrue, for numbers have fled, but numbers of those that remain are as guilty as they.

I am told that a man by the name of Hamilton in Washington county, who had been very active in the late disturbances, was informed on. A person who knew him well, undertook to describe his dress. A number of troops were set to guard the house, and if he came out and attempted flight, their orders were to shoot him. In the mean time the cunning rogue was busy changing his dress for that of some domestic, very different from his own, and walked out the house with apparent carelessness and unconcern, and spoke with the soldiers and officers, and indeed answered some questions that they put to him regarding Hamilton, with such adroitness, that he escaped through them, and fled. This story seems improbable, but I am told it is true. Pittsburgh is a handsome situation. I think I never saw two more beautiful rivers than the Monongahela and Alleghaney; I may add as a third, Youghiogeny, which did my heart good when I saw it, at the recollection of your former adventures before I was in being. Pittsburgh is amazingly crowded with quarters of Generals, Colonels, Aid-de-Camps, and other officers; the people are afraid of being eaten up if the army should rest here, but I believe there is not the most distant danger.

Inaccuracies you will pardon; though I should read over my letter ten times if I could, I fear they would escape my notice at present.

MARQUIS OF LANSDOWNE TO MAJOR WM. JACKSON, AT PHILADELPHIA.

Bowood Park, October 10th, 1796.

DEAR SIR:—I trouble you with the enclosed letter, from a very particular friend of mine, who is in every respect to be depended upon.

General Washington may perhaps not be sorry to know the circumstances contained in it — in which case, I am sure they cannot find their way to him through a more discreet channel than yours. He best knows the degree of importance which may attach to the personage in question, which is considered by many well-informed persons, as considerable; and I am certain that his magnanimity and wisdom render all solicitation on this, or any such occasion, altogether impertinent.

I shall be much obliged to you likewise, to communicate the enclosed to Mr. Bingham, with my very best compliments. I add no observations on the state of public affairs—not knowing when or how this may reach you.

I am, with great esteem and regard, dear sir,

Your most obedient, humble servant,

LANSDOWNE.

MR. COUTTS TO LORD LANSDOWNE.

(Enclosed in the foregoing Letter.)

Clifton, October 10*th*, 1796.

My Lord:—I believe I have had occasion to mention to your lordship the intimate acquaintance I have with the eldest son of the late Duke of Orleans; and I imagine the amiable character of the Duchess, his mother, is not unknown to you. I never knew much, personally, of the father; — and can only say, if he deserves the bad character I have often heard of him, he resembles very little his eldest son, who, I believe—those who know them most intimately, will agree with me — possesses the most engaging qualities, accompanied with the modesty becoming his years. He has constantly written to me since the French Revolution, and his conduct has been exemplary. He fought and behaved bravely, for the liberties of his country, till the murder of the king. He then left the army, and has lived in the greatest obscurity, on the most slender means. The most virtuous characters are too often calumniated. He has, to my knowledge, been hiding himself in Lapland, unknowing and unknown to almost everybody—at the same time that pamphlets and newspapers have placed him at Hamburgh and elsewhere, contriving with Dumourier plans of ambition—which he never thought of. The mother has lately procured the release from prison of her two younger sons, who are to go to America;* and the eldest, for whom I am interested, has, from dutiful

* In the Directory for 1798, after

"Dennis, Mr., *Taylor*, Pewter Platter Alley," appears the following:

"Dorleans, Messrs., *Merchants*, rear 100 South Fourth street."

These were Louis Phillipe and one of his brothers, who lived at the north-west corner of Fourth and Prune streets, in a house still standing, and now number 110.---*N. and Q.*, vol. viii, p. 168.

compliance with her orders, and to place himself out of all suspicion of European plots, set sail in an American ship lately from Hamburgh, for Philadelphia. Setting aside my personal affection for this young man, his misfortunes claim some regard from the world, so long as his conduct continues such as to deserve it, as hitherto it has invariably done. Your lordship knows he was born Duc de Chartres; and he does not mean to be unknown for who he is in America, though he may find it convenient to assume a less brilliant name; his wish being *privacy,* suited to the unhappy reverse of his fortune.

Under his uncommon calamitous fortune, I am confident your lordship would be glad to serve him—and it may be of great service, if you can procure for him a good recommendation to General Washington—also, that you would recommend him to any of your friends in the mercantile, or other respectable lines of life, at Philadelphia.

I flatter myself, with your usual kindness to me, you will excuse my writing to you in favor of a young person, for whom I have a very sincere regard; and believe the sentiments of respect with which I have the honor to be, my lord,

Your lordship's

Most faithful and obedient servant,

THOMAS COUTTS.

Any letters I procure for him, I mean not to send him to deliver, but to send them by the packet; and so leave it to the option of those they are addressed to, to take notice of my young friend, or not, as they think proper.

I shall, however, inform him that such letters have been written in his favor, and by whom.*

THE MARQUIS OF LANSDOWNE TO MAJOR WILLIAM JACKSON, AT PHILADELPHIA.

London, March 5th, 1797.

DEAR SIR:—Col. Markland and Mr. Richards arrived together, which brought me the favor of your two letters of the 28th November. I never received that to which you allude; which, with some others, I have reason to believe were either stopped or miscarried. But I have received the picture,† which is in every respect worthy of the original. I consider it as a very magnificent compliment, and the respect I have for both Mr. and Mrs. Bingham will always enhance the value of it to me and my family. I have just had the honor of writing to Mrs. Bingham my acknowledgments, but must depend on your making my excuses for not writing instantly, which can only be excused by the fact of an almost unceasing pain in my head. I am not alarmed at it, because I know the cause and the remedy, which last consists in the Bath water, with constant air, exercise and perfect leisure; but nothing could cure me, if Mrs. Bingham thought me wanting for a moment. This state of health, and many other circumstances, would make me consider it as a great calamity to return to my public situation. I know but *one* circumstance which could reconcile me to it, which is next to impossible: that I could have it in my power to

* An outline of his adventures in America is to be found in the spirited article on Louis Phillippe, reprinted from the *London Times*, in Appleton's Library.

† Portrait of Gen. Washington, by Stuart.

introduce a little more civilization among nations, and to put war at a greater distance. The weakness of Government and the extreme popularity of the sea service, added to old and false prejudices and habits, makes it difficult to render the commerce of neutral nations as sacred as it ought to be, but nothing should detain me from the attempt, if I saw a probability of succeeding. I cannot express to you the satisfaction I have felt in seeing the forts given up. I may tell you, in confidence, what may astonish you as it did me, that up to the very last debate in the House of Lords, the ministry did not appear to comprehend the policy upon which the boundary line was drawn, and persist in still considering it as a measure of necessity, not of choice. However, it is now indifferent who understands it. The deed is done, and a strong foundation laid for eternal amity between England and America.

General Washington's conduct is above all praise. He has left a noble example to sovereigns and nations, present and to come. I beg you will mention both me and my sons to him in the most respectful terms possible. If I was not too old, I would go to Virginia to do him homage. I am extremely obliged to your kindness and hospitality to Mr. and Mrs. Rigal. I believe them to be very worthy people. I beg to be remembered to them.

Mr. Richards appears a worthy, unaffected person. His stay in town was so short, that I did not see as much of him as I desired to do, but he has promised to come to me in the country.

Though I have not the honor of being known to Mrs. Jackson, I beg to offer my best wishes for her happiness, and that you will believe me always,

Your most faithful servant,

LANSDOWNE.

CHARLES COTESWORTH PINCKNEY TO MAJOR JACKSON, (IN THE CUSTOMS,) PHILADELPHIA,

Head Quarters, at Shepherd's Town,
May 15, 1800.

Dear Sir :—I am exceedingly obliged to you for a copy of the very elegant, pathetic and eloquent discourse you pronounced on our deceased Patron, Father and Friend. You knew him nearly and well, and could best declare his worth. I was greatly pleased when I first heard the Cincinnati had entrusted his eulogy to your talents, but I was enthusiastically delighted and affected when I perused your admirable oration. Again and again, I thank you for it.

What news from our envoys, or from Europe, or of our domestic politics?

The only injury we can now receive from the French is by their making a treaty with us; and I have no doubt but that they will complete the plan of their politics towards this country, by making such a one as will consequently draw us into a war with the coalition powers, or disarm, lull and completely humbug us, and afterwards observe it as long as they deem convenient. What are the Disunionists about? I trust the Federalists will not be over supine. When you have a leisure minute, devote me a line, and let me know what is going on. Mrs. Pinckney and my daughters, unite with me in best compliments to Mrs. Jackson and yourself, and we beg you will tender them, on our part, to Mr. and Mrs. Bingham and their family.

I remain, with great regard,

Yours, truly,
CHARLES COTESWORTH PINCKNEY.

JOHN SHIPPEN TO HIS FATHER, COL. JOSEPH SHIPPEN, AT PLUMLEY, CHESTER CO., PENNA.

Shippensburgh, December 13th, 1801.

DEAR AND HON. SIR :—When on the point of setting out to the Federal city, on the 26th October, I waited till the arrival of the mail in hopes of receiving a letter from you on your return from Philadelphia to Plumley. The mail did not disappoint my hopes, but brought me long, affectionate, satisfactory letters from you and sister Peggy, both of which I acknowledged by letter by Mr. Hall.

I then set out, and reached Chambersburg that evening. I went by way of Hagerstown, Fredericktown, Montgomery Court House, and Georgetown. After two or three days' stay at the city of Washington, I accomplished the objects of my mission thither; and, being but thirty miles from West river, I paid my relations there a visit, staying three days with them, and proceeding home by the way of Annapolis and Baltimore, having been absent thirteen days.

The city of Washington is elegantly situated as to inland view, and valuable as not being accessible by weighty, foreign men-of-war, and of being so distant from the sea coast up in the bosom of the country, as to be easy of defence, and difficult of attack by foreign invaders. Many merchants of capital must establish themselves there, and many Pennsylvania, German or other industrious tillers of smaller farms than are usually seen in Maryland or Virginia, must plant themselves in the surrounding country, before this great city can bid fair to progress.

How far these will be equally *consequences* as *causes* of its *progress,* is a matter of curious discussion. The truth is, everything must go hand in hand, and the warm advocates of that spot must not barely content themselves with building and improving the city, but should lend their attention seriously to the encouragement of merchants and farmers. Navigation and agriculture are the sources from whence must principally spring the advantages and greatness of any city. The plan is very extensive, and occupies a great space of country. Already (it is calculated, and I believe it) one thousand houses have been built there. These present themselves to one's view as a number of small villages, in respect of the scattered position of the houses; the most of which, however, are large and elegant. The lots and squares are, in my opinion, much too small, and are inconvenient for the want of alleys. I went by water to Alexandria, a very regularly built, handsome town. I returned by land on the Virginia side; from many hills on the road, we had fine prospects of the city of Washington, especially of the President's house and of the Capitol. In planning and plotting this city, and fixing the places for the public buildings, more attention was paid to the nature of the ground and views, than to any previous arrangement on paper or distances, and the sites chosen for the President's house and Capitol are the highest, and considered the best prospect. The distance between them is at least a mile. At a future day, when this city shall flourish and be generally pretty close built, it will have the advantage of most other cities in the world, in being all of a piece, and preserving the symmetry of a great original project. The public buildings are neither central nor convenient. The President's house, outside, exhibits great grandeur and simplicity of architecture. The inside (I went through it) is not equal to my expectations. The Capitol is only part built; from this, I can judge of the intended whole. Its architecture is not so simple; I think its decorations of wreaths and flowers, etc., cut in stone, are rather too profuse. It is, however, grand.

It struck me, the windows of the Capitol had the appearance of being rather small for the building.

I was very much pleased with its inside. The senate chamber is the most superb and grand room, and its architecture the most noble and elegant of any I ever saw. These two buildings are of a squared free stone, not a pure white, rather on the greyish order, or a tinge towards lead. They yield much to the marble of the Bank of Philadelphia. Three miles from Georgetown, just at the head of tide water, and at what are called the little falls, a bridge of single arch crosses the Potomac. It is composed of wood; erected by one Palmer, from Connecticut. I was told that it was formed by him in Connecticut and shipped in pieces. The abutments are a huge pile of massy square stones bolted together with great iron pins, and melted lead, a novel sight to me, and I take it, capable of resisting the most swollen floods of water. The Virginia side a high bank, Maryland side, low base of immovable, large and deep rocks. The fact is, here the Potomac is narrow and deep. People were busied in repairing the locks of the canal at the upper or great falls. I was very affectionately and kindly received and treated by my uncle Galloway, and my other relations at West River. I lodged at my uncle's, but he and I divided our time between his house, Tulip Hill, and Mrs. Cheston's. Mrs. Cheston is an uncommonly fine woman, and her daughters two of the most sensible young women I know. I felt extremely at home at these places, reflecting almost every moment that my dear mother had been wont in her innocent youth to frequent them, and that she drew her first breath at West River.

Last evening I had a letter from uncle Galloway, dated Hagerstown, 11th inst. He was on his way to Cumberland to visit his daughter Polly, (who married Captain Linn.) He mentioned his son John being with him. John has just returned from the Mediterranean. He is in the navy, and partakes of the honor of Captain Sterritt and crew in the late successful engagement.

Mrs. Cheston and the young ladies expressed a sincere desire that my sister Peggy would pay them a visit. This affectionate wish attached me still more to them. Mrs. Cheston is a most excellent manager of her farm and its concerns. Her farm is in the highest cultivation of any I observed in that part of Maryland. James Cheston, her only son, is a steady, promising young man. I was tired of the Maryland gates, but not of their oysters; which we had twice a day.

Your time, when in Philadelphia, must indeed have been pretty busily engaged, amidst the several interesting matters of business, and the many friends by whom you would be surrounded. As to the division of the Pegs' run lots, that may be somewhat tedious, but you will have fewer obstacles to combat. As to the sale of Plumley, I am in hopes you will be able to get your price for it, which, in my opinion, is not one farthing too high. Suppose you should not sell, still is it not necessary for your own sake and sister Peggy's, that you should move to Lancaster in the spring? I would give my vote for it. I am a friend to solitude, but I think at your time of life and that of sister Peggy, especially, when distress has taken some possession of the heart; a little change of cheerful company is absolutely necessary.

THE END.

www.ingramcontent.com/pod-product-compliance
Lightning Source LLC
LaVergne TN
LVHW021123110826
845150LV00005B/928

* 9 7 8 1 4 2 5 5 5 0 9 4 3 *